FROISSART'S CHRONICLES

Jean Froissart was born around 1337 at Valenciennes. When he was twenty the Lord of Beaufort asked him to write the *Chronicles* of the wars and feats of chivalry of his time, and this became a lifelong occupation. He went to England in 1361, where he joined the entourage of Queen Philippa, wife of Edward III of England. The Queen asked him to search Christendom for stories of knights and squires to complete his *Chronicles*. While in England he journeyed to Scotland and the Welsh Marches and revisited the Continent several times. In 1368 he went in the wedding retinue of Lionel of Clarence to Italy – Chaucer was in the same party and it is possible that he caught a glimpse of Petrarch. Coming back he received the news that Queen Philippa had died, and so decided to remain in the Netherlands, where he enjoyed the patronage of Wenceslas of Bohemia, Robert of Namur and Guy de Châtillon, under whose protection he took holy orders. He visited the brilliant court of Gaston Phébus, Count of Foix, in 1388, and in 1395 went back to England to be welcomed by Richard II. Five years later he recorded that monarch's downfall. The first book of the *Chronicles* was published in three versions, the second book was completed by 1388 and the third in 1390. He was revising the fourth when he died c. 1410.

John Jolliffe has worked for many years as a publisher, reviewer, editor and author. His most recent books have been histories of Duckworth publishers (for their centenary) and of Glyndebourne.

Froissart's Chronicles

EDITED AND

TRANSLATED BY

JOHN JOLLIFFE

PENGUIN BOOKS

PENGUIN BOOKS

Published by the Penguin Group
Penguin Books Ltd, 27 Wrights Lane, London w8 5tz, England
Penguin Putnam Inc., 375 Hudson Street, New York, New York 10014, USA
Penguin Books Australia Ltd, Ringwood, Victoria, Australia
Penguin Books Canada Ltd, 10 Alcorn Avenue, Toronto, Ontario, Canada m4v 3b2
Penguin Books India (P) Ltd, 11, Community Centre, Panchsheel Park, New Delhi – 110 017, India
Penguin Books (NZ) Ltd, Private Bag 102902, NSMC, Auckland, New Zealand
Penguin Books (South Africa) (Pty) Ltd, 5 Watkins Street, Denver Ext 4, Johannesburg 2094, South Africa

Penguin Books Ltd, Registered Offices: Harmondsworth, Middlesex, England

First published by Harvill Press Ltd 1967
Published as a Classic Penguin 2001

1

The frontispiece showing the betrothal of Isabel of France and Richard II is from an
illuminated manuscript in the British Museum [Vol. IV, p. 270 of *Froissart's Chronicles*] and is reproduced
by courtesy of the Trustees. Photograph supplied by the magazine *New Knowledge*

Maps and genealogical tables drawn by Jean Emerson

Printed in Great Britain by CPI UK

In memory of my mother and my father

Acknowledgements

I should like to thank Professor Armel Diverres,
of the University of Aberdeen, for many useful
suggestions, especially with regard to the
abridgement of the text; and Mrs Desmond
Guinness for her unique hospitality while I was
working on it.

J.H.J.

Contents

Contents

Contents

Contents

Contents

Contents

BOOK III

Contents

BOOK IV

Contents

Introduction

FROISSART'S LIFE

John Froissart, French historian and poet, priest, Canon and Treasurer of the collegial church of Chimay, and sometime chaplain to Guy of Châtillon, Count of Blois, was born in about 1337 at Valenciennes, where a statue was erected to his memory five hundred years later. The neighbourhood was rich in romantic associations: spreading almost up to the walls of the town lay the forest of Ardennes, its depths permeated by the shades of Pepin, Charlemagne and Roland. One of the many early manuscript copies of the *Chronicles* describes the author as a knight, but he himself tells us nothing of his origins, except for indicating that his father was a painter of armorial bearings. No doubt the copyist invested him with the title as a mark of his personal admiration and respect. Destined for the Church, and educated for it, Froissart showed neither early nor late any liking for an austere or disciplined regime. His inclinations were consistently romantic.

At that time, of course, the clergy were less inhibited in their way of life than they later became. Froissart mirrors his times, faithfully, naively, and as a rule without comment. Hearing and telling stories, versifying, gallantry and pleasure, these were his preoccupations from the start. He was only twenty when his lord and patron, Robert of Namur, suggested that he write a history of the recent wars, in particular those following the battle of Poitiers, of which he was to write a masterly description in the *Chronicles*. Froissart's constant expeditions to the scenes which he describes, and his interviews with eye-witnesses and participants in the battles and campaigns, no doubt served to distract him from pining much over the constant, unrequited romantic love that, as in the case of Petrarch, is the burden of his song as a lyric poet. Towards the end of the *Chronicles* we hear of Froissart's presenting a book of his lyric poems to Richard II at Eltham.

Early in his life, Froissart succeeded in becoming attached, as a page, to the English court. To what extent his early wanderlust was due to some romantic rebuff we cannot tell, but we may perhaps be guided by a pleasant generalization of his contemporary, Christine de Pisan, who warns against taking a lover's protestations too seriously: 'Although they all talk of dying,' she observes, 'I have yet to see the cemetery where they are buried.' His native country had close ties with England: in 1361 Philippa of Hainault, a native of Valenciennes like himself, put him under her special protection, and the whole English court seems to have enjoyed his poems and stories of gallant and chivalrous deeds.

Nevertheless, his restlessness returned, and the Queen provided him with money and horses to enable him to revisit his home and the light of his life. But he was soon back at the English court, this time for five years, and he refers to his return in the *Chronicles* with gratitude and affection. Later, he visited Scotland, about which his feelings were very different. On the return journey, he passed by Carlisle, which he thought of as Carlyon, King Arthur's capital, and Westmorland, where he noted that the ancient British language was still spoken. Back in London, he acted as secretary to King John of France, who was held prisoner there at the time along with a large number of the French nobility. It was probably in these surroundings that Froissart perfected his technique of extracting information from everyone he met. He liked to hear both sides of every story, and his appetite for the details of every little cavalry skirmish, every siege, every gallant action even, was such that the modern reader may find difficulty in following him everywhere without occasional lapses of attention.

After visiting Brussels and Brittany, he then followed the Black Prince to Bordeaux, and after further travels, he attended in 1378 the wedding of the Duke of Clarence to the daughter of Galeazzo Visconti in Milan. Chaucer, Boccaccio and Petrarch were also present. The unfortunate bridegroom only survived the wedding by a few months. Froissart moved on to Bologna, and from there accompanied King Peter of Cyprus to Venice. At Rome, in the following year, he heard of the death of Queen Philippa, and later movingly described it in the *Chronicles*.

He now settled down for a time as a priest at Lestines, in his own country, but the quiet life in general, and his pastoral duties in particular, seem to have been an unwelcome change, and he next became a clerk in the establishment of Wenceslas, Duke of Brabant. Wenceslas was himself a poet, and together they began to compile a kind of romantic novel, in verse, called *Méliador, or The Knight of the Golden Sun*. Wenceslas, however, died in 1383 before the work was completed, and Froissart moved on to the household of Guy of Châtillon, Count of Blois, who instructed him to continue writing his history. They went to Blois together and, after attaching himself briefly to the Duke of Berry, Froissart next hurried off to Sluys, where the French were gathering a vast fleet in the vain hope of repeating the Norman invasion of England. From there he went on to Ghent, and later devoted a long section of the *Chronicles*, written at Valenciennes, to the disasters that had lately overtaken Flanders in general and Ghent in particular.

He then paid a visit, in 1386, to Gaston Phoebus, Count of Foix, to learn details of the recent wars in that district at first hand from the knights of Gascony and Bearn. He rode to Gaston's castle at Orthez, stopping at various abbeys and castles on the way and accompanied for much of the journey by a knight called Espaing du Lyon, a veteran of many campaigns, which he was never reluctant to describe. He was also an authority on almost every town and castle that they passed on the road, and Froissart goes so far as to say that 'all the stories of Sir Espaing du Lyon gave me such satisfaction and pleasure that I found the journey far too short . . . as soon as we dismounted at an inn, I wrote down all he had told me, whether it was late or early, for posterity to enjoy; for there is nothing like writing for the preservation of events.'

Froissart was warmly received at Orthez, and when he left, loaded with presents from the count, it was for the wedding of his host's niece, the Countess of Boulogne, to the aging Duke of Berry. For the next five years, his peregrinations continued wherever his lively historical curiosity led him—chiefly to the courts of the great princes of the day, whose feasts, jousts, and tourneys formed the backcloth to his life. Sometimes he merely made the acquaintance of eye-witnesses: on one occasion he went to see an elderly Portuguese knight in Zeeland, who corrected the impressions that Froissart had formed of the wars in Spain, since up till then his only informants had been knights of Spain and Gascony.

By this time, the Count of Blois had been ruined by his extravagance, and Froissart now had recourse to another important patron of long standing, Albert, Duke of Bavaria, who probably enabled him to make another journey to England in 1393. He found the atmosphere very different from what it had been in the days of Queen Philippa. Most of his old friends were dead, but he was warmly, or at least attentively, received by Richard II. His account of the troubled months leading up to the King's deposition and death is inaccurate in the extreme, and shows no signs of the careful revising that he had lavished on the earlier parts of the *Chronicles*. Indeed, on his return to Flanders, Froissart did not long survive the unhappy King, whose melancholy fate is almost the last event that he describes. To judge by the abrupt ending of the last book, Froissart's death must have been sudden and unforeseen, but we know neither its exact date nor any other details.

THE CHRONICLES

Froissart's personality is reflected clearly in his work, which in turn bears living witness to the age he describes. The *Chronicles* are without artifice. The straightforward candour of Froissart's sentiments is matched by the often naive simplicity with which he expresses them. The colour and charm of chivalry was what excited him, and the qualities that he so eloquently and whole-heartedly extols are the traditional qualities of chivalry: valour, loyalty, distinction on the field of battle, and a gallant attitude towards women. Indeed, he asserts elsewhere that

> *Toute joie et toute honour*
> *Viennent d'armes et d'amour*

On the other hand, the less appealing characteristics of the age do not seem to have worried him unduly. Barbarous cruelty, senseless destruction of villages and towns together with their inhabitants, a permanent state of war often more or less for its own sake—only occasionally does Froissart feel moved to express regret at these ceaseless horrors, to such an extent were they taken for granted as part of the normal course of events. And of course, in the middle of all these horrors, as must happen in any war, there are still heroes, or at least demi-heroes, with the noble qualities that Froissart loved to admire. And once a character in the *Chronicles* has made up his mind on a course of action, just or unjust, cruel or kind, he follows it up to the hilt. There is no holding back, no flinching, no corruption.

Naturally, Froissart's account is not always correct, any more than it is complete. In any case, neither dates nor proper names nor the exact sequence of events were treated by the chroniclers of those days in a spirit of exactitude, and the many early copies of the manuscript contain endless variations, which it would be a life's work to sift and evaluate. In this edition, I have only tried to comment in the briefest possible way on those errors, obscurities, and other problems that might be a source of distraction or perplexity to the general reader and student, whose only equipment may be a reasonably robust appetite for the period. The scholar with a more discerning approach must naturally have recourse to the original texts himself and reach his own conclusions by comparing them. But the reader who finds this too daunting a prospect may find here a general picture of the events described.

Numerous cuts have been made, and those passages that have been omitted are only briefly summarized. This is partly to avoid the excessive length and the repetitions of the original, and partly to deal only briefly with those passages whose general importance or interest seems to be minimal. Opinions on this point will inevitably differ, and there will be no pleasing everybody. In the chapters translated in full, some long-winded passages have been shortened, but every effort has been made to omit nothing of importance.

With regard to the visit to Orthez, there may be those who would wish for a fuller version of what is one of the more entertaining chapters of the *Chronicles*, but it seems to me that the episodes and stories related in it were of more interest to the chronicler himself than they can be of importance to his readers; in any case the whole story can be found in the translations of both Berners and Johnes. But like the string of stories that Froissart heard on the way to Orthez, his subsequent stay at the castle, though I have not reproduced it in full, is not without bizarre features that add to the reader's picture of the period. Even by the standards of the middle ages, the Count of Foix's way of life was eccentric. He rose at noon and had supper at midnight, instead of the usual medieval habit of having dinner at ten o'clock in the morning and supper at five in the evening. And in spite of telling us a number of gruesome stories about the uncivilized habits of the count, Froissart calmly concludes that the count was 'perfect in all things, and as wise and perceptive as any high prince of his time.'

The real value, however, of Froissart's chronicle, to quote

Coulton, lies in his 'lively interest in things great and small, and in his power of vivid narrative.' It is not for nothing that he has been described as the Herodotus of a barbarous age. In contrast to the inhuman cruelty of the sack of Limoges, Froissart suddenly gives us an account of how the Black Prince behaved after the battle of Poitiers, when he refused to sit at the same table as his prisoner, the King of France, but waited at the table like a servant, in recognition not only of his position as a reigning monarch, but also of his bravery in the field of battle. Fourteen years later, after the capture of Limoges, the same Prince did not lift a finger to stop the general massacre that took place in revenge for the action of the bishop and the principal citizens in going over to the French side. Nowadays, the ideal of justice is represented by an unvarying mean; in the Hundred Years' War, the pendulum swung, and swung with a vengeance.

Another fact that will strike the general reader is that in the fourteenth century there was no French nation in the modern sense of the word. France was a collection of different nations, often at war with one another, and seldom capable of closing their ranks against a common enemy. Even after a long period of war with England, the fiercest fighting was still often between one French nation and another, and it was accompanied, as Coulton points out, by at least as much ravage and brutality as there has been in the last century between France and Germany, though it is also interesting to note what Froissart says about the feelings of these two countries about each other at that time.

The *Chronicles* are far from being a mere monument to medieval chivalry, as Shears describes them, though they certainly give a wonderful and detailed picture of it, warts and all. As Shears hastens to add, they put the reader in touch with a far wider cross-section of fourteenth-century life, for all their author's preoccupation with his favourite qualities—courage, self-assurance, pride of bearing, and outspoken yet courtly diction. Froissart, in his chosen calling, had to trim his sails to more than one passing breeze, or he would have sunk without trace, and we would not have his life's work. This helps to account for his aristocratic leanings and epicurean tastes, and also provides them with an excuse, even a *raison d'être*. Nor did they blind him to the fact (which he passes on to us without concealment, if sometimes only implicitly) that there was at least as much evil, suffering, poverty, and misery, relatively speaking, in the world of the fourteenth century as in any other era. Kings, princes, and prelates are chastised wherever Froissart can afford to chastise them, and his spirit of enquiry, his rationalizations and his awareness of his own self are all modern qualities that prevent him from being a stranger to the modern reader. But perhaps his most important quality of all is his realization that facts alone, though essential, are not enough in themselves. To have the maximum effect on us, they must be transformed into scenes of absorbing dramatic interest, and it was to achieve this that Froissart went back over his material, enlivening it further wherever he could. The first book of the *Chronicles* he rewrote twice, and had he lived he would no doubt have added still more to the rest of his great work. The words that open the fourth book give the key to his approach to his task, and make a fitting end to this brief introduction:

'Plus y suis et plus y laboure, plus me plaist.'

Footnotes to the text are the editor's comments unless otherwise attributed.

Maps & Genealogical Tables

The maps showing the expedition of Edward III
and the first and second expeditions of Charles VI
with the Bishop of Norwich's Crusade are drawn
from maps in Volume XXIV of Kervyn de
Lettenhove's *Oeuvres de Froissart*; those of France at
the Peace of Bretigny and of Europe in 1360 are
from *Muir's Historical Atlas, Mediaeval and Modern.*

EUROPE
IN 1360

—— boundary of the Holy Roman Empire

WEDEN

psala
Stockholm

Visby
AND
ar

agen
and

ANIA

Danzig

Kulm

Thorn
Posen

LITHUANIA

Warsaw

Vistula

KINGDOM

Oder

LE S I A

OF
Lemberg

gue

EMIA
rünn

POLAND

UKRAINE

Carpathians

MORAVIA

ZIPS

Vienna
Pressburg

IA

HUNGARY

Budapest Bistritz Jassy

Drave

Kalocsa TRANSYLVANIA

MOLDAVIA

ROATIA

Hermannstadt

Galatz

Kaffa
(to Genoa)

Tergovist

BOSNIA

Belgrade

WALLACHIA
(to Hungary 1368)

Cherson

Constantsa

VENICE

Danube Tirnova

Varna

B L A C K   S E A

STEPHEN

Nish

BULGARIA

TIC

Ragusa

SERVIAN

Kossovo

Sofia

Adrianople

Constantinople

Sinope

Amisus
(to Genoa)

Uskub
(Skoplje)

Amasra
(to Genoa)

ALBANIAN

PRINCES

Amasia

Durazzo

Philippopolis

E. EMPIRE

Pera (to Genoa)

PRINCIPALITY

Thessalonica

Nicaea Angora

Taranto

DUSHAN

Gallipoli

Brusa

Ottoman Turks

Corfu

Janina D. of Athens

Lesbos
(to Genoa)

Konia

Seljuk Turks

Sis

COUNTY OF
CEPHALONIA

LATIN STATES

Negroponte
(to Venice)

Smyrna

Chios
(to genoa)

Ephesus

(Eight Emirates)

Taurus

Armenians

Reggio

PR. OF ACHAIA

Kts. of St. John

Tarsus

racuse

Modon
(to Venice)

D. of
Naxos

Rhodes

KINGDOM OF
CYPRUS

Famagusta

Antioch

cily)

S E A

Tripolis

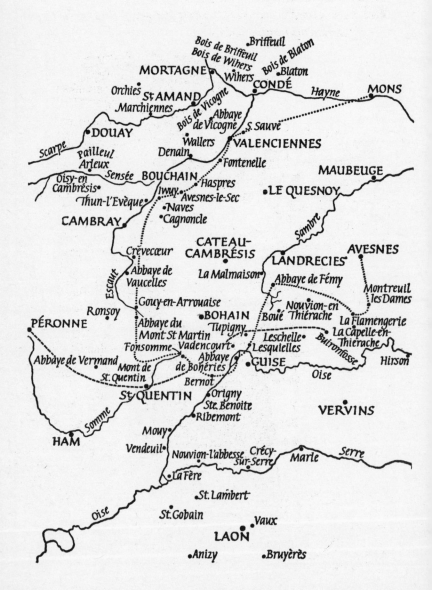

HAINAUT and THIÉRACHE

The March of the English army MONS–AVESNES ··········
The March of the French army PÉRONNE–Buironfosse ------

Bois de Briffeuil
Briffeuil
Bois de Wihers
MORTAGNE
Wihers
Bois de Blaton
Blaton
CONDÉ
Hayne
MONS

Orchies
St AMAND
Marchiennes
Bois de Vicogne
Abbaye de Vicogne
S. Sauvé

DOUAY
Wallers
VALENCIENNES

Scarpe
Pailleul
Arleux
Denain
Fontenelle
MAUBEUGE

Oisy-en-Cambrésis
Sensée
BOUCHAIN
Iwuy
Haspres
Avesnes-le-Sec
LE QUESNOY

Thun-l'Evêque
Naves
Cagnoncle

CAMBRAY
Sambre

CATEAU-CAMBRÉSIS
LANDRECIES
AVESNES

Crèvecœur
La Malmaison
Abbaye de Fémy
Montreuil les Dames

Abbaye de Vaucelles
Nouvion-en-Thiérache
La Flamengerie

Escaut
Gouy-en-Arrouaise
Boué
La Capelle-en-Thiérache

Ronssoy
BOHAIN
Tupigny
Leschelle
Buironfosse
Hirson

PÉRONNE
Abbaye du Mont St Martin
Vadencourt
Lesquielles
GUISE

Abbaye de Vermand
Fonsomme
Abbaye de Bohéries
Oise

Mont de St. Quentin
Bernot

St QUENTIN
Origny
Ste Benoite
VERVINS

HAM
Somme
Mouy
Ribemont

Vendeuil
Nouvion-l'abbesse
Crécy-sur-Serre
Marle
Serre

La Fère

St. Lambert

Oise
St. Gobain
Vaux

LAON

Anizy
Bruyères

FRANCE AT THE PEACE OF BRETIGNY, 1360

≡ Lands ceded to England at Treaty of Paris, 1259
▤ Lands held by England at accession of Edward III
⣿ Lands ceded to England at Treaty of Bretigny
--◄-- Edward III's march to Calais

Canterbury
Dover
Sandwich
Sluys
Calais
Bruges
FLANDERS
Ghent
Courtrai
S. Omer
BRABANT
Tournai
ARTOIS
Douai
PONTHIEU
Somme
S. Valery
Crécy
Arras
HAINAULT
Abbeville
Eu
St Quentin
English Channel
Amiens
Barfleur
St Vaast
Seine
Rouen
Reims
Guernsey
COTENTIN
Oise
CHAMPAGNE
Moselle
Jersey
Caen
Elbeuf
la Roche Derrien
St Lo
Lisieux
Evreux
Poissy
Paris
Châlons
St Malo
NORMANDY
Verneuil
Chartres
Marne
Morlaix
Dinan
Seine
BRITTANY
MAINE
Poissy
Bretigny
Sens
Carhaix
Rennes
Orleans
Pontigny
Hennebont
Le Mans
BLOIS
ORLEANS
Auxerre
Auray
Pontvallain
Angers
Tours
Blois
Guillon
Nantes
ANJOU
Loire
Vierzon
Dijon
Bourgneuf B.
Clisson
Chinon
Cher
Bourges
BURGUNDY
Thouars
Poitiers
Châteauroux
Châlon
La Rochelle
POITOU
Châtellerault
BERRY
Lusignan
Lussac
Auvergne
BOURBON
Taillebourg
Limoges
Loire
Saône
BAY OF
Saintes
ANGOUMOIS
Limousin
Lyons
Gironde
Charente
Angoulême
Rhône
BISCAY
Périgueux
Auberoche
DAUPHINE
PERIGORD
Bordeaux
Dordogne
Bergerac
Rhône
La Teste de Buch
GUYENNE
AGENAIS
Lot
Rodez
Avignon
Bazas
Agen
Cahors
ROUERGUE
Tarn
Dax
Adour
ARMAGNAC
Toulouse
Arles
Bayonne
GASCONY
Narbonne
BEARN
BIGORRE
COMMINGES
Carcassonne
Vitoria
Sulvatierra
NAVARRE
PYRENEES
Ebro
Pamplona
Burgos
Logrono
Najera
ARAGON

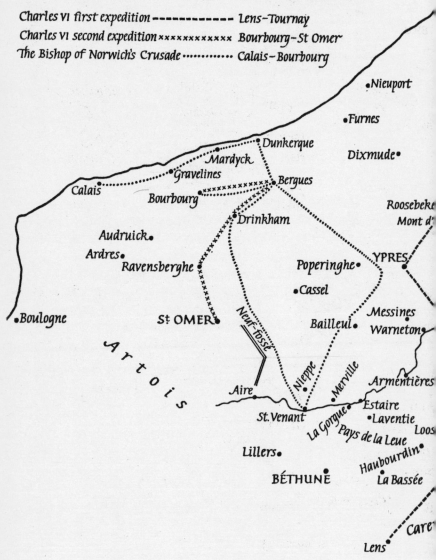

THE TWO EXPEDITIONS OF CHARLES VI
& THE BISHOP OF NORWICH'S CRUSADE

Charles VI first expedition ------------- Lens–Tournay
Charles VI second expedition ××××××××× Bourbourg–St Omer
The Bishop of Norwich's Crusade ·········· Calais–Bourbourg

Nieuport

Furnes

Dunkerque

Dixmude

Mardyck

Gravelines

Calais

Bourbourg

Bergues

Roosebeke

Mont d'

Drinkham

Audruick

Ardres

Ravensberghe

YPRES

Poperinghe

Cassel

Boulogne

St OMER

Neuf-fossé

Messines

Bailleul

Warneton

A r t o i s

Nieppe

Aire

Merville

Armentières

St. Venant

Estaire

La Gorgue

Laventie

Loos

Pays de la Leue

Lillers

Haubourdin

BÉTHUNE

La Bassée

Care

Lens

THE KINGS OF ENGLAND IN THE 14th CENTURY

with the dates of their reigns

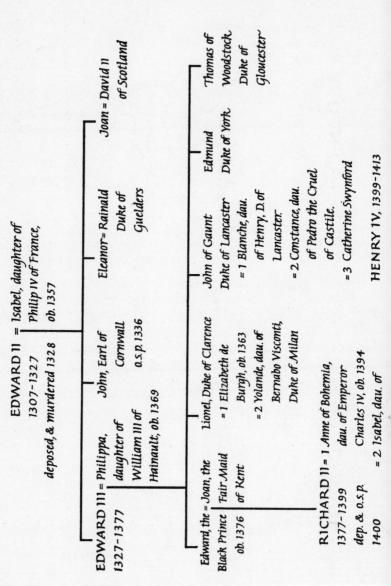

EDWARD II = Isabel, daughter of
1307–1327   Philip IV of France,
deposed, & murdered 1328   ob. 1357

EDWARD III = Philippa, daughter of William III of Hainault, ob. 1369
1327–1377

John, Earl of Cornwall
o.s.p. 1336

Eleanor = Rainald Duke of Guelders

Joan = David II of Scotland

Edward, the Black Prince = Joan, the Fair Maid of Kent
ob. 1376

Lionel, Duke of Clarence
= 1 Elizabeth de Burgh, ob. 1363
= 2 Yolande, dau. of Bernabo Visconti, Duke of Milan

John of Gaunt Duke of Lancaster
= 1 Blanche, dau. of Henry, D. of Lancaster
= 2 Constance, dau. of Pedro the Cruel of Castile.
= 3 Catherine Swynford

Edmund Duke of York

Thomas of Woodstock Duke of Gloucester

RICHARD II = 1 Anne of Bohemia, dau. of Emperor Charles IV, ob. 1394
1377–1399   = 2 Isabel, dau. of
dep. & o.s.p.
1400

HENRY IV, 1399–1413

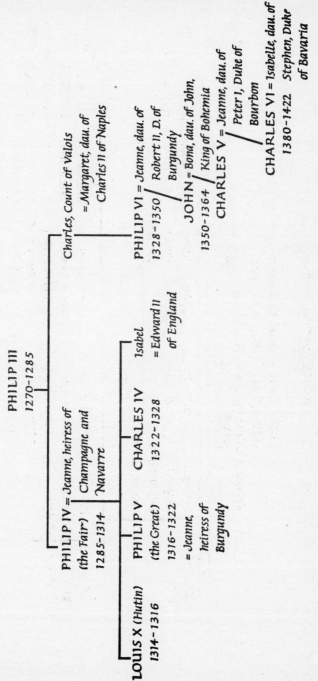

THE KINGS OF FRANCE IN THE 14th CENTURY

with the dates of their reigns

PHILIP III
1270–1285

Charles, Count of Valois
= Margaret, dau. of
 Charles II of Naples

PHILIP IV = Jeanne, heiress of
(the Fair)   Champagne and
1285–1314   Navarre

PHILIP VI = Jeanne, dau. of
1328–1350   Robert II, D. of
             Burgundy

JOHN = Bona, dau. of John,
1350–1364   King of Bohemia

CHARLES V = Jeanne, dau. of
             Peter I, Duke of
             Bourbon

CHARLES VI = Isabelle, dau. of
1380–14-22   Stephen, Duke
             of Bavaria

Isabel
= Edward II
 of England

CHARLES IV
1322–1328

PHILIP V
(the Great)
1316–1322
= Jeanne,
heiress of
Burgundy

LOUIS X (Hutin)
1314–1316

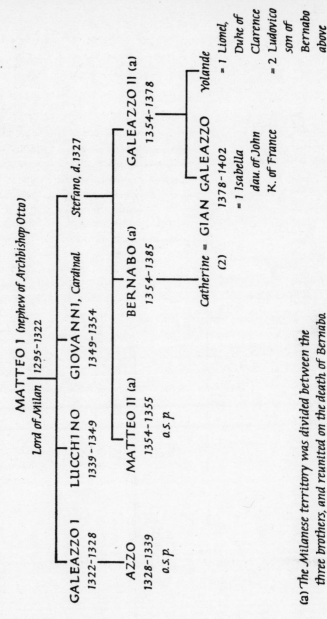

THE VISCONTI

Lords of Milan in the 14th Century

MATTEO I *(nephew of Archbishop Otto)* 1295–1322
Lord of Milan

GALEAZZO I
1322–1328

LUCCHINO
1339–1349

GIOVANNI, *Cardinal*
1349–1354

Stefano, d.1327

AZZO
1328–1339
o.s.p.

MATTEO II (a)
1354–1355
o.s.p.

BERNABO (a)
1354–1385

GALEAZZO II (a)
1354–1378

Catherine = **GIAN GALEAZZO**
(2)   1378–1402
= 1 *Isabella*
dau. of John
K. of France

Yolande
= 1 *Lionel,*
Duke of
Clarence
= 2 *Ludovico*
son of
Bernabo
above

(a) *The Milanese territory was divided between the three brothers, and reunited on the death of Bernabo.*

BOOK I

Book I

~~~~~~

1

Here begins the prologue of John Froissart, to the Chronicles of France, England and the neighbouring countries.

In order that the honourable adventures and noble feats of arms achieved in the wars of France and England may be memorably set down and perpetually recorded, whereby brave and honourable men may have an example to encourage them, I, John Froissart, will compose a history of great praise. But before I begin, I ask the Saviour of this world, who created all things out of nothing, to give me such grace and understanding that I may persevere so that whoever reads or hears this work may find in it both pleasure and good example. It is truly said that all buildings are composed of countless stones, and all great rivers are swelled and increased by many different springs and sources; in the same way all sciences are extracted and compiled by different scholars, one of whom may perhaps be ignorant of what another has written. But by the famous writing of ancient authors all things are known in one place or another. So to succeed in my enterprise, I will begin first by the grace of God and the Blessed Virgin Mary, from whom all comfort and consolation proceed, by taking as my foundation the true chronicles compiled by the right reverend, discreet and wise master, John le Bel, formerly Canon of Saint Lambert's at Liège, who gladly and diligently fulfilled his task in writing this noble chronicle, and continued it till the end of his life, following the truth as faithfully as he could, and toiling earnestly to acquire a perfect knowledge of it. In his own day he was in high favour with Sir John of Hainault and was in his privy council, the same Sir John who is often mentioned in this book; for he played the chief part in many fine and noble adventures and it was from him that the said John le Bel knew and heard of many noble deeds, which will be described hereafter. Having undertaken to compose this book, I have, in accordance with my natural inclination, frequented the company of various great and noble lords, both in France and in England, Scotland, and other countries. So, as far as I have been able, I have sought out the truth concerning the deeds of war and adventures that have occurred, especially since the great battle of Poitiers in which the noble King John of France was taken prisoner; for before that time I was young both in age and understanding. However I took it upon myself, on finishing my school days, to write an account of these wars in verse; and when it was compiled I took it to England and presented it to my lady Philippa of Hainault, the noble Queen of England, who received it most kindly, to my great profit and advantage. It may be that this book is not yet perfected nor corrected as accurately as the case requires, for when feats of arms are hard won, the honour that they earn ought faithfully to be given to those who by their valour and fortitude have deserved it. Therefore to succeed in that aim and to follow the truth as near as I can, I, John Froissart, have arranged this history on the aforesaid plan and true foundation, at the earnest request of my well-beloved lord Robert of Namur, knight, lord of Beaufort, to whom I owe all love and obedience, and may God grant that I may fulfil his pleasure. Amen.

2

First, the better to embark on this honourable and pleasant history of the noble Edward, King of England, he was crowned in London in the year of our Lord God 1326, on Christmas Day, although the King his father, as well as the Queen his mother, was still alive. Since the time of King Arthur it has often been observed in England that between two valiant kings there has most commonly been one less sufficient both in wit and valour. And this was made quite apparent by King Edward III[1], for his grandfather, King

---

[1] *For clarity, the usual numbers have been inserted to distinguish between different kings, popes, etc., of the same name, though Froissart never gives them.*

Edward I, was valiant, prudent, wise, and bold, and was adventurous and fortunate in all feats of war. He had great trouble with the Scots, but conquered them three or four times, for the Scots could never be victorious or successful against him. And after his death, his son by his first wife, who was father to the said good King Edward III, was crowned King and called Edward II: he resembled his father neither in wit nor valour, but ruled the country in an unbridled fashion, and relied on the advice of certain evil persons, whereby he had in the end neither advantage nor land, as you shall hear later. For soon after he was crowned, Robert the Bruce, King of Scotland, who had several times given great trouble to King Edward I, attacked him vigorously and reconquered all Scotland and the good city of Berwick as well, and burned and plundered a great part of the kingdom of England, venturing four or five days' journey into the country, and defeating the King and all the barons of England in pitched battle at a place in Scotland called Stirling, on the feast of Saint John the Baptist,[1] in the year of Our Lord 1314. The pursuit after this defeat lasted two days and two nights, and the English King escaped with only very few of his troops to London. But since this is no part of our subject, I will say no more of it.

3

This English king whom I speak of now, who suffered defeat in Scotland, had two brothers:[2] one was called the Earl Marshal, and was of wild and wicked character. The other was Sir Edmund, Earl of Kent, who was wise, gentle and amiable, and much loved by good people. This King had by his wife, the daughter of Philip the Fair, King of France, two sons and two daughters. Of the two sons the elder was called Edward and

[1] *June 24th.*
[2] *They were in fact his half-brothers by Edward I's second wife, Margaret, daughter of King Philip III of France. His first wife was Eleanor, daughter of King Ferdinand III of Castile.*

became King of England by the acclamation of all the barons while his father was still alive, as you have already heard. The second son was called John and died young. The elder of the two daughters was called Joan and was married when still a child to the young King David of Scotland, son of Robert the Bruce, by agreement of the two countries, in the cause of peace. The other daughter was married to the Duke of Guelders: they had two sons, Rainald and Edward, and two daughters, one the Countess of Blois, and the other the Duchess of Juliers.

4

King Philip the Fair of France had three sons, besides the beautiful Isabel, the Queen of England, and they were very handsome, and great knights. The eldest was called Louis le Hutin, who in his father's lifetime was King of Navarre; the second son was called Philip the Tall, and the third Charles. All three were to be Kings of France, succeeding each other after the death of King Philip their father, and having no legitimate male heirs. After the death of the last of them, Charles, the twelve peers and the barons of France would not give the crown to their sister who was Queen of England; for they held and maintained, and still do, that the kingdom of France is so noble that it cannot go or descend to a woman, or pass through the female line. For this reason the twelve peers and the barons of France gave the throne by common accord to the lord Philip of Valois, the son of the lord Charles of Valois, who was the brother of Philip the Fair, leaving out of the succession the Queen of England and her son who was the next male heir, being nephew to Charles, whereas Philip of Valois was only his first cousin. This is the point from which the afflictions and tribulations of war afterwards arose; for that is the true foundation of this history, to tell of the great events and feats of arms that followed. Not since the time when Charlemagne was Emperor of Germany and King of France had such great adventures and wars befallen the kingdom of France.

5

King Edward II, father of that King Edward with whom our
history deals, truly governed his country with great cruelty and
injustice, by the advice of Sir Hugh Despencer, with whom he had
been brought up since childhood. This Sir Hugh and his father
had by their exertions become the most powerful barons in
England, by reason of their money and the uses to which they
put it. In particular Sir Hugh the younger had gained so much
influence over the King, and had so moulded his opinions, that
nothing was done without him, and everything was done by him;
the King paid more attention to him than to anyone else. Sir
Hugh and his father wanted to gain supremacy over all the knights
and barons of England. For which reason great evils and disasters
later afflicted the country and the Despencers themselves as
well.

For after the great defeat at Stirling, bitter hatred and discontent arose between the noble barons and the King's council,
that is to say against Sir Hugh Despencer. They asserted that it
was through his advice that they had been defeated, and that he
had treacherously favoured the King of Scotland. And on this
point the barons had several meetings together, to hear each
other's opinions and discuss what could be done. Thomas Earl
of Lancaster was chief among them. Now Sir Hugh saw the discontent he had aroused, and being so high in the king's esteem,
and being, indeed, his particular favourite, he went to the King
and said that these knights were making an alliance against the
King and that if he did not take care they would put him out of
his kingdom. The result of this subtle and malicious report was
that the King had all those knights arrested when they were
assembled together for discussion, and without any more delay
and without even charging them, he had twenty-two of the
greatest barons of England beheaded. Among them was Thomas
Earl of Lancaster, the King's own uncle, a wise and saintly man,
who has since caused many miracles at the place where he was

beheaded.[1] For this deed Sir Hugh earned the deep hatred of the whole country, and especially of the Queen and of the King's brother, the Earl of Kent.

Sir Hugh continued to encourage the King in his misdeeds. For when he saw the displeasure of the Queen and the Earl of Kent, Sir Hugh maliciously caused such discord between the King and the Queen that for a long time the King would neither remain in the Queen's company nor even see her at all. Then the Queen and the Earl of Kent were told secretly of the danger they were in from Sir Hugh Despencer, and of their probable destruction, unless they took good care of themselves. And the Queen, pretending to go on a pilgrimage to the shrine of Saint Thomas at Canterbury, went on to Winchelsea, and there embarked on a ship that was made ready for her, with her son Edward, the Earl of Kent, and Sir Roger Mortimer, taking with them provisions in another boat. They had a fair wind and the next morning arrived at the harbour of Boulogne.

6

When the Queen of England arrived at Boulogne with all her company, she gave thanks to Our Lord, and went on foot to the Church of Our Lady, and made her offering and her devotions. And the captains of the town and the Abbot welcomed her with joy, and gave her lodging and hospitality; and they rested and refreshed themselves there for five days. On the sixth day, they left Boulogne with all their company, riding on horses and donkeys which they had brought from England. The Queen was escorted and accompanied by all the knights of the surrounding country who had come to see her and entertain her, since she was the sister of their lord the King. The Queen continued her journey till she reached Paris; and many of the nobles came out to meet her and to welcome her and her young son. She was escorted to the palace by Lord Robert of Artois, the Count of

---

[1] *Pontefract.*

Dammartin, the Lord of Coucy, the Lord of Montmorency and several others. And when the King of France saw his sister, whom he had not seen for a long time, he went up to her as she came into his chamber and took her right hand and kissed her and said: 'Welcome, my fair sister, and your fine son.' The Queen, who had little joy in her heart except at being near her brother the King, tried to kneel down two or three times at his feet, but the King would not allow her, and kept hold of her right hand, and enquired most kindly how she was and what had brought her. The Queen answered him calmly, and told him sadly of all the injuries and felonies committed by Sir Hugh Despencer, and asked his aid and comfort. And when King Charles heard his sister's troubles, he took great pity on her and comforted her most kindly, and said: 'Fair sister, stay with us; do not be distressed or downhearted. We have enough for you as well as for ourselves. And we will find some remedy for your condition.' The Queen knelt down and thanked him deeply, and afterwards she stayed with all her company with the King at Paris, and he had everything necessary supplied to her. And the Queen of England spent much of her time with the King and Queen of France, and the news she told them from England gave them little pleasure.

7

The influence of Sir Hugh Despencer, and the affection the King felt for him, increased every day. He had such a hold on the King that the whole country was amazed. Nor could anything be done at court without the agreement of Sir Hugh. And he behaved cruelly and wickedly towards many Englishmen, for which he was well hated. But nobody dared to mention or raise any complaint, for whoever it might be, earl or baron, that he suspected, Sir Hugh would have him seized, and under the royal authority would have him beheaded, without any appeal. The suspicion that he felt for others and the hatred that he inspired were almost beyond belief. And all the barons and thoughtful people in the country saw that it was not to be endured, and that they could no longer tolerate his wicked, outrageous behaviour. They debated among themselves secretly and decided to send for the Queen of England and ask her to return, for she had been in Paris for three years. They wrote and put it to her that if she could by any means contrive to raise an armed force, even a thousand men, and if she would bring her son and all her company to the kingdom of England, they would rally to her side, and would obey her and her son as their sovereign. For they could not and would not endure any longer the general disorder and the misdeeds of the King, which were all inspired by the advice of Sir Hugh and his followers.

When the Queen heard the news, she secretly consulted her brother King Charles, who willingly listened to her and advised her to press on boldly, for he would help her and lend her as many men as she wanted, and he would also lend her all the silver and gold she needed. With that, the Queen left him and returned to her lodging to make what provision she could for the future. And she secretly sought the help of those of the greatest barons in France whom she trusted most, and who would voluntarily support her—the ones, that is, whom she thought she could depend on. Then she sent a secret message to the barons in England who had communicated with her.

But this could not be kept secret from Sir Hugh Despencer. And in the course of time he was so active with messages and presents and promises that King Charles was won over, and told his sister Queen Isabel as definitely and clearly as he could to stay quiet and to abandon her project. When the Queen heard this she was, naturally, amazed and astounded, and she saw that the King was now disposed against her, for nothing that she could say would alter his decision or help her case. And so she left him, sadly and sorrowfully, and returned to her lodging; but she did not abandon her plans, and the King her brother was angry that she ignored his words. And he gave orders that nobody, on pain of exile, should help nor accompany the Queen his sister.

8

When the Queen heard this she was sadder than ever before, and with reason. She did not know what to think or do, because everything was, and had been for so long, against her, and those who should have come to her help were failing her, through wicked advice. She became desperate, she had no comfort, and she did not know what to do or what would become of her. And she often prayed and beseeched God to give her help and guidance. Soon afterwards she was told, in all truth, that if she did not behave discreetly, the King her brother would have her sent back to her husband the King of England, and her son with her, because it did not please the King of France that she should stay away from her husband. At this the Queen was more appalled than ever, because she would rather have been dead and dismembered than fall again into the power of her husband and Sir Hugh. She had great need of good advice. And she decided to leave France and go down into Hainault to see the Count of Hainault and Sir John his brother, who were most honourable knights, of the highest reputation. She hoped to find in him every comfort and good advice; he was her nearest relation.

Such was the Queen's plan; and she informed her people of her decision, and paid for everything she had had. Then she left her lodging as quickly and quietly as she could, with her son, who was then about fifteen years old, the Earl of Kent, Sir Roger Mortimer and all the other English knights that had come away with her. They passed right through France, to Vermandois and the region of Cambrai, and came to Ostrevant, in Hainault, to a castle called Brigincourt, of which Sir Nicolas of Ambrecicourt was lord. And his squires and his wife gladly and nobly welcomed into the castle the Queen of England, her son and her company. And they found everything at their disposal.

The news soon reached the Count of Hainault and his brother Sir John at Valenciennes that the Queen of England was lodging with Sir Nicolas at Brigincourt. And when the two knights heard this, they discussed what they should do. First Sir John left Valenciennes, well escorted with knights and squires, and rode all the way to Brigincourt in Ostrevant; and there he found the Queen, and did her all the honour and reverence he could. The Queen, in sorrow and despair, and without anyone to advise her with the exception of God and himself, began to tell him her troubles and hardships and all that had happened to her, weeping most pitifully; first, how she had been driven out of England with her son, and had come to France under the protection of her brother the King; and how she had thought she would be provided with armed troops by her brother, to return in strength and take her son back to his kingdom, as her friends in England had bidden her; and how her brother had been so advised that he had prevented this project and forbidden any nobles to accompany her, on pain of exile and of losing their lands. And she told him how, and with what hardship, she had fled there with her son, not knowing from whom or from what country she might find comfort or assistance.

And when the good Sir John heard the Queen's sad lament, and saw that she was in tears, he took great pity on her, and gently comforted her with these words: 'Madam, you may count on me as your own knight; I will stand by you to the death, even though everyone else fail you. I will do all in my power to see you and your son restored to your rightful position in England, with the help of your friends there, as you say yourself. And I, with everybody that I can enlist, will stake my life in your service.' The Queen, who was seated when she heard him speak these noble and encouraging words, would have fallen on her knees from the great joy and gratitude that she felt, but the noble knight would not let her, and got up and took her in his arms and said: 'By the grace of God, the Queen of England shall not think of kneeling before her knight. But be comforted, madam, and all your company as well, for I shall not break my promise. You will come and see my brother and my sister-in-law, your cousin the Countess of Hainault, who have asked me to bring you to them.' This the Queen agreed to, and said: 'Sir, I find in you more love and comfort than in the whole world. And for what you say and offer, I thank you a thousand times. We will never do you any disservice, but if in time we are restored, as I hope, by the comfort and grace of God and yourself, you will be richly rewarded.'

With these words Sir John took leave of the Queen and her son and of the Earl of Kent, and the other knights, and went to lodge at the Abbey of Denaing. And the Queen stayed at Brigincourt, greatly comforted, as the guest of Sir Nicolas of Ambrecicourt, who did all he could for her, for which the Queen was most grateful to him.

In the morning, Sir John heard mass, and after breakfast he left Denaing and rode back to Brigincourt, where he found the Queen and her company already prepared for the journey. They all left together, and Sir John took them on the road to Valenciennes, where they were gladly and gallantly welcomed. The count's hall was made ready for the Queen and her retinue. For at that time the count was living in the Hôtel de Hollande, with all his household. The Queen stopped at the hall and was well lodged and entertained. And the Countess of Hainault came to see her, and did her all honour and reverence, as she well knew how to do. And so did William, Count of Hainault, although he was suffering from gout and rode only with difficulty. Nevertheless he honoured and feasted the Queen nobly all the time she was at Valenciennes, which was about three weeks.

During all this time she prepared for her journey and attended to her affairs in general. And Sir John wrote warmly to those knights and companions whom he trusted the most in all Hainault, in Bohemia, and in Brabant. And he besought them, for the sake of their friendship, to come with him in this enterprise. From one district and another many came from love of him, though many refused, for all his entreaties. And in the same way Sir John was much rebuked by his brother, and his other advisers, because his plan seemed so bold and perilous to them, in view of the prevailing discord and hatred among the barons and the common people of England, and since the English are generally ill-disposed towards foreigners who gain the advantage over them and invade their country. So that everybody feared that neither Sir John nor any of his companions might ever come home again. But in spite of endless contrary advice and harsh words, the good knight would not be dissuaded. For he said that he could die only once, and that it was in the hands of Our Lord; but he had promised this noble lady to escort her back into her kingdom, and he would support her to the death. And he would just as soon die with that noble lady, who had been forced to leave her country, as anywhere else. For it was the solemn duty of every knight, especially when appealed to, to help ladies in distress.

9

So the English Queen and her company left Valenciennes, having made all the necessary preparations for the journey. And she took leave of Count William of Hainault and his wife, and thanked them deeply, humbly, and graciously for their kind and noble hospitality. And they set out under the protection and escort of Sir John and reached Dordrecht, in Holland. There they fitted out and provisioned ships and vessels both large and small, such as they could get, and shipped their horses and baggage and provisions. And when they had a fair wind, they entrusted themselves to Our Lord and embarked and weighed anchor and put to sea. They were not more than three hundred armed men in all.

And now, consider the boldness and daring of this enterprise of Sir John, going to attack and forcibly enter a kingdom where he knew nobody and nothing, and where he had no idea what he might find. But such was his courage and his trust in God that he considered that the voyage would turn out successfully and to his credit. He had everything before him, being then in the fine flower of his youth; and so all the more eagerly and boldly did he undertake the task.

Now I will name all the knights of Hainault who went with him on this voyage, in answer to his request. First, Henri d'Antoing, Robert de Bailleul, afterwards lord of Fontainnée, Fastres de Rue, Michel de Ligne, Sanses de Boussac, Perceval de Semeris, Sanses de Biauriu, the lords of Warguy, Potellée, Monteguy, Gommegnies, and Ambrecicourt, and various other gentlemen, who were eager to venture forth with Sir John and to advance their reputations. There were also a few others of Brabant and Bohemia.

They sailed with a good wind. They had intended to land at a certain port but were prevented by a storm that sent them off their course, so that for two days they did not know where they were. And in this God was merciful, and helped them; for if they had landed at the port they had chosen, or anywhere near it, they would all have been lost, and fallen into the hands of their enemies, who knew of their approach, and were waiting there to put them all to death, including the Queen and the young Prince. But God would not allow it. He altered their course by a miracle, as you have heard.

So it happened that at the end of two days the storm was over and the sailors sighted land in England. They made for it gladly and landed on the sands on the open seashore[1] without any harbour or port. And they stayed for three days on the sands, with few provisions, while they unloaded their horses and baggage. And they did not know what part of England they were in, nor whether they were in the power of their friends or their enemies. On the fourth day they set out, putting their trust in God; and they suffered bitterly from hunger and from the cold at night and from constant anxiety. But they went on riding over hill and dale till they came to villages and to a great monastery of the Dominicans called Saint Edmund's, where they stayed and refreshed themselves for three days. And they paid particular attention to their horses, for they thought that they would soon be needing them.

[1] *Near Harwich.*

10

The news of their arrival spread over the country until it reached those who had communicated with the Queen and invited her back. And they immediately prepared to come and see her, and her son whom they wanted as their sovereign. And the first to reach them, who gave their followers the most comfort, was Henry Earl of Lancaster, who had a twisted neck; he was the brother of Thomas Earl of Lancaster who had been beheaded, as you have heard above, and father of the Duke of Lancaster who was such a valiant knight[1] and so well respected, as you will hear later in this history. Thus Henry Earl of Lancaster came with a great company of men-at-arms and after him from one place and another came earls, barons, knights and squires with so many men-at-arms that the Queen's men thought they were out of all danger. And as they advanced, their numbers increased every day.

Then the Queen took counsel with the barons and knights and squires who had come to join her, and decided to go straight to Bristol, where the King and the Despencers were. It was a good town, large and rich and well enclosed, with a good seaport. And there is a very strong and powerful castle there, with the sea beating all round it. And in the castle were the King and Sir Hugh Despencer the father, who was about ninety years old, and his son Sir Hugh, the chief adviser of the King, who encouraged him in his wicked deeds and schemes, and the Earl of Arundel who was married to the daughter of Sir Hugh the younger, and several other knights and squires attending the King's court. The Queen and all her company set out for Bristol, with Sir John of Hainault and the earls and barons of England. In every town they entered they were honoured and feasted and new supporters joined them, right and left, from every side; they reached the city of Bristol and laid siege to it.

[1] *Froissart presumably refers to John of Gaunt, who was the son-in-law, not son, of Henry Earl of Lancaster.*

The King and Sir Hugh the younger held the castle, and Sir Hugh the elder and the Earl of Arundel held the town, with their supporters. And when the people of the town saw how powerful the Queen had become, and that almost all England was on her side, and clearly understood the danger they were in, they took counsel to give themselves up, and the town as well, in order to save their lives and their possessions. And they sent envoys to the Queen and her advisers, who, however, would not agree to their surrendering unless they gave up Sir Hugh Despencer and the Earl of Arundel, for it was to destroy them that she had come.

When the people of Bristol saw that they could have no peace otherwise, and could not save their possessions nor their lives, they reluctantly agreed, and opened their gates, so that the Queen, Sir John and all the barons, knights and squires entered and lodged in the city of Bristol. Those who could not get in stayed outside. Sir Hugh the elder and the Earl of Arundel were taken and brought before the Queen, for her to do what she liked with them. And her other children, her son John and her two little daughters were brought to her, for they were found there in the keeping of Sir Hugh. The Queen was overjoyed, since she had not seen them for a long time, and so was everyone else who was an enemy of the Despencers. There was general rejoicing that the King and Sir Hugh the younger who were shut up in the castle would be in great trouble, seeing the obvious and imminent danger that they were in. They could see that the greater part of the country was won over to the side of the Queen and her elder son, and drawn up in opposition to the King; so that if the King and Sir Hugh were worried and frightened and distraught, it was not without reason.

11

When the Queen and all her barons and other supporters were settled in at their ease, they approached as near as they could and laid siege to the castle. And the Queen had Sir Hugh the elder and the Earl of Arundel brought before her elder son, and all the barons that were there, and told them that she and her son would see that law and justice were done to them, according to their deeds. Then Sir Hugh answered: 'Madam, may God give us a good judge and a good judgement. And if we may not have that in this world, may we have it in the next.' Then Sir Thomas Wake stood up, a good knight, wise and courteous, who was marshal of the army, and read out all their deeds; and he turned to an old knight, sitting on his right, and asked him to say on oath what judgement should be passed on those who were guilty of such crimes. This knight took counsel with the other barons and knights, and reported it as their definite opinion that the defendants deserved death for the many horrible crimes with which they had been charged, and which were believed to be clearly proved. And that they deserved, from the cruelty of their own deeds, to suffer in three ways: first to be dragged to a place of execution, then to be beheaded, and then displayed on a gibbet. According to this sentence they were executed before the castle at Bristol, in full view of the King and Sir Hugh the younger. This execution took place in the year 1326, on the feast of Saint Denis, in October.[1]

12

After this execution took place, as you have heard, the King and Sir Hugh, seeing the terrible situation they were in, and not knowing of any relief that might come to them from any quarter, embarked with a few others in a small boat, and put out to sea from the castle, and tried to escape to Wales. But it was not the will of God that they should escape, for their sins were many. And they suffered terrible adventures; for they were in the boat for eleven days, and in spite of all their efforts they could make no headway against the wind, which by the will of God was against them; and every day they were driven back to within a mile of the castle from which they had set out.

[1] *October 19th.*

In the end Sir Henry Beaumont, son of one of the leading English Barons, boarded a barge with several others, and rowed so vigorously that the King's boatmen could not escape and were overtaken. And the King and Sir Hugh were taken back to Bristol, and handed over to the Queen and her son as prisoners.

So the Queen won back the whole kingdom of England with the help and support of Sir John of Hainault and his men. And great honour was won by him and his company, in this great adventure, for when they had embarked at Dordrecht they had numbered only three hundred men-at-arms. But for love of the Queen they acted so boldly and bravely, going on board ship and crossing the sea, few though they were in number, that they conquered as mighty a country as England, in spite of the King and all his men.

Thus ended this bold and noble enterprise; and Queen Isabel reconquered her entire kingdom and destroyed her enemies. And the King was captured by a turn of fate, as you have heard; at which the whole country rejoiced together, except the few who supported Sir Hugh Despencer.

When the King and Sir Hugh were brought to Bristol by the said Sir Henry Beaumont, the King was sent, by the advice of all the barons and knights, to the strong castle at Berkeley, on the Severn, and was handed over to the lord of Berkeley Castle, to be closely guarded. He was ordered to serve the King and look after him well and honourably, with proper people in attendance on him, but on no account to let him leave the castle. Those were his orders. And Sir Hugh was handed over to Sir Thomas Wake, the marshal of the army.

The Queen, with all the army, set out for London, which is the principal city of England. Sir Thomas Wake had Sir Hugh tied on to the meanest and poorest horse he could find; and he had him dressed in a tabard over his clothes, embroidered with the coat of arms that he bore, and so conducted him along the road in the Queen's procession as a public laughing-stock. And in all the towns they passed through, he was announced by trumpets and cymbals, by way of greater mockery, till they reached the good city of Hereford. There the Queen and all her company were received most respectfully and joyfully. And the Queen kept the feast of All Saints there with great solemnity and ceremony, out of love for her son and respect for the foreign nobles who were with him.

13

When the feast was over, Sir Hugh, who was not popular in that district, was brought before the Queen and all the barons and knights in full assembly. A list of all his misdeeds was read out to him, to which he made no reply, and the barons and knights passed sentence on him which was carried out as follows: first, he was dragged on a conveyance[1] through all the streets of Hereford, to the sound of trumpets and clarions; then he was taken to the market-place where all the people were assembled. Then he was tied on a tall ladder in full view of all the people both high and low, and a large fire was lit. Then his private parts were cut off, because he was held to be a heretic, and guilty of unnatural practices, even with the King, whose affections he had alienated from the Queen. When his private parts were cut off they were thrown in the fire and burned. Then his heart and entrails were cut out and thrown on the fire to burn, because his heart had been false and treacherous and he had given treasonable advice to the King, so as to bring shame and disgrace on the country, and had caused the greatest barons in England to be beheaded, by whom the kingdom should have been supported and defended; and he had encouraged the King not to see his wife or his son, who was to be their future king; indeed, both of them had had to leave the country to save their lives. When the other parts of his body had been disposed of, Sir Hugh's head was cut off and sent to London. His body was then divided into quarters, which were sent to the four next largest cities in England.

[1] *The word is* bahut, *a box, coffer or box-shaped trailer, used especially for the display of prisoners.*

After the execution, the Queen and all the lords, with a great number of the common people, set out for London, and travelled there by easy stages. And when they arrived, great crowds of the people of London, from the highest to the lowest, came out to meet them, and received the Queen and her son, and all those who accompanied her, with great reverence. And the citizens gave handsome presents to the Queen, and to those of her retinue who seemed to be the most deserving.

After fifteen days had passed in entertainments and feasts, the companions of Sir John of Hainault were anxious to return home, for they thought that their task was accomplished and that they had won great honour. They took leave of the Queen and the nobles, who begged them to stay a little longer, to consider what ought to be done with the King, who was then a prisoner; but they had such a desire to return home that these entreaties had no effect. When the Queen and her council saw this, they implored Sir John to stay at least until after Christmas, and to persuade as many of his companions as he could to stay on with him. This gallant knight wanted to leave no part of his mission unaccomplished, and courteously agreed to stay as long as the Queen wanted. And he kept as many of his companions with him as he could; but these were only a few, for the rest refused to stay, which displeased him very much. Even when the Queen and her council saw that nothing would induce his companions to stay, they were still shown every mark of respect. And the Queen ordered a large sum of money to be paid to them for their expenses and for their services, and jewels of great price, to each according to his rank, with which they were all perfectly content. And she had them all paid in ready money for their horses, which they decided to leave behind, accepting their own estimate of the value without any question.

Sir John stayed on in England with a few of his companions, at the Queen's earnest request; and the English paid them all the respect in their power. There were at this time a great number of countesses, and other noble ladies and maids of honour attending the Queen, and others who came there daily, who were not slow

to pay him honour, feeling that the gallant knight well deserved
it.

14

After most of the companions of Sir John had returned home,
leaving him in England, the Queen gave permission to many of
her own people to return to their homes and to their own affairs,
except for a few barons and knights whom she kept with her as her
council, ordering them to come back to London on Christmas
Day, to a great court which she intended to hold. And all those
who left promised to attend, as well as many others who received
notice of it. When Christmas came, a great court was held, as
the Queen had ordered, and it was attended by all the earls,
barons, and knights, the entire nobility of England, as well as the
prelates of the church and the chief officers of the principal towns.
At this assembly it was decided that the country could no longer
remain without a sovereign, that an account should be written of
all the actions and deeds of the King, then in prison, whether
caused by his own will or the evil counsel of others, and of all his
misdeeds, and his misgovernment of the country; that this account might be read out in public to all the nobles, and the best
advice would be taken on how, and by whom, the country was to
be governed in future. And when all the acts done or authorized
by the King, and all the details of his private life, had been read
out, the chief members of the assembly consulted together, and
came to the conclusion from their own experience that the greater
part of this account was true, and that such a man was not
worthy to wear the crown and be called King. But they agreed
that his elder son, and true heir, should be crowned instead of his
father, and that he should take wise and loyal counsel for the
better government of the country; and that his father should be
well guarded and kept prisoner, having every attention paid to his
rank, for the rest of his life.

All this was done according to the will of the great barons and
the chief officers of the biggest towns. And the young King

Edward, afterwards so successful in battle, was crowned with the royal crown in the palace of Westminster on Christmas Day, 1326; his sixteenth birthday was on the feast of the Conversion of Saint Paul,[1] 1327.

At this coronation the gallant knight Sir John of Hainault and all his companions, princes, nobles and commoners, were greatly feasted, and presented with many rich jewels. And they all remained during these grand feasts, to the delight of the lords and ladies present, until the feast of the Epiphany, when he heard that his brother, the Count of Hainault, and the King of Bohemia and a great number of the nobility of France had arranged a tournament to be held at Condé. Sir John, therefore, would stay no longer, in spite of their entreaties, for he greatly desired to go to the tournament, and to see his brother and the other lords who would be there, especially the gallant and generous prince, Charles, King of Bohemia.

When the young King Edward, the Queen, and the barons saw that Sir John would stay no longer, for all their entreaties, they gave him leave to go, though much against their will. And by the advice of the Queen, the King gave him an annuity of four hundred marks sterling, and to his heirs, to be held in fee, payable at the city of Bruges. He also gave a hundred marks a year to Philip of Châteaux, the chief squire and counsellor of Sir John, to be paid at the same time. He also gave a large sum of money to cover the expenses of their return journey, and a large escort of knights as far as Dover, and arranged his passage free of all cost, and he presented the Countess of Garennes, sister of the Count of Bar, with many rich jewels, when they took their leave.

Sir John and his company arrived at Dover and took ship to attend the tournament at Condé. And they took with them fifteen young and gallant knights from England, whom they would escort to the tournament and introduce to the lords and knights that they would find there. Sir John and his companions paid

---

[1] *January 25th. But in fact his sixteenth birthday was on November 13th, 1326.*

the fifteen young knights every possible attention, and the young men held two tournaments at Condé.

15

When Sir John and his companions had left them, the King and his mother ruled the country by the advice of the Earl of Kent, the King's uncle, and Sir Roger Mortimer, who held vast estates in England to the value of £700 a year. Both of them had been banished with the Queen. They also took the advice of Sir Thomas Wake, and of several others who were reputed to be the wisest in the land. This inspired a great deal of envy, which they say never dies down in England: and, indeed, it thrives there as freely as in other places.

So the winter passed, and the season of Lent, in perfect peace, until Easter; by that time King Robert of Scotland, who, though brave, had suffered much at the hands of the English, and had often been driven out and defeated by King Edward I, the grandfather of this young King, had grown old and now suffered from epilepsy. When he heard of the events in England, that the King had been deposed and his advisers put to death, he decided to defy the new King (seeing that he was still young and that the barons were not on good terms with one another) and conquer part of England. And so about Easter time, in the year 1327, he sent a challenge to the young King Edward and his whole country, announcing that he would enter the country and sack and burn it as he had done after the defeat of Stirling, where the English had suffered so much.

When the King and his council received this challenge, they made it known throughout the kingdom and gave orders that all nobles and others should come, properly attended according to their rank, and assemble on the following Ascension Day at York. He also sent a considerable force of men-at-arms to guard the Scottish border, and messengers to Sir John of Hainault, begging him most affectionately to come and assist and accompany him in his hour of need, and to meet him at York on Ascension Day, with as many men-at-arms as he could muster.

When the lord of Beaumont, Sir John, received this request, he sent out letters wherever he thought he could collect good companions, to Flanders, to Hainault and to Brabant, beseeching them to meet him, as well mounted and equipped as could be, at Wissant,[1] to embark there for England. All those he wrote to came willingly, as well as others who were not sent for, in the expectation that they would bring back as much money as those who had gone with him on his first expedition to England.

When he arrived at Wissant with all his company, Sir John found the ships and vessels that had brought them back from England all in a state of readiness; and they embarked with their cavalry as quickly as possible, and crossed to Dover. They continued to advance without pausing till they reached York, three days before Pentecost, where the King and his mother had assembled a great number of barons to advise and attend on him, all awaiting the arrival of Sir John of Hainault and his company, and of the men-at-arms, archers and common people of the various towns and cities. And as they arrived in their great companies, they were quartered in the villages all over the vale of York, to a distance of seven or eight miles, ready to advance to the Borders.

Sir John arrived with his company, and they were splendidly feasted by the King and his mother and all the barons. They were given the best quarters in the city, and Sir John was given an abbey of White Friars as his headquarters.

16

In order to entertain the foreign knights and all their company, the young King held a great court on Trinity Sunday, at the house of the Black Friars, where he and his mother were lodged,

---

[1] *A port between Boulogne and Calais, often used at this time for channel crossings.*

keeping their households separate—the King with his knights, and the Queen with her ladies, of whom there were a great number. The King had six hundred knights, lodged in the hall and the cloisters, and he created fifteen new ones. The Queen held her court in the dormitory, where at least sixty ladies sat at her table, whom she had assembled to entertain Sir John and the other knights. A large number of nobles were to be seen there, well served with many ingenious dishes, so disguised that no one could tell what they were. And the ladies were superbly dressed, with rich jewels, taking their ease.

But there was to be no continuation of the feast, or dancing, for immediately after dinner a violent quarrel broke out between the servants of the army of Hainault and the English archers, who were lodged with them. When these servants began fighting with the English, all the other archers in the town who were in the same quarters as the Hainaulters, assembled together, with their bows strung; a cry of alarm went up, and they started shooting at the Hainaulters, making them retreat into their lodgings. Most of the knights and their masters, who were still at court, knew nothing of the matter. But as soon as they heard of this affray, they hurried back to their quarters. Those who could not enter were left outside in great danger, for the archers, who were at least two thousand in number, were quite beyond control and were shooting indiscriminately at masters and servants alike.

It was supposed that this was all planned and executed in revenge by some friends of the Despencers and of the Earl of Arundel, whose deaths had been caused by Sir John of Hainault. For the English in whose houses the Hainaulters were lodged shut and barred the doors and windows and would not let them in. Nevertheless some of them entered the lodgings at the back, and quickly armed themselves, but did not dare go out into the street for fear of the arrows. Instead they slunk out at the back, through the gardens, trampling and breaking down the hedges and enclosures. And they waited for their companions in a square, till they amounted to a hundred in number, all armed, with as many more unarmed, who had failed to enter their lodgings.

The armed men hastened all together to the aid of their companions, who were defending their quarters in the main street as best they could; they then reached the lodging of the Lord d'Enghien, which had great gates opening onto the street at the front and at the back, and they fiercely attacked the archers. Many of the Hainaulters were wounded.

There were present there the good knights Sir Fastres de Rue, Sir Perceval de Semeris, and Sir Sanses de Boussac, who though unable to get back to their lodgings, fought as stoutly as those who were armed. They took great oak staves from the house of a carter, and dealt such fierce blows that nobody dared approach; and they knocked down sixty men, or so the story goes. In the end the archers were beaten, and three hundred were left there dead, all from the diocese of Lincoln.

I believe that God never granted better fortune to anyone than he did to Sir John of Hainault and his company. For the archers intended nothing less than to murder and rob them, even though they had come on the King's business. And the foreigners were never in such danger and trouble as during their time at York; nor were they completely safe till they returned to Wissant. For the surviving archers hated the Hainaulters even more than the Scots, who all this time were burning their country! And the knights and barons of England alerted the lords of Hainault (who felt no hatred for them) for their information and protection, that the archers and other common people of England, to the number of six thousand, were plotting and threatening to burn and kill the Hainaulters in their lodgings, by day or by night; and that there would be nobody on the side of the King or the barons that would dare to come and assist them. So it is not surprising that they were deeply troubled and alarmed. Nor could they think how to deal with this situation: they had no hope of returning to their own country, nor did they dare leave the King and the barons. They could find no comfort nor hope; all they could do was to sell themselves dearly and defend their lives, all joining together in the common cause.

The knights of Hainault made many prudent rules for their

own safety: always to sleep fully armed at night, to patrol the fields and roads round the town and the suburbs at night, and to send scouts a mile or two outside the town to see if the archers were coming, as they had been warned on reliable authority. And if the scouts were to hear troops moving towards the town, they were to return to the detachments in the fields, to give them warning, so that they could mount their horses and arm themselves, each rallying to his banner at a prearranged alarm post.

They remained in this state of unrest in the suburbs for four weeks, and they were only a handful of men by comparison with the host of the common people of England assembled there. None of them dared leave their lodgings or their arms nor enter the city, except the lords who went to see the King and the Queen and their council, to join the feast and to learn the news.

If this unfortunate and dangerous quarrel had not broken out, they would have passed the time very agreeably. For there were such abundant supplies in the city and the surrounding country that the King and all the nobles of England, and the foreigners and their troops, to the number of sixty thousand people, stayed there for six weeks without provisions becoming any dearer; as much could be bought for a penny when they left as before they arrived. There was good wine from Gascony, Alsace, and the Rhine, very cheap, and poultry and all kinds of other provisions as well. Hay, oats, and straw, of good quality, and cheap, were brought to their quarters.

17

When they had stayed there for three weeks after the affray, the King made a proclamation by his marshals that during the following week everyone should provide himself with carts and tents and all other necessities for the march to Scotland, for the King would remain there no longer. So everyone equipped himself as best he might, according to his rank, and when everything was provided, the King and his barons set out and encamped eighteen miles outside the city. Sir John of Hainault and his company were encamped next to the King, partly as a mark of honour and partly to prevent the archers, who were their bitter enemies, from taking advantage of them. The King and his advance troops stayed there two days to wait for the stragglers and to make certain that nothing was lacking.

On the third day, the whole army struck camp before daybreak and made a long day's march to the city of Durham, at the entrance to a country called Northumberland, a wild country full of deserts and mountains, and very poor in everything except cattle. Through it runs the River Tyne, full of stones and large rocks, and on this river is situated the town of Newcastle. The Earl Marshal of England was there with a large army to guard the country against the Scots, who were waiting in camp to enter England. At Carlisle there was also a large Welsh contingent, under the command of the Earl of Hereford and Lord Mowbray, to defend the crossing of the river Eden. For the Scots could not enter England without crossing one of these rivers.[1]

The English could learn no definite news of the Scots till they arrived at this place, but there they could see smoke rising from the various hamlets and villages in the valleys, which the Scots were burning. They had crossed the river so secretly that no news of their crossing had apparently reached either Carlisle or Newcastle, the distance between them being about fifty-seven miles.

The Scots are tough, and very bold and active in the use of arms and in fighting. At this time their opinion of the English was low, as it still is to the present day. When they make their forays into England, they cover sixty to seventy miles at a stretch, either by night or by day, though people who are unaware of their habits may find this difficult to believe.

[1] *Froissart's predecessor, Jean le Bel, thought that the Eden at Carlisle and the Tyne at Newcastle were both the same river, but Froissart himself discovered that the Tyne flows not towards but away from Carlisle, as we know from the revised version of Book I of the* Chronicles *in the Vatican MS.*

It is certain that on these expeditions they are all mounted on horseback, except the camp followers, who are on foot. The knights and squires are well mounted on good bay horses, and the common people on ponies. They never take transport on wheels with them, because of the wild mountains that they have to cross in Northumberland. And they take no provisions of bread or wine, because their habits are so austere that in time of war they subsist for quite a long time on half-cooked meat, with no bread, and river water, without wine. And they take no pots or pans, for they cook the meat of cattle inside the skin, after they have removed it from the carcass. And as they know they will find plenty of cattle in the country where they go, they take no provisions with them, except that each of them carries a flat stone under his saddle flaps, and a little bag of oatmeal behind the saddle: when they have eaten so much meat that their stomachs feel weak and ill, they put the stone on a fire and mix a little oatmeal with water. When the stone is hot, they lay this thin paste on it and make a little cake, like a biscuit, which they eat to ease the stomach. And it is not surprising that they make longer journeys than other people, since they all ride on horseback except the meanest of their followers.

In this manner the Scots had entered England, and were despoiling and burning the countryside, and they found more cattle than they knew what to do with. They had at least three thousand men-at-arms, knights and squires, mounted on good fast bay horses, and twenty thousand men of war, bold and alert, armed in the manner of their country and mounted on little ponies that are never tied up nor hobbled, but are turned out after the day's march to graze in the fields and bushes and heaths. The army was commanded by two excellent captains, for King Robert, who had been very brave, was now extremely old and suffering from epilepsy. He had put in command a gallant and brave prince, the Earl of Moray, whose shield was argent, three pillows gules, and Sir James Douglas, who was reputed to be the boldest and most ambitious knight in the two kingdoms, and whose shield was azure, on a chief argent three stars gules. These were the two highest and most powerful barons in the kingdom of Scotland, and the most renowned for their valour in feats of arms.

18

When the English King and his army saw the smoke rising from the villages, they knew that the Scots had entered the country. The alarm was immediately sounded, and everyone ordered to strike camp and follow the banners. They all advanced over the fields, armed and ready to give battle immediately. They formed into three battalions of infantry, each battalion including two wings composed of five hundred men-at-arms on horseback.

It was said that there were eight thousand knights and squires, and thirty thousand armed men, half of whom were mounted on ponies; the other half were countrymen on foot, sent and paid for by the towns according to their size. There were also twenty-four thousand archers, besides the camp followers.

Thus drawn up they advanced after the Scots, towards the place where the smoke was rising, till nightfall. Then the army halted in a wood, by a little river, to rest and to wait for their baggage and provisions. All day long, the Scots burned the country within a very few miles of the English, without the latter being able to catch up with them. At dawn the next day they were all drawn up again, each battalion with its banners, and advanced all day over mountains and valleys in good order, without ever being able to get near the Scots, who were burning everything before them. There were such deep woods and marshes and such wild country, full of mountains and steep valleys, that the troops were forbidden on pain of death to advance in front of the marshals with their banners.

When it was night again, all the troops—infantry, cavalry and baggage trains—were so exhausted that they could go no further. And the commanders realized that they were toiling in vain, and that if the Scots ever waited for them they would choose a mountain, or some position so advantageous that the English would not be able to fight them without grave risk. The King gave his orders, through the marshals, to encamp for the night and consider what should be done next day. So the army encamped in a wood by the side of a river, and the King lodged in a poor monastery near by. The whole of his army was quite worn out.

When each of them had chosen a place to camp, the lords retired to consider how they could bring the Scots to battle, in view of the nature of the country. It seemed probable that the Scots were returning to their own country, burning everything as they went, and that it would be impossible to fight them among these mountains except at a great disadvantage. But the Scots would have to cross the Tyne on their way home, and it was decided in full council that by starting before midnight and making haste the next day they could cut off the Scots from the place where the river could be crossed and force them either to fight at a disadvantage, or to remain cut off in England.

This decision being taken, every man retired to his quarters to eat and drink what he could; at the first sound of the trumpet, the horses were to be saddled and made ready; at the second, everyone was to arm himself, and at the third they would all mount their horses and fall in under their banners. They were to take only one loaf of bread each, carrying it slung behind them like hunters; and they were to leave behind all their equipment, including their baggage and its transport, and their provisions, as they thought they would be joining battle next day, at whatever cost, to win or lose all. These orders were carried out and by midnight all was ready, though few had had much sleep after a hard day.

Dawn broke as the battalions were forming. The banners advanced over the moors and mountains, over the valleys and rocks, without meeting any level country. On top of the mountains, as well as in the valleys, there were bogs and marshes, so difficult to cross that it was a miracle that any got through. For each man rode on ahead without waiting for his lord or for his companions. Those who fell into the mud found difficulty in getting help. Many of the banners stuck fast, and a number of the horses were unable to extricate themselves.

There were many cries of alarm that day, as if the front ranks had engaged the enemy: those further back, believing this to be the case, made all speed through the marshes, through the rocks and stones, up hill and down dale, armed in their helmets and shields, with a lance or a sword in their hands, not waiting either for father or brother or friend. When they had covered a mile or two and reached the hue and cry, they found to their disappointment that it was only herds of deer or bears or other wild beasts (of which there were a great number in those woods and wild moors) that were fleeing before the banners and horsemen. The hue and cry after these animals caused the rear to think that the van had caught up with the enemy.

So the young King and his army rode that day through the wild mountains, without following any road or path, and without finding any towns, but taking their direction from the sun. About the time of vespers they reached the Tyne, which they thought the Scots would have to cross again; and they stopped there exhausted as can be imagined, and then forded the river with great difficulty owing to the large rocks and stones lying in it. Once across, they encamped wherever they could along the bank. And the sun was setting as they encamped. Few of them had hatchets or hooks to cut wood or make any shelter. Many of them had lost their companions, and did not know what had become of them, and were naturally ill at ease. Meanwhile, those on foot were far behind. They did not know where they were, nor was there anyone to ask, but those who knew the country best said that they had covered twenty-eight miles that day, galloping on without ever stopping except when absolutely necessary. And so they lay that night on the river bank, fully armed and keeping hold of the reins of their horses, for there was nowhere to tie them up. The horses had no oats or forage that night, or the day before either, nor did the men have anything to eat except the loaf that each one carried, which was soaked by the sweat of the horses. Nor had they anything to drink but the river water, except some of the lords who had provided themselves with bottles; nor had they any fire or light, or any means of getting them, except a few lords who had torches with them. They spent the night miserably, without either taking their armour off or unsaddling their horses. When the long-awaited day dawned in which they hoped to find some relief and comfort for themselves and for their horses— either in finding food and lodging, or in fighting the Scots, which they were so keen to do, to get out of their miserable situation— it began to rain; it rained so heavily that by midday the river on which they were encamped was in such spate that no one could be sent to find out where they were, or to get food and litter for the horses, or bread and wine for their own sustenance. So they had to fast that day, and the next night as well, and the horses could only graze on the leaves of trees and heather. The men cut branches off the trees with their swords to tie their horses to, and brushwood to give themselves a little shelter.

About midday they found some poor peasants who told them that they were forty-two miles from Newcastle and thirty-three from Carlisle, and that there was no town nearer where they could get accommodation. This was reported to the King and the lords, who sent off men with horses to fetch provisions. A royal proclamation was made at Newcastle that whoever wanted to make money should bring bread, wine, oats and other provisions, and he would be paid instantly, and given safe conduct to the army. They were also informed that the army would not leave the district till they discovered where the Scots were.

Next day the messengers returned about midday with the provisions that they had been sent for, though they had not been able to procure much; and with them came people of the country with ponies and mules loaded with poorly baked bread in baskets, and some thin wine in large barrels, and other provisions, which brought a little relief to the army. And so it went on for eight days, which they spent on the river bank, surrounded by the mountains, while they waited for the arrival of the Scots, who were themselves equally ignorant of the whereabouts of their enemies.

Thus they had been three days and three nights without bread, wine, candles, oats or any other forage; and for the next four days they had to pay sixpence for a badly baked loaf that was worth only a penny, and two and sixpence for a gallon of wine worth only sixpence. Yet they were still so hungry that they snatched the food out of each other's hands, causing frequent arguments and quarrels.

All that week the rain added to their troubles, and their saddles and girths and harness became all rotten, and most of the horses developed sores on their backs. There was nothing to shoe the horses with, and no shelter for them except for their trappings. Most of the men had nothing to protect them from the rain and cold except their chain mail and armour, and there was nothing to make a fire except wood that was so green and wet it was nearly useless.

They remained in these conditions, between the mountains and the river, without hearing any news of the Scots, who they thought must pass that place, or somewhere near it, in order to return to Scotland. Great murmurs arose in the army. Those who had advised coming to that place were widely accused of having done so to betray the King and his army. So the lords in council gave orders for the army to prepare to move off and cross the river some twenty miles higher up, where the ford was easier. Orders were given for everyone to be ready to move on the next day and to follow the banners. It was also proclaimed that the first to succeed in bringing the King exact information of where the Scots could be found, would be rewarded with land to the value of one hundred pounds a year, and would be knighted by the King.

The offer of this reward was joyfully received, and fifteen or sixteen knights and squires left the army in their eagerness to win the prize, crossed the river at no small danger to themselves and climbed up into the mountains. There they all went off in different directions, each taking his own course.

The next day the army struck camp, and made a reasonable day's march, considering the state of the horses, which were far from fresh, were badly harnessed and shod, and had sores on their backs and mouths. With great difficulty they succeeded in recrossing the river, which was swollen with rain. Many fell into the water, and some were drowned. When they were over, they encamped there, finding forage in the fields; and they spent the night by a village that had been burned by the Scots. After all they had been through, this seemed to them as luxurious as being in Paris. Next day, they rode over hill and dale all day till they came to some more villages that had been burned, and some fields where there was corn and grass; there they spent the night. The third day they rode on in the same manner, having by now no idea where they were.

The fourth day began in the same way, but at nine o'clock a squire rode up to the King and said: 'Sir, I have news. The Scots are encamped on a mountain nine miles from here, waiting for you, and they have been there eight days. They knew no more of you than you did of them. What I say is true. For I rode so close to them that I was taken prisoner and brought before their chiefs. I gave them news of you and said that you were looking for them, to give them battle. And they soon let me go, when I told them of the reward you had offered anyone who could find out where they were, if he brought back news straight away. They say they are as eager to fight as you. And there you will find them without fail.'

As soon as the King heard this, he halted his army by a field of corn, to feed the horses, near a burned-out monastery of white monks, that had been called, since the days of King Arthur, Blanche Lande.[1] The King made his confession, and everybody prepared himself as best he could. And by his orders, a number of masses were said, in order that those who so desired might receive communion. He granted land to the value of a hundred pounds a year to the squire, and knighted him before the whole army. When they had all rested and eaten, the trumpets sounded. They all mounted their horses, and the banners advanced in the

[1] *Blanchland Abbey, south of Hexham.*

direction that the young knight showed them. Each battalion advanced straight ahead in close order, without making any detours round mountains or valleys. And they marched on till they came in full view of the Scots, so that each side could see the other clearly.

As soon as the Scots saw them, they came out of their camp on foot and quickly formed into three battalions on the brow of the mountain where they had been encamped. Past the foot of the mountain flowed a strong and rapid river, full of rocks and large stones, which it would have been dangerous to cross in haste. And even if the English had succeeded in crossing it, there was no room for them to form up between the river and the mountain. The Scots had drawn up two of their battalions each in a defile in the mountain, at the top of the rocky slope which it was not easy to climb to attack them: if the English had crossed the river, they would have been pelted with stones from above by the Scots, and would not have been able to turn back.

When the English lords saw how the Scots were drawn up, they ordered their men to dismount, remove their spurs and form into three battalions as before. A great number of new knights were made, and when the army had formed up, some of the chief lords escorted the young King as he rode past the lines to encourage the men. He spoke to them all most warmly and asked them to win honour both for him and for themselves. And he gave orders that no one, on pain of death, should advance in front of the banners or make any move before the order was given. Soon afterwards, the army was ordered to advance on the enemy without breaking ranks. This was done, and each battalion moved a considerable distance forward to the foot of the mountain on which the Scots were drawn up. The purpose of this advance was to see if the Scots would make a move, either forwards or backwards. But they did neither, and the armies were so close together that details of their armour could be distinguished.

The English halted, to make a new plan. And some of the troops mounted their horses to skirmish with the enemy and to examine the possibility of crossing the river, and to get an even closer view of the enemy position. Heralds were sent to tell the Scots that if they would come over the river and fight on the level ground, the English would retire and give them room to form up on the next morning. The Scots considered this offer and rejected it, telling the heralds that the King and his barons could see that the Scots were in his country, and had laid it waste and burned it; and that if this displeased the King he could come and take action, for they would stay there as long as they pleased.

When the King's council heard this answer, orders were given for the army to encamp on the spot; and so they spent the night there, lying very uncomfortably, fully armed, on the hard ground, among the rocks. They could get hardly any posts to tie up their horses, nor could they procure litter or forage, or brushwood for fires. When the Scots saw how they were placed, they left part of their army where the battalions had been drawn up, and the rest retired to their quarters, where they lit a number of fires, which were a marvellous sight to see. And all night long they made such a tremendous noise, blowing their horns and howling, that it seemed to the English as if all the devils in hell were coming to strangle them. Thus they spent the eve of the feast of St. Peter,[1] 1327.

The next day, St. Peter's day, mass was said, and everybody armed himself, and the men formed up round the banners, as on the day before. When the Scots saw this they too took up the same positions as they had before. All day the two armies faced each other, neither side daring to advance against the other. Again, some of the English crossed the river both on horseback and on foot to skirmish with the Scots, a few of whom came down to meet them, so that a number were wounded and killed, and a few prisoners taken, on both sides. In the afternoon, the lords gave orders for everyone to retire to their quarters, as they were achieving nothing.

So it continued for three days, the Scots never leaving their

[1] *August 1st.*

mountain, though there was a little skirmishing every day, with quite a number killed and captured. And at night the Scots always lit great fires, and made a hellish noise with their horns and with their howling. The intention of the English lords was to keep the Scots besieged on the mountain, since they were in no position to fight them. They assumed that they could starve the Scots out, since no provisions could reach them, and they could not get out to return to their country. The English knew, from the prisoners they had taken, that the Scots had no bread, wine, or salt, though they had caught plenty of cattle, which they could eat either boiled or roasted, though without bread or salt. Admittedly they do not mind that—they moisten a little oatmeal, as you have heard. The English, too, are sometimes reduced to this on their expeditions.

But on the fourth morning the English looked up the mountain and saw nobody: the Scots had left in the middle of the night. The commanders were amazed, and could not think what had happened to them. Scouts were sent out, both on foot and on horseback, and at about four o'clock they found the Scots encamped on another mountain, even more secure than the first, and overlooking the same river. They had camped in a wood, to be hidden, so that they could come and go secretly, as they pleased. As soon as this was known, the English were ordered to move, in battle order, and take up a position on another mountain, opposite the Scots. They formed into battalions, as if to attack, but the Scots, as soon as they saw the English formations approaching, came out of their quarters and took up a position near the river, facing the English, but still unwilling to come down or attack. Nor could the English attack them in this situation without the gravest risk. The English commanders sent heralds several times, asking them either to give or accept a stretch of level ground on which to fight. But the Scots would never agree to these proposals; and both armies suffered great discomfort in their respective positions.

On the first night that the English spent on that second mountain, Sir James Douglas, a very valiant, bold, and enterprising knight, taking with him about two hundred men-at-arms, crossed the river at some distance from the English army and, unobserved, boldly broke into the English camp, crying 'Douglas! Douglas! You will all die, you English barons!' And they killed more than three hundred men, and spurred on right up to the King's tent, still shouting and yelling 'Douglas! Douglas!' And as they left, they cut two or three of the guy-ropes of the King's tent. They lost a few of their number, but most of them got away back to the mountain.

Nothing more of this kind was attempted, and from then on the English kept a strong and vigilant guard, with sentries, to keep the army informed of anything they might hear. Most of the English knights slept in their armour, and every day skirmishes were made by all who had a mind to do so; many were wounded and taken prisoner on both sides, and many lives were lost.

On the twenty-second day, a Scots knight was captured who was forced against his will to give information about the state of the enemy. Under close examination he revealed that the Scots commanders had given orders that morning that everyone should be armed by the evening and should all follow the banner of Sir James Douglas, wherever he led them, and that this was to be kept secret. The prisoner knew nothing more for certain. The English knights held a council on this, and decided that it could mean that the Scots might come and attack and break into their camp on two fronts, making it a fight to the death, as a result of the starvation that they could endure no longer. The English formed three battalions, and each took up a position in front of the camp, and lit a large number of fires in order to see better; they left all the pages in the camp to look after the horses. And all that night they remained fully armed, each drawn up under his standard or banner, to await the outcome.

Towards daybreak, two Scots trumpeters came upon one of the outposts that guarded the English camp, and were captured and brought before the lords of the council, to whom they said: 'Sirs, what are you doing here? You are wasting your time. For we swear by our lives, the Scots left for home before midnight, and are now twelve or thirteen miles away. They took us with them for three miles, for fear we should give them away to you, and then they let us come and tell you.' On hearing this the English held a council and saw that they had been mistaken in their assumptions. They decided that it would be useless to follow after the Scots, as they would never catch them. For fear of being misled, the knights detained the two trumpeters and did not alter the position of the battalions till four o'clock; but when they saw that the Scots had in fact gone away, they let every man return to his quarters at his ease; and the lords held a council, to decide what was to be done.

Then some of the English troops mounted their horses and crossed the river, dangerous though it was, and rode up the mountain that the Scots had left in the night. They found the carcasses of five hundred fat cattle, which the Scots had killed, though unable to use them, simply in order to prevent their falling into the hands of the English alive. They also found more than three hundred cauldrons, made of skins with the hair still on the outside, hanging over fires, all full of meat and water, ready to boil; and more than a thousand spits, with meat on them, ready for roasting; and more than ten thousand old shoes, also made of undressed skins, which the Scots had left there. And they found five poor English prisoners, whom the Scots had bound naked to the trees, and two more with their legs broken. After releasing the prisoners they went back to the camp, at the moment when the whole army was preparing to return to England at the orders of the King and his council. All that day they followed the banners of the marshals, and halted quite early in a fine meadow where there was abundant forage. This was sorely needed, for the horses were so weak and exhausted by hunger that they could hardly move.

Next day they moved on again, and reached a large monastery about five miles from the city of Durham. There the King spent the night, with his army occupying the surrounding fields, where they found plenty of useful forage—grass, vetch, and corn. The next day they rested, while the King and the lords went to Durham Cathedral, where they paid homage to the bishop; the King also gave presents to the city and the burgesses, which he had not done before. In that city, they found all their carriages and carts and baggage, which they had left in a wood in the middle of the night thirty-two days previously, as you have heard. The inhabitants of Durham had found them and brought them into the city at their own expense, and had stored them in some empty barns. Each carriage had a little flag attached to it as a means of identification. The lords were delighted at finding their carriages and baggage, and they stayed in Durham for two days, with the army encamped in the surrounding country, for there was no room for them all inside the city. Then the horses were shod, and the King set out for York with the army, making such haste that they reached it in three days. There the King found his mother, the Queen, who welcomed him with great joy, as did the ladies of the court and the burgesses of the city.

There the King gave permission for the army to disband and for everyone to return to his home, and he gratefully thanked the earls, barons, and knights for their service. He kept with him Sir John of Hainault and his company, who were well entertained, especially by the Queen, and also by the knights and ladies of the court. The Hainaulters made out accounts for their horses, which were all weak and broken down—some had even died— and for their expenses, for which Sir John personally accepted full liability, because the King and his council could not at once raise the money to pay for all the horses. But they were paid enough for their immediate expenses, and for their return journey home. And in the course of the year they were all fully repaid the value of their horses.[1]

---

[1] *Rymer (Foedera I, p. 243) and* Calendar of Close Rolls, *Edward III, vol. I, 160 (H.M.S.O., 1896) quotes an order from the King to his treasurer, dated York, August 20th, 1327, to pay Sir John of Hainault on his arrival in London four thousand pounds for the loss of his horses, and to pawn the jewels in the Tower if there was not enough ready money available for the purpose.*

When the Hainaulters had received this advance for their horses, they bought ponies, to ride more comfortably, and sent all their grooms and trunks and baggage back by sea in two boats that the King provided for them, which landed them at Sluys, in Flanders. They took leave of the King and Queen, of the Earls of Kent and Lancaster, and of the barons, who paid them great honour. The King gave them an escort of twelve knights and two hundred men-at-arms to protect them against the archers, from whom they still did not feel safe, as they had to pass through their district, the diocese of Lincoln.

With this escort Sir John of Hainault set out with all his company, and eventually reached Dover, where they embarked in ships that were waiting ready for them; there their escort left them and all returned home. The Hainaulters arrived at Wissant, where they waited for two days, seeing to their horses and their armour. During this time Sir John and some of the other knights made a pilgrimage to the shrine of Our Lady at Boulogne. Then they all went back to their homes, except Sir John who went to visit his brother at Valenciennes. His brother, who was much attached to him, received him with great delight, and Sir John related to him the account of his whole expedition.

19

Such was the expedition that King Edward made against the Scots in the first year of his reign. Shortly afterwards the King and Queen, the Earls of Kent and Lancaster, Sir Roger Mortimer and the other barons in the council made a plan for the King to marry. They sent a bishop, two knights banneret, and two clerks to Sir John of Hainault to ask for his help in approaching his brother the Count of Hainault and Holland about the matter, that the Count might send one of his daughters. For the King would love her all the more dearly for his friendship with Sir John. Sir John gave magnificent feasts and honours to these messengers from the King, as he well knew how to, and then escorted them to his brother at Valenciennes, who also received them with great honour, and entertained them so elaborately that it would be tedious to relate.

When they had finished feasting, and explained their mission, the count answered them courteously, and said that he gave many thanks to the King and Queen, and to the lords by whose council they had been sent there to do him such honour; he added that they had sent such a distinguished embassy that he agreed to their request, subject to the permission of the Holy Father the Pope, and the Holy Church.

This answer was satisfactory, and two knights and two clerks were sent to the Pope at Avignon to seek a dispensation for the marriage. This was made necessary by the degree of their consanguinity, for their mothers were first cousins, being the daughters of two brothers. As soon as they reached Avignon their business was done, for the Pope and the College of Cardinals readily gave their consent.

When the messengers returned to Valenciennes from Avignon with their sealed documents from the Pope, the marriage was at once arranged and settled on both sides. Immediate preparations were made for the dress and personal possessions of the lady who was to be Queen of England. When all was ready she was married by virtue of a procuration which was brought from the King. She then set out for London, where her husband was awaiting her, and where she was to be crowned. She embarked at Wissant, and landed with her retinue at Dover. Her uncle, Sir John, conducted her to London and was most nobly received and feasted and honoured by the King and his court. There were great crowds of the nobility assembled, with jousts, dances, and feasts every day for three weeks in her honour.

Then Sir John took his leave and returned to Hainault with his company, richly loaded with jewels, which had been presented to them on all sides. Few of her countrymen remained with the young Queen besides a young man called Walter de Manny, who stayed to carve and wait on her at table. He later found such favour with the King and the nobles that he was included in the royal council. And afterwards he performed noble feats without number in many different places.

20

After the Scots had left the mountain, during the night, where they were besieged by King Edward and the English, they rode sixty-five miles at a stretch through that wild country, and crossed the Tyne[1] not far from Carlisle, returning to their own country. There, by the orders of their chieftains, they all disbanded and went to their own homes. Soon afterwards, some of the lords and wise counsellors arranged negotiations between the Kings of England and Scotland, resulting in a truce that lasted for three years.

During this truce King Robert of Scotland, who had been a very valiant knight, became so old and ill that he felt that death was near. He sent for all his chief counsellors among the barons of Scotland and told them he was dying, as they could see, and he begged and charged them, on their honour, to defend the country loyally, on behalf of his son David, and to obey him and crown him King when he came of age, and to arrange a marriage for him suitable to his station. Then he called the gallant Sir James Douglas, and said to him in front of the others: 'Sir James, my dear friend, you know what hardships and difficulties I have been through in my time to maintain the rights of this kingdom. And at the time when I was most occupied, I made a vow that I have never fulfilled. This makes me very uneasy. I vowed that once I had finished the war in such a way that I could govern this country in peace, I would go and help fight the enemies of Our Lord and adversaries of the Christian faith, to the best of my power. This was my heart's desire, but God willed otherwise: He has given me so much else to do in my time, and has recently afflicted me with this terrible disease, so that, as you see, I am on

---

[1] *Froissart probably means the Eden, but see note on p. 29.*

the point of dying. Since my body cannot go and achieve my heart's desire, I wish to send my heart in its place, to fulfil my vow. And since I know of no knight in my kingdom more honourable than yourself or more fit to carry out my vow for me, I beg of you, my dear and special friend, as earnestly as I can, to undertake this journey, for love of me, and to acquit my soul before Our Saviour. I know your valour and your loyalty: if you undertake it, you will not fail, and I shall die more contented. But it must be done as follows:

'As soon as I am dead, take my heart from my body and have it embalmed; and take as much money from my treasury as you shall think necessary for the journey, for yourself and for all those whom you want to take with you. And take my heart to the Holy Sepulchre where Our Lord was buried, since my body cannot go. Spare no expense, and provide yourself with such company and equipment as befits your rank. And wherever you go, let it be known that you are carrying the heart of Robert King of Scotland over the seas at his command, since his body cannot go.'

All those present wept out loud, and when Sir James found his voice, he said: 'Gallant sir, I thank you a hundred thousand times for the great honour you do me, and for the noble and priceless treasure that you entrust to me. I will most willingly do as you command, with the utmost loyalty in my power—never fear, however unworthy and inferior I may feel for the task.'

'Gallant sir,' said the King, 'I thank you. I have your promise?' 'Certainly, sir, most willingly.' And he gave his promise as a loyal knight. Then said the King: 'Thanks be to God! I shall die more peacefully, now that I know that the most valiant and accomplished knight in my kingdom will achieve for me what I have been unable to achieve for myself.'

Soon after, the valiant Robert the Bruce, King of Scotland, left this world, and was buried with all honours. His heart was taken and embalmed, as he had commanded. He was buried in the monastery at Dunfermline, having died on November 7th, 1327. Soon afterwards the valiant Earl of Moray also died, one of the most gallant and powerful princes of Scotland.

With the arrival of spring, the favourable season for sea voyages, Sir James Douglas made all the necessary preparations to carry out his expedition. He embarked at Montrose and sailed straight to Sluys, in Flanders, to find out if anyone was crossing the sea to Jerusalem in the Holy Land, so that he could join their company. He remained there for twelve days, refusing to set foot on shore, and staying on board ship the whole time, keeping a magnificent table, attended by trumpeters and drummers, just as if he had been the King of Scotland himself. He had with them a knight banneret, and six of the most valiant knights of Scotland, besides the rest of his staff. All his plate was of gold and silver—pots, basins, dishes, goblets, bottles, barrels, and everything else of that kind. He had twenty-six young and noble squires from the highest families in Scotland to wait on them. All those of any importance who came to see him were entertained with two kinds of wine, and two kinds of spices.

After spending twelve days at Sluys, he heard that King Alfonso of Spain was at war with the King of Granada, who was a Saracen, and he decided that by going there he would be making better use of his time and his journey, on the way to performing the task entrusted to him. He left Sluys and went straight to Spain, landing at the port of Valencia, and at once joining the King of Spain who was with his army on the frontier, quite near to the Saracen King of Granada.

Soon after their arrival, the King of Spain left his camp to approach nearer to his enemies. The King of Granada did the same, so that the two Kings confronted each other with all their banners. They began to form up their battalions and Sir James with his company took up a position on one of the flanks, to make his contribution the more conspicuous. When he saw the troops on both sides all drawn up, and the King of Spain's battalion advance a little, he thought that they were going to attack. And, in his anxiety always to be among the foremost, he and all his company spurred on their horses till they reached the King of Granada's battalion and made a violent attack on it, thinking that they were followed by the King of Spain and all his troops.

But this was not so, and he was deceived, for none of them followed him. The gallant knight, with all his company, was completely surrounded. And in spite of exceptional feats of arms and valour on their part, not one of them escaped, and all were killed. This was a terrible misfortune, and showed great cowardice on the part of the Spaniards, for which they were held to blame by all who heard tell of the affair: for they could easily have come to the rescue of the Scots if they had wished. So ended the voyage of Sir James Douglas.[1]

About the time this expedition left Scotland, a number of nobles and others, in the cause of peace between that country and England, arranged a marriage between the young King David of Scotland and the sister of the young King of England, which took place at Berwick with great feasts and celebrations on both sides.

21

King Charles IV of France, son of Philip the Fair, was married three times but left no male heir, to the detriment of his country, as you shall hear. His first wife was one of the most beautiful ladies in the world, the daughter of the Count of Artois. But she was not a good wife to him, and went mad; for a long time she was kept a prisoner in the Château Gaillard, before her husband was King. But when he came to the throne, the twelve peers of France were unwilling to allow the country to remain without a male heir. They strongly advised him to marry again, and he agreed, and married the daughter of the Emperor Henry of Luxemburg, sister of the gallant King of Bohemia; his first marriage, to the lady who was now in prison, being annulled by the pope of the day. By his second wife, who was most prudent and humble, he had a son, who died as a baby, and the mother died soon afterwards, at Issoudun, in Berry. The circumstances

---

[1] *His body was brought back to Scotland, where he was buried in the church of Douglas in the family vault. The heart of Robert the Bruce was buried at Melrose.*

of their deaths were suspicious, and a number of accusations were later made. The King afterwards married his third wife, Joan, the daughter of his uncle by marriage, Louis Count of Evreux; her brother was then King of Navarre. Before she bore him a child, the King was already on his deathbed. And, realizing that he was about to die, he gave orders that if the child should be a son, his cousin Philip of Valois should be the child's guardian, and regent of the country till the new King became of age. But if the child should be a daughter, the twelve peers of France, and the chief barons, were to take counsel together and give the crown to whoever appeared to have the best right to it. King Charles died about Easter in the year 1328, and soon afterwards a daughter was born to the Queen.

Most of the people of France were much upset and disturbed by this; and when the twelve peers of France heard of it, they met at Paris as soon as they could, and gave the crown by common consent to Philip of Valois. They passed over Isabel, Queen of England, and her son King Edward III, although she was the sister of the late King Charles. The reason they gave was that the kingdom of France is so noble that it must not pass to a woman, nor through the female line, as you heard at the beginning of this history. Philip was crowned King at Rheims on Trinity Sunday 1328, and, as a result, terrible wars and great desolation befell the kingdom of France, as you shall hear.

Soon afterwards King Philip VI summoned his barons and men-at-arms and went with a powerful army to Cassel to make war on the Flemish; and especially on those round Bruges and Ypres and those who lived in the district round Dunkirk and Gravelines. These were all unwilling to obey their lord, the Count of Flanders, and were in open revolt. He had been driven right out of his country and was reduced to living in miserable circumstances at Ghent.

King Philip defeated a Flemish army of at least sixteen thousand under their bold and intrepid commander, Colin Dannequin. The Flemish had put the garrison of Cassel under the command of the towns named above, to guard the frontier and keep it intact. I will now explain how the Flemish were defeated through their own bad tactics.

22

They left Cassel one day, at supper-time, to attack the King and his army. They moved very quietly, in three battalions, of which the first went straight to the King's tent and nearly took him by surprise as he sat at supper with his whole household. The second battalion went straight to the King of Bohemia's camp, and nearly caught him in the same situation. The third battalion went to the Count of Hainault's camp, and also narrowly missed catching him unawares. They pressed him so hard that his troops and those of Sir John his brother, the Lord of Beaumont, hardly had time to arm themselves. These three battalions came on the camp so quietly that the commanders scarcely had the chance to prepare themselves to fight, or their troops to assemble. They would all have been killed had not God miraculously come to their rescue; but by His grace, each of these lords defeated their attackers so completely in the space of a single hour that of the sixteen thousand Flemish troops not one survived[1]; and their captain was killed with them. None of these lords had any news of the others until the attack was over. Of all the Flemish soldiers, not one retreated; they were all killed on the spot and their bodies lay in three great heaps. The battle was on Saint Bartholomew's Day[2] in 1328.

After this victory the French came to Cassel and planted the banners of France there. The town surrendered to the King, and so did the towns of Poperinghe and Ypres and the territory under the castle of Bergues, and Bruges. They received Count Louis, their lord, with an enthusiastic welcome, and swore loyalty and allegiance to him for ever.

---

[1] *The figures are grossly exaggerated:* '*The loss on the Flemish side was probably less than four thousand.*' G. C. Macaulay.

[2] *August 24th.*

When King Philip had reinstated the Count of Flanders in his country, he disbanded his troops and went back to France to spend some time in Paris and the neighbourhood. He was much praised and honoured for this campaign in Flanders, and for the service he had done to Count Louis of Flanders, his brother. He lived in great prosperity, and much increased the royal power; and no King of France, so it was said, had ever lived in such royal state as King Philip.

23

The young King of England was ruled for a long time by the advice of his mother and of Edmund Earl of Kent and Sir Roger Mortimer, as you have heard. At length jealousy arose between these two lords, to the extent that Sir Roger Mortimer, with the connivance of the Queen Mother, advised the King that the Earl of Kent was going to poison him, if he was not careful, in order to inherit the throne to which he was next in line of succession. For the King's younger brother, John of Eltham, had recently died.[1] King Edward believed this report, in the way that young lords are often all too ready to believe their advisers, especially in the case of bad reports rather than good ones; and soon afterwards he had his uncle the Earl of Kent arrested and publicly beheaded, before any plea could be made on his behalf. Everyone in the land, nobles and commoners alike, was deeply troubled and concerned by this, and felt strongly against Sir Roger Mortimer ever after. They thought that it was through his advice and false testimony that this punishment had been inflicted on the gallant Earl of Kent, whom they regarded as both prudent and loyal. Sir Roger Mortimer was never so popular again.

[1] *Froissart is not quite right. John of Eltham survived the Earl of Kent by six years, and the King had another brother, Thomas of Brotherton, Earl of Norfolk; so there could have been little question of the Earl of Kent actually inheriting the throne.*

Not long afterwards great infamy fell on the Queen Mother, whether justly or not I do not know, because it was reported that she was with child by Sir Roger Mortimer. These rumours finally reached the ears of the King; he was also reminded that it was by the false evidence and jealousy of Mortimer that he had put to death his own uncle the Earl of Kent, who had been regarded all over the country as a prudent and loyal man. The King had Mortimer arrested and brought to London before him, and convened a great assembly of the barons and nobles. A knight read out all the deeds of Sir Roger Mortimer from a declaration. And when everything had been read out, the King asked everyone to give his judgement and say what ought to be done to him. Judgement was soon given, for everyone already had the facts on good information. They replied that Mortimer should suffer the same fate as Sir Hugh Despencer, and this sentence was carried out without delay or mercy. Mortimer was dragged through the streets of London on a hurdle, and then tied to a ladder in an open square. His private parts were cut off and thrown onto a fire, as were his heart and entrails, since he was guilty of treason in thought and deed. His body was then quartered and sent to the four largest cities in England, the head remaining in London.[1] Such was the fate of Sir Roger Mortimer; may God forgive him his sins.

The King then, on the advice of his council, had the Queen Mother shut up in a castle, with a number of servants and ladies to wait on her, as well as knights and squires of honour, in keeping with her rank. He also made her a handsome allowance to keep her for the rest of her life in the state to which she was accustomed. But he would not allow her to leave the castle or show herself except when any entertainment was given before the castle gates. The Queen Mother passed her time quite comfortably there, and the young King visited her two or three times a year.

[1] *According to Dugdale, Mortimer's body was left hanging for two days and two nights by the King's command, and was then given to the Grey Friars who buried it in their church, from where it was eventually moved to Wigmore. Froissart appears to have merely repeated the fate of Sir Hugh Despencer.*

24

After the King had carried out these two executions, he took new advisers from among the wisest and most highly regarded of his subjects, and kept the country at peace by following their good advice.

About a year after the coronation of Philip of Valois, when all the barons and tenants of the crown in France had done him fealty and homage except the young King Edward, who had neither appeared nor been summoned, the King of France was advised to send for the English King to come and do homage to him, as was his duty. And he sent the lord of Anceris and the lord of Beausault with two clerks of the Parliament of Paris called Simon of Orléans and Peter of Maisiers to London to take this message to the King. These four messengers accordingly left Paris with a large retinue and crossed over by Wissant and Dover, where they spent a day waiting for their horses and baggage to be landed. They then went on to Windsor, where the King and Queen were in residence. The four messengers told the King their business, and who had sent them. King Edward, to do honour to his cousin the French King, gave them an audience and received them honourably, as did the Queen. Afterwards they stated their business and were given a ready hearing. The King answered that he had not got his council with him, but that he would send for them, and they might go on to London where a sufficient answer could be given them. To their great delight they dined with the King and Queen, and then left, spending the night at Colnbrook on their way to London.

The King followed them shortly afterwards, and went to his palace at Westminster. He summoned his council, and they in turn sent for King Philip's messengers; and when they had presented the letters sent by their lord, the King of France, they withdrew, and the King asked his council what was to be done. It was decided to send an answer in accordance with past precedent, to be delivered by the Bishop of London as follows: 'My lords, you are the emissaries of the King of France, and I bid you welcome. We have heard your speech, and read your letters, and considered them with all attention. We inform you that we have advised our lord, the King, to go and visit his cousin, the King of France, who has sent this message in such friendly style, and to perform his homage to him in accordance with his bounden duty. You will return to France and tell your lord the King that the King of England will soon be with him to do his solemn duty.'

The messengers were delighted with this answer, and took their leave of the King and Queen; before they left, a feast was held in their honour at the Palace of Westminster, and as they left, the King gave them rich presents and fine jewels, as a mark of his affection and regard for his cousin, the King of France. They soon left, and went straight back to Paris, where they found King Philip and gave him their news. The King was very pleased, and said that he would be delighted to see his cousin King Edward, whom he had never seen before.

The news spread throughout France that the King of England was coming to do homage to King Philip, and the dukes, counts, and other nobles made elaborate preparations for his visit. King Philip wrote to his cousins, King Charles of Bohemia and King Louis of Navarre, specifying the day on which King Edward was coming and inviting them to be present; these two kings accordingly arrived with great magnificence. The King of France was advised to go and meet his cousin in the city of Amiens. Great preparations were made there—rooms, houses, and provisions for the King and all his staff, as well as for the Kings of Bohemia and Navarre, the dukes of Brittany, Burgundy, and Bourbon, who were coming with more than three thousand horse, and the King of England, who was to bring six hundred. He did not omit to equip himself suitably, as befitted his high estate, for his visit to the King of France. He brought with him the Bishops of London and Lincoln, the Earls of Derby,[1] Salisbury, Warwick, and

---

[1] *The King's first cousin, son of Thomas, Earl of Lancaster.*

Hereford, and six barons—Sir Reginald Cobham, Thomas Lord Wake, the Marshal of England, Richard Lord Stanford, Lord Percy, Lord Mohun, and Lord Mowbray—besides forty knights.

There were over a thousand horse in all, and the crossing from Dover to Wissant took two days. When they were all across, the King and his company rode to Boulogne, where they spent one day.

The news of his arrival at Boulogne soon reached King Philip and the French lords, who were already at Amiens. King Philip was delighted, and sent his constable with a number of knights to meet King Edward, who was at Montreuil. After receiving a very warm welcome, the King of England was escorted to Amiens, where King Philip was ready to receive him with all due ceremony, attended by the Kings of Bohemia, Navarre, and Mallorca, and a marvellous array of dukes, counts, and barons. All the twelve peers of France had come to do honour to the King, to entertain him and to witness his homage. King Philip received him honourably and magnificently, as did the other Kings and the nobility of France, for the space of fifteen days.

Many conferences and diplomatic exchanges took place, and it seems to me that King Edward did homage by word of mouth alone, without putting his hands between those of the King of France, or of any prince or prelate nominated by him. But by the advice of his council, the King of England would proceed no further with his homage without going back to England to examine such precedents as would clarify the whole question of homage and of what was due from the King of England to the King of France. The latter did not press him, but replied: 'Cousin, we do not wish to deceive you; what you have already done is quite sufficient until you shall have returned to your country and discovered from the undertakings of your predecessors what you should do.' King Edward replied: 'Sir, I thank you.'

After spending a reasonable time with him, King Edward took his leave amicably of King Philip and the other nobles, and returned to England; he went to Windsor, where Queen Philippa welcomed him with joy, and asked after King Philip, her uncle, and her French relations. The King told her of the great reception he had been given, and of the great honours paid to him, which could not have been met with in any other country but France.

Soon afterwards the King of France sent the following emissaries to London from his privy council: the Bishops of Chartres and Beauvais, Louis of Clermont, the Duke of Bourbon, the Count of Harcourt and the Count of Tankerville, besides other knights and clerks of the law, to confer with King Edward on the matter in London. For on his return the King had examined the question of how his predecessors had paid homage for the land they held in Aquitaine, of which they were dukes. A number of people in England were complaining that King Edward came before King Philip in line of succession to the French throne. Nor were King Edward and his counsellors unaware of this. But a great parliament and assembly took place on the subject, and the French King's ambassadors remained there all winter, till the following May, without getting any definite answer. But in the end the English King, in accordance with his privileges, by which he set great store, was advised to write the following letters patent, sealed with his great seal, in recognition of the homage that he owed to the King of France.

'Edward, by the grace of God King of England, lord of Ireland and Duke of Aquitaine, to all those who may see or hear of these letters, sends greeting.

'Be it known, that when we did homage at Amiens to our excellent and well beloved lord and cousin Philip King of France, it was said and required of us on his behalf that we should acknowledge the said homage to be liege homage, and that in doing it we should expressly promise to bear faith and loyalty to him, which at the time we did not do, not having information that it was due. We did homage to the King of France in general terms only, saying that we entered into his homage in the same way as our predecessors, as Dukes of Guyenne, had done to the Kings of France of the time. We have since ascertained the truth, and we acknowledge, by these presents, that the said homage we did in general terms to the King of France at Amiens, was, and ought to be, liege homage, and that we owe him faith and loyalty, as Duke of Aquitaine, peer of France, Earl of Ponthieu and Montreuil. And we promise henceforward to bear faith and loyalty to him. So that no disputes may arise over this matter in the future, we promise for ourselves and our successors, as Dukes of Aquitaine, to do homage in the following manner.

'The King of England, as Duke of Aquitaine, will put his hands between those of the King of France; and the person who speaks on behalf of the King of France, and addresses the King of England as Duke of Aquitaine, shall say as follows: "You become liegeman to my lord the King of France, as Duke of Aquitaine and peer of France, and you promise to bear him faith and loyalty. Say: *Yes.*" And the King of England, and his successors, shall say: *Yes.* Then the King of France shall receive the King of England, by faith and by mouth.[1] Moreover when the said King and duke enters homage as Earl of Ponthieu and Montreuil to the King of France, he shall put his hands between those of the King of France, and the person who speaks on behalf of the King of France shall say: "You become liegeman of my lord the King of France, as Earl of Ponthieu and Montreuil, and you promise to bear him faith and loyalty. Say: *Yes.*" And the King of England, as Earl of Ponthieu, shall say: *Yes.* The King of France shall receive liege homage from the King of England, by faith and mouth.

'In this manner shall all future homage be paid and renewed. For this cause we and our successors, Dukes of Aquitaine, after doing homage, will present letters patent, sealed with our great seal, if the King of France so requires. We also undertake to keep the peace between the Kings of France and the Dukes of Aquitaine. So it shall be done, and the said letters will be renewed by the succeeding Kings of England, whenever they pay homage as Dukes of Aquitaine and Earls of Ponthieu and Montreuil to the

---

[1] 'Homage de foi et de bouche' *was the usual form.*

succeeding Kings of France. As proof of this, we have added our great seal. Given at Eltham, the 30th of March, 1330.'[1]

The lords mentioned above took this letter back to France, having taken their leave of the King. And the King of France ordered it to be deposited in his chancery.

25

Robert, Count of Artois, was the man above all others who helped King Philip come to the throne; he was one of the highest barons of France, and of most noble lineage, being descended from kings. He had married the King's younger sister, and had always been his special companion and friend in all his fortunes. For three years he had managed everything in France, and nothing was done without his approval.

It then happened that King Philip took a violent hatred against the count, by reason of a suit that was brought before him regarding the County of Artois. Count Robert tried to win this suit by means of a letter that he produced, and which, by all accounts, was forged. And if he had been arrested in the first flush of the King's rage, he would inevitably have been put to death. So in spite of his exalted rank and position, he decided to leave France and go to his nephew, Count John, his sister's son, at Namur. When he had gone, and the King saw that he had escaped, he arrested his own sister, who was Count Robert's wife, and her two sons John and Charles, and imprisoned them, swearing that they would never be released as long as he lived. And in spite of various appeals on their behalf, they were never released, for which the King was much blamed, though not openly.

The King was extremely angry on discovering that Count Robert had gone to Namur, and in his rage sent a message to

---

[1] *This text has been rationalized: the Froissart MS is inconsistent in its mentions of the dukedoms of Guyenne and Aquitaine.*

Raoul, Bishop of Liège, asking him to attack and make war on John, the Count of Namur, unless he expelled Count Robert from his country. This bishop was extremely fond of the King of France, and thought little of his neighbours, and he sent a message to the young Count of Namur saying that he would make war on him if he did not expel his uncle, Count Robert. The Count of Namur reluctantly sent away his uncle, for fear of worse happening. Count Robert, in great distress, decided to go and see his cousin the Duke of Brabant, who was powerful enough to support him, and who welcomed him with great joy, and gave him every comfort. On learning this, King Philip sent a message to the duke that if he supported Count Robert or allowed him to remain on his territory, then he would have no worse enemy than the King of France, and he would do him all the harm in his power. The duke then no longer dared support Count Robert openly, but sent him in secret to Argenteuil, till he could see how the King would react.

The King, who had spies everywhere, discovered this, and in his rage made an alliance against the duke of Brabant composed of the King of Bohemia (though he was the duke's first cousin), the Bishop of Liège, the Archbishop of Cologne, the Duke of Guelders, the Marquis of Juliers, the Count of Bar, the Count of Los, the Lord Fauquemont, and several other lords. They all challenged the duke and entered his country near Hasbaing, and went straight to Hannet. And they burned the countryside twice, as they pleased. The King sent with them the Count of Eu, his constable, with a great number of men-at-arms, to show that he had instigated the whole campaign.

At this point William, Count of Hainault, decided to intervene; he sent his wife (who was also a sister of King Philip), and his brother Sir John, Lord of Beaumont, to the King to ask for a truce between him and the Duke of Brabant. After making endless difficulties, the King agreed, on condition that the duke should submit to the decisions of the King and his council with regard to the duke's relations with the King and his allies, and that he should evict Count Robert from his country by a certain date, which he agreed to do only with extreme reluctance, being left with no alternative.

26

Meanwhile King Edward decided to make war on his brother-in-law the King of Scotland. The three-year truce between the two countries had been kept, and peace lasted for another year after that, making the longest break in hostilities for two hundred years. But King David had now seized the city of Berwick-on-Tweed, which was properly part of England, and which had been peacefully held for a long time by Edward I and Edward II. King Edward III was also informed that the kingdom of Scotland was held in fief to his own crown, and that the young King of Scotland, his brother-in-law, had never acknowledged this or paid homage for it. He therefore indignantly sent ambassadors to King David, asking him to withdraw his people from the city of Berwick, and to restore it to him, because it had always belonged to the Kings of England, his ancestors, from whom he had inherited it; he also asked him to come and do homage for the kingdom of Scotland, which King David only held in fief.

King David took the advice of his barons and chieftains, and sent back the following reply: 'My lords, I and my barons are much surprised by the request that you bring from the King my brother-in-law. For we cannot find that the kingdom of Scotland has ever been subject to that of England, either by homage or in any other way. The late King, my father, of happy memory, never paid homage to the King of England, whatever wars were fought over the matter, and I have no intention of doing so myself. As for the town of Berwick, King Robert my father won it by open war from the late King of England, and kept possession of it for his whole life, as I intend to do to the best of my power. I would ask you to request the King, whose sister I have married, to allow me to enjoy the same powers as my ancestors enjoyed, and to keep what my father won and held peacefully all his life; and not to listen to any evil counsel. For if anyone wishes us harm, the

King should assist and support us, for the love of his sister who is my wife.'

The ambassadors replied: 'Sir, we have understood your answer, and will faithfully take it back to our lord the King.' And they returned to the King, who was far from pleased with this answer to his request. He summoned all the barons, knights, and councillors to a parliament, to give their considered opinion on the matter.

Meanwhile Count Robert of Artois came to England disguised as a merchant, following the advice of the Duke of Brabant. King Edward received him kindly, made him a member of his council, and created him Earl of Richmond, a title that his ancestors had had.[1]

When those who had been summoned had assembled for the parliament, the King made public his request to the King of Scotland, together with the answer. He then asked for such counsel as would maintain the honour of the crown. The final consensus of the council was that the King could not honourably endure the wrongs that the King of Scotland was inflicting on him; and they advised him to take a sufficiently powerful force, not only to recapture Berwick, but to invade Scotland in such a way that King David would be only too glad to pay homage and satisfaction. They added that they would willingly accompany him under his command.

The King was delighted by this reply and by the goodwill of the people. He thanked them and asked them to be ready and equipped, on a given day, at Newcastle. Each returned to his home to make preparations. The King himself prepared for the campaign, and sent further ambassadors to King David to give him due notice and, provided King David had not changed his mind, to defy him.

As the appointed day drew near, King Edward arrived at Newcastle with his army, and waited for three days until their

---

[1] *This is a mistake. The earldom of Richmond had long been in the family of the Dukes of Brittany, according to Dugdale.*

number was complete. On the fourth day they set out for the border, passing over the lands of Lord Percy and Lord Neville, who are two great barons in Northumberland. They marched forward with Lord de Ros, Lord Mowbray, and also Lord de Lisle; the King approached the city of Berwick, for King David sent the same answer to the second embassy as he had to the first, and so had been properly summoned and defied. The King entered Scotland, crossing the Tweed, and was advised not to stop at Berwick but to ride on and burn and lay waste the country, as his grandfather had done in the past. He succeeded in laying waste all the flat country, including a number of towns surrounded with dikes and palisades, and he took the strong castle of Edinburgh, placing his own garrison inside. And they crossed the second river[1] of Scotland below Stirling, overrunning the country as far as Perth and Aberdeen, and burning and sacking the town of Dunfermline. But the monastery they left unharmed, by order of the King. They conquered the country to the east as far as Dundee and westwards as far as Dumbarton, a very strong castle on the border of the Highlands, where the King and Queen had retired. Nobody withstood the English, for all the Scots retired into the forests of Jedworth, which are impenetrable to those who do not know the country. They carried all their movable possessions there, abandoning everything else. It is not surprising that the Scots were frightened, and fled, for they had no experienced commanders, as they had had in the past: King David was only fifteen or sixteen years old; the Earl of Moray was still younger; and a boy named William Douglas, nephew of the Douglas killed in Spain, was the same age, so that the kingdom of Scotland was without good captains and completely at the mercy of the English. The whole plain of Scotland was therefore laid waste, and a number of castles were captured and garrisoned by King Edward.

When this had continued for six months, and the King still met with no opposition, he retired in good order to Berwick,

---

[1] *The Forth.*

capturing Dalkeith Castle on the way. This is the ancestral home of the Earl of Douglas, and lies about five miles from Edinburgh. King Edward appointed a governor and a strong garrison. And by short marches he came to Berwick, which is situated at the entrance to Scotland, on the border of Northumberland. He surrounded the city and besieged it, saying that he would not leave until either he had taken it or the King of Scotland had come at the head of his army to raise the siege.

The King spent a long time before Berwick, for the city was well fortified and garrisoned by King David's men, and an arm of the sea runs up to it on one side. All this time there were assaults and skirmishes outside the city walls nearly every day, for the townsmen were constantly expecting to be relieved; in this they were disappointed, though a few Scots knights did ride up with the intention of surprising the English in the evening, or at daybreak. But all in vain, for the English army was so much on the alert that the Scots could not have made an effective attack without suffering heavy losses.

When the people of Berwick could see that there was no hope of relief, and that provisions were failing, and that they were so closely besieged by land and sea that nothing could enter, they decided to negotiate with the King for a truce of one month. And if King David or his men did not come and raise the siege during that month, they would surrender the city, on condition that their lives and goods were spared and the soldiers allowed to return to their native land without loss or damage.

This truce was not immediately concluded, for the King would have preferred an unconditional surrender, to punish as he pleased those who had held out so obstinately against him. But finally he yielded to the good advice of his council, and especially of Count Robert of Artois, who had been at his side throughout the whole campaign, constantly pointing out how good his legal right was to the French throne, since he was heir to his mother's brother, the late King Charles. Count Robert wanted the King to move the scene of war to France, to avenge his losses there, and to leave Scotland. By these and other arguments the

King was persuaded to ratify the Treaty of Berwick. The truce was granted, and after a month the people of Berwick informed their lord King David and his council of their position, from which they could think of no conceivable way of fighting the King of England or raising the siege. The town of Berwick was therefore given up at the end of the month, together with the fine, strong castle that stands outside it. The marshals of the army took possession of both in the name of the King. The burgesses came out to do homage and fealty to the King, and to acknowledge that it was from him that they held the town. Then the King made his ceremonial entry into the town to the sound of trumpets, and stayed there twelve days. He appointed a knight called Sir Edward Balliol as governor, and left several young knights and squires with him to help preserve the conquests he had made from the Scots, and to defend the frontier.

The King then turned back towards London, giving leave to his troops to disband, and he himself went to Windsor, which was his favourite residence, taking with him Count Robert of Artois, who reminded him incessantly, night and day, of his right to the French throne. The King listened to him readily.

So ended King Edward's expedition against the Scots. He laid waste the greater part of their country[1] and at long last the English captured a number of castles from the Scots, the most important being that of Berwick. The King stationed in them a number of able and expert knights, of whom Sir William Montagu and Sir Walter de Manny are most worthy of mention. They led the chief skirmishes and minor expeditions against the Scots, in most of which they are said to have been successful, and to have won the favour of King Edward and his barons.

The better to secure their entry and retreat on their forays into Scotland, Sir William Montagu fortified the Tower of Roxburgh, on the border, and made it a strong castle, capable of resisting any attack. He gained so much favour by this that the King made him Earl of Salisbury, and found him a noble and

[1] *An obvious exaggeration.*

64

honourable wife. He also knighted Sir Walter de Manny, and made him a member of his council, and showed him great favour at court. Sir Walter did many great feats of arms afterwards, as you will hear later in this history. But the noble knights of Scotland frequently disturbed the English. They kept to the wilder parts of the country, in deep marshes and high forests, where no one could follow them; but they harassed the English so continually that there were skirmishes and alarms almost every day and in one of these Sir William Montagu lost an eye through his exceptional boldness.

It was in these same great marshes and forests that the gallant King Robert the Bruce had taken refuge when King Edward I had overrun and conquered the kingdom of Scotland. Several times he had been so hard pressed that he could find nobody to give him shelter, in castle or fortress, for fear of King Edward I, who conquered the whole of Scotland so effectively that there was no town or castle or fortress that stood out against him.[1] When Edward I returned to England, the gallant King Robert rallied all his people from wherever they were to be found, and won back all the castles, fortresses and towns as far as Berwick, some by force of arms and others by diplomacy and natural affection. When Edward I heard of this, he was very angry, and summoned his host and went on until he had defeated the Scots a second time, and reconquered their kingdom. So it went on between the two Kings, and I have heard it said that King Robert regained his country five times. These two Kings were regarded as the most gallant knights in the world, and they maintained their efforts until the death of Edward I, which occurred at Berwick. On his deathbed Edward publicly summoned his eldest son, who was afterwards King, and made him swear by the Saints that as soon as he was dead, he would have his body boiled in a cauldron until the flesh should be separated from the bones, and that the flesh should be buried and the bones preserved. And that every time the Scots rebelled, he would summon

---

[1] *'Hammer of the Scots' is inscribed in Latin on his tomb.*

his army and carry with him the bones of his father. For he firmly believed that as long as his bones were carried against the Scots, the English would never be defeated. However, King Edward II did not fulfil his oath, but had his father's body carried back to London, and buried there. For this he suffered great harm, as you have heard, beginning with his defeat at the battle of Stirling.

27

After the King of England had done homage to him, King Philip of France, out of grace and devotion, went to see the Holy Father Pope Benedict XII who lived and ruled at Avignon at that time. King Philip also wanted to visit those parts, to divert himself, and to make himself familiar with the cities and towns and castles, and to acquaint himself with the nobles of his kingdom. After making elaborate preparations he left Paris with the Kings of Bohemia and Navarre, accompanied by a great retinue of the nobility, keeping great state at considerable expense. He passed through Burgundy and came to Avignon, where he was honourably received by the Pope and the whole College of Cardinals, with whom he stayed some time, at Villeneuve near Avignon. The King of Aragon also came to the court of Rome at that moment, to join in the great festivities that celebrated their arrival, and they all remained there for the whole of Lent.

News then reached the court of Rome that the enemies of God were marching in great force against the Holy Land, and had reconquered most of the northern part of Serbia, and cruelly martyred the King, who was a convert to Christianity; and the infidels were threatening the whole of Christendom. The Pope was greatly disturbed, and on Good Friday, in the presence of the above-mentioned Kings, he preached a sermon on the Passion of Our Lord, and warmly encouraged them to take up the Cross and attack the enemies of God. The King of France was so deeply moved that he took up the Cross, and asked the Pope's consent, which he granted, giving the King and all who went with him absolution for all their sins, if they would truly confess and repent of them. Out of devotion and friendship for the King, the Kings of Bohemia, Navarre, and Aragon put on the Cross, as did a number of dukes, counts, barons and other nobles who were there, and also the Cardinals of Naples, Périgord, and Ostia, and Cardinal Blanc. This crusade was made public and announced everywhere, amid general rejoicing, and the delight especially of those who took pleasure in feats of arms and did not know how otherwise to occupy themselves.

When the King of France and the other kings had spent some time with the Pope, and had completed most of their business, they took their leave. The King of Aragon went back to his own country, and the King of France went to Montpellier with his company, where he spent a considerable time. While he was there he made peace between the Kings of Aragon and Mallorca, between whom there had been a dispute. He then returned by easy stages to Paris, visiting cities, towns, castles, and fortresses, of which he had a great number, on the way. He passed through Auvergne, Berry, Beauce, and Gatinois, and was royally welcomed when he returned to Paris. The kingdom of France was at that time powerful, rich and compact, the people were prosperous, and there was no talk of war.

The crusade that was undertaken by the King of France, and which he commanded, was joined by other lords as well, and by some of them out of true devotion. King Philip assembled the greatest and most magnificent expedition ever to cross the seas— even in the days of Godfrey de Bouillon nothing had exceeded it. He had fitted out, in the ports of Marseille, Aigues-Mortes, and Narbonne, and from the neighbourhood of Montpellier, sufficient galleys and ships of all kinds to carry sixty thousand men with all their provisions—biscuits, wine, fresh water, salted meat and all the equipment necessary for an army, enough to last for three years if necessary.

The King of France sent ambassadors to the King of Hungary, a most valiant man, asking him to make all preparations for letting God's pilgrims pass through his country; the King of Hungary willingly agreed. In the same way he communicated with the King of Cyprus, the valiant Hugh de Lusignan, and the King of Sicily, who both also agreed, and made the necessary preparations. The King also sent word to the Venetians, asking them to open their frontiers, and to collect guards and provisions, which they willingly did, as also did the Genoese and all the inhabitants of that coast. The King sent the Grand Prior of France to Rhodes, to collect supplies there. And the knights of Saint John arranged with the Venetians to provide supplies in the island of Crete, which is part of their territory. In short, preparations were made everywhere to receive the pilgrims of God; and over three hundred thousand people put on the Cross, and embarked on this crusade.

28

At the time when this crusade was so much in the air that nothing else was spoken of, Count Robert of Artois was in England, in exile from France, staying with King Edward; he had been with him at the capture of Berwick and on other expeditions in Scotland, from which they had just returned. He was continually encouraging the King to defy the King of France, who was withholding his inheritance from him. And the King was in constant consultation with his privy council, deliberating how to maintain his right to the French throne of which he had been deprived in youth, but to which he was the rightful heir, as Count Robert of Artois had informed him. The twelve peers and the barons of France had unanimously given the throne to Philip of Valois. And if King Edward challenged his right to it unsuccessfully, as would probably happen, and were afterwards rebuffed and did not press his claim, he would be more blamed than ever. He saw quite clearly that it would be impossible for him to overcome the might of France with only such forces as he could bring from his own country; he would need to enlist, by means of money, powerful help in the Empire and other places. He therefore constantly consulted his privy council, without whose advice he would make no move.

Finally, his council gave this unanimous reply: 'Sir, this matter is such an important one that we dare not give you a final opinion; but we recommend that you send fully briefed ambassadors to the gallant Count of Hainault, whose daughter you have married, and to his brother, Sir John, who has so valiantly assisted you; and that you implore them to give their advice, for they are better informed in this kind of affair than we can be; and they are bound, by the affection they have for you, to protect your honour and your cause. And if they agree with you, they can advise you what lords can give you best assistance, and how you can best win their support.'

The King agreed to this proposal, and asked the Bishop of Lincoln to undertake this embassy out of affection for him, together with two knights banneret and two clerks learned in the law. They all agreed readily, and set out after making their preparations, and crossed the Channel to Dunkirk, from where they continued and rode through Flanders to Valenciennes. There they found the Count of Hainault lying ill in bed with gout and arthritis; and also there at Valenciennes was Sir John, his brother. They were, naturally, entertained most hospitably, and afterwards explained to the two brothers the reason for their embassy, together with all the doubts and hesitations that the King had expressed to his council.

The Count of Hainault answered: 'If the King succeeds in this, in God's name I will be pleased. As you may imagine, I care more for the man who married my daughter than I do for King Philip, who has never done anything for me, even though I did marry his sister. In fact, he secretly prevented the marriage of the young Duke of Brabant to my daughter Isabel. So I will not fail my dear son-in-law the King of England, if his council advises this undertaking. I will give him every assistance, and so will my brother John here, who has helped him before. But he will need other support, more powerful than ours, for Hainault is a small country compared to the kingdom of France, as you know. And England lies too far away to be able to help it.'

'Certainly, sir, you have given us very good advice, and shown us great affection and goodwill, for which we thank you on behalf of our lord the King,' replied the Bishop of Lincoln. 'But, dear sir, will you tell us the names of those lords who can most easily help our King, and whom he can trust best, so that we may inform him?'

'Upon my soul,' said the count, 'I cannot think of any lords who can give him such powerful assistance as the Duke of Brabant, who is his first cousin, the Bishop of Liège, the Duke of Guelders, who married your King's sister, the Archbishop of Cologne, the Marquis of Juliers, Sir Arnold of Bacqueghen and the lord of Fauquemont. I know of no lords in the world who can raise a larger number of men-at-arms in a shorter time. They are warlike themselves and can muster eight thousand fully armed men, if they choose, provided they are paid first; for they love profit. And if the King, my son-in-law, can acquire the support of these lords, he could come over here and cross the Oise and give battle to King Philip.'

This advice delighted the English lords, and they took leave of the Count of Hainault and his brother, and made their way back to report it to King Edward. They returned to London and were given a great feast by the King when they told him their news, for it brought him great joy and comfort. Rumours of this reaction soon reached France, and were so exaggerated that King Philip's enthusiasm for his crusade cooled, and he was advised to protect his own kingdom and people instead. He cancelled the orders he had given to his officers, who were now making elaborate preparations, until such time as he could find on what footing King Edward's expedition would be, seeing that he was busily raising an army.

The King of England ordered ten knights banneret and forty other knights bachelor to accompany the valiant Bishop of Lincoln across the sea to Valenciennes, to negotiate with a number of lords of the Empire named by the Count of Hainault, and to carry out the instructions of the count and his brother Sir John.

When they arrived, the great state that they kept was marvelled at by all; they spared no expense, and they could not have done more to gain glory and renown if the King had been there in person. Some of the young knights bachelor covered one of their eyes with a piece of cloth, having vowed to various ladies at home that they would see out of only one eye until they had performed some feat of arms in France. They would answer no questions on the subject, and their appearance caused much mystery.

After being entertained at Valenciennes, the Bishop of Lincoln and most of his company went to negotiate with the Duke of Brabant, as they had been advised. The duke entertained them magnificently, and promised to support the King, who was his first cousin, with all the means in his power, and to let him come and go through his territory, armed or unarmed, whenever he liked. And for a round sum of florins he agreed that if King Edward defied the King of France, and invaded his kingdom, and obtained the support of those lords mentioned above, then he would join him with a thousand men-at-arms.

The ambassadors returned to Valenciennes well pleased. And by means of their negotiations and their King's money, they arranged that the Duke of Guelders (King Edward's brother-in-law) the Marquis of Juliers (who also represented the Archbishop of Cologne) and his brother Waleran, and the Lord of Fauquemont should all come to Valenciennes to have talks with them in company with the Count of Hainault, who was too ill to ride on horseback, and his brother Sir John. And by means of a considerable distribution of florins they made a pact to defy the King of France, and to accompany the King of England whenever he pleased and to provide him with a certain number of men-at-arms with crested helmets.[1] And the above-named lords undertook to be the King's allies, along with other lords from beyond the Rhine, who were in a position to bring large numbers of

[1] *Up to this point, Froissart has referred to men-at-arms as 'crested helmets,' but from here on he calls them 'lances' or 'coats of mail.'*

troops with them, provided they were paid in advance. These lords from Germany then took their leave and went home, but the English lords stayed on at Valenciennes with the Count. They sent further deputations to the Bishop of Liège, whose support they wanted, but he would do nothing against the King of France, being his liegeman and having done fealty to him. The King of Bohemia was not approached, since his son John, Duke of Normandy, had married Bona, the French King's daughter, and this connection would have prevented him from entering any alliance against France.

29

At the time of which I speak there were great dissensions between Louis, the Count of Flanders, and his Flemish subjects; they were in open rebellion, and it was at great danger to himself that he remained in Flanders. There was at this time a man at Ghent called Jacques van Artevelde, who had been a brewer of mead, and he had gained so much both in favour and in fortune all over Flanders that no one dared oppose him or contradict his orders. Whenever he went out into the city of Ghent he was attended by sixty or seventy armed ruffians, of whom two or three were his most trusted lieutenants. And whenever he met somebody whom he suspected or disliked, he had him killed; for he had instructed his most trusted followers that whenever he made a certain sign on meeting somebody, they should kill the man at once, no matter what his rank, without another word. This happened frequently, and many of the leading citizens had been killed. He was so much feared that nobody dared speak out against any of his actions, or even think of contradicting him.

When his bodyguard conducted him to his house, each of them used to go home for dinner, and immediately afterwards would come back and make a noise and brawl in the street outside his house until he should want to go round the town and amuse himself. They escorted him like this until supper-time, and they were each paid four Flemish groats a day for wages and expenses, which was paid to them regularly once a week. He also employed sergeants and soldiers in every town and fortified place in Flanders to carry out his orders and to see if rebellion was being plotted or speeches being made against him. As soon as any such person was discovered, he was either banished or killed immediately. In the same way he banished a number of powerful knights and squires and burgesses whom he suspected of supporting the Count of Flanders in any way, and seized half of their revenue, leaving the other half to their wives and children. Most of those banished, of which there were a considerable number, went to live at Saint Omer and were called Exiles.[1]

To put it briefly, there was never a ruler—duke, count, or prince—in Flanders or any other country with such absolute power as Jacques van Artevelde. He collected rents, duties on wine, and all the other lawful revenue belonging to the count, all over Flanders; and he raised special levies, which he spent and gave away as he pleased, without keeping any accounts. When he said he needed money, people were wise enough to take him at his word, and no one dared contradict him; nor when he wished to borrow money did anyone dare refuse him.

The English ambassadors, who had kept such great state at Valenciennes, as you have heard, thought it would be very much in the King's interest in this undertaking to have the aid of the Flemish, who were then on bad terms both with the King of France and the Count of Flanders, their rightful lord. The Count of Hainault, when consulted by the ambassadors, agreed that it would be the greatest possible help, but he could not see how it could be done without winning over Jacques van Artevelde. They replied that they would do all in their power to win his friendship, and they set out from Valenciennes by four different roads, some for Bruges and some for Ypres, but most for Ghent, spending so liberally all the time that the money might have been falling from the skies. They tried to win the friendship of all, and they made promises on every side where they thought they could

[1] 'Les avoillés.'

further their ends. It was the Bishop of Lincoln and his company, who went to Ghent, who succeeded—by making fine speeches and in other ways—in winning the friendship and support of Jacques van Artevelde, and considerable favour in the town, particularly with an old knight called De Siger, a nobleman of Courtrai who was much respected in the town. He was a knight banneret, and was regarded as the most gallant knight and fearless soldier in Flanders, and he had valiantly served the other knights. He kept company with the English knights and entertained them, as every loyal knight should do to strangers. But in the end he suffered for it, for it was reported to the King of France that he was entertaining the English; and the King sent strict instructions to the Count of Flanders to have this knight arrested and beheaded, by any means that he could. The count carried out these orders, not daring to disobey them; this caused general distress, since the knight had been held in great affection and regard, and it added to the unpopularity of the count.

The English lords were so successful in their negotiations that Jacques van Artevelde called several meetings with the chiefs of the provincial towns to discuss with the English the business on which they had come, and the privileges and alliance offered by the King of England. The result of these discussions was as follows: the chiefs of the towns gave their consent that the King of England and his troops could pass through Flanders whenever he pleased. But the Flemish were under obligations to the King of France not to offend him or enter his kingdom without forfeiting a large sum in florins. They asked the ambassadors to be satisfied with this answer for the present, and the English lords returned, quite content, to Valenciennes. They had been in constant touch with the King their master, informing him of developments. The King had kept them supplied with quantities of gold and silver for their own expenses and for distribution among the German lords, who asked for nothing better.

About this time the gallant William Count of Hainault died, on June 7th, 1337; he was buried at the church of the Cordeliers at Valenciennes, and the Bishop of Cambrai sang the mass. There

was a great congregation of dukes, counts and barons, for he
was much loved and respected by all. On his death he was
succeeded in Hainault, Holland, and Zeeland by his son William,
who had married Joan, daughter of the Duke of Brabant. She
had received as her dowry rich and valuable lands at Binche,[1]
and her widowed mother, Jeanne de Valois, went to stay at the
monastery of Fontenelles, on the Scheldt, where she lived a devout
and charitable life.

30

King Philip was informed of all these alliances, and of the pacts
that King Edward had made overseas, and would gladly have
won the Flemish over to his side. But Jacques van Artevelde had
dominated them so completely that nobody dared to act against
his wishes. Even the Count, their lord, could not stay there in
safety, but sent his wife and their son Louis into France. However, certain knights and squires were in garrison on the island of
Cadsand,[2] and defended it against the English. The English
knights in Hainault knew that if they went home by that route
they might be attacked. Nevertheless they rode over the country
of Flanders, visiting the large towns, under the protection of
Jacques van Artevelde, who gave them all the honour and
support that he could. They later embarked at Dordrecht, to
avoid passing the island of Cadsand. They made their best way
home, as secretly as they could, and the King received them very
gladly. They gave him a full account of their activities and the
alliances they had made, all of which delighted the King, though
he was deeply grieved by the death of the count, his father-in-law.
When he heard about the garrison of Cadsand harassing his men,
he said that he would soon settle it. He told his cousin the Earl of
Derby, and Sir Walter de Manny, who had fought so boldly in
Scotland, and other knights and squires to advance on the garrison of Cadsand and attack it. They collected a number of men-

---

[1] *Between Mons and Charleroi.*   [2] *Between Sluys and Flushing.*

at-arms and archers and embarked on the Thames at London; they numbered about five hundred men-at-arms and two thousand archers. They weighed anchor and lay the first night off Gravesend; the next day they reached Margate, and on the third tide they hoisted their sails and crossed over to Flanders, and after collecting and drawing up their vessels they arrived at Cadsand in the afternoon of Martinmas,[1] 1337.

31

Seeing that their objective lay before them, and that wind and tide were in their favour, the English decided to approach, in the name of God and Saint George. They sounded their trumpets, put on their armour, and drew up their ships. Then, with the archers in the prows, they set sail for the town. The sentinels and guards in the garrison had plainly seen the approach of this large army and, realizing that it was the English, had already armed and manned the dikes and dunes, with their banners ranged in front of them. They also created sixteen knights. Their full number was probably about five thousand, brave knights and bachelors, as they later proved themselves. Among them was Sir Guy of Flanders, the bastard brother of Count Louis, a brave and gallant knight who urged on his men and encouraged them to distinguish themselves, and many other bold knights and bachelors, all eager to do battle with the English.

There was no preliminary parleying, for the English were as eager to attack as their enemies were to defend themselves. The battle-cry went up and the archers were ordered to draw their bows, which they did with such effect that the defenders were forced willy-nilly to retire, many of them being struck by the first shower of arrows. The English landed, and fought hand-to-hand with battle-axes, swords and lances. Many noble feats of arms were done, and the Flemish defended themselves bravely against an attack that was conducted in the true spirit of chivalry. The

[1] *November 12th.*

gallant Earl of Derby dashed to the forefront of the first assault with lances, and was wounded. Sir Walter de Manny did him a vital service by moving him out of danger, from where he lay, crying 'Lancaster for the Earl of Derby!' The two armies closed with each other, and many were wounded, especially on the Flemish side, for the English archers were particularly effective with their continuous discharge of arrows.

The battle at Cadsand harbour was fiercely fought, for the Flemish were good fighters, and expert in arms; they had been specially selected by the Count of Flanders and posted to guard this passage against the English, and they were determined to acquit themselves nobly and do their duty in every respect, which they did. Chief among the English barons and knights were the Earls of Derby and Suffolk, Sir Reginald Cobham, Sir Lewis Beauchamp, Sir William Fitzwarren, Lord Berkeley and Sir Walter de Manny, besides many others who vigorously assaulted the Flemish.

There was fierce hand-to-hand fighting, and in the end the Flemish were put to flight, and lost more than three thousand killed, in the harbour as well as in the streets and houses. Sir Guy the Bastard was taken prisoner, and about twenty-six other knights and squires were killed. The town was taken and pillaged, all the contents being removed to the boats along with the prisoners; after that it was burned. The English returned home without further loss, and King Edward was delighted with their success. Sir Guy was made to pledge himself to remain a prisoner, but that same year he became English and did homage to the King, to the extreme annoyance of his brother the Count of Flanders.

32

The news of this defeat spread far and wide. The Flemish claimed that the Count had placed that garrison there without consulting them and against their will. Van Artevelde, who had taken over the entire government of Flanders, was not displeased by the result of the battle, and sent ambassadors to King Edward recommending himself with all his heart, advising him to cross over to Antwerp since the Flemish were eager to see him, and saying that if he crossed the sea his interests would be served more profitably.

King Edward was of the same opinion, and made elaborate preparations: in the following spring he embarked with a great company of earls, barons, and knights, and crossed over to Antwerp, which was held at that time for the Duke of Brabant. When he was known to have landed, crowds gathered from all sides to see the great state that he kept, and when he had been well entertained, he sent word to his cousin the Duke of Brabant, his brother-in-law the Duke of Guelders, the Marquis of Juliers, Sir John of Hainault, the lord of Fauquemont, and all those from whom he hoped for support, to confer with them; and they all assembled at Antwerp soon after Whitsun. When the King had entertained them, he explained his purpose, and asked them to state their intentions clearly. For that was his purpose in coming there, and any delay would be greatly to his disadvantage, since he had made all his preparations. The German lords had a long consultation among themselves, trying to settle their differences, and eventually gave the King the following answer: 'Dear Sir, we came here for the pleasure of seeing you, rather than for anything else. And we are not in a position to provide the answer you require; but we will all return to our people, and come back here on a day to be named by you, and give you a firm answer, so that the matter will no longer rest with us.' The King saw no alternative, and named a day in the middle of July; but he clearly indicated to them the great expense that he would incur in the meantime, for he had expected them to provide the answer on his first arrival. He added that he would not go back to England before discovering their intentions. The lords departed, and the King stayed quietly at the monastery of Saint Bernard. Some of the English knights stayed at Antwerp to keep him company, and the rest went about the country amusing themselves in great style, all over Hainault and Flanders; and they were well received and feasted wherever they went. The Duke of Brabant spent a long time at Louvain, sending frequent messages to the King of France, asking him not to believe any unfavourable reports about him. The day arrived when King Edward expected the answer of the lords mentioned above; but they made excuses and sent a message to him that they were all ready, with their followers, as they had undertaken, provided the Duke of Brabant was also ready, since he was the nearest to France, and yet seemed the most lukewarm about the whole affair. As soon as the duke should be ready to move, they too would set off and would not lag behind him.

At this, King Edward spoke to the duke, his cousin, and showed him the communication sent by the other lords. He begged him, out of friendship and as a relation, not to cause any delay, since he seemed to be rather cool and indifferent to his cause. He added that if this were the case he might lose the support of the German lords. The duke, in some embarrassment, said he would summon his council. After long deliberation he said that he would be ready as soon as need be—but that he must first see the other lords, whom he then asked to meet him at Halle, to suit the convenience of the young Count of Hainault and his uncle, Sir John.

When the lords of the empire were assembled at Halle, after long consultation they made the following statement to the King of England: 'Dear Sir, we have given this weighty problem much thought, and, all things considered, we see no cause for us to defy the King of France with you unless you can obtain the support of the Emperor of Germany and unless he commands us to do so on his behalf. For he has a perfectly good case against the King, as we shall explain. We should in that case act immediately and give you the assistance that we promised you. The Emperor's case is this: there is an old covenant, sworn and sealed, which states that no King of France shall ever occupy or hold any possessions of the empire. But King Philip has broken this covenant, by taking possession of the castle of Crèvecoeur, near Cambrai, and that of Arleux, in Artois, and several other properties in the region of Cambrai, for which the Emperor has a good case for challenging him through us who are his subjects. We advise and beg you to obtain his agreement, in order to save our honour.'

The English King decided to follow their advice, though it would be tedious to report all their speeches and consultations. It was eventually decided that the Marquis of Juliers should go and speak to the Emperor, taking with him knights and advisers from the King, and also some from the Duke of Guelders. The Duke of Brabant, though he would not send any envoys, lent the King his castle at Louvain to reside in until the following summer, if he so wished. For the King had said that on no account would he return to England without having accomplished some part of his enterprise, for the shame that he would feel, after the great stories that had been circulated. The Marquis of Juliers found the Emperor at Nuremberg, and succeeded in achieving the object of his visit, partly through the cooperation of Margaret of Hainault, who was married to Louis of Bavaria, the head of the Holy Roman Empire. It was then that the Marquis of Juliers was raised to the rank of marquis from that of count, and the Duke of Guelders was created a duke, having also until then been a count. The Emperor gave a commission to four knights and two clerks of the law, who were members of his council, to make the King of England his vicar over the whole German Empire, with instructions that he should be obeyed as faithfully as the Emperor himself. These knights took with them legal instruments to this effect, sealed and confirmed by the Emperor.

33

At this time the young King David of Scotland, who had lost a great part of his kingdom to his brother-in-law the King of England, and could not recover it, left Scotland in secret, with the Queen. They put to sea and landed at Boulogne, and went on to Paris, where King Philip was waiting for the arrival of a challenge from King Edward and the lords of the German Empire. King

Philip was delighted and received him magnificently, for he saw that King Edward was making every possible preparation for making war on him and driving him out of his country. When King David stated his position and his needs, King Philip soon came to terms with him, because, like many great lords, he was fully capable of coming to an agreement when there was some advantage to be gained from it for himself. He gave King David a castle to live in for as long as he pleased, on condition that he did not make any pact or agreement with the King of England without his consent. He entertained the King and Queen of Scotland for a long time, providing everything that they needed, for they had brought few resources from Scotland to support themselves. He also sent ambassadors to the lords in Scotland who were carrying on war against the English garrisons, and offered them considerable assistance, provided they did not come to any terms with the English not approved by him and by the King of Scotland, who had given the same undertaking.

The Scots knights considered this request from the French King and willingly agreed to it, and swore to the same agreement as their King had already made, and sealed it. This is how the alliance was first made between King Philip of France and King David of Scotland that lasted for so many years. The King of France sent troops to Scotland to fight the English, under Sir Arnold of Andreghen, the Marshal of France, and Lord de Garencières, and other knights and squires, for he thought that the English would be too busy with the Scots at home to be able to cross the sea, except in numbers too small to do him any harm.

34

After conferring with his allies at Halle, King Edward went back to the castle at Louvain, which he was preparing for his residence. He sent a letter to Queen Philippa asking her to join him, since he would not be able to return to England that year; and he sent back a number of knights to guard the country, and the Scots border in particular. The Queen was delighted, and made preparations for the journey. Meanwhile, the other English knights who had come to Brabant with the King dispersed all over Flanders and Hainault, keeping great state and living in high style. They spent money as if it came down from the clouds, and gave fine jewels to the lords and ladies, to win their goodwill and favour. They soon became very popular with them, and even with the common people, to whom they gave nothing, but who rejoiced to see such magnificence.

The Marquis of Juliers returned from the Emperor about All Saints' Day.[1] He sent a message to King Edward giving thanks to God for the success of his mission. The King was overjoyed, and asked him to come on the feast of Saint Martin, when all the other lords would be there. He asked his cousin the Duke of Brabant where he would like the meeting to take place. The duke did not want it to be in his own territory, nor did he wish to go as far as Trèves, which would have been most convenient for the lords of the empire. So he asked for it to be held at Herck, in the county of Loos, near his own country. The King was ready to make any concessions the Duke might ask, to attain his object, and agreed to the meeting place, summoning all his allies there on the feast of Saint Martin.

The town was overflowing with people, and the market hall, where bread and meat were usually sold, was decorated with rich hangings, like the presence-chamber of a king. The King sat with a rich gold crown on his head, on a throne erected on a butcher's block five feet above the rest of the assembly. Never was the hall put to such exalted use. The letters from the Emperor were read out to the assembled lords and people, proclaiming King Edward Vicar and Lieutenant of the Empire and granting him full judicial powers to act in the Emperor's name, and to mint gold and silver coinage; also commanding the princes of the Empire and all subjects to obey his Vicar as himself and to do fealty and homage to him as Vicar of the Empire.

The lords then swore fealty to King Edward as Vicar, and various litigants pleaded their causes, receiving judgement as if

[1] *1328.*

they had come before the Emperor. An old statute was renewed, which had been enacted long before at the Emperor's court; it was to the effect that anyone who intended to injure or attack an enemy must give three days' notice of his intentions or otherwise he would be in the wrong. When all this was settled, the lords took their leave and undertook to fulfil their obligations by being ready, with all their men fully equipped, three weeks after the feast of Saint John, to besiege the city of Cambrai, which rightly belonged to the Empire but had been annexed by the French King. The lords all set out for home, and King Edward, as Vicar of the Empire, returned to Louvain, where he found the Queen had just arrived with many of the nobility, and accompanied by numerous ladies in waiting. They held court there in great style all that winter, and had quantities of gold and silver money minted at Antwerp.

The Duke of Brabant did not fail, however, to make his excuses to the King of France, sending to him his special adviser, Sir Louis of Travehen. The Duke instructed him to make his excuses and to contradict any reports that might be circulating against him. Sir Louis did not dare disobey the Duke's orders but did everything in his power to carry them out. In the end he was ill rewarded, for he was killed in a duel in France. When it became quite clear that all the Duke's eager protestations were untrue, Sir Louis was so embarrassed that he would never return to Brabant, but lived in France to kill any suspicion that might attach to him.

35

Winter passed, summer returned, and the feast of Saint John the Baptist drew near. The lords of Germany began preparations for the campaign, and the King of France also made preparations against them, for he knew something of their intentions, even though he had not yet received a formal challenge. King Edward's stores and provisions were collected in England and shipped across with his men-at-arms. He himself went to Vilvoorde,[1] and assembled them there when they landed; and when the town was full, he made his men encamp in tents in the fields along the river. They stayed there from the feast of Saint Mary Magdalen until that of Our Lady in September,[2] waiting week by week for the arrival of the other lords, especially for the Duke of Brabant, for whom all the others were waiting. When King Edward saw that they did not come, he wrote drawing their attention to the obligations that they were under, and summoning them to Mechelen on Saint Giles's day, at the same time asking the reason for their delay.

King Edward stayed on at Vilvoorde, incurring great expense, very much against his will: he had to support, at his own expense, sixteen hundred men-at-arms, who had crossed the sea with him, and ten thousand archers, not counting the other followers of the army. This was a very heavy expense; and he had also paid over large sums to the German lords, who were so far merely delaying him with promises; and in addition he had to keep up a large force against the privateers from Genoa, Normandy, Brittany, Picardy, and Spain whom King Philip maintained at sea to harass the English under the command of Sir Hugh Quiriel, Sir Peter Bahucet, and Barbenoire, guarding the crossings from England to France. These corsairs were only waiting for the news that the King of England had defied the King of France to land in England (they had already decided on a landing-place) and lay waste the country.

The lords of Germany answered the King's summons and came to Mechelen with the Duke of Brabant and Sir John of Hainault, though they did not bring their troops or equipment with them. But after further discussions they agreed that the King would be able to set out in a fortnight, when their preparations would be complete. To put a better face on it they decided to send a challenge to King Philip from the following nobles: first King Edward, then the Duke of Guelders, the Marquis of Juliers,

---

[1] *A small town on the Senne, a few miles north of Brussels.*
[2] *July 22nd to September 8th, 1329.*

Count Robert of Artois, Sir John of Hainault, the Marquis of Nuys, the Marquis of Blanckenburg, the lord of Fauquemont, Sir Arnold of Bacquehem, the Archbishop of Cologne and his brother Waleran, and all the lords of the Empire, who were champions of King Edward's cause. The challenge was written and sealed by everyone except the Duke of Brabant, who again excused himself and said he would play his part in the proper time and place. The Bishop of Lincoln was entrusted with the delivery of this challenge; he performed his role blamelessly, and was given safe conduct back to the King, his lord, at Mechelen.

36

Sir Walter de Manny performed two notable feats of arms in the very week that the challenge was sent to the King. As soon as he thought it could have reached the King, he collected forty lances, whom he knew he could depend on, and rode night and day to Hainault, where he entered the woods of Blaton. His followers were as yet unaware of his intention, but he then explained to his closest lieutenants that he had taken an oath in England, before various lords and ladies, that he would be the first to make war on French soil, and that he would take a castle or a fortified town, and perform some gallant feat. He now intended to ride to Mortagne, which is in French territory, and take the town by surprise. His followers cheerfully agreed to go with him, so they tightened their girths, buckled on their armour and rode in close formation through the woods of Blaton, reaching Mortagne a little before sunrise. It so happened that they found the wicket-gate open. Sir Walter dismounted, and led them through quietly, leaving guards at the gate so that they should not be disturbed. He then marched down the street with his pennon to the great tower and the ramparts. They found the tower poorly guarded, but they failed in their attempt on it because both gate and wicket were shut. The guard heard the noise and saw them from his post, and was amazed. He began to blow his horn and to cry out: 'Treason! Treason!' The soldiers and inhabitants woke up, but did not venture out of the fortress.

When Sir Walter de Manny heard the townsmen moving, he beat a hasty retreat towards the city gates, first setting fire to the houses in the street next to the fortress, sixty of which were burned down; the inhabitants were much alarmed, thinking they would all be captured. But Sir Walter rode off with his men and after crossing the Aisne went straight to Condé. They then took the road towards Valenciennes, but left the town on their right, and so came to Denaing, where they put up at the monastery. Then they crossed over towards Bouchain and persuaded the governor to open the gates to them. They crossed a river which rises near Arleux and flows into the Scheldt, and came to a fortified castle called Thun-l'Evêque, which belonged to the Bishop of Cambrai. This castle was completely taken by surprise, since the country was not conscious of being at war, and the guard was so inadequate that the castle was captured with the governor and his wife inside. Sir Walter left a strong garrison there, with his brother Sir Giles de Manny in command. Sir Giles gravely disturbed the inhabitants of the district of Cambrai, for the castle was only three miles from the town. Sir Walter returned to the King at Mechelen, having fulfilled his object, and his enterprise gave the King great pleasure.

37

As soon as King Philip received the challenge from King Edward, he saw that war was inevitable. He collected soldiers and men-at-arms from every direction and sent a strong force to garrison Cambrai, where he thought the first attack would be made. He put in command of it Lord Gallois de la Baume, a knight from Savoy, with Lord Thibault of Marneil and the Lord of Roye. Including the Savoyards, they were perhaps two hundred lances. King Philip also sent a force to capture the county of Ponthieu, which King Edward held by right of his mother. He also sent deputations to a number of lords of the empire, the Count of Hainault, the Duke of Lorraine, the Count of Bar, and the

Bishops of Liège and Metz, asking them not to start hostilities against him or his country. Most of them agreed not to do so, but the Count of Hainault, in a very courteous reply, said that although he would be ready to help King Philip at any time, against any enemy, nevertheless King Edward was making war on behalf of the empire, as Vicar and Lieutenant of the Emperor, and he could not refuse to assist King Edward, since he held part of his land from the Emperor, and was therefore bound to obey him and his Vicar as well. The King readily accepted this answer, and was not much perturbed by it, for he felt sufficiently powerful to withstand his enemies.

When Sir Hugh Quiriel and his corsairs heard of the outbreak of war between England and France, they were delighted: they set out with a force of about twenty thousand soldiers of every description and landed in the harbour of Southampton on a Sunday morning when the people were at Mass. The Normans and Genoese entered the town and robbed and pillaged it, murdering the inhabitants and raping their women. They loaded their plunder into the vessels and retired with a following wind to Dieppe, where they divided their spoils.

38

King Edward left Mechelen and came to Brussels to confer with his cousin the Duke of Brabant. A large body of Germans, numbering at least twenty thousand, joined the King, who asked the Duke whether he was coming with them or deserting their cause. The Duke replied that as soon as he knew that Cambrai was besieged, he would come with twelve hundred lances, stout men-at-arms. This answer pleased the King very much.

The King left Brussels and stayed the night at Nivelles. The next day he came to Mons, where he found the young Count of Hainault, his brother-in-law, with his uncle Sir John, who received them gladly, together with Count Robert of Artois, who all this time had been very close to the King and in his privy council, and sixteen or twenty of the chief knights and barons of England who were in waiting on the King and advising him. The Bishop of Lincoln, who was renowned for his courage and good sense, was also with them. The King spent two days at Mons, where he was well entertained by the Count. The English then pushed on, camping at night in the open country. There were plentiful supplies for them to buy: some paid for them, and others did not.

The King then came to Valenciennes, which he entered with only a dozen knights. The Count of Hainault had already arrived, with Sir John and the Lords of Enghien, Faguinelles, Verchin, and Havareth, and a number of others, who greeted the King. The Count took him by the arm and led him to the great hall, which was all decked out to receive him. As they were mounting the steps the Bishop of Lincoln raised his voice and called out: 'William of Ausonne, Bishop of Cambrai, I call on you as proctor to the King of England, Vicar of the Empire, to open the gates of the city of Cambrai. Otherwise you will forfeit your lands and we will enter by force.' No reply was made, as the Bishop of Cambrai was not present. The Bishop of Lincoln continued: 'Count of Hainault, we admonish you on behalf of the Emperor to come and serve the King of England his vicar, before Cambrai, with all your forces.' The Count answered: 'Willingly.' With these words they entered the hall and took the King to his room. Soon afterwards a large and magnificent supper was served. The next morning the King left Valenciennes and came to Haspres. He stayed there two days, waiting for his men to arrive. He then went on to Cambrai, after most of his troops had arrived, and surrounded the city and besieged it with his troops, who grew in number all the time.

The Count of Hainault and Sir John his uncle arrived and took up their quarters near the King; as also did the Duke of Guelders, the Marquis of Juliers, the Marquis of Nuys, the Marquis of Blanckenburg, the Count of Mons, the Count of Saumes, the lord of Fauquemont, Sir Arnold of Bacquehem, and all the other lords of the empire with their troops.

On the sixth day that they were encamped before Cambrai, the Duke of Brabant finally arrived with a fine array. He had nine hundred lances besides large numbers of other armed men. He went into quarters at Ostrevant on the river Scheldt, over which a bridge was built for communication between the two armies. When the Duke of Brabant arrived, he sent a challenge to King Philip, who was at Compiègne; Sir Louis of Travehen, who was his representative with the King, died soon after this action.

During the siege of Cambrai there were a number of assaults and skirmishes. Sir John of Hainault and the Lord of Fauquemont usually rode out together, and burned and destroyed much of the surrounding countryside. These two lords, with five hundred lances and a thousand other fighting men, came to the castle at Oisy, near Cambrai, and launched a formidable attack on it. Had it not been for the valiant defence of the knights and squires inside, who held it for the Lord of Coucy, they would have taken it. As it was, little damage was done, and these lords returned to their quarters. The Count of Hainault, who was most chivalrous, and a good ruler of his people, came on a Saturday to the gate of Saint Quentin, and made a great assault on it. John Chandos, who was then still a squire, flung himself between the barrier and the gate, and fought most valiantly at the length of a lance against a squire from Vermandois called Jean de Saint Dizier. Other notable feats of arms were achieved and the Hainaulters got possession of the barrier. With the Count were his marshals Sir Gerard of Verchin and Sir Henry of Antoing, and many others who pressed on boldly in the quest for honour. At another gate, called the Porte Robert, were assembled Sir John of Hainault, the lord of Fauquemont, and Sir Walter de Manny with their troops, making a determined assault. But the men of Cambrai and the French troops were equally vigorous in their defences, so that the attackers gained no advantage, but withdrew to their quarters, beaten and exhausted. The young Count of Namur came to serve under the Count of Hainault at his request, and said that he would continue to serve so long as they remained in the empire, but once they entered French territory he would be obliged to go and join the King of France, who had retained him. The Count of Hainault also gave strict instructions, on pain of death, that no damage should be done in the kingdom of France.

While the King of England was outside Cambrai, with at least forty thousand troops, and was busily engaged in assaults and attacks, King Philip assembled his forces at Peronne, in the Vermandois, to attack the English. Whereupon King Edward called a council of his own countrymen, which was also attended by Count Robert of Artois, in whom he had particular confidence, to decide whether it was better to invade France and go to attack King Philip, or to stay at Cambrai till they took it. In view of the strength of the city, and of its being so well provided with men, artillery and provisions, they decided that its capture would be a long and uncertain business. Winter was approaching, no brilliant successes had been won in the field, and their expenses were enormous. All things considered, they decided to strike camp and move on. For in France they would find plentiful provisions and better forage. This counsel prevailed, and the lords were told to move their tents, baggage, and belongings of all kinds. Then they all set out for Mont Saint Martin, on the French border, advancing by companies, each lord with his people. The marshals of the host were the Earls of Northampton, Gloucester, and Suffolk, and the Earl of Warwick who was the Constable of England. Near Saint Martin the troops of England, Germany, and Brabant crossed the Scheldt without difficulty, as it is not too wide at that place.

When the Count of Hainault had escorted the King of England to the frontier, he took his leave and said he could ride no further with him. King Philip, his uncle, whose hatred he did not want to incur, had asked him to go and serve with him in France, in the same way as he had served King Edward in the Empire. The King replied, 'May God assist you!' So the Counts of Hainault and Namur left the King, and returned to Quesnoy. The Count of Hainault dismissed most of his troops, but asked them to re-

main in readiness as he would shortly be wanting to go to assist
King Philip, his uncle.

39

When he had crossed over into France, King Edward summoned Henry of Flanders, who was a young squire, and knighted
him, giving him two hundred pounds sterling a year, with
security in England. The King stayed for two days in the
monastery at Mont Saint Martin, and his troops camped in the
surrounding country. The Duke of Brabant stayed in the
monastery at Vaucelles. When the King of France, who was at
Compiègne, heard that King Edward was nearly at Saint
Quentin, he increased his forces everywhere and sent his
constable, Count Raoul of Eu and Guines, with a large body of
men-at-arms, to Saint Quentin to defend the town and the
frontier; and he sent the lords of Coucy and Ham into their own
districts. He sent troops also into Guise, Ribemont, Bouchain
and the neighbouring fortresses to defend them. He went himself
to Peronne in the Vermandois with a great number of nobles and
men-at-arms. Every day his troops increased in number, and they
took up a position on the beautiful river Somme, between Saint
Quentin and Peronne.

While King Edward was at Mont Saint Martin, his troops
overran the country as far as Bapaume, quite near Peronne and
Saint Quentin. They found it prosperous and rich, untouched by
war. To achieve honour in the first flush of his knighthood, Sir
Henry of Flanders joined several other knights including the lords
of Fauquemont, Bergues, and Vandresen under the leadership of
Sir John of Hainault, numbering in all about five hundred. They
formed a plan to attack the neighbouring town of Hennecourt,
where most of the local population had fled with their goods,
trusting in the strength of the walls. Sir Arnold of Bacqueghen
and Sir William of Duvenvoorde had already been there with
their troops, but without success; as a result, all these lords had
gathered together with the intention of doing their utmost to

capture it. But there was a certain abbot in the town of great courage and good sense, and he had wooden barriers erected outside the city gates, and also across the main street with upright poles only six inches apart. He armed all the inhabitants and posted them on the battlements, providing them with stones and quicklime and suitable defensive artillery of that kind. And when these lords approached Hennecourt in battle order, he posted his men between the gates and the barrier, and opened the gates behind them. The lords dismounted, and, sword in hand, approached the barrier, which was very solid. They attacked the defenders vigorously with their lances, and received equally severe blows in return. The abbot, too, exchanged stern blows with the attackers, in the front rank; many gallant feats were performed, and savage attacks made, in the course of which there were many killed and wounded, as the stones and beams and quicklime rained down from the battlements.

Sir Henry of Flanders, sword in hand, laid about him with a will. But the abbot caught hold of his sword and pulled him towards the barrier with such force that he dragged Sir Henry's arm through it, between the poles; for he would not demean himself to let go of the sword. If the grating had been wider, the abbot would have had him through, for Sir Henry's whole arm was through, and he was in great pain. But his companions pulled in the opposite direction, and, after a prolonged struggle, eventually succeeded in dragging him to safety, though he left his sword in the abbot's hands. At the time of writing, it was shown to me in the great hall, where it is proudly preserved by the monks.

Hennecourt, then, was severely attacked all that day, till the evening. There were many casualties, and in particular Sir John of Hainault lost a knight from Holland called Sir Herman, who bore for arms a fess componé gules, and in chief three buckles azure. When the troops of Flanders, Hainault, England, and Germany saw that they could not triumph over the resolution of the defenders, but that they were beaten, they retired to their quarters, carrying the wounded with them.

Next morning the King left Mont Saint Martin, having given

instructions, which were duly followed, that nobody, on pain of death, should harm the monastery. They entered the Vermandois, and encamped in battle order at Mont Saint Quentin, where the inhabitants of Saint Quentin could have attacked them had they wished; but they had no intention of leaving the town. The English scouts went up to the barricades and skirmished with the defenders, who were under Count Raoul the Constable of France and Sir Charles of Blois, who drew up their people in order of battle before the barricades. And when the English, who included the Earls of Suffolk and Northampton, Sir Reginald Cobham and Sir Walter de Manny, saw that there was nothing to be gained from the situation, they retired to the main army of the King, which remained in camp on the hill until the early morning. A council was then held to decide whether to advance into France or to go towards Thiérache, along the frontiers of Hainault, where they could get provisions every day. Following the advice of the Duke of Brabant, they chose the latter course. If King Philip followed them with his army, as might be expected, they would wait for him and give him battle in the plain.

So King Edward left Mont Saint Quentin, and took the road with his army in close order, in three battalions. The marshals and the Germans led the first, King Edward led the second, and the Duke of Brabant the third. They advanced only ten or twelve miles a day, burning and laying waste the country as they went. A troop of English and Germans crossed the Somme and entered the Vermandois, burning and doing great damage to the country. Another troop, under Sir John of Hainault, took a different route and came to Origny Saint Benoît,[1] quite a good town, but not strongly fortified. It was soon captured, robbed and burned, and a convent of nuns violated. The Germans then left and took the road to Guise and Ribemont. King Edward stayed at Vervins for a day, while his men advanced and burned the country. News reached him that King Philip had left Peronne with a hundred thousand troops. So King Edward left

---

[1] *About nine miles from Saint Quentin.*

Vervins and took the road for La Flamengerie, to go to L'Eschelle, in Thiérache. The marshals, with the Bishop of Lincoln, at the head of five hundred lances, crossed the river Oise and entered the district of Laon, towards the Lord of Coucy's lands; they burned Le Fêre, Saint Gouvin and the town of Marle, and went to spend one night at Van, below Laon. Next day they rejoined the army, for they learned from their prisoners that King Philip had reached Saint Quentin and would cross the Somme there. They burned the good town of Crécy-sur-Seller, which was unfortified, as well as a number of other towns and villages in the neighbourhood.

Now as for the followers of Sir John of Hainault, who numbered a good five hundred fighting men, they came to Guise, where they burned the town and destroyed the mills. Sir John's daughter Joan, who was the wife of Count Louis of Blois, was in the fortress, and she begged him to depart and to spare the inheritance of his son-in-law. But in vain, for Sir John would not depart till he had completed his purpose. Then he returned to the King, who was staying in the abbey at Fervaques, while his men overran the countryside.

The lord of Fauquemont came with a hundred and twenty German lances to Lounion, in Thiérache, a large, flat town, whose inhabitants had retreated to the woods with their belongings, and fortified a position by cutting down trees. The Germans, under Sir Arnold of Bacqueghen, rode up and attacked them. They defended themselves as best they could, but were overpowered and put to flight, leaving forty dead or wounded, and losing all their belongings. Thiérache was thus laid waste without hindrance, the English doing as they pleased.

40

King Edward left Fervaques and spent the first night at Montreuil.[1] Next day he came to La Flamengerie, where he pitched

---

[1] *In Aisne, as opposed to Montreuil in the Pas-de-Calais.*

camp, surrounded by all his troops, to the number of forty thousand; he decided to wait there for King Philip, and whatever the circumstances to offer battle. King Philip advanced to Vironfosses, where he was joined by his nephew the Count of Hainault, who gave satisfactory reasons for having fought against his uncle at Cambrai. King Philip was joined by the Kings of Bohemia, Navarre, and Scotland, and their armies were drawn up opposite those of King Edward, neither side having any advantage over the other in position. King Edward had discovered the proximity of the enemy, and took the Duke of Brabant's advice that the only honourable course of action was to fight. This decision was conveyed to King Philip by a herald, who returned, laden with fur mantles given him by the French in their delight at his message. King Philip named the following Friday for the day of the battle, it being then a Wednesday. On the next day Lord de Fagnolle rode out from the French army to view their enemies, but his horse ran away with him and he fell into the hands of some German troops, who obtained a rich ransom for him from the Count of Hainault, from whose force he had come.

41

On Friday, after hearing mass, the two armies made themselves ready. The English army consisted of three battalions led by the Dukes of Brabant and Guelders and King Edward. The English contingent, which was the largest, included the Bishops of Lincoln and Durham, the Earls of Derby, Salisbury, Northampton, Gloucester, Suffolk, Richmond, and Hereford, with Count Robert of Artois, Sir Reginald Cobham, Lord Percy, Lord de Ros, Lord Mowbray, Sir Louis and Sir John Beauchamp, Lord Delaware, Lord Basset, Lord Fitzwalter, Sir Walter de Manny, Sir Hugh Hastings, and many others. On the wing of his army was another force under the Earls of Warwick and Pembroke, Lord Berkeley, and Lord de Molins, to rally those who might be thrown into disorder. The King created a number of knights, including Sir John Chandos, who, as you have heard, had performed feats of unprecedented glory. The King rode up and down the ranks, begging his lords and companions to help him maintain his honour; in his battalion there were six thousand men-at-arms and the same number of archers.

The King of France was attended by the following nobles, apart from the three Kings mentioned: the Dukes of Normandy, Brittany, Burgundy, Bourbon, Lorraine and Athens; the Counts of Alençon, Flanders (the King's brother), Hainault, Blois, Bar, Forêts, Foix, Armagnac, Longueville, Estampes, Vendôme, Harcourt, Saint Pol, Guines, Boulogne, Roussy, Dammartin, Valentinois, Auxerre, Sancerre, Genève, and Dreux; and the Dauphin of Auvergne; and from Gascony and Languedoc, counts and viscounts beyond number. It was indeed a most beautiful sight to see the banners and pennons flying in the breeze over the plain, with the mantled horses, and the knights and squires armed and accoutred to perfection. On the French side there were fifteen thousand men-at-arms and twenty thousand infantry.

42

It may well seem amazing that two such substantial armies could separate without fighting. But the French were in two minds: some said that it would be shameful and culpable for the King not to fight when he could see his enemies all drawn up in his own country, and when he had followed them for that very purpose. Others said that it would be folly for him to fight without being certain that there would be no treachery on his own side. For if things went against him, he would be putting his whole kingdom in danger, and even if he won, he would be no nearer gaining the territory either of the King of England or of any of his allies from the Empire.

So the morning passed in argument; but about noon a hare happened to run through the French camp, and those who saw it set up a great hue and cry, which made those at the rear think that the battle was beginning, and made them put on their helmets

and draw their swords. A number of new knights were created—
fourteen by the Count of Hainault alone, who were always
afterwards called 'Knights of the Hare.' Nothing more happened
that Friday except that a letter arrived from King Robert of
Sicily to the French King: King Robert was a great astrologer
and had several times examined the horoscopes of the Kings of
England and France, from which he deduced that the King of
France would inevitably be defeated if he fought the King of
England. So, recognizing in his wisdom the danger that threatened his cousin King Philip, he sent this letter warning him never
to have a battle with the English when King Edward was present.
This letter increased the existing doubts of the French nobles, and
although King Philip was anxious to give battle, the day passed,
on their advice, without an attack being made.

Seeing that there was to be no battle, the Count of Hainault
retired to Quesnoy. King Edward and the Duke of Brabant, with
their allies, collected their baggage and retreated that evening to
Avesnes. Next day, the detachments from Brabant and Germany
took their leave and went home, King Edward accompanying
the Duke of Brabant. His cousin King Philip was disappointed
that there had been no battle, but his counsellors pointed out how
he had nobly and valiantly succeeded in expelling the enemy
from his country, and that it would take King Edward a great
many expeditions of that kind before he conquered France. King
Philip gave leave for the whole army to disperse, and thanked the
nobles most courteously for having come to serve him. Thus
ended this great expedition, and King Philip went to Saint Omer,
and sent troops to all the towns along the frontier of the empire,
in particular in Tournai, Lille, and Douai. He sent Sir Godemar
du Fay to be in command at Tournai, and Sir Edward of Beaujeu
to Mortagne, and returned himself to Paris.

43

King Edward went to Brussels, escorted by his chief allies among
the nobles, to discuss the future conduct of the war. They held a

parliament to which Jacques van Artevelde was summoned and gladly came, together with all the councils from the principal towns of Flanders. It appears that King Edward was advised by his allies to ask the Flemish to assist him in the war, to defy King Philip and accompany him wherever he wanted them; in return, he would help them to recover Lille, Douai and Béthune.[1] The Flemish, after consultation, gave the following reply: 'Sir, this is not the first time that you have made this request. We would willingly agree to it, but we are pledged on oath not to make war on any King of France, under penalty of forfeiting two million florins, now deposited in the Papal Chamber, and on pain of excommunication. However, if you take the coat of arms of France, quartering it with that of England, and call yourself King of France, we will regard you as King of France, and obey you as such; and we will ask to be released from this bond, which you will grant us. Thus will we get a dispensation, and will follow you wherever you command.'

The King took counsel carefully at this, for it was a grave matter to assume the arms and title of France without having conquered any part of it. On the other hand the Flemish could be of more assistance to him than anyone else, and he was reluctant to lose their help. So he consulted all his privy councillors, including the Count of Artois, and the German lords as well, and after weighing the issue carefully, replied to the Flemish that if they would seal and swear to their part of the bargain, he would do as they suggested—to which they agreed.

Many questions were discussed at this conference at Ghent, and it was decided to besiege the city of Tournai. The Flemish were delighted, for they thought that they were powerful enough to capture it, and that afterwards they could easily recapture the other cities wrongfully held at that time by the French. It was noted with satisfaction that Hainault would be on their side, though the Count had been unable to attend the parliament,

[1] *Then occupied by the French.*

although summoned; however, he sent satisfactory reasons for his absence.

Such was the position when the lords dispersed to their homes. King Edward went to Antwerp; but the Queen remained with her court at Ghent, where she was often visited and encouraged by Jacques van Artevelde and the nobles of Ghent.

Soon afterwards the English fleet was made ready at Antwerp, and the King embarked with the greater part of his forces, leaving the Earls of Salisbury and Suffolk at Ypres to show that the English and Flemish interests were identical. They garrisoned the town and made vigorous attacks in the neighbourhood of Lille all that winter. King Edward reached London about Saint Andrew's Day,[1] 1339, and was warmly greeted after his long absence. Complaints reached him of the damage done by the Normans and Picards at Southampton, which distressed him deeply; he replied that the invaders would pay dearly for it, as indeed they did in the following year.

44

King Philip had disbanded his army, but he had greatly reinforced his navy, which already included detachments from Genoa, Normandy, Picardy, and Brittany. During the winter they made frequent raids on Dover, Sandwich, Winchelsea, Rye, and the Kentish coast, with a force of over forty thousand soldiers on board. The English did not dare leave their ports, for fear of being plundered at sea and killed; and they suffered heavy losses that winter, including that of a fine large ship the *Christopher*, carrying money and wool to Flanders. The Normans captured it, stole the cargo, and threw the crew overboard; the French boasted triumphantly about this success.

King Philip was continually thinking how he could take revenge on his enemies, and particularly on Sir John of Hainault, who had done him great disservice, especially by escorting King

[1] *November 30th.*

Edward to the district of Cambrai and Thiérache, and burning the country. He therefore wrote to the Lord of Coucy, to the Vidame of Chalons, Sir John de la Bone, and Sir Gerard of Loire, asking them to collect an expedition, invade Hainault and burn the country. They marched on Chimay with five hundred men, and took rich plunder, for the inhabitants never imagined that the French would advance beyond the forest of Thiérache. But they burned the suburbs of Chimay, and a number of neighbouring villages—in fact almost the whole territory of Chimay except the fortress. They then retired to Aubenton, in Thiérache, with their spoils. Sir John of Hainault heard the news at Mons, where he was staying with the count, his nephew, and was, not unreasonably, very angry, as was the count, from whom these lands were held. Nevertheless they made no open plan of revenge against the kingdom of France.

The French garrison at Cambrai sent some troops out to a small fortress near the town, called Relenques, which belonged to Sir John of Hainault, and was held by his illegitimate son with about twenty-five men. The attack was beaten off; but the dikes were frozen over, so that anyone could come right up to the castle walls: in view of this, the men inside decided that they would not be able to hold out, and they left Relenques in the middle of the night and set fire to it. Next day, it was entirely destroyed by the troops from Cambrai, and those who had been defending it retired to Valenciennes. Meanwhile Sir Giles de Mauny, who had been put in command of the garrison at Thun-l'Evêque by his brother Sir Walter, continued to harass the country round Cambrai, advancing right up to the city gates.

One day Sir Giles came up to Cambrai with over a hundred men-at-arms, causing grave alarm to those inside. The garrison armed themselves and rode to the gate where the skirmish had begun, and where Sir Giles had driven back the men of Cambrai. Among the latter was a man from Gascony called William Marchant, who rode out fully armed to the fray on a good charger. When Sir Giles was near him, he spurred on vigorously to meet him, lance in hand, fearing nothing. Sir Giles had his shield pierced, and all the armour round his heart, and the lance went right through his body. He fell to the ground, mortally wounded. This caused as much dismay to his own side as delight to his enemies. The encounter was very sharp, with many wounded, and numerous feats of arms performed. Finally the garrison of Cambrai were victorious, and drove off the attackers. They kept the body of Sir Giles, who died two days later, though everything was done to save his life. His body was sent to his brothers Sir John and Sir Thierry, who were in garrison at Bouchain in Ostrevant. For though Hainault was not at war, the French frontier was heavily defended. A handsome coffin was made, and the body was escorted by two monks, and was afterwards buried in the church of the Cordeliers at Valenciennes. The two brothers then came to Thun-l'Evêque, and carried out a vigorous campaign against the men of Cambrai in revenge for their brother's death. . . .

SUMMARY
44-49

Partly at the request of the Bishop of Cambrai, King Philip allowed a number of French knights to invade Hainault. They destroyed the countryside with fire and sword, even robbing and burning a monastery at Haspres. The Count of Hainault had the bells rung at Valenciennes, and called a parliament at Mons with his uncle; they decided to defy King Philip, in view of the damage done with his connivance in Hainault. The Abbot of Crespin took the challenge to King Philip, who said that Hainault richly deserved all it had suffered. After a great battle, the count and Sir John captured and destroyed Aubenton, in Thiérache, killing two hundred Frenchmen. Forty other towns and villages were destroyed before the count returned to Mons, where he arranged a definite alliance with King Edward, and made his uncle governor of Holland and Zeeland.

King Philip was furious when he heard of the trick by which King Edward had won the support of the Flemish. He persuaded Pope

Benedict XII[1] 'to put such a curse on the Flemish that no priest dared say mass there.' The Flemish were only slightly reassured when King Edward undertook to bring priests over who would say mass whether the Pope liked it or not.

King Philip ordered his garrisons at Tournai, Lille, and Douai to overrun Flanders. They burned the town of Courtrai, and took five hundred prisoners to hold to ransom. They also took ten thousand sheep and an equal number of pigs and cattle.

Jacques van Artevelde planned a joint attack on Tournai with the Earls of Suffolk and Salisbury. Disregarding the advice of their guide, the English fell into an ambush on their way to the meeting place, and Salisbury and Suffolk were taken prisoner. The attack was called off. Meanwhile the Duke of Normandy, King Philip's eldest son, invaded Hainault at Easter, 1340, and burned twenty-five villages between the rivers Selle and Honneau, as well as twelve more around Valenciennes, but the only fortress that he captured was Escandoeuvres, which fell by treason. The castle was pulled down and the stones used to repair the town of Cambrai. Many more villages were burned by the garrisons of Douai and Lille. The count sought help in England and Bavaria, as did Sir John in Brabant and Ghent. Thunl'Evêque was besieged by the Duke of Normandy, but the siege was raised by the Count of Hainault; rather than joining in pitched battle with the latter, the French preferred to continue a war of attrition, thinking that the coalition of their enemies would eventually be broken.

50

King Edward had meanwhile set sail in order to help his brother-in-law in Hainault fight against the French. He sailed on the eve of the feast of Saint John the Baptist,[2] 1340, and made straight for Sluys. Sir Hugh Quiriel, Sir Peter Bahucet and Barbenoire were at that time lying between Blanckenburg and Sluys with

---

[1] *According to Froissart, Clement VI; he was not made Pope, however, until 1342.*

[2] *June 24th.*

over a hundred and forty large ships (not counting provision-boats) manned by forty thousand men from Normandy, Genoa, and Picardy, waiting for the return of King Edward, and determined to prevent it.

King Edward saw such a number of masts in front of him that it looked like a wood. When he asked his ship's captain what it could be, he replied that it must be the Norman fleet that King Philip kept constantly at sea, which had done such great damage at Southampton, capturing the *Christopher* and killing her crew. King Edward declared that he had long wanted to fight them, and now, please God and Saint George, he would be able to, for they had done him such harm that he longed for revenge. He drew up his ships in line so that there was one shipload of men-at-arms between every two of archers, with a number of additional vessels full of archers kept in reserve, as replacements. There were on board a large number of noble ladies on their way to Ghent to attend the Queen, whom they had not seen for a long time. They were well escorted by three hundred men-at-arms and five hundred archers, provided by the King, who besought them all to defend his honour.

When King Edward had properly deployed his fleet, he manœuvred it so that the wind was on their starboard quarter, in order to have the advantage of the sun, which had previously shone full in their faces. The Normans, unable to understand these manœuvres, thought that the English were trying to avoid giving battle; but they were delighted to see that King Edward's standard was flown, for they were eager to fight him. They drew up their own ships, with the *Christopher*, which they had captured earlier that year, in the van, now manned with Genoese crossbowmen. The fleet advanced to the sound of trumpets and other warlike instruments.

A fierce battle broke out, each side opening fire with crossbows and longbows, and hand-to-hand fighting began. The soldiers used grappling irons on chains in order to come to grips with the enemy boats. Many noble feats of arms were achieved, both captures and rescues. The great *Christopher* was recaptured by the English, and all her crew killed. There was great hue and cry and the *Christopher* was manned by archers and joined the battle against the Genoese.

The battle that followed was cruel and horrible. Sea-battles are always more terrible than those on land, for those engaged can neither retreat nor run away; they can only stand and fight to the bitter end, and show their courage and endurance. Sir Hugh Quiriel and his companions were bold fighters, and had done great damage to the English in the past, and killed many of them. The battle lasted from early in the morning till noon, and in that time the English were hard pressed, for they were outnumbered four to one, and their enemies were all experienced sailors. King Edward, who was in the flower of his youth, proved himself a gallant knight, and he was supported by the Earls of Derby, Pembroke, Hereford, Huntingdon, and Gloucester; Sir Reginald Cobham, Sir Richard Stafford, Lord Percy, Sir Walter de Manny, Sir Henry of Flanders, Sir John Beauchamp, Lord Felton, Sir John Chandos, Lord Bradestan, Lord Delaware, Lord Melton, and Count Robert of Artois, now Earl of Richmond, and many other gallant knights whose names I cannot remember. But they fought so valiantly, with the help of those from the neighbourhood of Bruges, that they won the day. Their enemies were all killed or drowned, and not one escaped. The news soon spread through Flanders and Hainault, and came to the two armies before Thun-l'Evêque. The allies were as delighted as the French were distressed.

After this victory, which was on the eve of Saint John's day, King Edward spent the night, with his fleet, off Sluys; there was a great sounding of trumpets and other instruments. The Flemish came to visit the King when they heard of his arrival; he asked news of Jacques van Artevelde from the inhabitants of Bruges, and was told that he had gone to help the Count of Hainault, with over sixty thousand Flemish troops, against the Duke of Normandy. Next day the King landed, and set out on foot on a pilgrimage to Our Lady of Ardembourg, attended by a great number of knights. He heard mass and went on, in the evening, to Ghent, where the Queen welcomed him with delight. The army and baggage gradually followed him to the same place.

King Edward sent word to the nobles who were besieging Thun-l'Evêque, and when they heard of his arrival and his victory at sea, they dispersed. The Count of Hainault also disbanded his troops, except for the principal lords, whom he took to Valenciennes, where he entertained them lavishly, especially the Duke of Brabant and Jacques van Artevelde. The latter made a speech in the market-place, before all the nobles, explaining King Edward's right to the French throne, and also the strength of an alliance between Flanders, Hainault, and Brabant. His great eloquence won the approval of all who heard him; they said that he spoke with wisdom and experience, and that he was fully worthy to govern the county of Flanders. These lords then took their leave and agreed to meet the King at Ghent eight days later. He welcomed them and entertained them splendidly, as did the Queen, who had recently given birth to a son, called John, who was afterwards Duke of Lancaster by right of his wife Blanche, daughter of Henry Duke of Lancaster. A conference was then arranged at Vilvoorde.

When King Philip heard of the defeat of his army on the sea at Sluys he was distressed, and he withdrew to Arras, sending squadrons to defend the frontiers of Hainault and of Flanders, for these were the countries he feared the most.

51

King Robert of Sicily, who was on the throne at this time, had a great reputation as an astrologer, and constantly warned King Philip not to fight with the King of England, for the latter would be sure to win. King Robert was so much attached to the French crown that he would have hated to see any calamity overtake it. He was visiting the Pope and College of Cardinals at Avignon at this time, and he informed them of the great dangers that threatened France from the war between the two Kings. He also implored the Pope to act as a peacemaker between them, which he undertook to do, provided the Kings would listen to him.

52

The conference at Vilvoorde was attended by all King Edward's chief allies from the Low Countries and the empire. Three or four representatives from each of the principal towns of Flanders, Hainault, and Brabant came too, and these three countries made a pact of mutual assistance, so that if one of them was attacked, she could count on the help of the other two. If any disagreement arose between two of the three countries, the third would act as arbiter. If this failed, the case would be brought before King Edward, in whose hands this covenant was declared and sworn, and who in the last resort would make peace between them. A number of clauses were agreed and sworn to, but afterwards broken. But as a confirmation of love and friendship, they had coins struck that were to be valid in all three countries and were called 'companions,' or 'allies.' It was also settled that before Michaelmas King Edward should lay siege to the city of Tournai. All the lords present undertook to be there, as well as detachments from the principal towns. Each man then set off for his home, to prepare himself for the siege according to his estate.

53

King Philip was fully informed of the agreements made at Vilvoorde, and he proceeded to fortify Tournai, and to fill the town with enough provisions to stand a long siege. Towards harvest-time, King Edward set out from Ghent with four thousand men-at-arms and nine thousand archers, not counting foot soldiers. The army was commanded by seven English earls, twenty-eight bannerets and two hundred knights. The Duke of Brabant supported him with an army of twenty thousand, and the Count of Hainault brought the fine cavalry of his country, as well as a large army from Holland and Zeeland. Jacques van Artevelde came next with sixty thousand Flemish troops, not counting those from Ypres, Cassel, Poperinghe, and Bruges. The German lords also brought their armies, and between them all they completely surrounded the town of Tournai.

54

The siege lasted a long time, for the town was well prepared and gallantly defended. The Count of Hainault led several expeditions into the surrounding countryside, burning villages and looting the country. The Flemish attacked the town from the river, with boats, but were repulsed. At the same time, in Gascony, the Count of Lille recaptured Aquitaine for the French and besieged Bordeaux with the help of the Count of Périgord and the chief nobles of the district.

55

Meanwhile, in Scotland, the part of the country not occupied by the English was governed by the following knights: Sir William Douglas (brother of Sir James who was killed in Spain) the Earl of Moray, Patrick Earl of Dunbar, the Earl of Sutherland, Sir Robert Erskine, Sir Simon Fraser, and Sir Alexander Ramsay. For seven years they lived in hiding in Jedworth Forest, summer and winter, making what expeditions they could against the towns and fortresses garrisoned by King Edward, and often winning great renown and glory by their gallant and adventurous campaigns.

During the siege of Tournai, King Philip sent some troops over to Scotland, who arrived safely at Perth. He begged the King of Scotland to make such vigorous war on England that King Edward would be obliged to come home and leave the siege of Tournai. King Philip promised the Scots lords every assistance and support, and they accordingly prepared a great expedition against the English. They left Jedworth Forest and crossed Scotland to recapture as many fortresses as they could. They passed by Berwick, crossed the Tyne and entered Northumberland, which was formerly a kingdom on its own. There they found plenty of fat beasts; they laid waste the country as far as the city of Durham, and even further. They went back by a different way, still destroying the country, so that all the land within three days' journey of the border was completely devastated. They then went back into Scotland, recapturing all the fortresses held by the English except Berwick and the three other strongest castles in the country, Stirling, Roxburgh, and Edinburgh, which might be called the sovereign castle of Scotland. Indeed one could hardly find stronger castles than these in any country, and they were valiantly defended as well as having excellent natural positions. The castle at Edinburgh stands on a high rock from which the whole neighbouring countryside can be seen, and the rock is so steep that nobody can climb it without stopping to rest two or three times. The governor of it was a valiant English knight, Sir Walter of Limousin, whose brother Sir Richard had fought so bravely at Thun l'Evêque against the French.

Sir William Douglas formed a bold and subtle plan which he communicated to the Earl of Dunbar, Sir Simon Fraser (who had been guardian and tutor to King David of Scotland) and Sir Alexander Ramsay; and they all agreed to it. They collected two hundred savage Highlanders, and put to sea with a good supply of oats, oatmeal, and coal. They landed peacefully at a port about eight miles from Edinburgh, and set out by night with a dozen of their most trusted companions, all dressed in tattered clothes and old hats, like poor merchants. They loaded twelve little ponies with sacks full of oats, coal and meal; and they made their other men hide themselves in a ruined abbey at the foot of the hill on which the castle stands. At daybreak the 'merchants,' secretly armed, made their way as best they could with their horses to the castle. When they were halfway up the mountain, Sir William Douglas and Sir Simon Fraser went ahead and approached the porter, telling him that they had brought, at great risk to themselves, supplies of coal, oats, and meal, which they would sell at a cheap price. The porter replied that the garrison were in need of these things, but that it was too early to wake the governor or his steward. But he told him to bring up the provisions, and opened the outer gate, through which they all passed quietly. Sir William Douglas had noticed that the porter had all the keys of the great door into the castle, and had asked the porter, with a pretence of indifference, which key opened the great door and which the wicket. When the outer gate was opened they brought in the ponies and unloaded the first two sacks of coal right in the gateway, so that it could not be shut again. They then killed the porter so quickly that he did not utter a sound, took the keys and unlocked the great door. Sir William Douglas sounded a blast on his horn as a signal, and the twelve 'merchants' took off their ragged disguise and emptied the rest of the coal in the doorway to prevent it from being closed.

When the men in hiding heard the horn, they rushed up to the castle. The castle guard was awakened by the horn, and seeing the armed men running up to the castle, sounded the alarm crying, 'We are betrayed,' at the top of his voice. The whole garrison armed themselves and came to the door, but Sir William and his companions prevented them from shutting it again. The fighting grew fiercer, but the attackers held their ground till they were reinforced. The garrison, and in particular their governor, defended themselves valiantly when they saw that they had been deceived. But in spite of their killing and wounding many of the attackers, Sir William Douglas and his men took the fortress, killing all the English except the governor and six squires whom they spared. The Scots remained in the castle all that day and appointed as governor Sir Simon Erskine, who was a squire of that country, and they left with him a garrison of his countrymen. The news of this capture reached King Edward at Tournai.

56

King Edward had altogether, from all the different countries, an army of a hundred and twenty thousand men. The commanders in the city besieged by King Edward, now that provisions were running low, ordered all those who had not brought in enough supplies for themselves to leave the city. They were driven out and had to pass through the army of the Duke of Brabant, who took pity on them and gave them safe conduct. King Philip remained at Arras all this time, while the garrison at Tournai was in dire need of relief; but he now issued a summons to raise troops all over France and also in many parts of the empire, to such good effect that the King of Bohemia, the Duke of Lorraine, the Bishops of Metz and Verdun, and the Counts of Bar, Montheliard, Geneva and Savoy all answered his call with all the troops they could muster. He also won the support of the Dukes of Brittany, Burgundy, and Bourbon; the Counts of Alençon, Forêts, Armagnac, Flanders, Harcourt, and Dammartin; the Lord of Coucy, and other knights and barons too numerous to mention. The Kings of Navarre and Scotland also joined him, in accordance with the homage they paid him.

57

King Philip then left Arras with this great army and made for Tournai. When he was nearly at Pont-à-Tressin, two German knights rode out from their garrison at Bouchain with about twenty-five lances and attacked a French force of about a hundred and twenty who had collected a large quantity of loot, which they were taking to Mortagne. Nearly all the French were killed in the violent battle that ensued, and the loot they had taken was returned to its rightful owners.

58

King Philip encamped near the bridge of Bouvines, and a force under Sir Robert de Bailleul left the French camp and crossed the Pont-à-Tressin, where they met a company of Hainaulters under Sir Robert's brother, Sir William, on their way through the foggy marshes to attack the quarters of the King of Bohemia and the Bishop of Liège. Sir William's troops were driven back after a sharp struggle, through mistaking Sir Robert's banner in the mist. Sir William escaped with the loss of a large number of his men, including Sir Vauflart de la Croix, who was captured after hiding all night in the reeds, and was later put to death by the people of Lille, to whom King Philip had handed him over.

59

The Count of Hainault soon afterwards set out from the army besieging Tournai with about six hundred of his countrymen to attack the town of Mortagne, which was defended by the Lord of Beaujeu. This lord stationed himself at the weakest part of the defences, armed with a very stout lance with a steel hook attached to the end, so that he could fix the hook into the armour of any attacker and drag him into the river. By this method he accounted for twelve of the attackers in the course of the day. The men of Valenciennes constructed an excellent catapult, which threw stones into the town, to the distress of the inhabitants, and meanwhile another machine was made to extract the piles from the river so that they could row up and attack the town by water. This, however, proved too laborious. There was also a very able engineer in Mortagne who, after considering the damage caused by the catapult, constructed a similar one, not large but so well made and accurate that it was only used three times. The first shot landed a stone within twelve yards of the machine used by the men of Valenciennes; the second was even nearer, and the third was so well aimed that it struck the machine on the shaft, and broke the case. The soldiers of Mortagne cheered, and the Hainaulters, having failed for two days and nights to capture any part of Mortagne, returned to Tournai.

SUMMARY

60-61

A body of men from Valenciennes attacked the fortress of Saint
Amand, but without success: their alliance with the English was de-
rided by the defenders, who cried out 'Go away and drink your good
ale!' Next day the Count of Hainault came from Tournai and took the
town by battering down part of the abbey walls. Later, he crossed
into France and burned a fortified monastery at Marchiennes. The
siege of Tournai continued, and it was thought that the Duke of
Brabant allowed provisions to get through into the town. In an attack
on the French at Pont-à-Tressin the Germans captured Sir Charles de
Montmorency and eighty other French knights.

62

Sir Robert of Artois and Sir Henry of Flanders had under their
command forty thousand Flemish troops from Ypres, Poperinghe,
Cassel, and Bergues; one day, about three thousand of them set
out, lightly armed, and destroyed a number of houses in the
suburbs of Saint Omer. The alarm was sounded, and the lords
of the town set out with about eight hundred men and made a
circuit round the outside of the town till they came up with the
Flemish who were busy looting the town of Arques, nearby, in
some disorder. The French attacked them unawares, with cries of
'Clermont, Clermont, for the Dauphin of Auvergne!' The
Flemish dropped their loot and fled, pursued by the French who
cut them down in great numbers: of the three thousand Flemish,
eight hundred were killed and four hundred captured and
imprisoned in Saint Omer. The few that escaped rejoined their
leaders, but were shown little sympathy, since they had acted
without orders, with no one in command. And about midnight,
while they were asleep in their tents, an extraordinary general
panic came over them; and they all got up and struck camp with

all possible speed. Tents and pavilions were pulled down and bundled into wagons, and the army took to its heels, in complete disorder, without waiting for anyone. When the two commanders were told what was happening, they got up immediately and had great fires and torches lit; and they set off and overtook their troops and asked, 'What is the matter? Why are you running away? No one is chasing you. Come back, for God's sake! What you are doing is very wrong.' But the troops paid no attention and all fled straight back to their homes. Sir Robert of Artois and Sir Henry saw that there was nothing to be done, and packed up their baggage and went back to the siege at Tournai, where their story was heard with great surprise. The general verdict was that the troops had been bewitched.

SUMMARY

63-72

Partly by the personal efforts of Joan of Valois, sister of King Philip and mother of the young Count of Hainault, a truce was made in 1341, and the siege of Tournai called off after eleven weeks.

Both sides claimed victory: the French because Tournai had not fallen, and the English because they had done such widespread damage for so long in France, and forced the French to seek a truce. King Edward and the Count of Hainault both went home, and King Philip dismissed his troops.

At the council of Arras that followed, the Cardinals of Naples and Clermont tried to make a permanent settlement between the Kings of England and France and their numerous advisers. But neither side would make any concessions, though the French agreed to give up Ponthieu, Queen Isabel's dowry. The truce was extended for two years.

Soon after the truce of 1341, the Duke of Brittany died, leaving no children. His half brother, the Earl of Montfort, disputed the succession with his niece, who had married Count Charles of Blois. Montfort succeeded in establishing himself at Nantes and proceeded to seize a quantity of treasure that had been secretly amassed by his late brother at Limoges.   He assembled an army and captured Brest, Rennes, Hennebont, Vannes, and Carhaix.   He then crossed to England and did homage to King Edward at Windsor for the duchy of Brittany. King Edward accepted this, thinking he might enter France more successfully from Brittany than from Flanders.

Charles of Blois meanwhile complained to King Philip that his wife was the lawful heiress. Montfort was summoned before the King and his peers, and denied having done homage to King Edward, but maintained his claim to Brittany. He was ordered to stay in Paris pending the King's decision, but after 'sitting and imagining many doubts,' left secretly for Brittany. This annoyed the King, and the peers and barons decided against Montfort's claim.

Charles of Blois collected the Dukes of Normandy, Burgundy, and Bourbon, the Count of Alençon, and others, at Angers, and after taking Champtocé laid siege to Montfort at Nantes.   The town surrendered and Montfort was taken to King Philip and imprisoned in the Louvre where he eventually died.[1] His widow, 'who had the courage of a man and the heart of a lion,' retained the loyalty of his supporters.

73

It has already been described how, during the siege of Tournai, King Edward was informed of the activities of the Scots, how they

---

[1] *Froissart is wrong: Père Morice's*, Histoire Ecclésiastique et Civile de Bretagne (*1750*), *explains how in 1345 the Earl of Montfort escaped from the Louvre after three years' imprisonment and made his way to visit King Edward at Westminster. The King was intent on the preparations for his war in Gascony, but thought it wise to give Montfort some troops, under the command of William Bohun, Earl of Northampton, to support him against Charles of Blois.*

Montfort paid homage to the King for the duchy of Brittany, in the Archbishop's rooms at Lambeth. He then set out for Brittany and after an unsuccessful attack on Quimper, died in the castle at Hennebont on September 26th, 1345, appointing in his will the King of England as guardian of his son John of Brittany.

recaptured a number of towns and fortresses, and were still besieging Stirling Castle. In the month of October, King Edward set out again, having given orders for troops and archers to meet him at York, which they did. When they heard of his approach, the Scots redoubled their attacks on Stirling, both with siege-engines and cannons, to such effect that the garrison surrendered, saving their lives but not their possessions. This news reached the King at York, and he marched to Durham and on to Newcastle. He billeted his troops in the neighbourhood, and stayed there over a month, waiting for the provisions that they had sent round by sea. But many of these ships were lost in the November weather, and others were carried by adverse winds to Holland and Friesland. King Edward's army, which numbered six thousand cavalry and forty thousand infantry, was therefore in great distress: they could not advance, for winter had set in, and there were no provisions to be had, since the Scots had gathered all their cattle and corn into their fortresses.

After the capture of Stirling, the Scots lords retired to Jedworth Forest, but when they heard that King Edward had reached Newcastle with a large force to burn and ravage their country, as he had done twice before, they assembled to consider the best means of defence. They were few in number, and they had been fighting for over seven years, without a leader, often lying out in woods and fields, to their great discomfort. Their own King was not in the country, and they were in despair. They therefore sent a bishop and an abbot to King Edward, to ask for a truce. These ambassadors reached the King and his barons at Newcastle, and put their case with such eloquence that a truce of four months was granted, provided the Scots sent a message to their King in France, to the effect that unless he returned to Scotland by the following May, with sufficient power to defend the country against the English, they would become subjects of the King of England, and never regard him as their sovereign lord again. These were the terms of the truce, with which the Scots were quite satisfied. They then sent Sir Simon Fraser, Sir Robert Erskine, and two other knights to take the news to their King in

France. King Edward had stayed at Newcastle with his army in acute distress from lack of provisions, which made him more eager to accept the truce. He now turned homewards and dismissed his troops.

The ambassadors from Scotland passed through England on the way to their King in France, and took ship at Dover. King David, who had been in France for seven years and knew that his country had been destroyed and ravaged, as you have heard, decided to take leave of King Philip and go back to comfort and assist his people. In fact, he set out with his Queen before the ambassadors reached him; he embarked at a different port and landed at Moray before any of the lords knew of it. When they heard, they were overjoyed, and gave a great feast to welcome him, with all due ceremony; they then escorted him nobly to Perth, where the good salmon are caught in such abundance.

74

News of the arrival of King David and his wife Joan soon spread, and his people came from all parts to see him and to celebrate. Afterwards they all put before him complaints of the damage and destruction that King Edward and the English had done in Scotland; King David was horrified at the extent of the destruction, and tried to comfort them by saying that he would get his revenge, or lose his throne, and his life as well, in the attempt. He sent messengers to all his friends both near and far asking for their help. The Earl of Orkney, a great and powerful baron who had married the King's sister, was the first to answer the call. He came with a great following, as did several other great barons and knights from Sweden, Norway, and Denmark, some out of friendship and others for money. In all, sixty thousand foot-soldiers assembled at Perth on the day ordained by the King, and three thousand knights-at-arms from every part of Scotland all mounted on rough ponies.

When all were assembled, they set out to do as much harm as they could in England, for the truce had expired. They left Perth in regular order and spent the first night at Dunfermline. They then crossed the Firth of Forth and came to Edinburgh, and pushed forward past Roxburgh Castle, which they did not attack, although it was held by the English, for they did not want to risk their forces or to expend their artillery; they did not know what resistance they were going to meet, and they wanted to achieve some notable success before returning to Scotland. They also passed by Berwick without attacking it, and crossing into Northumberland they went on as far as Newcastle, burning and destroying the country as they went. There King David and the army halted for the night, to see what advantage was to be gained. Some local knights who were in the town left it secretly at dawn with about two hundred lances to attack the Scots. They went straight for the quarters of the Earl of Moray, whose arms were argent, three pillows gules. He was still asleep, and they captured him and killed a great number of his men before the army roused itself, and after taking considerable booty they went back rejoicing into the town, and delivered their prisoner to Sir John Neville, the governor. When the army awoke and armed themselves, they rushed on the town like madmen and made a violent assault on the gates; this achieved nothing, and they lost a number of troops, for the defence was very capable and drove them off with heavy losses.

75-76

When King David saw that there was nothing to be gained by continuing the siege of Newcastle, he led his army into the bishopric of Durham, burning and laying waste the country as he went. They made violent assaults on the city of Durham in their frenzy to avenge the capture of the Earl of Moray. When King Edward heard of this,[1] he gave orders that all knights and squires, and anyone else between the ages of fifteen and sixty, were to

---

[1] *The news was brought to him by Sir John Neville, who covered the distance between Newcastle and Chertsey on horseback in five days.*

set out without fail for the north to defend the realm against the Scots. While these orders were being carried out, the Scots, by their furious attacks, captured Durham, and cruelly put to death all whom they found inside, sparing neither women nor children nor priests; nor did they leave any house or church standing. It was a great and terrible shame so to ravage Christendom and to destroy the churches in which God is served and honoured.[1]

77

King Edward reached Wark Castle on the same day that the Scots left, and he was furious to find them gone, for in his eagerness to fight them, he had come in such haste that both his men and his horses were exhausted. He ordered his army to encamp, for he wished to see the castle and the noble lady who held it, as he had not seen her since before her marriage. Taking ten or twelve knights with him he went to salute the Countess of Salisbury and to examine the damage done by the Scots' attacks.

When the countess heard that the King was coming, she had the gates opened, and went out to meet him so richly dressed that no one could look at her without wonder and admiration at her noble appearance, her great beauty, and her warmth of expression. When she came to the King, she made a deep curtsy, thanking him for coming to her aid, and led him into the castle to entertain him fittingly. Everyone was dazzled by her; the King

[1] *This is one of the few occasions on which Froissart is moved to comment on the horrors of war. But the passage is doubtful history, for there are no references in any English chronicles to the sack of Durham. Chapter 76 of the narrative goes on to say that 'King David retired towards Carlisle, passing on the way a castle belonging to the Earl of Salisbury (Wark Castle) then held by his nephew Sir William Montagu, who attacked the Scots' rearguard and carried off plunder. The castle was then assaulted; the Earl of Salisbury was at that time held prisoner in France, and the countess was looking after the garrison. After several fruitless attacks the Scots retired to Jedworth Castle, fearing that King Edward was on his way.'*

The whole passage, however, is muddled and inconsistent.

could not take his eyes off her, and thought he had never seen a
lady so noble and beautiful, and at the same time so gay and
attractive. A spark of love was kindled in his heart that was to
remain burning a long time, for he did not think that anywhere
in the world could there be a lady so worthy of love. They entered
the castle hand in hand, and first she led him into the great hall,
and then to his room, which was as richly furnished as might be
expected. All this time the King gazed at her so ardently that she
became embarrassed. After looking at her for a long while, he
went to a window and leaned on it, reflecting deeply. The
countess, thinking no more of it, went to entertain the other
knights and to see to the preparation for dinner. She then
returned to the King, who was still lost in thought, and cheerfully
enquired: 'Sir, what is it that you are pondering so deeply? So
much meditation does not suit you, if I may be so bold. You
should be feasting, and in high spirits: you have driven off the
enemies who dared to attack you.' The King answered: 'Ah,
dear lady, since I came here, something has struck me of which I
had no notion, and I must reflect on it. I do not know what will
be the result, but I cannot take my mind off it.' 'Ah, dear sir,' replied the countess, 'you should always be in good spirits, and feast
with your friends and encourage them, and leave off thinking and
musing. God has helped you so much in all your enterprises and
given you so much grace, that you are the most feared and renowned prince in Christendom. And if the King of Scotland has
done harm to your kingdom, you can repay him when you like, as
you have done before. So come into the hall to your knights, if
you please, for dinner will soon be ready.' 'Ah, dear lady, something else touches my heart—it is not what you think. It is that
your sweet nature, your perfect sense, your noble and exceptional
beauty have so struck me that I am in love with you. I beg of
you to return my love, which nothing can quench.' The countess
was taken aback: 'Dear sir,' she said, 'do not mock me, and do
not tempt me. I cannot believe that you mean what you have
said, nor that so noble and gallant a prince as yourself could
think of dishonouring myself and my husband, who is such a

valiant knight and has served you so faithfully, and is at this
moment in prison for your cause. Certainly, sir, this would not
add to your glory, nor benefit you. Such a thought has never
entered my mind for any man, nor will it, please God. If I were
guilty of such a thing, it is you who ought to blame me and
punish my body with death.'

This admirable lady left the King much astonished and went
to hasten dinner in the hall. She afterwards returned to the King,
with some of his knights, and said: 'Sir, come into the hall. The
knights are waiting for you, to wash their hands. They have
fasted too long, as you must have too.' The King left his room and
went into the hall, and washed, and sat down to dinner with the
knights and their hostess. But he ate little, for his mind was on
other things, he remained pensive, and cast his eyes in the
direction of the countess whenever he could. The others thought
it was the Scots who had escaped him that were the object of his
anxiety. The King stayed in the castle all day, thoughtful and
worried, for he did not know what to do. Sometimes he blamed
himself, since honour and duty forbade him to harbour these
false thoughts of dishonouring this valiant lady and her loyal
husband who had always served him so faithfully. On the other
hand, his passion for her was so violent that it overwhelmed
all thoughts of honour and duty. His mind was occupied with
this all that day and night. In the morning he made his army
strike camp and pursue the Scots, to chase them out of his
country. He took leave of the countess with the following words:
'Dear lady, God protect you till my return; and I beg you to
change your mind.' 'Dear sir,' she replied, 'may God the Father
protect you, and drive all wicked and dishonourable thoughts
from your heart, for it will always be my wish to serve you in every
way that is consistent with my honour and yours.'

The King departed, confused and ashamed. He went after the
Scots with his whole army, beyond Berwick, and encamped
about ten miles from Jedworth Forest, where King David and all
his men had retired to their stronghold. King Edward stayed
there for three days to see if the Scots would come out and fight.

On each day there were skirmishes, and many were killed and taken prisoner. Sir William Douglas was always in the forefront, performing many gallant feats, and was a constant thorn in the flesh of the English.

78

During these three days, various discreet advisers on both sides tried to arrange a truce between the two Kings, which was finally settled to last for two years subject to the agreement of the King of France, for the King of Scotland was in such close alliance with him that he could not make any settlement without his approval. If King Philip should refuse his assent the truce would last only until the first of August. The Earl of Moray would be released on condition that King David should obtain from the King of France the release of the Earl of Salisbury, before the feast of Saint John the Baptist.[1]   King Edward agreed more readily to the truce since he was engaged in fighting in France in Gascony, Poitou, Saintonge, and Brittany, and had soldiers everywhere.   King David departed and sent ambassadors to the King of France, to confirm the truce. King Philip gave his consent, and sent the Earl of Salisbury back to England, whereupon King Edward sent the Earl of Moray back to King David, who was delighted.   The two great armies withdrew without further delay.

SUMMARY

79

In Brittany, the Count of Blois laid siege to Rennes in the following spring. The Countess of Montfort, who was at Hennebont, appealed to King Edward for help; he sent Sir Walter de Manny with three thousand archers, but they were delayed for two months by the weather. Rennes fell in May 1342.

---

[1] *June 24th.*

80

When the city of Rennes was captured and the townsmen had done homage to Count Charles of Blois, he was advised to set out for Hennebont, where the Countess of Montfort lived; for now that the Count was in prison the war would be at an end once the countess and her son could be captured. She had with her at Hennebont the Bishop of Léon, uncle of Sir Hervé de Léon who was attached to the Count of Blois; also Sir Yves de Trésiquidi, the Governor of Guingamp, the two brothers de Quirich, Sir Henri and Sir Olivier de Pennefort and several others. When they heard that they were about to be besieged they had the alarm bells rung and gave orders that everyone should arm himself for the defence of the town.

When Charles of Blois discovered the strength of the fortifications at Hennebont, he prepared for a siege. Some of his troops, who came from Spain and Genoa as well as from France, advanced to the barriers to skirmish; they were opposed by some of those inside, and as frequently occurs in such circumstances, the Genoese lost more in the conflict than they gained. About the time of vespers, each side drew back to make a strong assault, to try out the defence and to see if any advantage was to be gained. On the third day they attacked fiercely, early in the morning; but the defenders resisted so stoutly that by midday the attackers were forced to retreat a little, leaving many of their number dead and carrying back many wounded. Their commanders were enraged by this retreat, and made their troops return to the attack more fiercely than ever, while the defenders remained equally determined to acquit themselves well.

The countess herself was clad in armour, and well mounted. She made the womenfolk in the town tear up stones from the streets and carry them to the battlements to drop on their enemies; and pots of quicklime were put to the same purpose. The countess also performed another very gallant deed: she had climbed a tower, to watch how her troops were acquitting themselves, and she noticed that all the lords and their followers had left their camp outside and had come to join the assault. She therefore collected three hundred horsemen who were guarding one of the gates at which no attack was being made; she rode out of the gate, at the head of her men, and galloped up to the tents and lodgings of the attackers, and cut them down and burned them with impunity, for they were guarded only by boys and servants who fled at their approach. When the French saw their camp on fire, and heard the hue and cry, they ran back astounded, crying, 'We are betrayed!' so that the assault on the town was broken off. The countess saw them, and rallied her men; and deciding that she could not get back into the town without too great a risk, she set out for the castle of Brest, which is not far away. Lord Louis of Spain, who was marshal of the army, seeing her galloping away from the blazing tents with her men, set off in pursuit with a large force. He cut down some of the stragglers who were less well mounted than the rest. But the countess succeeded in reaching Brest with the greater part of her force, where they were received with great delight. When Lord Louis discovered from prisoners he had captured that it was the countess who had led this attack, and escaped, he reported the news to the army, who were very much amazed; in the town, there was great anxiety, when neither she nor any of her companions returned, and no one knew what had become of her.

Next day the lords of France, having lost their tents and their provisions, decided to make huts of branches and leaves, nearer the town, which they occupied in some discomfort. They called out repeatedly to those inside: 'Come on, my lords, go and look for your countess! She is lost, and it will be a long time before you find her.' The townsmen were much distressed, and they had no news of her for five days.

Meanwhile, the countess had been so active that she had collected a force of five hundred men, well armed and mounted, and, leaving Brest, about midnight, they reached Hennebont at sunrise. Skirting the enemy's flank they entered by one of the city gates, to the great delight of the townsmen and to the sound of horns and trumpets. The French were amazed. They armed themselves, and made another violent assault on the town, which was defended with equal vigour. The attack lasted till noon, but the French lost more than they gained. When they eventually retired (for their men were being killed and wounded to no purpose) Charles of Blois held a council and decided to go and besiege the castle at Auray, which had been built and fortified by King Arthur. He was accompanied by his brother and the Duke of Bourbon, Sir Robert Bertrand, Marshal of France, and Sir Hervé de Léon, with the Genoese under his command. Lord Louis of Spain was to stay by Hennebont, with the Vicomte de Rohan and the rest of the Spanish and Genoese troops. They sent for twelve large siege-engines, which they had left at Rennes, to bombard the castle with stones, for they realised that they were not achieving anything by their assault: half the army remained at Hennebont and the other half went and encamped at Auray.

Charles of Blois ordered an attack and a skirmish to be made against the castle, which was well defended by two hundred loyal subjects of the countess, under the command of Sir Henri de Pennefort and his brother Olivier. Twelve miles from the castle lies the town of Vannes, which was held for the countess by Sir Geoffrey de Malestroit, a brave and valiant knight. On the other side lies the good town of Dinan,[1] which was as yet only fortified by a ditch and a palisade. The commander there was the Governor of Guingamp, who was however at that time with the countess at Hennebont. But he had left his wife and daughters at Dinan, and with them, as his lieutenant, his son Sir Reginald.

Between these towns lies a strong castle that belonged to Charles of Blois,[2] which he had garrisoned with troops from Burgundy under a young commander called Gerard of Malain,

[1] *This cannot mean the present town of Dinant, which is about sixty miles north-west of Auray, near Saint Malo. It presumably refers to the small Breton village of Saint Sauveur de Dinan.*
[2] *La Roche Perion.*

who had with him another bold knight called Sir Peter Porte-
boeuf. These two had harassed and devastated the surrounding
country and had pressed the towns of Vannes and Dinan so hard
that no provisions could be brought into them except at grave
risk. For they made constant excursions, one day towards Vannes,
and another day towards Dinan, so regularly that Sir Reginald of
Guingamp captured Gerard of Malain in an ambush, with
twenty-five of his followers, rescuing at the same time fifteen
merchants, with all their goods, who had been captured and
were being taken back to the garrison at La Roche Perion. Sir
Reginald escorted them all to Dinan, for which he was much
commended.

To return to the siege of Hennebont, Lord Louis of Spain had
battered and destroyed the walls to such an extent that the inhabitants began to lose heart and wanted to come to terms, for
they could see no hope of rescue. So it came about that the
Bishop of Léon (uncle of that Sir Hervé through whom, it was
said, the Count of Montfort was captured) had a long secret discussion with his nephew on various subjects; and it was agreed
that the bishop should try to win over the townsmen to surrender
to Charles of Blois. Sir Hervé, on his side, was to obtain a pardon
for the townsmen from Count Charles, and an assurance that they
would lose none of their property. The bishop went back to the
town. The countess was suspicious, and begged the other lords
of Brittany, for the love of God, not to doubt that help would
come within three days. But the bishop spoke so eloquently that
the lords were in two minds; next day, too, he spoke again so
reasonably that nearly everyone was persuaded. Sir Hervé was
already near the town when the countess, who was looking out to
sea from a window, cried out with delight: 'I can see the relief
coming that I have longed for so dearly!' She repeated this shout,
and everyone in the town ran to the windows and battlements;
and they could clearly see a great number of ships both large and
small approaching Hennebont. They were much comforted by
this, for they rightly assumed that it was the fleet from England
that had been held up for two months by contrary winds.

81

When the Governor of Guingamp and the other lords saw the fleet approaching, they told the bishop that he could stop trying to persuade them, for they had no intention of following his wishes. The bishop was very angry and replied: 'Sirs, I will leave your company, and will go to the side that appears to me to be in the right.' He sent his defiances to the countess and all her supporters, and went to give an account of the position to his nephew Sir Hervé. The latter was furious, and gave orders that the largest siege-engine available should be brought up as close to the walls as possible, and should bombard the town incessantly, day and night. He then presented his uncle to Lord Louis of Spain and Count Charles of Blois, who received him courteously.

The countess had rooms prepared for the English lords, and sent a noble deputation to greet them; and when they landed and came before her, she welcomed them most graciously, and feasted them and showed her gratitude by doing everything she could to entertain them. She put them all up in the castle, until they could find suitable lodging in the town. The next day she gave them a great dinner, and all night long, and next day as well, the siege-engine never ceased firing on the town.

After this show of hospitality, Sir Walter de Manny, who led the English troops, had a great desire to go and destroy the siege-engine which was so near the walls and was doing such damage all the time, if anyone would follow him. Sir Yves de Trésiquidi replied that he would not fail him in this, his first onslaught. All Sir Walter's men armed themselves, as did the Breton knights, and they all left quietly by one of the gates, taking three hundred archers with them. The archers shot so well that the men guarding the machine fled, and some of them were killed by the men-at-arms attached to the archers, who also destroyed the great siege-engine and broke it to pieces. They then dashed up to the tents and lodgings, and burned them, killing and wounding many of their enemies, whom they took by surprise. Then they retired in good order, and when the enemy were mounted and armed they came galloping after them like madmen. When Sir Walter saw them coming in pursuit with a great hue and cry, he exclaimed: 'May I never again be kissed by my dear lady, if I go back into the castle without knocking down one of these gallopers!' He turned to face them, spear in hand, with a number of his companions, and attacked the first-comers. Many of them kicked their legs in the air, and some of his own men were unhorsed as well.

The fighting became heavy, with reinforcements pouring in from the camp, and the English and Bretons had to retire to the fortress walls, where many brilliant feats of arms, captures and rescues were accomplished, with Sir Walter ever in the forefront. Other archers, who had not taken part in the assault on the siege-engine, now poured out of the town and took up positions on the banks of the ditches, and drove back the attackers with a rain of arrows, killing and wounding a great number of men and horses. The attackers, seeing that they were having the worst of it and losing men to no purpose, retired, and afterwards the troops from the town re-entered it and dispersed. The countess was to be seen coming down from the castle and kissing Sir Walter and his companions two or three times, each in turn, valiant lady that she was.

SUMMARY

82-99

The French abandoned the siege of Hennebont, and the war dragged on in Brittany, first one side capturing towns, then the other. The siege was later renewed, and, after arranging a diversion to occupy the enemy, Sir Walter de Manny brilliantly rescued two English knights, John Butler and Matthew Trelawney; they had been captured by the French, and the English had been warned by a spy that their execution was imminent.

Later, after the capture of Jugon by Charles of Blois, a truce was called, and the Countess of Montfort crossed to England, where feasts and jousts were held in London in honour of the Countess of Salisbury.

A sea battle was fought at Guernsey between Louis of Spain and Robert of Artois, Earl of Richmond, who was bringing support for the Countess of Montfort; the battle was indecisive and was ended by a violent storm.

The English captured Vannes, which was later recovered by the French; Robert of Artois was wounded, and died after returning to England. King Edward again besieged Vannes till the winter of 1342, when a three-year truce was concluded through the efforts of two cardinals sent by Pope Clement VI.

100

At this time[1] King Edward decided to restore and rebuild the great castle at Windsor, first built by King Arthur, who instituted the noble Round Table there, from which so many good and valiant knights went out into the world to engage in brave and gallant feats of arms. King Edward also founded an order of knighthood, consisting of himself and his sons and the most gallant knights in the land, up to the number of forty. They were to be called the 'Knights of the Blue Garter,' and they were to hold a feast once a year at Windsor, on Saint George's Day. He therefore summoned earls, barons and knights from all over his country and told them his intention. They welcomed it, for it seemed honourable to them, and likely to increase love and friendship. Forty knights were elected,[2] reputedly the bravest in the land, and they swore and sealed a declaration that they would keep the feast and the statutes that had been ordained. The King founded a chapel of Saint George at Windsor, and appointed canons to serve God, endowing them generously. And so that the feast might be known far and wide, he sent heralds to France, Scotland, Burgundy, Hainault, Flanders, Brabant, and the Em-

---

[1] *1344.*

[2] *The original Knights of the Garter were in fact only twenty-six in number, including the King and the Prince of Wales.*

pire. And he gave all knights and squires that wanted to come to the ceremony safe conduct for fifteen days afterwards. The celebration was fixed for Saint George's day, 1344;[1] the Queen was to be present, attended by three hundred ladies and maids in waiting, all of high birth, and richly dressed in matching robes.

SUMMARY

101-114

At the feast on Saint George's day at Windsor, King Edward received ambassadors from Gascony who asked for his support in view of the weakness of their country and the danger they were in from the French. The King agreed and sent a force under the Earl of Derby, with the Earls of Pembroke and Oxford and Sir Walter de Manny.

The Earl of Derby took a number of towns in Gascony, including Bergerac, Auberoche, Aiguillon, and La Réole, where Sir Walter found his father's tomb; he also took Castelmoron, and Villefranche in Périgord, and the city of Angoulême. During the winter, the English troops were split up to garrison the various towns that had been captured.

115

Jacques van Artevelde of Ghent was at this time still ruling the country of Flanders, and enjoying great power and prosperity. He was on such close terms with King Edward that he actually undertook to make him his heir over Flanders, and settle it on the Prince of Wales, making it a duchy.

In view of these promises, King Edward went to Sluys about Saint John's day,[2] with a large number of barons and knights from England, taking with him the young Prince of Wales. The King remained with his fleet in the harbour of Sluys, where he held his court. Several discussions took place between the King

---

[1] *April 23rd.*   [2] *June 24th, 1345*

and his Flemish friends on the one hand and councillors from the principal towns on the other. The latter were not in agreement either with the King or with van Artevelde, who was in favour of disinheriting Count Louis and his young son, the rightful heir, in favour of the Prince of Wales. This the Flemish were on no account willing to do. At the final conference, which was held at Sluys on board the King's ship, the *Catherine* (the size of which was marvellous to behold) they stated their unanimous decision: 'Dear sir, the request that you have made is a very oppressive one, and could in the future be a severe burden to Flanders and to our successors. It is perfectly true that we know of no lord in the world whose success and advancement we would rather see than yours. But this we cannot achieve by ourselves, without the agreement of the whole people of Flanders. We will each of us return to our own towns, and lay this question before the inhabitants; and we will abide by the decision of the majority. We will return within a month with an answer that we hope will satisfy you.' Neither the King nor van Artevelde could get a more definite answer, nor a shorter time appointed. The King therefore agreed, the conference ended, and the councillors returned to their own towns.

Jacques van Artevelde stayed a little longer with the King, who had further confidences to exchange with him. And Jacques, in his turn, undertook to win his countrymen over to his point of view, though in this he was to fail. For he made a mistake in staying behind, and not going to Ghent with the councillors.

When these latter reached Ghent, they called a general meeting in the market-place, and publicly explained the subject of the conference at Sluys, and the aims that King Edward was hoping to achieve with the help and advice of van Artevelde. The whole assembly then began to murmur against him, and received the request unfavourably, saying that please God they would never be found so disloyal as to seek to disinherit their natural lord in favour of a foreigner. They left the market-place in great discontent, and with feelings of deep hatred for van Artevelde—whereas if he had gone to Ghent first, instead of to

Brussels and Ypres, to state the case for the King of England, the inhabitants would all have fallen in with his opinion, as they did in the two other towns. But he had such confidence in his position and power that he thought he could get back to Ghent in time. After making his tour he reached Ghent about midday, to find the inhabitants assembled in the street leading to his house. As soon as he appeared, they began to murmur, putting their heads together and saying: 'Here is the man who is too powerful and who wants to rule Flanders as he pleases; it is too much to bear.' As well as all this, a rumour had been spread in the town about the great treasure of Flanders, which had been amassed by Jacques in the nine years and more during which he had effectively ruled the country: he had kept no account of the revenues, but had deposited them secretly and had also received all fines and forfeits himself, passing on nothing to the count, but sending some of it secretly to England, and thereby giving the people of Ghent a severe grievance.

As he rode down the street, he noticed a new and hostile atmosphere: those who in the past had bowed and raised their hats to him now turned their backs and went into their houses. His suspicions were aroused, and as soon as he got inside his house, he had the doors and windows shut and barred. His servants had hardly done this when the whole street in which he lived was filled with people of all kinds, and especially with workmen of the meanest sort. The house was surrounded, and attacked on every side, and broken into by force. Those inside did all they could to defend it, wounding many of the attackers. But in the end they could not hold out, so violent was the attack—nearly three-quarters of the population of the town took part in it. When Jacques van Artevelde saw the vigour of the attack, he came to a window looking onto the street and began to speak humbly and eloquently, with his head bared: 'My good people, what is the matter? Why are you so furious? How have I displeased you? Tell me, and I will put it right.' Those who heard him answered with one voice: 'We want an account of the treasure that you have unlawfully collected.' Van Artevelde tried to soothe them by replying: 'Gentlemen, I have not touched a penny of it. I beg of you, go back to your homes, and come back tomorrow morning. I will then give you a full and sufficient account.' But they answered with one voice: 'No, no, we want it now. You will not escape us like this. We know that you have emptied the treasury, and sent money to England without telling us. Therefore you must die.'

When van Artevelde heard this, he clasped his hands together, and weeping bitterly, said to them: 'Gentlemen, I am what you have made me. Before, you swore that you would protect and support me against all comers; now, you want to kill me for no reason at all. And if you want to, you can: for I am only one man against you all. But in God's name, think better of it. Remember all the advantages and benefits I have given you in the past. Small thanks you are giving me for them! You know that when trade was dead in this country, I revived it. And afterwards I governed you so peaceably that under me you had everything you wanted, corn, wool, riches, and all the different kinds of merchandise that have made you so wealthy.' At this, they began to shout out, all at once: 'Come down, do not preach to us from up there; we want an account immediately of the great treasure of Flanders; you have governed too long without giving us any accounts. It is not right for anyone in office to receive the rents of a lord, or a country, without giving account.'

When Jacques van Artevelde saw that he had failed to pacify them, he shut the window, and decided to leave by a back way, through a church adjoining his house. But his house was battered and broken into at the back, and there were four hundred people in it clamouring for him. In the end they caught him and killed him without mercy, the death stroke being given by a saddler, Thomas Denis by name. Thus did Jacques van Artevelde end his days, who before had been such a great ruler in Flanders. Poor men first gave him his position, and wicked men killed him in the end. The news of his death soon spread, and when they heard it some were sorry and some were glad. Count Louis of Flanders was at Dendremonde at the time, and was very glad to hear of the death of Jacques van Artevelde, who had been such a thorn in his flesh. Nevertheless he did not yet have sufficient confidence in the Flemish to return to Ghent.

All this time King Edward had been waiting at Sluys for the return of the Flemish deputies; and when he heard of the death of his great friend and ally Jacques van Artevelde at the hands of the men of Ghent, he was greatly enraged. He left Sluys and put out to sea, vowing vengeance on the Flemish for the death of his friend. The Flemish deputies, fully aware of his fury, went with representatives from Bruges, Ypres, Oudenarde, and Courtrai and called on the King at Westminster to point out that they were guiltless; they also hinted at a possible marriage between the King's daughter and the son and heir of the Count of Flanders. So, little by little, the King was pacified, and the death of Jacques van Artevelde forgotten.

SUMMARY

116-122

Count William of Hainault was killed on a campaign in Friesland, and his nephew Sir John was persuaded by the King of France to change sides, on the grounds that the English were going to stop his pension.

In the autumn, the Duke of Normandy collected a large army at Toulouse against the Earl of Derby. After Christmas they captured Miremont and Villefranche, and besieged Angoulême, where the English commander, John of Norwich, was granted a truce. He and his troops escaped to Aiguillon, and Angoulême surrendered. The Duke of Normandy vigorously laid siege to Aiguillon, which was defended with equal tenacity by Sir Walter de Manny.

King Edward set out from Southampton with a large army, including many of the chief earls and barons of England, and landed at Saint Vaast la Hougue, in Cotentin. The army advanced through Normandy in three battalions, burning and pillaging as it went. King Philip meanwhile mustered his allies from Lorraine, Bohemia, Luxemburg, Flanders, and the Empire. King Edward captured Barfleur, Cherbourg, Carentan and Saint Lô, and encamped at Ouistreham, at the mouth of the river Orne, ten miles from Caen.

123

The English rose very early in the morning, and prepared to set out for Caen.[1] The King heard mass before sunrise and then mounted his horse; with him were the Prince of Wales and Sir Godfrey of Harcourt, who was marshal and governor of the army and on whose advice the King had undertaken the expedition. The army advanced in battle order, with the marshal's banner at their head, towards the fine city of Caen.

When the inhabitants saw the English battalions approaching in serried ranks, with all their banners and pennons flying in the breeze, and heard the archers roaring—for they had never seen or heard archers before—they were so terrified that nothing in this world could have prevented them from fleeing. They ran from the town in disorder, heedless of the Constable of France, and falling over each other in their haste. The Constable of France and the Count of Tankerville safely reached a gate at the entrance to the bridge, for they realized that there was no chance of recovery, with the English already in the town and setting about them mercilessly. Some knights and squires who knew the way made for the castle, where they were taken in by Sir Robert of Wargny, the governor. The castle was large and well provisioned, so that those who could enter it were safe. The English men-at-arms and archers pursued the fugitives, slaying and giving no mercy.

The Constable of France and the Count of Tankerville, who had taken refuge behind the gate at the entrance to the bridge, were appalled by the slaughter, and were extremely anxious not to fall into the hands of the archers, who would not know who they were. But they saw an English knight with one eye, called Sir

[1] *At this time, according to Michael of Northburgh, Caen was 'greater than any city in England except London.'*

Thomas Holland, with five or six other knights whom they had met before in campaigns in Granada and Prussia, and they called out to him to take them prisoner. Sir Thomas was delighted, both by the thought of saving their lives and by the thought of the ransom they would fetch, which would be worth a hundred thousand sheep. Sir Thomas dismounted and advanced towards the gate with sixteen others; they climbed to the top, and found the two lords, with twenty-five other knights, who all surrendered to Sir Thomas. Leaving them under a sufficient guard, Sir Thomas returned to the fray, and prevented many acts of horrible cruelty. The lives of many citizens were also saved by other English knights and squires, and many nuns were saved from violation.

It was to the advantage of the English that the tide in the river (which is capable of carrying large ships) was so low that they could ford it without all having to crowd onto the bridge. Thus did King Edward capture Caen, though not without suffering losses on his own side: some of the inhabitants had climbed up to the garrets and the attics of the houses above the narrow streets, and thrown down stones and benches and mortar, killing and wounding more than five hundred of the English. King Edward was very angry when he heard of these casualties, and gave orders that next day the town should be burned, and the inhabitants put to the sword. But Sir Godfrey of Harcourt said to him: 'Sir, please moderate your anger, and be satisfied with that you have already done. You still have a long journey to make before you reach Calais. There are a large number of inhabitants in this town who will defend themselves stoutly, if need be. It will cost you many lives to destroy this town, and might put an end to your expedition. Nor would it be creditable to you to have to return with your object not accomplished. Spare these people, and you will reap the advantage within a month. For, inevitably, King Philip will come and give you battle. You might meet with plenty of difficulties, assaults, and skirmishes, in which you will need all the men you have and more. We are already masters of this town, without further slaughter, and the inhabitants will willingly put all their goods at our disposal.'

The King knew that Sir Godfrey spoke the truth, and replied: 'Sir Godfrey, you are our marshal. Order the army as you please, for in this case we do not wish to overrule you.' Sir Godfrey then rode through the town, his banner before him, giving orders in the King's name that no one should dare kill or harm any man or woman, or set fire to any property. On hearing this, several of the townsmen invited the English into their houses, and others opened their coffers to them, giving up all they had, in return for their lives being spared. But in spite of the King's orders, many atrocious murders, thefts and acts of arson were committed, for in the kind of army that King Edward led there are always villains, rogues, and men of easy conscience. The English were masters of Caen for three days, and they amassed great wealth, which they sent down the river in barges to Ouistreham—cloth, jewels, gold and silver plate and many other treasures. They decided to send back their ships with the prisoners and spoils of war to England, and the Earl of Huntingdon was put in charge of them with two hundred men-at-arms and four hundred archers. King Edward ransomed the Count of Guines, who was Constable of France, and the Count of Tankerville from Sir Thomas Holland and his companions, for the sum of twenty thousand nobles.

124

Having sent the treasure that he had taken home to England King Edward took the road for Evreux,[1] but to no advantage, as it was well fortified. He went on to Louviers, a town prosperous in the wool trade, and undefended: the English took it without difficulty. After taking a great deal of plunder, the English marched through the county of Evreux, burning everything except the fortified towns and castles, which King Edward left alone, in order to save his men and artillery. He then made for the Seine,

[1] *About thirty miles south of Rouen, and fifty miles west of Paris.*

not marching directly to Rouen, but burning the towns of Gisors, Vernon, Mantes, and Meulan on the way, and ravaging the countryside. He advanced to Poissy,[1] where he found the bridge broken down, with the beams and posts lying scattered in the river. The King waited for five days, until the bridge was repaired and his army could cross over. His marshals advanced very close to Paris, burning Saint-Germain-en-Laye, Saint Cloud and Bourg-la-Reine.

The people of Paris were terrified, for the city was not at that time fortified. At last, King Philip acted. He first had all the out-buildings in the town pulled down, to facilitate movements of troops. He then went to Saint Denis, where he found the King of Bohemia, Sir John of Hainault, the Duke of Lorraine, the Count of Flanders, the Count of Blois and many other knights and barons. When the people of Paris saw the King leaving, they were even more frightened than before, and a deputation came to him, fell to their knees and said: 'Dear sir, noble King, what are you doing? Leaving your fine city of Paris? The enemy are not five miles off. As soon as they know you have left, they will be here. We cannot resist them, nor can we find anyone to defend us. Please stay and help us protect your fine city.' King Philip replied: 'My good people, have no fear. The English will come no nearer. I am going to Saint Denis to my army, for I want to ride out against the English, come what may.' Thus King Philip succeeded in calming the people of Paris, who had been in great fear of sharing the fate of the men of Caen.

King Edward stayed at the convent at Poissy over the feast of the Assumption.[2] On the day of the feast he sat at table in his scarlet sleeveless robes, trimmed with ermine. He afterwards took the field, and Sir Godfrey of Harcourt, one of his marshals, was on one flank with five hundred men-at-arms and twelve hundred archers. Quite by chance, Sir Godfrey met with a large force of the citizens of Amiens, some on foot and some on horseback, who were answering King Philip's call to arms. He im-

[1] *Less than twenty miles from Paris.*   [2] *August 15th.*

mediately attacked them with those under his command, and they put up a stubborn resistance, for they were very numerous, well-armed and in battle order, under the command of five knights of the district of Amiens. The battle was long and drawn out, and many were killed at the first onslaught. But in the end the English won the day, and the men of Amiens were nearly all killed or captured. The English took all their equipment and baggage, and much of it was very valuable, for they had been going to join the King excellently equipped, and had left their city not long before. At least twelve hundred were left dead on the field. Sir Godfrey rejoined the main army in the evening and the King was very pleased at his victory.

The King burned and destroyed all the flat country round Beauvais, as he had done in Normandy, and stayed one night in the rich monastery at Saint Lucien, not far from the town of Beauvais. Next day, after leaving, he looked back and saw the monastery in flames. Enraged by this, he halted the army and gave orders for twenty of those who had set fire to it to be hanged on the spot. For he had given strict orders that, on pain of death, no churches or religious houses should be violated or burned.

He passed by the town of Beauvais without attacking it, still anxious to preserve his men and artillery. He took up his quarters in the small town of Milly, and the two marshals rode right up to the outskirts of the town. They were unable to resist making an attack and skirmishing with the guards at the barriers. They divided into three companies, to attack the three gates, and the assault lasted till the afternoon, without much success, since the city was strong and well fortified, and provided with everything; the exertions of the bishop were worth even more than those of the rest of the defenders. When the English saw that they could gain nothing they retreated to the King's camp, after setting fire to the suburbs, which they burned right up to the city gates. Next day the King and his army marched on, burning and laying waste the countryside and spent the night in a large village called Grandvillier.

The day after that, the King moved to Argis. His scouts found the castle unguarded, and captured it without difficulty and burned it. They then moved on, always destroying everything they found, till they came to Poix, a fine town with two castles. They found no lords defending the place, only the two beautiful daughters of the Lord of Poix; they would soon have been violated had not two English knights, Sir John Chandos and Lord Bassett, defended them and brought them safely to the King, who looked after them chivalrously and enquired where they wished to go. They were then safely escorted to Corbie, in accordance with their wishes. The King spent the night at Poix.

That night the inhabitants of Poix as well as those of the castles had a conference with the marshals of the army, to save the town from being burned. They agreed on a sum of florins to be paid as ransom on the following day, as soon as the King should leave. The marshals left a few men behind to receive the ransom, and the army moved on. When the people of Poix saw how few had been left, and that the King and his army had gone, they refused to pay, and ran out to attack the English, who defended themselves stoutly and quickly sent to the army for help. Sir Reginald Cobham and Sir Thomas Holland, who commanded the army's rearguard, quickly turned back when they discovered what had happened, crying 'Treachery! Treachery!' They went back to Poix, and found their companions still fighting the people of the town. Almost all the inhabitants of Poix were killed, the town burned, and the two castles demolished. The English then rejoined the King's army at Airaines, where he had halted the troops and ordered them on pain of death to do no damage to the town, either by burning or in any other way; for he wished to spend a day or two there, to find out where he could most easily cross the river Somme, which, as you shall hear, it was necessary for him to do.

SUMMARY

125-126

King Edward found great difficulty in crossing the Somme, for all the bridges were heavily defended. King Philip advanced beyond Amiens with an army of a hundred thousand, hoping to cut off King Edward between Abbéville and the Somme. King Edward was shown a ford at Blanchetaque, in the tidal waters of the Somme, where he succeeded in overcoming an army under Sir Godemar du Fay, who strenuously opposed the English crossing. After capturing some ships at Le Crotoy, King Edward assembled his entire army near Crécy, about ten miles inland. His army was outnumbered eight to one by the French. That night at Abbéville, King Philip entertained all the princes and chief lords on his side at supper, and begged them 'always to remain friends, to be allies without jealousy, and chivalrous without pride.'

127

That Friday, as you have heard, King Edward encamped in the plain. The surrounding country was rich in provisions, and he had abundant supplies in reserve. The King gave supper to the barons and earls, and they made good cheer before retiring.

That night, so I have heard, when he was left alone with his lords of the bedchamber, the King went to his oratory and prayed devoutly that God would help him next day, and that if he fought his enemies, he would come off with honour. He went to bed about midnight and after rising early heard mass with the Prince of Wales. The majority of his army did the same, making their confession and receiving communion. After mass, the King gave orders that his men should all arm themselves, leave their camp, and take up a favourable position, which he had chosen the day before. At the rear he enclosed a large park with only one entrance, near a wood, in which he placed all his baggage train and wagons, together with the horses: all the men-at-arms and archers remained on foot.

The King gave orders, through his constable and two marshals, to divide the army into three battalions. In the first he placed his young son, the Prince of Wales, with the Earls of Warwick and Oxford, Sir Godfrey of Harcourt, Sir Reginald Cobham, Sir Thomas Holland, Sir Richard Stafford, Lord Mohun, Lord Delaware, Sir John Chandos, Sir Bartholomew Burghersh, Sir Robert Neville, Sir Thomas Clifford, Lord Bourchier, Lord Latimer, and other knights and squires whom I cannot name. There were about eight hundred men-at-arms in the Prince's battalion, with two thousand archers and a thousand others. They took up their position in regular order, each knight under his banner or pennon, surrounded by his men.

The second battalion included the Earls of Northampton and Arundel, Lord de Ros, Lord Lucy, Lord Willoughby, Lord Bassett, Lord Saint Aubyn, Sir Lewis Tufton, Lord Multon, Lord Lascelles, and many others; altogether there were about five hundred men-at-arms in this battalion, and twelve hundred archers. The third battalion was commanded by the King with a number of good knights and squires, in all about seven hundred men-at-arms and two thousand archers.

When these three battalions had been drawn up and given their orders, the King mounted a small white horse, and carrying a white stick, with his two marshals on either side, he rode at a walking pace through all the ranks, encouraging the earls, barons, and knights, and asking them to protect his honour and defend his right. He spoke in such a cheerful and gentle manner that all who had been dispirited took heart at once on seeing and hearing him. When he had completed the rounds of each battalion, it was ten o'clock. He rejoined his own battalion, and ordered the whole army to make a good meal, and drink a glass of wine afterwards. This they did; and after packing up their pots and barrels in the carts, they returned to their battalions, and sat down on the ground, their helmets and bows beside them, in order to be more fresh when the enemy arrived. For the intention of the King of England was to wait there for the King of France, and fight him with all his power.

128

That same Saturday, the King of France rose early and heard mass in the monastery of Saint Peter's at Abbéville, where he was lodging. With him were the King of Bohemia, the Count of Alençon, the Count of Blois, the Count of Flanders, the Duke of Lorraine and all the chief nobles. There was not enough room for the whole army at Abbéville, and many of them were lodged at Saint Riquier. The King set out with his army at sunrise, and when he had advanced five miles was advised to form his army in battle order, and to let those on foot go ahead, so as not to be trampled underfoot by the horses. The King sent four valiant knights ahead, Lord Moyne of Bastelburg,[1] the Lord of Noyers, the Lord of Beaujeu and the Lord of Anceris; they rode so far ahead that they could easily make out the English position; and the English were aware that they had come to reconnoitre, but paid no attention and let them return without attacking.

When King Philip saw them coming back, and pushing through the crowd to reach him, he asked: 'Sirs, what news?' They all looked at each other, none liking to speak first. In the end the King asked Lord Moyne, who was attached to King Charles of Bohemia, and who was acknowledged as one of the most valiant and chivalrous knights in Christendom, having performed many noble deeds.

'Sir,' said Lord Moyne, 'Since it is your wish, I will speak, but I do so under correction of my companions. We advanced far enough to reconnoitre your enemies. They are drawn up in three battalions, and are evidently awaiting you. If there is no better suggestion, my advice is that you should halt your army here for the rest of the day. For by the time your rearguard arrives and the army is properly drawn up, it will be late. Your

[1] *In Bohemia.*

troops will be tired, and in disarray, but you will find the enemy fresh and alert, and fully aware of what they must do. In the morning you can draw up your line of battle better, and reconnoitre more easily, and discover where you can most advantageously attack; for you may be sure that they will wait for you.'

The King gave orders that this should be done, and his two marshals rode up and down giving the command 'Halt banners, the King's command, in the name of God and Saint Denis.' Those that were in front halted; those at the rear did not, but still pressed forward, saying that they would not halt until they were as far forward as the front, and those in front of them were pushed forward in their turn. This disorder was entirely caused by pride, every man wishing to surpass his neighbour, in spite of the marshal's words. Neither the King nor the marshals could stop them, since every lord was eager to show off his own power. So they advanced, in complete disorder, till they came in sight of the enemy. It would have been far better had the front rank stood firm: but on seeing the enemy they immediately retired, in complete disarray, which alarmed the rear, who thought they must have been fighting, and been turned back. There was then room for them to advance, had they so wished, and some did advance, while others held back. All the roads between Abbéville and Crécy were blocked with common people who, when they got within eight miles of the enemy, drew their swords and cried out 'Kill, Kill.' Nobody who was not present or has not had leisure to examine the whole affair can possibly imagine the confusion of that day, and in particular the chaotic state of the French. I owe my own knowledge of it mostly to the English, who were well able to observe the confusion, and to the men of Sir John of Hainault, who were always near the King's person.

129

The English, who had been drawn up in three battalions, sitting quietly on the ground, calmly rose to their feet, when they saw the French approaching, and formed their ranks. The Prince's battalion was in front, with its archers drawn up in a triangular formation, with the men-at-arms behind. The Earls of Northampton and Arundel, who commanded the second battalion, were drawn up in good order on the Prince's flank, to support him if necessary.

You must realize that on the French side, the kings, dukes, counts and barons did not advance in any regular order, but one after another, as they pleased. As soon as King Philip came in sight of the English, his blood began to boil, such was his hatred. He cried out to his marshals: 'Order the Genoese forward and let the battle begin, in the name of God and Saint Denis.' There were about fifteen thousand[1] Genoese crossbowmen; but they were quite unready for battle, being very tired and having marched over fifteen miles in full armour, carrying their crossbows. They told the constable that they were in no condition to fight, and the Count of Alençon, when he heard of it, said, 'This is what one gets for employing such rabble; they fail us in the hour of need!' Meanwhile a violent storm broke from the heavens, with tremendous thunder and lightning. Before the rain came, an immense flight of crows had passed over both armies, indicating the severity of the coming storm. Several wiseacres explained that this was the sign of a great battle and of fearful bloodshed. The storm soon passed, and the sun came out, bright and clear, shining straight in the eyes of the French, whereas the English had it behind them.

When the Genoese were in some kind of order, and were ready to attack the English, they began to shout extremely loud in order to dismay the English, who, however, held their ground and paid no attention. They cried out a second time, loud and clear, and went forward a little, but the English did not move. A third time they shouted, extremely loud, and advanced, aimed their crossbows and began to shoot. The English archers then took a pace forward, and let fly their arrows in such unison that they

---

[1] *G. Villani, a far more reliable authority, puts the number at six thousand, in his* Historia Universalis, 1348.

were as thick as snow. The Genoese had never experienced such archery, and when they felt the arrows pierce their arms, heads, and coats of mail, they were much taken aback; some cut the cords of their crossbows, others flung them to the ground, and all turned tail and fled. The French had a large body of men-at-arms on horseback to supervise the Genoese. And when the latter tried to run away, they were prevented. For the King of France, seeing them turn back in disorder, cried out in a fury: 'Kill all this rabble, kill them! They are getting in our way and they serve no purpose.' Then you might have seen the men-at-arms laying about them, killing all they could of the runaways. The English kept up their hail of arrows as strongly as ever, shooting into the thick of the enemy; the arrows fell among the men-at-arms and their horses, bringing many of them down, horses and men together: once down, they were quite incapable of rising to their feet.

The valiant and noble King Charles of Bohemia was the son of the noble Emperor, Henry of Luxemburg; although the latter was nearly blind, he had the order of battle explained to him; and he enquired from his knights the whereabout of his son, the Lord Charles. They replied: 'Sir, we do not know; he is fighting in another part of the field.' Then this valiant prince said: 'Gentlemen, you are my men and my friends and my companions. I beg of you to lead me into the fight this day, that I may strike a blow with my sword.' The knights nearest him did as he asked, though Lord Moyne and a number of good knights of Luxemburg wanted to leave him behind; but in order not to lose him, several knights tied their reins together, and advanced with their King at their head, to achieve his object. The truth is that in spite of the great number of lords and knights in the King of France's army, very few notable feats were achieved by them, for the battle began late in the day and the French arrived already weary. All the same they pressed on, preferring death to the dishonour of flight. Charles of Bohemia, who already called and signed himself King of Germany, and bore those arms, reached the field of battle in good order. But when he saw that the French were doing badly, he went away, by what road I do not know. Whereas the King his father advanced far into the fray, and struck four strokes or more with his sword, and fought as valiantly as his companions. So far forward did they advance that all were killed; their bodies were found next day, round the King their lord, with the reins of their horses knotted together.

King Philip was furious that his army was being cut down by a handful of Englishmen, and in spite of being advised by Sir John of Hainault to retreat, he advanced without a word to join his brother, the Count of Alençon, whose banner he could see on a little hill. There the Count of Alençon was advancing in good order against the English, and after riding past the archers, he succeeded in engaging the Prince of Wales's battalion, and fighting long and valiantly, as did the Count of Flanders in another part. The King of France was most anxious to join them, but there was a great hedge of archers and men-at-arms in front of him that remained unbroken. That morning, King Philip had given Sir John of Hainault a fine black charger, and he in turn had mounted Sir John de Fusselles on it, to carry his banner. This horse took the bit between its teeth and brought its rider, still carrying the banner of Hainault, right through the English army. And when he was at last able to turn, the horse stumbled and fell in a ditch, being hit by an arrow; there Sir John de Fusselles would have died had not his page followed him, making a detour round the battalions. The page found him in the ditch, unable to rise because of the horse but otherwise in no danger, for the English would not break their ranks to take prisoners. The page helped him up and they returned by a different way.

This battle, fought between Crécy and La Broye, was a very cruel and murderous affair, and many feats of arms went unrecorded. It was already late when the battle began, which hindered the French more than anything else, for towards nightfall many knights and squires lost their commanders, and they wandered about in small parties attacking the English, but before long they were all wiped out. For the English had decided that morning to take no prisoners and hold no one to ransom, so great were the numbers against them.

The Count of Blois, nephew of King Philip and of the Count of Alençon, came with his men under his banner to fight the English, and acquitted himself nobly, as did the Duke of Lorraine. Many people say that if the battle had begun in the morning, there would have been many notable feats of arms achieved on the French side. For a number of French knights and squires, as well as others from Germany and Savoy, broke the lines of archers in front of the Prince's battalion, and engaged, hand to hand, with the men-at-arms; upon which the second battalion, under the Earls of Northampton and Arundel, came to their aid, and none too soon, or they would have been hard pressed.

The first battalion, seeing the danger they were in, sent Sir Thomas Norwich to the King, who had taken up a position on a little hill, by a windmill. 'Sir,' said Sir Thomas, 'Lord Warwick and Lord Oxford and Sir Reginald Cobham, who are with your son, are hard pressed by the French; they beg you to come to their help with your battalion, for they think that if the numbers of the French increase, the Prince will be overwhelmed.'

'Sir Thomas,' replied the King, 'is my son dead, or fallen, or so badly wounded that he cannot help himself?'

'No, sir, thank God, but he is so hard pressed that he needs your help.'

'Well, Sir Thomas, go back to him and to those that sent you, and tell them not to ask for any help from me while my son is still alive. Say that I want them to let the boy win his spurs, for I am determined, please God, that the day shall be his, and that the honour and glory of it shall be won by him and by those to whom I have entrusted him.'

Sir Thomas returned to his lords, and told them what the King had said. This answer gave them great encouragement, and they regretted having asked for help. They were inspired to even greater feats of valour than before, and held the position, to their great credit.

There were no doubt many great feats of arms of which I have no knowledge. But one thing is certain: Sir Godfrey of Harcourt, who was in the Prince's battalion, made every effort to save the life of his brother, having heard that his brother's banner had been seen engaged fighting for the French, against Sir Godfrey's side. But Sir Godfrey could not reach him in time: his brother was killed on the field, and so was the Count of Aumale, his nephew. Elsewhere, the Count of Alençon and the Count of Flanders fought fiercely under their banners, with their people round them, but they could not resist the might of the English. There they were slain, and with them many other knights and squires who attended and accompanied them. Louis Count of Blois and the Duke of Lorraine, his brother-in-law, with their banners and troops, made a gallant stand in another part of the field; but they were surrounded by a troop of the English and Welsh, who showed them no mercy, and all their valour was in vain. The Count of Saint Pol and the Count of Auxerre were also killed, both gallant knights, and many others besides.

At the close of day, towards vespers, King Philip left the field utterly defeated, with only fifty barons round him in all; Sir John of Hainault was the chief among them, and nearest the King, with the Lords of Montmorency, Beaujeu, Aubigny, and Montfort. The King rode off, lamenting and bewailing, to the castle of La Broye. When they reached the gate, they found it locked, and the drawbridge up, for night had fallen—a dark, thick night. The King ordered the governor to be summoned, for he wished to enter. The governor was called, and appeared on the battlements, and asked who it was that called out at this time of night. King Philip heard his voice and called out; 'Open, open, governor; it is the unhappy King of France.' The governor recognized the King's voice, and already knew he had lost the day, from some fugitives who had passed below the castle. He lowered the bridge and opened the gate. The king entered, with his five companions, and they stayed till midnight. But the King would not shut himself up there or stay there; they drank a glass of wine, and then rode off, taking with them guides who knew the country. They left at midnight, and rode so hard that they reached Amiens at dawn. There the King stopped at a monastery, saying he would go no further till he found out which of his people lay dead on the field and who had escaped.

Now let us return to Crécy, and the position of the English. All that Saturday they never broke their ranks to pursue anybody, but held their position and repulsed the attacks that were made against them. This was the only reason why the King of France was not taken, for he stayed on the field till very late, as you have heard, with not more than sixty men around him, quite near the enemy. Then Sir John of Hainault had taken hold of the King's reins, having already remounted him once, when his horse was killed under him, and said: 'Sir, come away, it is high time. Do not expose yourself. Today you have lost, but another day you will win.' And he led the King forcibly from the field.

That day, the English archers brought a tremendous advantage to their side. Many people say that it was by their shooting that the day was won, although the knights achieved many noble deeds, fighting hand to hand, and rallying valiantly. But the archers certainly succeeded in one great achievement, for it was entirely by their fire at the beginning that the Genoese, and they were fifteen thousand in number, were turned back. And a great number of French men-at-arms, well armed and mounted and richly apparelled, were overthrown by the Genoese, who while running away, became entangled with them and brought them down so that they could not rise again. And on the English side there were a number of Cornishmen and Welshmen on foot, armed with large knives, who advanced between the archers and the men-at-arms (who made way for them) and came upon the French when they were in this plight; and they fell upon the earls, barons, knights, and squires and killed them mercilessly, great lords though they were. The King of England was afterwards much annoyed that these nobles had not been held to ransom.

130

By nightfall on Saturday, when there were no longer any shouts and battlecries to be heard, the English held the field, and their enemies were routed. They made great fires, and lit torches, for the night was very dark. King Edward, who had not put on his helmet all day, came down from his post with all his battalion towards his son, the Prince, and put his arms round his neck and kissed him. 'My fine son,' he said, 'God grant you perseverance! Indeed you are my son, and right loyally you have acquitted yourself. You are worthy of ruling a realm.' At these words the Prince bowed low and humbly, out of proper respect for his father.

The English were overjoyed at their victory: they gave praise and thanks to the Lord many times during that night for the successful outcome of the day. The night passed without rioting, for the King had forbidden it. On the Sunday morning there was such a thick fog that one could scarcely see half an acre of ground. The King gave orders that a detachment of five hundred men-at-arms and two thousand archers should go and see if any companies of French troops had rallied together.

That morning, the French forces from Rouen and Beauvais had left Abbéville and Saint Ricquier, knowing nothing of the defeat of the previous day. They fell in with this English detachment, thinking it was part of their own side. When the English realized this, they fell upon them, and a fierce battle followed. The French were soon put to flight, in great disorder. In this rout more than seven thousand were killed in the fields and among the hedges and bushes. Had the weather been clear, not one would have escaped.

Further on, the same English force came upon the Archbishop of Rouen, and the Grand Prior of France, who did not know of the battle either. They had understood that the King would not fight till Sunday, and made the same mistake of taking the English for their allies. A fresh battle began, for the two prelates were well supported with men-at-arms, but they could not withstand the English. They were defeated, and though a few escaped, nearly all were killed, with their two commanders. Not a prisoner was taken. In the course of the morning the English came across a number of Frenchmen who had lost their way on the Saturday, and spent that night in the fields with no news of their King or commanders. The English put to the sword all they met, and I am told that of the foot soldiers from the cities and towns, four times as many were killed on Sunday morning as in the great battle on Saturday.

131

This detachment returned to the King as he was coming out of mass, and told him all that they had seen and done. Once the King was sure that no army was being rallied against him, he gave orders for the dead to be examined. Two valiant knights were sent off, Sir Reginald Cobham and Sir Richard Stafford, together with three heralds to identify the coats of arms of the fallen and two clerks to write down the names. They took great pains, and spent all day in the field, so great was the number of the dead. They came back as the King was going in to supper, and made their report: they had found the bodies of eleven princes, twelve hundred knights and about thirty thousand common men.[1] Eighty banners had been left on the field.

The King and Prince and all the knights praised God for the great victory he had sent them, a mere handful of men in comparison with their enemies. The King lamented in particular the death of the noble King of Bohemia, and of his noble companions. The army remained there that night, and on Monday morning the order was given to leave.

---

[1] *Another of the Froissart texts gives the losses of men below the rank of knight as fifteen or sixteen thousand. Both figures are wildly exaggerated. Michael of Northburgh says that one thousand five hundred and forty-two were killed in the battle, and two thousand next day.*

The King ordered that the bodies of all the great lords should be taken and buried on consecrated ground at the monastery of Montenay, nearby. He proclaimed a truce for three days, to bury the dead. Then he rode to Montreuil, while his marshals rode to Hesdin, and burned Vaubain and Serain, though they could do nothing with the castle, which was too strong for them. They spent Monday night by the river at Hesdin, and the next day they crossed and rode towards Boulogne, burning the towns of Saint Josse and Neufchâtel, and Etaples as well. The army passed between the forests of Hardelon and the country round Boulogne, and came to the large town of Wissant, where the King, the Prince, and all the army lodged; and after a day's rest they came before the strong town of Calais.

SUMMARY

132-144

King Edward built quarters for his army outside Calais and decided to starve out the town without attacking it. The Governor of Calais expelled all the poor people from the town to make the provisions last longer. King Edward let them pass, giving them a free dinner, and twopence each, as alms.

The Duke of Normandy, who was still besieging Aiguillon, was summoned by King Philip to defend France. As the besiegers left, they were attacked from inside the town, and Sir Walter de Manny learned, from a prisoner who was taken, of King Edward's victory. Sir Walter was given a safe conduct to Calais as ransom for a Norman knight whom he captured. On the way he was imprisoned at Orléans, but was released, and dined with King Philip on his way to Calais.

The Earl of Derby captured Poitiers, as well as other towns and castles in Poitou.

Meanwhile, in 1346, encouraged by King Philip, King David of Scotland invaded England, but was defeated at Nevill's Cross,[1] near

---

[1] *Froissart says that Queen Philippa led the English army. This is most unlikely, and not mentioned in earlier English sources.*

Newcastle (October 17th). King David was captured by Sir John Copeland.

Louis, Count of Flanders, was forced by the Flemish to become engaged to Isabel, daughter of King Edward. He succeeded in escaping, however, and fled to King Philip.

Robert, Lord of Namur,[1] did homage to King Edward at Calais. War broke out in Brittany, and La Roche Derrien was captured by the English, who took Charles of Blois prisoner. King Philip came to Sangates to try to raise the English siege on Calais, but failed.

145

When King Philip left Sandgate, the people of Calais saw that all hope of rescue was gone and this caused such deep distress that even the boldest could hardly endure it. So they entreated their governor, Sir John de Vienne, to go up onto the battlements and make signs to the besiegers that he wished to speak to them. When King Edward heard of this, he sent Sir Walter de Manny and Lord Bassett to the governor, who said to them: 'Dear sirs, you who are such valiant knights are aware that the King of France our sovereign has sent us here with orders to guard this town and the castle against all damage; this we have done to the best of our ability. But now all hope of relief has failed; we are in such straits that we have nothing left to eat. Unless your sovereign, the noble King, takes pity on us, we must either die or go mad with hunger. I therefore ask you to beg of him to let us go, just as we are. He may take the town, and the castle, and everything in them; he will find it enough.'

To this Sir Walter replied: 'John, we know something of the King's intentions, for he has stated them. You must know that he does not intend to let you go like this: it is his wish that you should surrender completely to his will, whether it is to allow anyone their ransom, or to put them to death. For the people of Calais have done him such great harm by their obstinate defence,

---

[1] *One of Froissart's principal patrons.*

and cost him so many lives, and so much money, that he is very angry with them.'

Sir John de Vienne replied: 'These conditions are too severe. We are only a small number of knights and squires here, and we have loyally served the King, our sovereign lord, as you would have done, and we have endured many hardships and evils, and we will endure more sufferings than knights have ever endured before, rather than let the meanest boy in the town suffer any worse than the greatest of us. I entreat you, out of compassion, to go to the King of England and beg him to take pity on us. We have such hopes of his nobility that he may change his mind.'

Sir Walter and Lord Bassett returned to the King and told him what had been said. The King said that he had no intention of granting their request, but insisted on their unconditional surrender. Sir Walter replied: 'Sir, you may well be wrong, for you are setting a bad precedent. If you should order us to occupy one of your castles in the future, we would go less readily, if you put these people to death; for we would suffer retaliation, in similar circumstances.' Many barons who were present supported these words. The King answered: 'My lords, I do not want to hold my opinion alone against all of you. Sir Walter, you will tell the governor that the greatest favour that he can expect from me is that six of the chief burghers of the city shall come out, their heads and feet bare, and with halters round their necks, and with the keys of the town and the castle in their hands. These will be at my mercy, and the rest of the town shall go free.'

'Sir,' said Sir Walter, 'I will tell them willingly.'

He told them that this was all that was to be gained from the King, and Sir John de Vienne replied: 'Sir Walter, I believe you. I would now ask you to wait here until I have put this affair before the people of the town, for as they asked me to undertake it, it is right that they should know the result.'

He went to the market-place and had the bells rung to summon the entire populace to the town hall. They all assembled, men and women; they were burning for news, for the famine in the town had become almost unendurable. When they were all assembled, Sir John reported to them what had been said, and told them that he could not obtain any more favourable terms. This information caused such bitter and desperate lamentations that the hardest heart in the world would have been moved to pity; Sir John wept bitterly.

Soon afterwards, the richest burgher in the town, Sir Eustace de Saint Pierre, got up and said: 'Gentlemen, it would be a great shame to allow so many people to starve to death, if there were any way of preventing it. And it would be highly pleasing to Our Lord if anyone could save them from such a fate. I have such faith and trust in gaining pardon and grace from Our Lord if I die in the attempt, that I will put myself forward as the first. I will willingly go out in my shirt, bareheaded and barefoot, with a halter round my neck and put myself at the mercy of the King of England.'

At these words the crowd almost worshipped him, and a number of men and women fell at his feet weeping bitterly. It was a most affecting sight to witness. Another very rich and much respected citizen, called Jean d'Aire, who had two beautiful daughters, rose up and said he would keep him company. The third to volunteer was Sir Jacques de Wissant, who was very rich both by inheritance and by his own transactions; he offered to accompany his two cousins, and so did Sir Pierre his brother. Two others completed the number, and set off dressed only in their shirts and breeches, and with halters round their necks, as they had been told.

They took with them the keys of the town and the castle and followed Sir John, who, being scarcely able to walk, rode on a little pony, and led them to the gates. There was the greatest sorrow and lamentation all over the town, and they were accompanied by the most pitiful cries all the way to the gates, which were opened and then shut behind them. Sir John took them to Sir Walter de Manny, who was waiting for them at the barrier, and said: 'Sir Walter, as Governor of Calais, and on behalf of the unhappy people of this town, I hand over to you these six citizens. I swear that they are the most highly respected and honourable, both by birth and position, in the town. They have with them the keys. I beg of you, kind sir, to intercede for them with the King of England, that these good men may not be put to death.'

The barrier was opened. The six men went out, in the condition I have stated, with Sir Walter de Manny, who took them straight to the King's pavilion. Sir John went back into the town.

The King was at that moment in his chamber, with a large number of nobles. When he heard that the citizens of Calais were coming in the condition that he had ordered, he came out in front of his quarters, accompanied by his retinue, who were eager to see what would happen. The Queen of England, who was in an advanced state of pregnancy, followed her lord.

When Sir Walter presented the men of Calais to him, the King glowered at them in silence for he hated the inhabitants of Calais bitterly, for all the harm and trouble they had caused him at sea.

The six burghers knelt before the King and, joining their hands together, threw themselves on his mercy. The King remained speechless with anger for a time, and when he spoke it was to give orders for them to be beheaded. All the knights and barons present begged the King as earnestly as they could to show them mercy. But he would not listen to them.

Then Sir Walter de Manny spoke up and said: 'Ah, sir, please restrain your anger. You have a reputation for great nobility of soul. Do not therefore destroy it by an action of this kind, and give people cause to defame you. If you do not take pity on these men, but put them to death, the whole world will regard it as great cruelty. Of their own free will, these men have put themselves at your mercy to save their fellow citizens.'

The King replied in anger: 'Sir Walter, they will be beheaded. The people of Calais have caused the death of so many of my men that they too must die.'

The Queen of England, whose pregnancy was far advanced, then fell on her knees, and with tears in her eyes implored him: 'Ah! my lord, since I have crossed the sea in great danger, I have never asked you any favour. But now I humbly beg you, for the Son of the Blessed Mary and for the love of me, to have mercy on these six men!'

The King looked at her for some minutes without speaking, and then said: 'Ah, lady, I wish you were anywhere else but here. You have entreated me in such a way that I cannot refuse. Therefore, though I do it with great reluctance, I hand them over to you. Do as you like with them.'

The Queen thanked him from the bottom of her heart, and had the halters removed from their necks. She took them to her rooms, had them clothed and gave them a good dinner. She then gave them six nobles each, and had them escorted safely out of the camp.[1]

146

And so the stronghold of Calais was captured by King Edward, about Saint John's day in the month of August 1347, after a siege of about a year. After presenting the six citizens to the Queen, King Edward summoned Sir Walter de Manny and the two marshals, the Earls of Warwick and Stafford, and said to them: 'My lords, take the keys of the city and castle of Calais. You will imprison all the knights that you find there, or make them surrender on oath. They are good men and I will reward them. But all the other mercenary soldiers will be disbanded, and so will all the other inhabitants of the town, men, women, and children. I am going to repopulate Calais with Englishmen.'

These orders were carried out. Only three of the citizens were

[1] *'Froissart alone of his contemporaries relates this remarkable fact; and the simplicity of his style may give even to fable the appearance of truth. . . . The action of these six men . . . was sufficiently great to have been trumpeted through all France by the thousand and thousand voices of Fame. This action, however, brilliant as it was, and which the wretches driven out of Calais would have spoken of everywhere, was unknown in the capital. Had it been otherwise, the* Chronicle of Saint Denis, *and other histories of the time, would not have been silent on the subject; and yet not one mentions it.'* Lavasque.

allowed to remain in Calais, a priest and two other old men, who were versed in the customs, laws, and institutions of the city, and could point out the various properties. All this was done, and the castle made ready for the King and Queen to take up residence, and the other houses made ready to receive the King's people. The King and Queen then rode at the head of a glorious procession of nobles into the city, to the music of trumpets, drums, horns, and other warlike instruments. The King rode up to the castle, where he found everything in readiness. He gave a large dinner, the first night, to all the court and the nobles; and he stayed in the castle till the Queen gave birth to a daughter, who was named Margaret.

The King gave fine houses in the town to the principal nobles, and on his return to England sent thirty-six citizens of substance to inhabit the town, so that it should be wholly English. The fortifications were pulled down, and the damage inflicted during the siege was eventually repaired. The knights of Calais who had been taken prisoner, were ransomed after six months: but it was a terrible misfortune for all the inhabitants of Calais, high and low, some of whom had been there for generations, to be driven out with their wives and children. They had to leave their fine houses, and their possessions, taking nothing with them; nor did they receive any compensation from the King of France, for whom they had lost their all. Most of them later settled at Saint Omer.

Cardinal Guy de Boulogne, who was with King Philip at Amiens, procured a truce for three years between the Kings of England and France. The truce was agreed to by everybody except the rivals for the duchy of Brittany, but these two ladies still carried on the war against each other. King Edward returned to England with the Queen and her child, leaving as governor of Calais a Lombard, Sir Amery de Pavie. As well as the thirty-six citizens, he also sent from England four hundred other men of lesser position to live at Calais. Their number increased daily, for the King increased the extent and number of their privileges so much that many people were eager to go.

Count Charles of Blois, who claimed the duchy of Brittany and had been captured at La Roche Derrien, was taken to England and sent to the Tower of London. He was not kept in close confinement, but shared the same conditions as the King of Scotland and the Earl of Moray. Soon afterwards, however, at the request of the Queen, his first cousin, Count Charles was released on parole, and could ride wherever he liked in London. But he could spend only one night at a time away from the Tower, except when he was in the company of the King or Queen. The Count of Eu and Guines was also a prisoner, but he was such a gallant and amiable knight that he was constantly entertained by the King and the Queen and their court.

SUMMARY

147-158

Froissart deals very briefly with the events of the years 1347-1355, though later texts than the one followed in this translation do refer in passing to the Black Death, the Flagellants, the persecution of the Jews, and the 'Battle of the Thirties' in Brittany.

The truce of 1347 was broken by various brigands, who plundered towns and castles for their own ends, especially in Languedoc and Brittany. In 1349 King Edward discovered that the Governor of Calais, Sir Amery de Pavie, had secretly undertaken to sell the town back to the French. King Edward, under the banner of Sir Walter de Manny, defeated the French contingent who came to Calais in the hope of taking it over. The King fought with Sir Eustace de Ribeaumont in single combat and defeated him, but in recognition of his valour, gave him a chaplet of pearls.

In the same year King Philip married his second wife, Blanche, daughter of King Philip of Navarre. His eldest son, John, Duke of Normandy, also married a second wife in that year, Jane, Countess of Boulogne, widow of the Duke of Burgundy; besides Boulogne and Burgundy, she brought Artois, Auvergne, and various other lands into the hands of the King of France. King Philip died in August

1350, and his son John succeeded him. He revived the Order of the Star, comparable to that of the Garter. There was a great famine in France.

In 1352 Pope Clement VI died, and was succeeded by Innocent VI.

In 1355 the Prince of Wales besieged Carcassonne, and laid waste Narbonne. The three estates provided an army of thirty thousand for King John, to be paid out of a new *gabelle* (a tax on salt) and a capital levy of eightpence in the pound on all estates. When this proved insufficient, a graduated income tax was introduced.

In 1356 King John went to Rouen, had the Count of Harcourt beheaded, and the King of Navarre imprisoned in the Louvre, and captured some castles in Normandy belonging to the latter.

The Prince of Wales advanced through Auvergne, Berry, and Touraine, and captured the town of Romorantin, and also the castle, by means of Greek fire.

King John, hearing from observers of the great damage done by the Prince of Wales, advanced with an army of twenty thousand men-at-arms to Poitiers. The Prince of Wales sent a detachment of sixty men out on reconnaissance, who came upon a French force of two hundred, and succeeded in drawing them on till they were all either killed or captured by the main army of the Prince. He discovered from the prisoners taken that King John had advanced with a very large army.

158

. . . When the Prince of Wales learned that King John had advanced so far that a battle was unavoidable, he collected all the stragglers and gave orders that nobody on pain of death should skirmish or advance ahead of the banners of the marshals. The English army then advanced, all that Saturday, till they were within two miles of Poitiers.

The Captal[1] of Buch, Sir Haymenon of Pomier, Sir Barthol-

---

[1] *The hereditary commander of a fort* (cp., *in Scotland, the Captain of Dunstaffnage*).

omew Burghersh, and Sir Eustace of Ambrecicourt were then sent
out to reconnoitre the French position. They took with them two
hundred men-at-arms, all beautifully mounted, and advanced till
the large army of the French King was in full view. The whole
plain was covered with men-at-arms. The English could not
resist attacking the French rear, and unhorsed many of them and
took a number of prisoners, until the main army began to stir, and
news of what was happening reached King John, just as he was
about to enter the city of Poitiers. When the King heard that the
enemy were behind him, and not ahead, he was delighted, and
ordered his whole army to turn back and head for the open
fields, so that it was very late before his army was quartered there.
The English contingent returned to the Prince with a description
of the immense numbers of the French. The Prince was undismayed, and said: 'God be on our side! We must consider how
to fight them to best advantage.' The English were encamped in
a very strong position that night, among the vineyards and
bushes. Both armies were well guarded.

159

On Sunday morning King John was most anxious to fight. He
had mass sung solemnly in his pavilion, and received communion, with his four sons. After mass he held a large council
consisting of his brother the Duke of Orléans, the Dukes of
Bourbon and Athens, the Counts of Ponthieu, Eu, Tankerville,
Salzburg, and Dammartin, and many barons of France and other
great lords who held land in the neighbourhood. It was eventually decided that the army should advance into the plain, and
that each lord should unfurl his banner and advance, in the name
of God and Saint Denis, in battle order.

Trumpets were sounded, and the whole army armed and
mounted, and advanced to the place where the King's banners
stood fluttering in the breeze. There might be seen all the
nobility of France, in their brilliant armour, with banners and
pennons flying; all the flower of France was there, no knight or

squire daring to stay at home for fear of dishonour. By the advice of the constable and marshals, the army was drawn up in three battalions, with about sixteen thousand men in each, all experienced and well tried fighting men. The first battalion was under the Duke of Orléans, with thirty-six banners and twice that number of pennons. The second was under the Duke of Normandy and his two brothers, Louis and John; the third was under the King of France himself, and included many noble and outstanding knights.

While the battalions were forming, King John summoned Sir Eustace of Ribeaumont, Sir John of Landas, Sir Guiscard de Beaujeu and Sir Guiscard d'Angle, and said to them: 'Ride up to the English army, as close as you can, see how they are drawn up, and find out whether we had better fight them on foot or on horseback.' The four knights rode off, and after examining the English position, started back to the King who was waiting for them on his white horse, looking now and then at his troops, and thanking God that they were so numerous. Then he addressed his troops: 'Men of Paris, Chartres, Rouen and Orléans, you have always threatened what you would do to the English if you could set your hands on them. Now they are here, and I will lead you to them. Let us see how you take revenge for all the harm and damage that they have done you. We are going to fight them, without fail.' Those who could hear him replied: 'God be on our side! We will not fail.'

As the King was saying these words, the four knights made their way through the throng towards him. In answer to the King's questions they replied: 'Sir, the news is good: God willing, you will be victorious. We have observed the enemy's position, and they are perhaps two thousand men-at-arms, four thousand archers and fifteen hundred men on foot. They are in a very strong position, but they cannot make more than one battalion in all. Nevertheless they have shown great judgement in choosing a position, the other side of a lane, behind a long hedge which they can defend with their archers; and as that is the only road for an attack, we must pass through the middle of them.

The lane has no other entry, and it is so narrow that four men can scarcely ride abreast. At the end of the lane, surrounded by vines and thorn bushes, so that it is impossible to penetrate in any regular order, their men-at-arms are drawn up on foot, with the archers in front of them in a triangular formation. They have been clever, for it is impossible to attack them without running the gauntlet of the archers.'

The King asked Sir Eustace, who was the spokesman, how he would advise him to attack. 'Sir,' he replied, 'on foot, except for three hundred picked men-at-arms, the most expert and bold in your army; they must be extremely well mounted, in order to break the line of the archers. Then your battalions must follow up quickly on foot and engage the men-at-arms hand to hand. This is the best plan that I can think of; if anyone can suggest a better, let him do so.'

The King approved this plan, and his marshals proceeded to select three hundred knights and squires, the cream of his army, all well armed and mounted. Afterwards a battalion of Germans was formed, under the Counts of Salzburg, Neyde, and Nassau, to support the marshals. King John was armed in the royal armour, and nineteen others were similarly accoutred.[1] He put his eldest son under the care of the lord of Saint Venant, and his other three sons under the care of other good knights and squires. The banner of France was carried by Sir Geoffrey de Chargny, the most valiant and astute knight in the army.

160

When the army was drawn up, the men were ordered to shorten their lances to the length of five feet, to make them more manageable, and to remove their spurs, as they were to advance on foot.

---

[1] Cp. *Shakespeare, describing a scene 120 years later:*
> '*I think there be six Richmonds in the field:*
> *Five have I slain today instead of him.*'
>   Richard III, *Act V, Scene 4.*

Just before the attack was to be made, the Cardinal of Périgord rode up to the King at full gallop. He had left Poitiers early that morning, and now made a low bow to the King and begged him, with his hands joined, to wait a little, for the love of God, and hear what he had to say; he continued as follows: 'Most dear sir, you have here the flower of the chivalry of France assembled against the English, who are a mere handful of men by comparison with you. It would be far more honourable and advantageous to you to overcome them without having recourse to battle than to risk such a splendid army and such noble knights as you have here. Let me therefore, in all humility and for the love of God, go to the Prince and point out what danger he is in.' 'Sir,' said the King, 'You may certainly go; but come back quickly.'

The Cardinal rode off to where the Prince of Wales was surrounded by his men, in the thickest part of the vineyard. After exchanging greetings, the Cardinal began: 'Dear son, if you have carefully considered the mighty power of the King of France, you will allow me to make peace between you if I possibly can.' 'Sir,' was the reply, 'if my own honour and that of my army is kept unblemished, I will listen to any reasonable terms.' 'Well said, my son,' said the Cardinal. 'I will arrange a treaty if I can; for it would be a great pity if so many excellent people as are assembled here, should meet in battle.'

The Cardinal went back to the King, and said: 'Sir, you need be in no hurry to fight them, for they cannot escape; you can win a bloodless victory; I therefore beg you to allow a truce until sunrise tomorrow.' Part of the King's council would not agree to this, but the Cardinal spoke with such eloquence that the King finally agreed. He had a magnificent pavilion of red silk erected on the spot where he stood.

All that Sunday the Cardinal rode to and fro between the armies, determined to bring them to terms, if possible. But the only conditions that would satisfy the King were for four of the principal Englishmen to give themselves up to his mercy, and for the Prince and his army to surrender unconditionally. Various proposals were made: it is said on good authority that the Prince offered to surrender all the towns and castles that he had captured during the current campaign, to set free, without ransom, all his prisoners, and to swear not to take up arms against the King of France for seven years. But the King and his council refused this proposal, and declared finally that unless the Prince and a hundred of his knights surrendered as prisoners, they would not escape without a battle, and to this the Prince and his advisers would never have agreed.

Meanwhile, several spirited young knights on either side rode out to observe the positions of their respective enemies. In this way Sir John Chandos, a noble and valiant knight, met one of the marshals of France, Sir John of Clermont, near one of the flanks of the French army. They were both wearing the same badge on their surcoats, a blue Madonna worked in embroidery, surrounded by rays of light. When he saw it, Clermont said: 'Chandos, since when have you taken the liberty of wearing my badge?' 'It is you who have taken mine,' replied Sir John Chandos; 'It is as much mine as it is yours.' 'I deny it,' came the answer. 'And were it not for the truce between us, I would soon show you that you have no right to wear it.' 'Ha!' replied Chandos. 'To-morrow you will find me in the field, ready to defend and prove by force of arms that it is as much mine as yours.' Clermont replied: 'That is just like your English boasting: you can invent nothing new—whenever you see something fine belonging to someone else, you take it for your own.' With that they parted. The Cardinal, having failed to reconcile the King and the Prince, for all his efforts, returned to Poitiers late in the evening, while the English built mounds and ditches round the positions of their archers, to make them more secure.

On Monday morning the Cardinal returned to the field at sunrise in the hope of pacifying both sides: but without success. The French told him angrily to go back to Poitiers or anywhere else he liked, and not to bring them any more proposals, or it might be the worse for him.

The arrangement of the English army was exactly as had been

reported to the French King by the four knights: but the Prince now ordered a number of the most valiant and brilliant knights in his army to remain mounted, and in the same way as the French King, ordered three hundred men-at-arms, and as many mounted archers, to post themselves on a small hill on the right flank from which they could circumvent the battalion of the Duke of Normandy, who was himself at the foot of the hill.

The most illustrious knights in the Prince's army were the following: Thomas Beauchamp, Earl of Warwick, John de Vere, Earl of Oxford, William Montagu, Earl of Salisbury, Sir John Chandos, the Earls of Suffolk and Stafford, Sir Reginald Cobham, Sir Richard Stafford, Edward Lord Despencer, Sir James Audley and his brother Peter, Lord Berkeley, Lord Bassett, William Lord Fitzwarren, Lord Delaware, Lord Mohun, Lord Willoughby, Bartholomew Lord Burghersh, Lord Felton, Richard Lord Pembroke, Sir Stephen Cossington, and Sir Thomas Bradestan. From Gascony and Hainault there were other valiant knights, and in truth the Prince had with him the whole flower of chivalry. His army did not number more than eight thousand in all, whereas the French were altogether a good fifty thousand, of whom over three thousand were knights.

161-162

When the Prince of Wales saw that the efforts of the cardinal had been in vain, he addressed his troops as follows: 'My gallant men, we are only a few against the might of our enemies, but do not let us be discouraged by that. Victory goes not to the greater number, but where God wishes to send it. If we win the day, we shall gain the greatest honour and glory in the world. If we are killed, there will still be the King my father, and my noble brothers, and all your good friends, to avenge us. I therefore beg of you to fight manfully today; for, please God and Saint George, today you will see me act like a true knight.'

Sir James Audley and Sir Eustace of Ambrecicourt were the first to advance against the enemy, but Sir Eustace, after wounding a German knight, was taken prisoner by the Count of Nassau's men. Soon afterwards the fighting became general. The battalion under the French marshals advanced before those troops who were intended to break the line of the English archers; and it entered the lane where the hedges on both sides were lined with the archers, who began shooting with such deadly aim from both sides that the horses would not go forward into the hail of bearded arrows, but became unmanageable and threw their riders, who were then unable to rise to their feet in the confusion. Thus the marshals' battalion never reached that of the prince, though a few knights and squires were so well mounted that they succeeded in breaking through the hedge, but even these were unable to reach the prince's battalion. Sir James Audley, with his four squires, had taken up his position sword in hand in front of this battalion, and was performing wonders. He advanced so far that he actually engaged Lord Arnold of Andreghen, the Marshal of France, a valiant and brave knight, under his own banner, and fought him for a considerable time, wounding him severely. The marshals' battalion was soon routed by the archers with the assistance of the men-at-arms, who rushed among the French as they fell and seized or killed them as they pleased. Lord Arnold of Andreghen was captured, but not by Sir James and his squires, for they were continually fighting and pursuing their enemies and did not stop to take prisoners. Sir John of Clermont fought under his banner as long as he could, but was finally struck down and could neither get up again nor procure a ransom, but was killed fighting for his lord. Some say that his fate was the result of his exchange with Sir John Chandos on the previous day.

Seldom can a body of good fighting men have been so totally and speedily defeated as the battalion of the marshals of France, for they fell back on each other so fast that the army could not advance. And the rear were forced to fall back on the Duke of Normandy's battalion, which was broad and thick in front but soon thinned out at the rear, when the news of the marshals' defeat was known: for the soldiers mounted their horses and rode off. At that moment an English troop came down from a hill and, riding past the battalion with a large force of archers, fell upon its flank. The English archers were certainly of infinite service to their side, and caused great havoc. For their shooting was so accurate and so well concerted that the French did not know which way to turn, as the archers kept on advancing and gaining ground.

When the English men-at-arms saw that the enemy's first battalion was beaten, and that the Duke of Normandy's battalion was also beginning to waver, they hastily mounted and gave a shout, to dismay their enemies still further: 'Saint George for Guyenne!' Sir John Chandos then said to the Prince, 'Sir, sir, ride on ahead. The day is yours; thanks to God it will be in your hands. Let us make for our opponent the King of France, for the hub of the matter will lie there. He is brave and certainly he will not run. He will wait for us, God willing, but he must be well fought. You have said already that you would show yourself a good knight.' The Prince was roused by these words, and replied: 'Come on, John, you will not see me turn back, I will always be with the leaders.' Then he said to his standard-bearer: 'Banner, advance, in the name of God and Saint George.' The standard advanced. The battle raged furiously, and many knights fell; you must understand that no one who was unhorsed could get up again unless he was quickly assisted. As the Prince advanced with his men he saw Lord Robert of Duras lying dead by a bush, his banner beside him, surrounded by a dozen of his men. The Prince told two or three of his squires and archers to place the body on a shield and take it to Poitiers and present it from him to the Cardinal of Périgord, and say that he saluted him by that token. This was done. For the Prince had been informed that the cardinal's men had remained against him in the field, which was not fitting for a man of God. For churchmen, under pretext of doing good and bringing about a peace, may pass from one army to the other but ought not to take up arms on either side. The Prince was therefore angry with the cardinal, and sent him the body of his nephew Robert of Duras.

The Prince then charged the battalion of the Duke of Athens, the Constable of France. The encounter was very sharp, and many fell. The French, who fought in large companies, cried 'Mountjoy! Saint Denis!' and the English replied with: 'Saint George for Guyenne!' The Prince next met the German battalion, but they were soon overthrown. The English archers shot so quickly and well that nobody dared come within range of them, and many were killed without getting a chance of being ransomed. The Counts of Nassau, Salzburg, and Neyde, who commanded the Germans, were all killed, and many other knights and squires that followed them. In the course of the fighting Sir Eustace of Ambrecicourt was rescued by his own men and, after remounting, performed notable feats of arms and made many valuable captures.

Those lords who were in charge of the French King's sons decided to remove them from the field to a place of safety when they saw the Prince advancing on them. And on the return of these lords to the battlefield they met the Duke of Orléans and his battalion, still completely intact, having deserted their position behind the King's battalion; though it is certainly true that it contained a number of knights and squires who would certainly have preferred death to dishonour, even though their leaders had fled.

I have described earlier the battle of Crécy, and how the French were so ill favoured by fortune; they had equally ill luck at Poitiers, for they outnumbered the English by seven to one. But the battle of Poitiers was, truly, far better fought than that of Crécy, and the men-at-arms had far more opportunity to observe their enemies. For at Crécy, the battle did not begin till the late afternoon, and the army was in disorder, whereas at Poitiers it began early in the morning, with the French in good order; and many more gallant deeds were done. Fewer great lords were killed, and those who were captured or killed in the field fought so valiantly that their descendants are honoured for it to this day. King John of France was unalarmed by all that he saw and heard, and having ordered his men to dismount, he put himself at their head and ordered the banners to advance on the English, and the battle raged fast and furious.[1] Also in the King's battalion was Lord Douglas, of Scotland, who fought valiantly for a time: but when he saw that there was no hope left for the French, he made off as best he could, for he was determined not to fall into the hands of the English, preferring death to such a fate.

Sir James Audley was always in the thick of the fighting, with his four squires; he was severely wounded in the body, the head and the face. But as long as he had the strength, he went on fighting, and continued to press forward. Towards the end of the battle, when he was covered in blood, and weak from his wounds, his four squires took him behind a hedge, out of the battle, to let him regain his breath. They took off his armour, as gently as they could, dressed his wounds, and sewed up those that were most dangerous.

King John of France proved himself a valiant knight; and if a quarter of his army had acquitted themselves as nobly, the day would have been his. Nevertheless, those lords who remained with him fought to the best of their power, until they were all killed or captured. Scarcely any who dismounted and fought at his side tried to escape. . . .

163

It often happens, in the fortunes of love and war, that events turn out more favourably and wonderfully than could have been hoped or expected. And indeed, the battle of Poitiers, in the plains of Beauvoir and Maupertuis, was bloody and dangerous. Many splendid feats of arms may never have come to light and although the day ended favourably for the English, both sides suffered heavily. King John himself did wonders with his battle-

[1] *Here follows a list of the principal French knights who were killed, including the Duke of Bourbon, the Duke of Athens, and the Bishop of Châlons. The clergy fought on the battlefield in person until about 1540.*

axe. The Count of Tankerville was taken prisoner as he tried to break through the throng, quite near the King, as also were Jacques of Bourbon, Count of Ponthieu, and Sir John of Artois, Count of Eu; and a little further on, Charles of Artois and many other knights were captured under the standard of the Captal of Buch. The French were pursued right up to the gates of Poitiers, and terrible slaughter took place, for the inhabitants of the town shut the gates and would allow no one to enter and take refuge. The carnage was so frightful that some of the French surrendered as soon as they saw an Englishman; and a number of the English, archers as well as knights, took five or six prisoners each.

A great tumult surrounded King John, through eagerness to capture him. Those who were closest, and who knew him by sight, cried out: 'Surrender, sir, surrender, or you will die.' There was a young knight from Saint Omer present called Sir Denis of Morbèque, who had been on the English side for about five years, having been banished from France in his youth for causing the death of a man in a private affray at Saint Omer. This knight was lucky enough to find himself nearest to the King of France, and being large and strong, he forced his way up to him and said in good French: 'Sire, sire, surrender!' The King was in dire straits, and so hard pressed by his enemies that he asked the knight: 'To whom shall I surrender? To whom? Where is my cousin, the Prince of Wales? If I could see him, I would speak to him.' 'Sire,' replied Sir Denis, 'he is not here; surrender to me, and I will take you to him.' 'Who are you?' said the King. 'Sire, I am Denis of Morbèque, a knight of Artois. But I serve the King of England, for I cannot belong to France—I have forfeited all I had there.' The King then gave him his right glove, and said 'I surrender to you.' There was a great crowd round him, for everyone was eager to cry out, 'I have taken him.' The King and his young son, Philip, were unable to advance any further or to escape from the throng.

The Prince of Wales, his helmet on his head, was brave and cruel as a lion that day, and took great delight in fighting his enemies. Sir John Chandos, who never left his side all day, said to him, towards the end of the battle: 'Sir, I advise you to halt here, and set your banner above this bush. Your men are scattered, but they will rally to it, for, thanks be to God, the day is ours. I can see no banners or pennons of the French, nor any companies that can rally against us. You must refresh yourself a little, for I see you are much heated.'

The Prince agreed, and had his banner set over the bush, to rally his men; the minstrels sounded their horns, and the Prince took off his helmet. His lords-in-waiting were soon ready, and pitched a small crimson tent, which the Prince entered. Then wine was brought to him and his lords, who increased with every minute, and gathered round him with their prisoners.

As soon as the two marshals arrived, the Earls of Warwick and Suffolk, the Prince asked if they had any news of the King of France. 'None, sir,' was the reply. 'But we think he is either killed or captured, for he has not left his battalion.' Then the Prince quickly sent the Earl of Warwick and Sir Reginald Cobham to find out exactly what had happened to him.

These lords mounted their horses and rode off to the top of a little hill to look around them. They saw a great host of men-at-arms coming towards them very slowly on foot. The King of France was in the middle of them, and in some danger. For the English and the Gascons had taken him from Sir Denis, and the strongest were arguing, and shouting out: '*I* have captured him, *I* have.' But the King, to escape from this danger, said: 'Gentlemen, gentlemen, take me quietly to my cousin, the Prince, and my son with me: do not quarrel about my capture, for I am such a great knight that I can make you all rich.'

These words calmed them a little, but the quarrel soon began again, and they did not move a yard without rioting. But the two English lords, seeing the throng, spurred on their horses and came up and asked what was happening. 'The King of France is taken,' they were told. 'More than ten knights and squires are claiming him as their prisoner and challenging each other.'

The two lords pushed through the crowd, and ordered everyone to fall back, in the name of the Prince and on pain of death.

They dared not disobey these orders. The two lords dismounted and bowed low to the King, who was much relieved to see them, for they were delivering him from great danger.

164

Meanwhile the Prince had asked the knights round him: 'Does nobody know anything of Sir James Audley?' 'Yes, sir,' was the reply. 'He is badly wounded and lying in a litter quite near by.' 'I am very sorry that he is wounded,' said the Prince, 'and I would like to see him. See if he can be carried here; if not, I will go to him.' Sir James was told of this, and said: 'A thousand thanks to the Prince for thinking of such a humble knight as me.' And he called to some of his men to carry his litter to where the Prince was. When he reached him, the Prince bowed to him and received him with great honour, and said: 'Sir James, I owe you great honour. Your valour has won you renown and glory above us all today, and your courage has shown that you are the bravest of knights.' 'My lord, you may say what you like,' replied Sir James, 'but I only wish it were true. If I have exerted myself today in your service, it was only to fulfil a vow, and it should not be regarded as prowess.'

'Sir James,' said the Prince, 'we all look on you as the most valiant. To increase your renown and to equip you better to pursue your glorious career, I retain you as my knight for ever, with five hundred marks a year revenue, to be paid from my estates in England.' 'Sir,' said Sir James, 'may God make me deserve the great benefits you have given me.'

With these words he took his leave, for he was very weak; and he was carried back to his tent. He had not been carried far when Lord Warwick and Sir Reginald Cobham brought the King of France to the Prince's tent. The Prince bowed low before him, and received him most chivalrously, and sent for wine and food, which he presented to the King himself, as a mark of special affection.

165

Such was the battle of Poitiers; it began at nine in the morning, and was over by noon, though some of the English did not return from the pursuit of their enemies till late in the evening. It was reported that all the flower of the knighthood of France were killed, and the loss to the country was incalculable. As well as the King and his son the lord Philip, seventeen counts were taken prisoner, not counting barons, knights and squires, and between five and a half and six thousand were killed in the field. When the English had all reassembled, they discovered that the number of their prisoners was twice that of themselves. In view of the risk they might otherwise be running, they decided to ransom them on the spot. The French found their captors most obliging, and many were released on their own undertaking to come to Bordeaux with their ransom money before Christmas. Every prisoner was entirely at the disposal of his captor, to ransom or not as he pleased.

As may be imagined, all those who accompanied the Prince of Wales were much enriched, in wealth as well as in glory, not only by the ransom money which they obtained but also from the quantities of gold and silver plate, rich jewels, whole trunks full of belts heavy with gold and silver fittings, and furred coats. No one set much store by armour, for it was in plentiful supply: the French had come as richly and magnificently dressed as they could, as if victory had been a foregone conclusion for them.

166

When Sir James Audley was carried back to his tent, he sent for his brother and four of his cousins and also for the four squires who had attended him in the field. 'Gentlemen,' he said, 'My lord the Prince has been pleased to give me five hundred marks a year as a heritage. I have done very little to deserve it; but these four squires have served me most loyally. Any honour I have gained, especially in this battle, has been due to their bravery, Therefore I wish to reward them, and I would like you, my cousins, to be witnesses. It is my intention to make over to them the gift of five hundred marks, in the same form as my lord has given it to me. I disinherit myself of it and assign it irrevocably to them.'

The knights looked at each other and said: 'It is a characteristically noble gesture on the part of Sir James,' adding with one voice: 'Sir, may God remember you for it! We will bear witness of this gift to the squires wherever they go.'

167

In the evening the Prince of Wales gave a supper to the French King; for all the vast quantities of provisions that the French had brought with them had fallen into the hands of the English, many of whom had not tasted bread for three days. The Prince also invited the greater part of the counts and barons who had been taken prisoner. The King of France and his son Prince Philip were put at a well-laid table, set on a dais, with the Lords Jacques de Bourbon and John of Artois, and the Counts of Tankerville, Estampes, Dammartin, Granville, and Partenay. The Prince himself served the King's table, and all the other tables as well, with every mark of humility, and refused to sit at the King's table, in spite of numerous entreaties, saying that he was not yet worthy of such an honour, and that it would not be fitting for him to sit at the same table as so great a prince, and one who had shown himself so valiant that day. He then knelt before the King and added: 'Sir, do not dine miserably because God has not granted your wishes: the lord my father will certainly treat you with all the honour and friendship in his power, and will behave so reasonably that you will always remain the best of friends. In my opinion you have every reason to be glad, even though the day was ours; for you have today won a reputation of bravery that surpasses all your other knights. I do not speak, dear sir, to flatter you, for everybody on our side who saw the action agrees that this is your due, and awards you the laurels.' At this, murmurs of agreement and praise were heard from the English and French alike, that the Prince had spoken truly, and nobly, and that he would be one of the most gallant princes in the world, if God should grant him life to continue his glorious career.

SUMMARY

168-181

After the battle of Poitiers the Prince of Wales retired to Bordeaux with his army. The Three Estates temporarily took over the government of France; they consisted of twelve representatives of the clergy, twelve of the nobility, and twelve of the burghers. They asked the Duke of Normandy to release the King of Navarre from prison, but the duke would not agree to do so.

Fighting continued in the region of Cotentin; Sir Godfrey of Harcourt was killed, and his army defeated by the French. The Prince of Wales took the King of France back to England, but first had to distribute a hundred thousand florins among the barons of Gascony before they would agree to it. Pope Innocent VI sent two cardinals to England and they eventually procured a truce between England and France to last until midsummer 1359.

Shortly afterwards[1] the Treaty of Berwick was concluded between England and Scotland, and King David of Scotland, after nine years of imprisonment, was released on the following terms:

1 He should never bear arms against the King of England.
2 He should try to gain his subjects' consent that the crown of Scotland be held in fief and homage from the King of England, and failing that he should swear to keep a lasting peace with England.
3 He should pay an indemnity of five hundred thousand nobles within ten years.

[1] *October 3rd, 1357.*

4 Twenty young Scots nobles were to remain in England as hostages
until the sum was paid in full.

In May the Duke of Lancaster laid siege to Rennes, and Sir William
of Graville recaptured the city and castle of Evreux from the King of
France, who had taken them from the King of Navarre. The King of
Navarre was rescued from prison and made a speech in Latin in Paris,
complaining of his grievances. He soon became more popular than the
Duke of Normandy, who was acting as regent.

182

Soon after the King of Navarre was released, severe disorders
broke out in many parts of France, in the districts of Beauvais,
Brie, Laon, Soissons, and on the Marne. Some of the inhabitants
of the country towns assembled without any particular leader near
Beauvais, numbering at first not more than a hundred. Their
contention was that the nobility of France was betraying the
kingdom, and that it would be a public service if they were
destroyed; they all agreed to this, and cried 'Shame on the men
who prevent it!' Then, with no further discussion, they set off in a
body, armed only with iron-tipped sticks and knives, for the house
of a knight nearby. They broke into it and killed the knight, and
his wife and children as well, and burned the house; all through
Brie they killed young and old alike. They then moved on to another strong castle, took the knight who lived there and tied him
to a stake, and several of them raped his wife and daughter,
before his very eyes. They then killed the wife, who was pregnant,
and the daughter, and the other children as well, and last of all
they murdered the knight himself, with great cruelty. They also
destroyed and burned the castle.

They did the same in many castles and fine houses, and their
number increased to six thousand. Wherever they went, they
made new recruits of their own sort, who followed them. Meanwhile all the knights fled, with their wives and children and
squires, sometimes to a distance of fifty miles, where they thought

they would be safe. Their houses they left unguarded, with all the valuables inside.

These wicked people, without a leader and without ordinary weapons, plundered and burned every house they came to, like mad dogs, murdering every gentleman and raping every lady they could find, showing no mercy anywhere. Never was such cruelty shown in Christendom, or by Saracens either. Whoever perpetrated the most outrageous crimes, such as no human being should even imagine, was applauded the most. I dare not mention some of the inconceivably horrible atrocities that they committed against the women. They had chosen a king from among their number, whom they called Jacques Bonhomme. He came from Clermont, near Beauvais, and he was the blackest, most diabolical villain of them all. These wretches burned and destroyed more than sixty fine houses and strong castles in the region of Beauvais, and also in the neighbourhood of Corbie, Amiens, and Montdidier. Every knight and squire who could do so fled with his lady to Meaux, if he wished to avoid being assaulted and murdered; the Duchess of Orléans, the Duchess of Normandy, and many other ladies followed this course. These accursed men operated between Paris, Noyons, and Soissons, and all over the territory of Coucy, in the county of Valois. In the dioceses of Laon, Noyon, and Soissons, over a hundred castles and houses were destroyed.

183

When the gentry around Beauvais, Corbie, and the Vermandois saw their houses destroyed and their friends slaughtered, they appealed for help to their friends in Flanders, Hainault, Brabant, and Bohemia; and a number of gentlemen soon came from those parts and began to kill and destroy the brigands, whenever they found them, and to hang up their bodies all together on the nearest trees. In the same way the King of Navarre destroyed over three thousand of them in a single day, near Clermont, in the region of Beauvais. But their numbers had by this time so in-

creased that if they had all been collected in one place, they would
have amounted to a hundred thousand. When asked why they
behaved as they did, they replied that they did not know, but they
were merely doing the same as other people, and that they were
going to destroy all the nobles and gentlemen in the world.

At this juncture, the Duke of Normandy secretly left Paris;
he was suspicious of the King of Navarre, who appeared to have
formed an understanding with the Provost of the Merchants and
his party, and to be in complete agreement with him on every
issue. He came to the bridge at Charenton-sur-Marne, and
issued a general summons to the vassals of the crown, and sent a
defiance to the provost and his supporters. When the provost
heard what was afoot, he was afraid that the duke would return
by night and overrun Paris, which was not at that time a fortified
city; he collected as many workmen as he could, and made them
dig ditches all round the city, and then surrounded the town with
a wall, with gates at intervals. The work went on day and night,
and three thousand workmen were employed for a whole year, at
considerable expense. To surround a city the size of Paris with
adequate fortifications was an immense task, and it was the most
useful achievement that the provost accomplished in his life, for
otherwise Paris would have been overrun and pillaged several
times over by different factions in the subsequent years.

184

Meanwhile the Count of Foix and his cousin the Captal of Buch
had returned to France from an expedition to Prussia. They were
deeply disturbed to hear of the troubles prevailing in France; on
reaching Châlons they learned how the ladies mentioned above
had taken refuge in Meaux, and although the Captal was on the
side of the English, they decided to go to the assistance of these
ladies and support them to the best of their ability. The truce
between England and France was still in force, and the two
knights could go wherever they liked; their following consisted of

not more than forty lances, for they were returning from a pilgrimage. They were warmly welcomed at Meaux, for the ladies were in constant danger: the Jacquerie, who had heard of their presence in Meaux, had joined forces with the rabble from Valois, and were on their way to the town. In the same way their numbers were increased by brigands from Paris who had heard of the treasures in Meaux and flocked to join them; they amounted altogether to nine thousand, and their ranks were swelled at every step.

When the rabble reached the town, the inhabitants opened the gates to them, and they entered in such numbers that the streets were packed with them as far as the marketplace, in which the ladies had their lodgings. At the sight of such a crowd of ruffians advancing on them, the ladies were terrified; the houses in the market-place are quite strong, provided they are properly guarded, for the river Marne flows around them on three sides. The two lords, with their men, advanced to the gate of the marketplace, marched through under the banners of the Duke of Orléans and the Count of Foix, and faced the ill-armed rabble.

When the brigands saw this force properly drawn up against them, small though it was, they became less bold, and their leaders began to fall back. The gentlemen then pursued them, cutting them down with their lances and swords, and the brigands began to panic and flee, falling one on top of another under the weight of the blows. Then armed men of every kind rushed out of the gates and fell upon the brigands, striking them down like beasts, and soon clearing the town of them—for they kept no kind of regular order. They killed so many brigands that they became quite exhausted, and they flung the bodies in heaps into the river. Over seven thousand of them were killed, and not one would have escaped, if their opponents had chosen to pursue them.

When the men-at-arms returned they set fire to the town of Meaux, with all the rabble of the town inside it, for they had been on the side of the Jacquerie. And after being routed at Meaux, the brigands never rallied in any great numbers. For the young lord of Coucy, Enguerrand by name, had a number of troops under him who suppressed them mercilessly, wherever they were to be found.

SUMMARY

185-215

The Duke of Normandy laid siege to Paris, which was controlled by the party of the Provost of the Merchants, who eventually earned the suspicion of the inhabitants of Paris by his negotiations with the duke, the King of Navarre, and the remnants of the English army still in France. The provost secretly arranged to hand over Paris to the Navarrois and the English, but the plot was discovered and the provost killed.

The King of Navarre declared war on France, and his troops met with considerable success in Picardy, and plundered and burned the town of Amiens. A famine spread over France that lasted four years, and 'the whole country was in a state of warfare.' The Canon of Robesart valiantly defeated a party of Navarrois at Creil, near Laon.

Philip of Navarre, the King's brother, arrived with his army too late to relieve the garrison of Saint Valéry, which was taken after a long siege by the Constable of France. Sir Peter Audley narrowly failed to capture Châlons-sur-Marne. At last peace was made between the Duke of Normandy and the King of Navarre, but it was not recognized by Philip.

The fighting continued in France, and the truce between France and England expired; a peace treaty agreed to in London by the Kings of England and France was rejected by the Duke of Normandy, and King Edward invaded France in the summer. The Duke of Lancaster went ahead of him and they were joined by various knights of the empire. King Edward besieged Rheims, but without success, and later made a pact with the Duke of Burgundy. The King of Navarre made war on the Duke of Normandy, who refused battle. King Edward retired to Chartres, and the Peace of Brétigny was signed,[1] which laid down that an indemnity of six hundred thousand francs was to be paid by France, and hostages delivered.

[1] *October 24th, 1360.*

King John of France was released, and made a pilgrimage on foot from Calais to Boulogne accompanied by the Prince of Wales and his brothers. The captured provinces in France were returned to the French and King Edward ordered his garrisons to disperse, but they formed companies to plunder and destroy the country. Jacques de Bourbon was sent with an army to suppress them, but was defeated. These marauders captured Pont Saint Esprit, and Pope Innocent VI initiated a crusade against them from Avignon, under the command of the Marquis de Montferrat, who persuaded most of them, with promises of generous pay, to go and fight for him in the wars in Lombardy; they did so with some success.

216

At this time there died in England Henry, Duke of Lancaster,[1] to the great sorrow of the King and barons. He left two daughters: Maud, who married William, Count of Hainault, son of Louis of Bavaria and Margaret of Hainault; and Blanche, who married John of Gaunt, Earl of Richmond, the fourth son of King Edward III.

The young Duke Philip of Burgundy also died about this time. King John, as his nearest relation, succeeded him as Duke of Burgundy, with all rights over Champagne and Brie, to the great annoyance of the King of Navarre, who also claimed these territories, but without success.

The King of France then decided to visit the Pope and the College of Cardinals at Avignon, and to amuse himself by inspecting his new inheritance in Burgundy on the way. He left Paris at the end of June [1362], leaving his son Charles, Duke of Normandy, as regent in his absence; he was escorted by the chief knights of the land, and, travelling luxuriously, by easy stages, he reached Villeneuve, outside Avignon, about Michaelmas.[2] He was most sumptuously entertained, and his attendants as well, by the Pope and the Sacred College. The King stayed at

[1] *He died in the plague of 1360.*   [2] *September 29th.*

Villeneuve, and exchanged a number of visits with the Pope and the cardinals at Avignon.

At this time, the King of England's mother, Queen Isabel, died; she was the daughter of Philip the Fair, King of France. King Edward arranged a sumptuous funeral for her in London, at Christ Church, which was attended by all the prelates and barons of England, as well as by those French lords who were at that time retained in England as hostages. The Prince and Princess of Wales then left England, and after landing at La Rochelle and resting there for four days they were magnificently entertained by Sir John Chandos, who had governed Aquitaine for some time and now came to La Rochelle, with a fine company of knights and squires, to welcome the Prince. He then escorted the Prince to Poitiers, where the knights of Poitou and Saintonge came and paid homage and fealty to him. The Prince rode from town to town, receiving homage everywhere, till he reached Bordeaux, where he stayed for some time. The nobles of Gascony also all paid homage to him, and they were received with such courtesy and grace that they were delighted. Even the Count of Foix came to visit the Prince, who received him magnificently. Peace was also made between him and the Count of Armagnac, who had been at war a long time. Sir John Chandos was made Constable of the Duchy of Aquitaine, and Sir Guiscard d'Angle was made marshal. A number of English knights were made seneschals and bailiffs in the duchy, and they maintained greater state and magnificence than the inhabitants of the country could have wished.

217

About Candlemas,[1] 1362, King Peter of Cyprus came to Avignon, where he was warmly received at the papal court. He was escorted to the palace of Pope Urban by a number of cardinals, and was graciously received both by the Pope and by the King of

[1] *February 2nd.*

France, who was there at the time. The two Kings remained at Avignon, or in the neighbourhood, for the whole of Lent, and were frequently received by the Pope. In the course of these visits the King of Cyprus urged the Pope, in the presence of the King of France, and the cardinals, that it would be a noble and worthy undertaking for Christianity to make an expedition over the seas against the enemies of God. The King of France listened eagerly to this suggestion and said that he would willingly take part in the expedition himself, for two reasons: one was that his father, King Philip, had formerly vowed to do so, and the second was in order to remove from the kingdom of France all those men-at-arms, called the Free Companies, who were pillaging and robbing his country without a shadow of right, and thereby to save their souls. But this purpose the King of France kept to himself until Good Friday, when the Pope preached in his chapel at Avignon before the two Kings and the Sacred College of Cardinals. After the sermon, which was most humble and devout, the King of France showed his devotion by putting on the cross and humbly asking the Pope to confirm his action, which he gladly did. A number of other knights, some of them the highest in the land, did the same. The King of Cyprus was delighted, and gave thanks to Our Lord. . . .

SUMMARY

217-222

The King of Cyprus passed through the empire, visiting Prague, Brussels and Bruges, and enlisting support for the crusade as he went. He then visited England, and returned through France and Aquitaine. King John of France also came to London, where he fell ill and died. He was succeeded by his son, the Duke of Normandy, who immediately prepared to resist the King of Navarre. The Lord of Boucicaut and Bertrand du Guesclin captured Mantes and Menlan from the Navarrois by a trick; both of these towns command important crossings of the Seine. The King of Cyprus returned to Paris to condole with the

Duke of Normandy, and King John was buried in Paris at Saint Denis.

The French under Bertrand du Guesclin won an important and hard-fought victory over the forces of Navarre under the Captal of Buch at Bocheral, in Normandy.[1] A good many English fought on the side of Navarre.

223

On Trinity Sunday, 1364, Charles, the eldest son of the late King John of France, was crowned and consecrated King Charles V by the Archbishop of Rheims in the great church of Our Lady at Rheims, and with him his Queen, the daughter of Peter, Duke of Bourbon. The King of Cyprus, the Dukes of Anjou and Burgundy, Wenceslas of Bohemia, the King's uncle, who was Duke of Luxemburg and Brabant, the Count of Eu, the Count of Dammartin, the Count of Tankerville, the Archbishops of Paris and Rouen, and many other knights and prelates attended the coronation. There were great feasts and rejoicings at Rheims, where the King and Queen remained for five days, and it would take a long time to describe the celebrations and pageants that the people of Paris arranged on the return of the King and Queen. Superb presents were given to those foreign lords who had come for the occasion, most of whom now took their leave.

When King Charles returned to Paris he gave the Duchy of Burgundy to his youngest brother, Philip, who then left Paris, accompanied by a great retinue, to take possession of his duchy and to receive homage from its barons, knights, cities, castles, and towns. He then returned to Paris.

King Charles gave orders for Sir Peter of Sequainville to be beheaded for having fought on the side of Navarre. Sir William of Graville would have suffered the same fate had not his son, Sir Guy, given the following ultimatum to the King: whatever punishment was to be inflicted on his father, he threatened that

[1] *May 23rd, 1364.*

he would do the same to Sir Beaumont de Laval, a great lord of Brittany whom he held prisoner. Sir Beaumont's family then appealed to the King with such success that they obtained the exchange of Sir Beaumont for Sir William of Graville. About this time Bertrand du Guesclin won over the castle of Roulleboise, by offering the governor, Sir Vautaire Austard, a large sum of money, perhaps five or six thousand francs, to return to Brabant, whence he came.

Various fortresses in the regions of Caux, Normandy, Beauce and Perche were still in the hands of large companies of brigands, some pretending to support the King of Navarre, others unashamedly pillaging and destroying the country for their own ends. King Charles was constantly harassed by complaints against these brigands, and sent against them his brother, the Duke of Burgundy, who summoned a large number of knights and men-at-arms to join him at Chartres. He then took the field, accompanied by Bertrand du Guesclin, the Lord of Boucicaut, and a number of other distinguished knights, with over five thousand fighting men. In view of their numbers, they split into three battalions: one of them was commanded by Bertrand du Guesclin, who advanced with no more than a thousand men towards Cotentin, and the neighbourhood of Cherbourg, to guard the frontier and prevent the Navarrois from entering Normandy. He was accompanied by the Lord of Sancerre, Sir Arnold of Andreghen, the Count of Joigny and a number of other knights and squires from Normandy and Brittany. A second battalion was under Sir John de la Rivière, composed of a number of knights from Picardy and France, whom he took towards Evreux. The Duke of Burgundy himself commanded the third battalion, which was the largest, and went to besiege the fortress of Marcheville.[1] He surrounded the town with siege-engines brought from Chartres, which never ceased firing on the town by day and night.

[1] *In Beauce.*

224

Meanwhile Louis of Navarre, younger brother of the new King as well as of the late King Philip of Navarre, took it upon himself to continue the war, since it was being fought over a question of inheritance that concerned his family. Since the battle of Cocherel he had been so active in mustering troops that he could now put twelve hundred lances in the field. His troops increased in numbers every day, and were quartered in Languedoc, between the Loire and the Allier. About three thousand of them were detached under the command of Bertrand and Hortingo de la Salle. They crossed the Loire and quickly advanced to La Charité, a large and well-fortified town on that river.

They entered the town without difficulty before daybreak, and occupied part of it; but thinking that the inhabitants might have laid an ambush for them, they did not dare try to overrun the rest of the town till daybreak. The inhabitants took advantage of this respite and loaded all their most valuable possessions, together with their wives and children, into boats, which slipped downstream to Nevers, a distance of a dozen miles. The troops who had entered the town advanced at dawn, and on discovering the situation, decided to keep possession of the town and fortify it—for it would be a very useful base from which to attack the country on both sides of the Loire. Louis of Navarre sent Sir Robert Briquet with another three hundred armed men to reinforce them; and they were then in such strength that they began to inflict severe damage on the surrounding district. Their numbers increased daily. . . .

SUMMARY

224-231

The Duke of Burgundy planned several expeditions against Louis of Navarre in Beauce and Normandy, but was forced to return to

Burgundy, to defend it against the Count of Montbelhard. He then recaptured La Charité.

Meanwhile, in Brittany, the Count of Montfort besieged Auray, and King Charles sent Bertrand du Guesclin to help Charles of Blois resist him. Montfort however was joined by Sir John Chandos and other English knights, and they won a considerable victory near Auray,[1] in which Charles of Blois was killed. Montfort took Auray, Dinan, and Jugon. A peace was then concluded, by which the Count of Montfort's claim to the Duchy of Brittany was upheld. Peace was also made between the Kings of France and Navarre through the efforts of their respective Queens and the Captal of Buch. The Duke of Brittany married Joan Holland, daughter of the Princess of Wales by her earlier marriage to Thomas, Earl of Kent.

War broke out in Spain between Don Pedro of Castile[2] and his illegitimate brother Henry, to whose support John of Bourbon and Bertrand du Guesclin led the companies of brigands who were still marauding in France. With their aid and that of a number of English knights, Henry the Bastard was crowned King of Castile, and Don Pedro was excommunicated for a wide variety of crimes, which included poisoning his wife (a first cousin of the Queen of France) and seizing church revenues. He fled to Corunna and Henry was crowned King at Burgos. In desperation, Don Pedro appealed to the Prince of Wales for help.

232

When the Prince of Wales heard of the arrival of Don Pedro's emissaries at Bordeaux, he sent for them to discover their business. On being presented, they fell on their knees and gave him Don Pedro's letter. The Prince read it twice, and found that Don Pedro gave a most pitiful account of his situation, and of how he had been driven out of the kingdom of Castile, his rightful inheritance, by his bastard brother, who had formed powerful alliances first with the Pope, and then with the Kings of Aragon and the French marauders. He begged the Prince in the name of

---

[1] *September 29th, 1364.*   [2] *Pedro IV, called the Cruel.*

God, to take pity on him and restore him; for it was by no means right for a Christian King to be disinherited and to lose his throne to a bastard.

The Prince told the ambassadors from Castile that they could stay at his court till he was ready to answer them; he then sent for his chief counsellors, Sir John Chandos and Sir William Felton, who were respectively high constable and steward of Aquitaine. 'My lords,' he said with a smile, 'here is great news from Spain. Our cousin Don Pedro is complaining of his brother Henry the Bastard, who has driven him out and usurped the throne. He implores us to comfort him and assist him.' The Prince then read the letter aloud to them, and asked their advice, since they were his chief counsellors. The two knights looked at each other without speaking. 'Speak out,' cried the Prince, 'whatever your opinion may be.'

According to my information, the two knights then advised the Prince of Wales to send troops to Corunna, where Don Pedro was, to escort him back to Bordeaux, so as to learn more fully his needs and intentions. They could then decide better how to act. The Prince agreed to this suggestion, and sent Sir William Felton with twelve vessels full of men-at-arms and archers, commanded by four knights, to escort Don Pedro and the remnants of his men from Corunna, in Galicia, back to Bordeaux. They set sail, and stopped for five days at Bayonne to revictual their ships and await a favourable wind. When they were on the point of leaving, Don Pedro arrived there in person, having left Corunna in great terror; not daring to stay there any longer, he had brought with him a few of his men, and as much of his treasure as he could manage. Sir William Felton explained the situation to Don Pedro, who was delighted, and accompanied him back to Bordeaux.

The Prince of Wales rode out of the town to meet him, as a mark of special honour, and greeted him with great respect and deference. After taking refreshment, they rode into the town together, and the Prince insisted that Don Pedro should ride on his right hand—indeed, no prince of this time was so well versed in good manners and chivalrous behaviour. As they rode, Don Pedro told the Prince all his troubles: how his bastard brother had usurped the throne, and of the disloyalty of his subjects who had all deserted him except for one knight, Don Fernando of Castro. The Prince comforted him with great courtesy, and begged him not to be too downhearted. For it lay in God's power to restore to him everything that he had lost, and to give him revenge over his enemies.

Don Pedro was given a room at the monastery of Saint Andrew, where the Prince and Princess were staying. Before his arrival, a number of knights, English as well as Gascons, who were in the privy council of the Prince, had felt bound to offer him their loyal advice, which they had done as follows: 'My lord, you have often heard the proverb "All covet, all lose."[1] It is true that you are the most enlightened, esteemed, and honoured prince in the world, that you possess large territories on this side of the sea, and that you are at peace, thanks to God, with everyone. And no king, far or near, is powerful enough to dare anger you, so famed are you for valour and good fortune. And so it is reasonable that you should be content with what you have, and not seek to make enemies. We would add that Don Pedro of Castile, now driven out of his country, is now, and has always been, a man of great pride, cruelty, and wickedness. Through him the kingdom of Castile has suffered many wrongs, and many valiant men have been beheaded and murdered without any just cause. It is to these wicked actions, ordered or connived at by himself, that Don Pedro owes the loss of his throne. He is also an enemy of the Church, and has been excommunicated by the Holy Father. He has had the reputation, for a long time, of being a tyrant, and has always, without any justification, made war on his neighbours, the Kings of Aragon and Navarre, whom he has tried to dethrone by force. It is also generally rumoured and believed that he murdered his young wife, your cousin, the Duke

---

[1] 'Qui trop embrace, mal estraint,' *or, as Lord Berners puts it, 'He that to moche embraseth, houldeth the wekelyer.'*

of Bourbon's daughter. Consider these things, and reflect on them. For everything that he has suffered since is merely God's punishment, which may serve as an example to other rulers not to act in the same way.'

Such was the advice given to the Prince before the arrival of Don Pedro; but the answer that he gave was as follows: 'My lords, I am sure that your advice is inspired by feelings of the deepest loyalty. I may say that I am already perfectly informed on the character and conduct of Don Pedro, and I am well aware of the innumerable crimes he has committed, and for which he is now suffering. The reason which now induces me to want to help him is this; it is neither right nor reasonable for a bastard to inherit and keep a throne, and to expel his brother, the rightful and legitimate heir. No king, nor son of a king, ought ever to allow it, for it is prejudicial to the whole principle of monarchy. Apart from that, my father and Don Pedro have long been bound by pacts and alliances, by which we are committed to giving him our support, should he require it.'

These were the reasons that induced the Prince to help Don Pedro, and to answer his counsellors as he did. No attempt to dissuade him could succeed, and by the time Don Pedro arrived at Bordeaux, the Prince was even more unshakeable and firm in his intentions. Don Pedro approached the Prince with deep humility, and gave him rich presents, as well as promising him various advantages for the future; he undertook, among other things, to make the Prince's eldest son, Edward, King of Galicia, and to share with the Prince and his followers the great riches he had left behind in Castile, which were so securely hidden that nobody else would be able to lay their hands on them. The Prince's followers heard these words with great delight, for both the English and the Gascons are by nature extremely eager for money. The Prince was advised to summon all the barons of Aquitaine to a special parliament at Bordeaux, at which Don Pedro could state his position, and also his resources for rewarding them if the Prince undertook to restore him to his throne. Letters were written, and messengers sent off to all parts. . . .

SUMMARY

232-234

After the conference at Bordeaux, King Edward was asked to agree to the proposals for assisting Don Pedro, which he did. The Prince of Wales, wishing to lead his men through the pass of Roncevalles into Spain, asked the King of Navarre for safe conduct through his country. The King of Navarre eventually agreed, in spite of having already made an alliance with Henry the Bastard. The Prince of Wales summoned those English knights who had until then sided with Henry, while the latter obtained the solid support of the King of Aragon. The Prince persuaded the Count of Foix to allow the Free Companies to pass through Foix on their way to join his army; he melted down two-thirds of his gold and silver plate, and sent for more money from England, realizing that to restore a king against the will of his people is far harder than to drive one out. He retained a thousand lances of the Count of Albret. The Viscount of Narbonne and other French lords attacked the Free Companies on their way to join the Prince, but were defeated at Montauban. The Pope forbade those knights who were captured by the Free Companies to pay their ransom money.

235

The Prince of Wales had by this time enlisted all the Free Companies on his side, to the number of twelve thousand. Having engaged their services, he also had to pay for their subsistence from the end of August to the beginning of February. He also enrolled men-at-arms from any other quarter where they were available. He could get none in France, for because of the alliance between the French King and Henry the Bastard, all the soldiers in France were Henry's men, as well as those companies from Brittany who were retained by Bertrand du Guesclin. The

Prince might have employed mercenaries from Flanders, Germany, and Brabant, had he wished; but he sent them away, preferring to rely on his own vassals and subjects rather than on foreigners. A large body of troops came over from England, for the King gave permission to his son John, Duke of Lancaster, to join the expedition with four hundred men-at-arms and four hundred archers, at which the Prince was naturally delighted.

At this point the Prince was visited at Bordeaux by James, King of Mallorca. He was King in name only, having no possessions; for the King of Aragon had taken him prisoner, and had put his father to death in prison at Barcelona. King James, who had married the Queen of Naples, came from there to Bordeaux to avenge his father's death and recover his inheritance. He was warmly received by the Prince, who on hearing of the reasons for his visit, and the wrongs done to him by the King of Aragon, said: 'My lord King, on our return from Spain our first task will be to restore you to the throne of Mallorca, either by diplomacy or, if necessary, by force.' The King was overjoyed at this, and remained with the Prince at Bordeaux, waiting for his departure for Spain. As a mark of respect, the Prince equipped him as lavishly as he could, since King James was both short of money and far from home.

All this time the Prince continued to receive reports of the disgraceful behaviour of the Free Companies from the districts where they were quartered. He would willingly have hastened his departure, as he was begged to do, had he not also been advised to wait until after Christmas, when the worst of the winter would be behind him. He was more ready to listen to this advice, since the Princess his wife was expecting a child, and was deeply saddened by the thought of his departure, and he did not want to leave before the birth of the child.

Meanwhile quantities of supplies were collected, for little enough would be available where they were going. It appears that the Prince then countermanded the thousand lances which the Lord of Albret was to have provided, and wrote to ask him, partly on grounds of economy and partly to guard their own lands, to dismiss eight hundred of the thousand, and bring a mere two hundred on the expedition.

The Lord of Albret was making strenuous preparations for the campaign, and was utterly astonished at the Prince's letter: 'What's this?' said he. 'The Prince is making fun of me. How can he ask me to dismiss eight hundred knights, whom I have retained expressly at his command, and prevented from gaining other honour and advantage elsewhere?' And he answered the Prince as follows: 'My dear lord, I am quite amazed by your letter, which I hardly know how to answer. If I do as you ask, it will be highly damaging to me and to all my men, whom I have engaged at your special request, and who are even now ready to serve you. I have stopped them from advancing themselves in a number of different ways. Some of them were on the point of making expeditions across the sea to Prussia, and some to Constantinople and Jerusalem, and they will be gravely displeased at being now left behind! They cannot understand, any more than I, how I have deserved such treatment from you. My dear lord, please understand that I cannot separate them one from another. I am the least and the humblest among them, and if any are to be sent away, all the rest will follow in sympathy, as God is my witness. May He keep you under His holy protection!'

The Prince of Wales found this answer very presumptuous, and many of his knights agreed with him. He shook his head and said: 'The Lord of Albret is very high and mighty, to disobey my instructions in my own country! By God, he is mistaken. He can stay here, if he likes, for we will succeed very well without him or his thousand lances.' Some of the English knights then observed: 'Sir, you do not know these Gascons very well yet, nor what a high opinion they have of themselves. They have had little respect for us for a long time. Do you not remember their arrogance when King John of France was first brought here to Bordeaux? They boasted quite openly that it was through them that you won the battle of Poitiers and captured the King of France. They wanted to go even further, it was quite clear. It took you four months of diplomacy before they allowed the King to be brought to England, and you had to give in to all their demands to keep them on your side.'

The Prince said nothing, but he did not forget what had happened. This was the beginning of the enmity between him and the Lord of Albret, who was from then on in great danger; for the Prince's temperament was proud and overbearing, and his hatred was bitter. Right or wrong, he was determined that any lord who was under his command should be subservient to him. But the Count of Armagnac, the Lord of Albret's uncle, heard of the quarrel between his nephew and the Prince, their lord, and came to Bordeaux. He saw the Prince, and Sir John Chandos and Sir Thomas Felton who were his chief counsellors. He arranged things with such diplomacy that the quarrel was settled, and the Prince said no more. But the Lord of Albret nevertheless received orders to bring no more than two hundred lances with him, which pleased neither him nor his men. They never again felt the same affection for the Prince as before, but they had to bear this annoyance as best they could, for they had no alternative.

236

Meanwhile the Princess of Wales gave birth to a son, at Bordeaux, on the feast of the Epiphany,[1] 1367. Two days later, he was baptized by the Archbishop of Bordeaux, his godfathers being the Bishop of Agen and the King of Mallorca. He was given the name Richard, and afterwards became King of England.

The following Sunday, the Prince set out to join the main part of his army at Dax,[2] in Gascony, where his brother the Duke of Lancaster arrived with his army after paying a visit to his sister-in-law at Bordeaux. The two brothers were overjoyed at seeing each other again, and shortly afterwards they were joined by the Count of Foix, who, outwardly at any rate, paid deep respect to the Prince, offering the service of himself and his vassals. For the

---

[1] *January 6th.*   [2] *About thirty miles north-east of Biarritz.*

period of his own absence, the Prince entrusted the government of his lands in France to the Count of Foix. It was then rumoured that the King of Navarre was making a new treaty with Henry the Bastard, which astonished the Prince and deeply discouraged Don Pedro. In view of these reports, Sir Hugh Calverly entered Navarre with his troops and took the cities of Miranda and Puente-la-Reina. The King of Navarre was enraged at this violation of his territory, and wrote to the Prince, who paid little attention, on the grounds that the King of Navarre had broken his treaty with Don Pedro. The Prince therefore wrote back to the King, asking him to come and explain in person the rumours mentioned above, or else to send a suitable deputy.

The King of Navarre, on being accused of treachery, was more furious than ever, and sent his special envoy, Don Martin de la Carra, to Dax. Don Martin spoke so eloquently that the Prince was satisfied, and a meeting with the King was arranged at Peyrehorade.[1] When he heard that the King had set out, the Prince sent the Duke of Lancaster and Sir John Chandos to meet him at Saint Jean Pied de Port, and the King, after being most courteously received, held a long conference with them. At the subsequent meeting with the Prince and Don Pedro, the original treaty made at Bayonne was renewed, and the King of Navarre then knew for certain what was to be allotted to him from the kingdom of Castile. Don Pedro and the King swore to preserve peace and friendship with each other, and they parted amicably, having settled that the Prince could at any time pass through Navarre with his troops, and that provisions would be available to them on payment. The King of Navarre returned to Pamplona, and Don Pedro and the Prince to Dax.

A number of great barons in Poitou, Brittany, and Gascony had until then hesitated before joining the Prince, doubting if he would secure a free passage through Navarre. But after this pact had been made, they hastened to join their friends who were already with the Prince. Last, and most unwillingly, came the

---

[1] *Twelve miles south of Dax.*

Lord of Albret with his two hundred lances, accompanied by the Captal of Buch. Bertrand du Guesclin quickly set off to rejoin Henry the Bastard, followed by men-at-arms of all ranks.

237

Between Saint Jean Pied de Port and Pamplona lie the ravines and canyons of Navarre, which are most dangerous to pass through, for there are a hundred places among them where a whole army could be held up by thirty men. And since the army set out in the middle of February, it was bitterly cold. In order to pass through at all, the army had to split up into three divisions; the vanguard was under the Duke of Lancaster, with Sir John Chandos, and twelve hundred pennons, and they passed through on a Monday. Next day the Prince went through with the King of Navarre and Don Pedro, followed by at least four thousand men-at-arms. The march on the Tuesday was made still more unpleasant and difficult by the piercing wind and the snow; however, they crossed the mountains and reached Pamplona, where the King of Navarre royally entertained the Prince and Don Pedro to dinner. Next day the third division made the crossing, under the King of Mallorca, accompanied by the Count of Armagnac, the Lord of Albret, the Count of Périgord and all the independent companies, amounting to ten thousand horse. They had rather better weather for their crossing, and all those divisions encamped for a week in the Vale of Pamplona, where they found abundant provisions of every kind for themselves and their horses.

The Free Companies could not be restrained from pillaging, as they had always done in the past, and the King of Navarre was very angry at the damage that they did; he regretted, more than once, ever having opened his frontiers, but by then the harm had been done. However, as a result of his entreaties, the pillaging was less severe than would otherwise have been the case.

Henry the Bastard was kept informed of this advance by his spies, and raised troops as fast as he could in Castile, of which he now called himself King. Since he was very popular in the country, his vassals willingly obeyed his call, and troops flocked to the rallying-point, which he had fixed at San Domingo de la Calçada. Once he knew for certain that the Prince had come through the gorge of Roncesvalles with his army, he knew equally beyond all doubt that there would be a battle. And in order to let the Prince know that he was ready and waiting to defend his right, he wrote him the following letter:

'To the most mighty and honourable lord, the Prince of Wales and Aquitaine.

'We have heard that you have crossed the mountains at the head of your army, and have made alliances with our enemies, to take the field against us. This fills us with astonishment. For we have never harboured hostile intentions against you of any kind that would justify your advance on us, and your intention of taking from us what little inheritance God has given us. But since you are the most powerful and fortunate prince in the world, we hope that you glory in your strength. And since we know for sure that you are seeking battle with us, if you will have the kindness to inform us by which road you will enter Castile, we will come to meet you in the defence of our realm. Given, etc.'

When the Prince received this letter, he exclaimed: 'Truly, this bastard Henry is a bold and valiant knight to write me such a letter.' He could not agree with his council on what answer to give, and the herald was told to wait until it suited the Prince to reply. Sir William Felton was permitted to go ahead to reconnoitre the enemy position, and with him went a hundred and sixty lances and three hundred archers. A number of knights accompanied him, including Sir Hugh Stafford, Sir Simon Burleigh and Sir Richard Canston, none of them men to be forgotten. They advanced into the kingdom of Navarre under the direction of guides, as far as Logrono, on the river Ebro, which is deep and rapid at that point. After crossing it they encamped at a village called Navarretta, to learn King Henry's situation, and the strength of his army.

238

Meanwhile the King of Navarre was taken prisoner by a French knight, Olivier de Mauny,[1] while riding between two towns on the French side of his country. The Prince and the English were astonished, and some people thought that the King of Navarre had purposely allowed himself to be captured, not wishing to accompany the Prince of Wales any further in view of the previous alliance he had made with King Henry and the King of Aragon. At any rate, his Queen was much alarmed and distressed, until the Prince of Wales most gallantly comforted her. . . .

SUMMARY

238-241

The Prince of Wales advanced to Salvatierra, and Sir William Felton skirmished with the enemy while the two main armies approached each other. Bertrand du Guesclin arrived to support King Henry, whose brother, Don Tello, attacked the Prince's vanguard, and defeated Sir William Felton and his men.

Sir Arnold of Andreghen advised King Henry to starve out the Prince's army by preventing their supplies from crossing the mountains. The Prince answered King Henry's letter, explaining his reasons for supporting Don Pedro. The two armies met outside Navarretta, and Sir John Chandos was made a knight banneret.

241

. . . The sun rose on a wonderful scene: banners fluttered in the breeze, and the armour of the knights glittered in the sunlight: all the various banners and pennons, and the noble army beneath them, were a real delight to see. The armies began to move

---

[1] *A Breton and a supporter of King Henry.*

forward but, before they met, the Prince of Wales looked up to heaven, and joined his hands in prayer:

'True Father of Jesus Christ, Who hast created me, grant by Thy merciful grace that victory may attend me and my people this day; for Thou knowest that it was in the support of justice and reason, to restore this King to the throne from which he was driven, that I was bold enough to undertake this battle.'

After this prayer, he offered his right hand to Don Pedro and said: 'Sir, you will find out today whether you will ever hold anything in the kingdom of Castile.' Then he cried: 'Advance, banners, in the name of Saint George!'

The two armies advanced and the battalion of the Duke of Lancaster and Sir John Chandos engaged that of Bertrand du Guesclin and the Marshal of Andreghen, who had at least four thousand men-at-arms under them. At the first onslaught, there was a terrible clash of spears on shields, and it was some time before either side could make any impression on the other. Great feats of arms were performed, and many knights were un-horsed, never to rise again. The other battalions were not slow to join in the fray, and the Prince of Wales, accompanied by Don Pedro, and by Don Martin de la Carra, who represented the King of Navarre, attacked the battalion of Don Tello and Don Sancho. But when the Prince attacked this battalion, Don Tello suddenly panicked and fled in disorder, without striking a blow, taking with him two thousand cavalry. This flight was never explained, but the battalion no sooner fled than it was destroyed, for the Captal of Buch and the Lord of Clisson and their men fell upon the infantry of Don Tello's battalion and killed and wounded them in immense numbers.

The battalion under the Prince and Don Pedro then attacked King Henry's position, which was held by over forty thousand infantry and cavalry; and the battle raged fiercely on every side. The Spaniards and men of Castile used slings that threw stones with such force they could split a helmet in half, and many of their enemies were brought down. The English archers retaliated with devastating effect. The battle cry of 'Castile for King

Henry!' was answered by 'Saint George for Guyenne!' The French and Aragonese under Bertrand du Guesclin stoutly resisted the English attack.

Sir John Chandos showed exceptional bravery under his banner, and forged so far ahead into the fray that he was surrounded by the enemy and unhorsed. A huge man of Castile, Martin Ferrans by name, whose boldness and courage were far-famed, attacked Sir John, determined to kill him. But Sir John had not forgotten a knife that he had under his chain-mail; he now drew it and stabbed his attacker to death, when the latter was already on top of him. Sir John jumped up and his men rallied round him.

This bloody and terrible battle was fought between Najarra and Navarretta[1] .... Those nearest King Henry fought like men, following his own example. But when one company began to turn and run, he called out to them: 'My lords, I am your King. You have put me on the throne of Castile, and sworn that you would rather die than abandon me. In God's name keep your oath to me, and do for me what I would do for you: for I will not give a yard as long as I see you at my side.'

With these and similar words, King Henry thrice rallied his men, and by his own conduct in the field added greatly to the honour of his men.

Many were killed, wounded, and put to flight in this great battle. The English at first suffered severely from the Spanish slingers, who, however, soon became disorganized under the heavy fire of the archers. King Henry's men fought well, but the English and Gascons were the more experienced fighters. Indeed the Prince had with him the flower of chivalry, and the most renowned fighting men in the world. They all fought with all their might, as indeed was necessary. For from Spain and Castile there were nearly a thousand armed men, whose great numbers gave them encouragement; and indeed, in that great host there

[1] *Here follows a list of the knights on each side who were most conspicuous in the battle.*

were inevitably some good fighters who gave of their best. Don Pedro was beside himself in his anxiety to find his brother, and galloped about crying: 'Where is this son of a whore, who calls himself King of Castile?'

On the Spanish side, the division under Bertrand du Guesclin fought the best. For the English, Sir John Chandos was particularly to the fore, attending the Duke of Lancaster as he had attended the Prince at Poitiers, for which he received, not undeservedly, the highest praise. During the whole day, he never thought of taking prisoners on his own account, but gave his whole attention to fighting. But his men took innumerable prisoners, and all those who came from France and Aragon were either captured or killed. And through answering loyally to the rallying cry of King Henry, instead of putting their own survival first, more than fifteen hundred of his followers lost their lives.

After the defeat of Bertrand du Guesclin's battalion, the three English battalions joined forces and the Spaniards were no longer able to withstand them. They broke their ranks, and fled in disorder towards Najarra and the river that runs past that town. And when he saw that all his rousing words were in vain and that his men were defeated, King Henry galloped away not towards the town, where he might have been surrounded, but along another road. In this he showed his wisdom, for had he been captured he would have been killed without mercy. The English and Gascons fell pitilessly on the fleeing Spaniards, many of whom leaped into the river, which was both swift and deep, preferring to be drowned to being run through. The Grand Prior of Santiago and the Master of the Order of Calatrava, two monks who were also valiant men-at-arms, took refuge in Najarra in the course of this rout, but the English and Gascons took the town and pillaged it, gaining great riches in the process. For the Spaniards had come there in great state, and had had no opportunity after the battle to secure their property. Their defeat was complete and terrible, especially on the banks of the river, which I have heard was quite discoloured with the blood of their men and horses. This battle was fought on Saturday, April 3rd,

1367; on the Spanish side five hundred and sixty men-at-arms were killed, and seventy-five hundred soldiers of the ranks, not counting those who were drowned. But on the English side only forty soldiers were killed, and four knights.[1]

SUMMARY

242-245

Following this battle, Don Pedro was once more acknowledged King by the whole of Castile; he asked the Prince of Wales to stay at Valladolid while he procured money to pay the Prince for his army.

King Henry took refuge, along with his family, with the King of Aragon at Valencia, and later, after conferring with the Duke of Anjou at Montpellier, made war on Aquitaine with the aid of some of the Free Companies. Don Pedro was unable to raise money for the Prince, and complained that the Prince's Free Companies made his task impossible. The Prince, after spending the hottest months of the summer at Valladolid, grew unwell and retreated, in great displeasure with Don Pedro, to Aquitaine.

King Henry retired to Aragon, and the Prince's Free Companies entered France. The Barons of Gascony, Poitou and Aquitaine complained to the King of France about '*forage*,'[2] a new hearth-tax imposed by the Prince. King Henry advanced to Burgos, where the gates were at once opened to him, as they were soon after at Valladolid. The whole of Galicia returned to his side, and he was joined by an army of two thousand under Bertrand du Guesclin, lately ransomed. The whole of Spain wavered in its new allegiance to Don Pedro, who however collected, from the Kings of Portugal and Granada, an army of forty thousand, composed of Jews and Saracens as well as Christians.

---

[1] *These figures seem highly improbable in view of Froissart's account of the fighting.*
[2] *Levied on every chimney or household fire in his dominions.*

245

. . . News reached King Henry, who was besieging the city of Toledo, that Don Pedro was advancing on him with an army of forty thousand assorted troops. At the council that King Henry called, Bertrand du Guesclin advised him to advance on Don Pedro with as many troops as could be spared from the siege, with a view to taking Don Pedro's army by surprise on the road. King Henry willingly left his brother, Don Tello, in charge of the siege, and set off after Don Pedro. He had spies on the move everywhere, who reported to him the details of Don Pedro's movements and the condition of his army.

Don Pedro had no idea of his brother's intentions, and his army advanced slowly and without much order. After being hospitably entertained at the castle of Montiel, Don Pedro had set out very early in the morning, and was advancing in his usual haphazard order, not expecting to fight that day, when he was suddenly confronted with King Henry, with his brother Don Sancho, Bertrand du Guesclin, and his other commanders advancing with banners flying, fully prepared for action, and followed by six thousand men. They advanced in close order, at full gallop, and fell heavily on Don Pedro's van, with cries of 'Castile for King Henry!' and 'Our Lady for Guesclin!' They overthrew and defeated the vanguard, carrying all before them, and killing and bringing down a large number. No prisoners were taken, on the instructions of Bertrand du Guesclin, in view of the great number of Jews and infidels in Don Pedro's army.

Don Pedro himself, who was advancing with the largest division, was amazed to hear of the sudden defeat of his van, and saw that he was in danger of losing everything, for his troops were widely scattered. But like the bold and resourceful knight that he was, he planted his banner, for his troops to rally to, and sent orders for the rear to join him with all speed, for the engagement had begun. This they did, and the battle became more general.

Many of Don Pedro's army were unhorsed, and killed, so valiantly did King Henry and his men acquit themselves. However, the battle was not over at once, for Don Pedro's men were six to King Henry's one, but Don Pedro had been taken quite unawares, and suffered the most terrible losses.

Among the many valiant knights on King Henry's side were a number from Aragon, including the Viscount of Rocaberti. And there were some outlandish folk among their opponents, such as Saracens and Portuguese: the Jewish contingent soon took to their heels, but the men from Granada and Benmarin made good use of their bows and lances, while in their midst Don Pedro laid about him with his battle-axe to such good effect that none dared come near him.

King Henry made a frontal attack on his brother's army in close order, and his men cried out loudly and attacked vigorously, so that Don Pedro's lines began to falter, and his chief lieutenant, Don Fernando of Castro, soon saw that they would lose the day, so unnerved was their army by the suddenness of the attack. He therefore advised Don Pedro to retire to the Castle of Montiel, which he had left that morning, and where he might again be safe, whereas if he were captured on the field, no mercy would be shown him. Don Pedro followed this advice, and when he arrived there with a mere eleven followers, he found the gates of the castle open. But even after this, the Saracens in his army, who were quite unfamiliar with the country, and were just as ready to die in the field as to endure a long pursuit, kept up the fight and sold their lives dearly.

King Henry and Sir Bertrand were delighted by the report that Don Pedro had retired to Montiel, and they advanced on the castle, killing whoever they came on with animal ferocity, until they were exhausted with the slaughter. They pursued the fugitives for nearly ten miles, and over twenty-four thousand men were killed in all.[1] The very few who escaped were local in-

[1] *Another text of Froissart says that 'the pursuit lasted over three hours, and over fourteen thousand men were killed or wounded.'*

habitants who knew the country. The battle was fought below Montiel on August 13th, 1368.

King Henry and Sir Bertrand encamped below the castle, and surrounded it with their men, sending the main part of their army back to Toledo to reinforce Don Tello. Montiel was a strong enough castle to have held out a long time if it had had enough provisions. On Don Pedro's arrival, however, to his great sorrow, there was only enough food for four days, and the castle was so closely watched that not even a bird could have escaped from it unobserved.

Don Pedro fully realized that there was no question of coming to terms with his enemies, and in view of the lack of provisions in the castle, and his generally dangerous situation, he decided to try to escape from the castle at midnight with his eleven companions, putting his trust in God. The night was dark and thick, and the watch was kept by the Bègue[1] de Villaines, who had three hundred men under him. Don Pedro and his men left the castle, and advanced down a path so quietly that they hardly made a sound. The Bègue, however, was very much on the alert, in his anxiety not to lose the whole object of his watch, and thought he heard the sound of footsteps on the path. 'Keep still, my lords,' he ordered. 'I hear someone, we will soon know who it is. It may be men with provisions, for they are very short of food in the castle.' The Bègue advanced, dagger in hand, with his men behind him, and challenged a man very close to Don Pedro. 'Who are you? Speak, or you are a dead man.' The man addressed, who was English, refused to answer, and dashed forward. The Bègue let him pass, and next addressed Don Pedro, whom he examined carefully, and thought he recognized, in spite of the darkness, by his resemblance to his brother King Henry. He put his dagger to Don Pedro's chest, and asked: 'And who are you? Tell me, or die.' With these words he took hold of the horse's bridle to prevent him from escaping.

---

[1] *This title does not occur elsewhere, but it presumably indicates some minor local lord or commander of troops.*

Don Pedro saw the large number of men before him, and saw that there was no escape. He said: 'I am Don Pedro, King of Castile, and much harm has been attributed to me by those who wish me ill. I give myself up, with my men, as your prisoners. I beg you to put me in a place of safety, and you may have whatever ransom you ask, for thank God I still have enough, if you keep me from falling into the hands of Henry the Bastard.' The Bègue replied, according to my information, that he could come in safety, and that Henry would know nothing of what had happened. They set off for the Bègue's lodgings, and had not been there an hour when they were joined by King Henry and the Viscount of Rocaberti, with a few of their men.

On coming into the room where Don Pedro was confined, King Henry asked: 'Where is that son of a Jewish whore who calls himself King of Castile?' Don Pedro, who was fearless as well as cruel, replied: 'It is you who are the son of a whore—I am the son of King Alfonso.' And with these words he set hands on King Henry and began to wrestle with him, and being the stronger, he forced King Henry down onto a couch. He reached for his knife and would have killed King Henry had not the Viscount of Rocaberti seized Don Pedro's foot and turned him over, with the result that King Henry, now having the upper hand, drew his long dagger and plunged it into Don Pedro's body. His attendants then rushed into the room and made short work of Don Pedro. With him was killed an English knight called Sir Ralph Holmes (who was called the Green Squire) and a squire called James Rowland, who had come to his defence. But no harm was done to Don Fernando of Castro and the rest of Don Pedro's men, who remained the prisoners of the Bègue de Villaines and Sir Yon de Laconet.

So perished Don Pedro of Castile, who had once ruled in such prosperity. His body was left lying on the spot for three days, which on grounds of humanity seems to me much to be regretted. The news of his death soon spread abroad to the delight of his enemies and the anger of his friends. But when the news reached his cousin the King of Portugal, he was greatly enraged, and swore vengeance. He immediately sent a challenge to King Henry, and made war on him, occupying the outskirts of Seville for a whole season. This however did not prevent King Henry from pursuing his own ends: he returned to Toledo, which soon surrendered to him, along with the rest of the country. Even the King of Portugal did not wish to continue the war for long, and soon came to terms. After this King Henry ruled over Castile in peace. A number of knights from France and Brittany remained with him, including Bertrand du Guesclin and Olivier de Mauny; he treated them handsomely, as was indeed their due, for without their help he would never have achieved his object. Bertrand du Guesclin was made Constable of Spain, and granted the estate of Soria, which was worth twenty thousand florins a year, and his nephew Sir Olivier was given the estate of Crecte, valued at half that sum. The other knights were also liberally rewarded. The Kings of France and Aragon were delighted by the outcome of the war, as was the Duke of Anjou.

About this time occurred the death of Lionel, Duke of Clarence, who had joined his brother's expedition and married the daughter of Galeas Visconti, the ruler of Milan. As his death did not appear to have been natural, his companion, Sir Edward Despencer, declared war on Galeas and killed many of his subjects. But in the end they were reconciled by the Count of Savoy.

SUMMARY

246-247

The lords of Gascony, who were less ready than those of Poitou and Saintonge to submit to the taxes imposed by the Prince of Wales, appealed again to the King of France, although it was indicated to them that they had no right of appeal to anyone except the King of England. The French king was unwilling to take any action that would lead to war, but on re-examining the terms of the Peace of Brétigny he was persuaded that he had a good case. He therefore summoned the Prince of Wales to appear before the Parliament of Paris.

The summons was taken to the Prince at Bordeaux and read out to him by two emissaries.

248

When the Prince heard the French King's letter read out, he was completely amazed, and shook his head, looking fiercely at the Frenchmen. After a few minutes' thought he replied: 'We shall willingly attend on the appointed day at Paris, since the King of France commands it, but it will be with our helmet on our head, and sixty thousand men behind us.'

At this, the Frenchmen went down on their knees and said: 'Dear Sir, have mercy, for God's sake, and do not be too angry at this request. We are only messengers sent by our lord the King to whom we owe all obedience, as your own subjects do to you. In bringing you this request we are only following his instructions, and any reply you give us we will willingly take back to him.'

'No,' said the Prince, 'it is not to you that I bear any ill will, it is to those who sent you. Your King has been ill advised to meddle with our subjects and to set himself up as judge in matters that do not concern him and over which he has no jurisdiction. It will be shown him quite clearly that when he gave possession of the Duchy of Aquitaine to my father, he surrendered all his rights without exception; all those who are now appealing against us have no other court to appeal to except the court of England, to our lord and father. And it will cost a hundred thousand lives to change the position.'

With these words the Prince went to his room, leaving the Frenchmen speechless. Some English knights then advised them to leave, as their message had been delivered, and they would receive no other answer. The Frenchmen later set out for Toulouse, to inform the Duke of Anjou of what they had done. . . .

SUMMARY

249-271

The Prince of Wales, on second thought, had the Frenchmen overtaken and imprisoned on a spurious charge. The French King was indignant at all that had happened, and although fully aware of the risk involved in war with England, he was reluctantly forced into it by the lords of Gascony and Guyenne, and by the continual damage done by the English in his realm.

The Dukes of Berry and Bourbon, and other French hostages, had returned to France from London; the Duke of Bourbon had earned his release by obtaining from Pope Urban the bishopric of Winchester for King Edward's chaplain, and close adviser, William of Wykeham.

The Prince of Wales's health grew worse, and he sent for Sir John Chandos, whom he installed at Montauban.

The French King sent his defiance to King Edward by a kitchen servant, which greatly offended him. Ponthieu and Abbéville were reconquered by the French before King Edward could defend them. Sir Guiscard d'Angle, on his return from Rome, joined the Prince of Wales.

King Edward strengthened the garrisons along the Scots border and the South Coast. The Dukes of Berry and Anjou ordered their vassals to attack the Prince of Wales, who at the King's orders was joined by the Earls of Cambridge and Pembroke at Angoulême. Fighting broke out in Quercy, Périgord, and Languedoc. Cahors and several neighbouring towns joined the French.

The Dukes of Guelders[1] and Juliers sent their challenges to the King of France, whose brother, the Duke of Burgundy, had married the daughter of the Count of Flanders. Sir Robert Knolles was appointed commander of the Prince of Wales's men, and with Sir John Chandos and others captured Gramat, Rocamadour and Villefranche, but failed to take Durmel or Domme.

The Earls of Cambridge and Pembroke captured Bourdeilles,[2] and

---

[1] *Son of Edward III's sister.*   [2] *In Périgord.*

the Free Companies took Belleperche,[1] where the mother of the Queen of France and the Duchess of Bourbon was living. An English force including Sir James Audley, captured La Roche-sur-Yon, on the borders of Anjou. The Duke of Lancaster came to Calais, and the Duke of Burgundy encamped opposite him, at Tournehem. Sir John Chandos laid waste Anjou, and the young Earl of Pembroke was besieged at Puirenon in Poitou.

272-3

Between six and nine o'clock in the morning, when the attack reached its fiercest point, the French grew indignant at the stubbornness of the English defence and at their own failure to win the day. They sent to the neighbouring villages for pickaxes and mattocks to undermine the house in which the English had taken refuge, for it had no moat and was enclosed by only a stone wall. This was what the English were most afraid of, and the Earl of Pembroke drew aside one of his most trusted squires, and said to him: 'My friend, get on my horse and leave by the back gate, which we will open for you. Ride flat out for Poitiers, tell Sir John Chandos the danger that we are in, and give him this ring for me as a token—he will recognize it at once.' He took a gold ring from his finger and gave it to the squire, who was much honoured by this commission, jumped on the fastest horse he could find and set off by the back gate for Poitiers. The French did not let up but continued their attack with great vigour, which was only equalled by the English defence; this was indeed necessary, or the English would not have held out for two hours.

Another squire had previously been sent off from Puirenon to Poitiers, at about midnight, but had lost his way in the dark, and found it only at dawn, by which time his horse was tiring. He did not reach Poitiers until nine o'clock, and found Sir John Chandos at mass. Kneeling down beside him, he delivered his message; but Sir John, who was still vexed with the Earl of Pembroke for

[1] *On the Garonne.*

having refused to join him on an earlier expedition, was not particularly inclined to help him, and merely replying 'We could hardly reach him in time' heard the rest of the mass. After mass, tables were laid and dinner prepared. Sir John was asked if he would dine. 'Yes, since it is ready,' was the reply. He went into the hall, where knights and squires had gone ahead with water to wash his hands. While he was washing, the Earl of Pembroke's second messenger arrived, who went up to Sir John with the gold ring and said: 'Dear sir, by this token the Earl of Pembroke recommends himself to you, and begs you to come to his assistance and rescue him from the great danger that he is in at Puirenon.'

Sir John Chandos took the ring and, recognizing it, answered: 'It will hardly be possible for us to reach him in time if he is in the situation that you describe. Come, let us dine. Even if they are all captured or killed, we must still have our dinner.'

Sir John and the others finished the first course. When the second course was brought, and they had already begun to eat it, Sir John, who had been wrapped in thought, looked up at his men and to their delight spoke as follows: 'The Earl of Pembroke is a lord of high birth and long lineage; he has married the King's own daughter, he is a brother in arms, as in all else, with my lord of Cambridge. He entreats me so earnestly that I must grant his request and go to his aid if there is still time.' He then pushed the table back and said 'To horse! To horse! I am going to Puirenon.' These words were heard with joy, and all his men put on their armour. Trumpets sounded, and every man-at-arms in Poitiers mounted as best he could. Word soon went round that Sir John Chandos was going to the aid of the Earl of Pembroke, and in the end he was followed by over two hundred lances, their numbers increasing all the time.

The news of Sir John's approach soon reached the French at Puirenon, who had kept up the pressure of their attack from dawn right up to midday. The most sensible of the French captains then took the view that their men were worn out by the relentless attack to which they had been subjecting the English, and decided to retreat, with their prisoners and the rest of the spoils that they had captured, rather than to have to face the onslaught of Sir John Chandos and his fresh troops.

Seeing their retreat, the Earl of Pembroke and his men said to each other: 'Chandos must be on the march; for the French are retreating, and dare not wait for him. Quick, quick, let us leave this place, let us head for Poitiers and meet him.' This they did as best they could, some on foot, some on horseback, and some riding two on the same horse. They had scarcely gone two miles before they met Sir John Chandos; great joy was shown on both sides at the meeting, but Sir John was very angry at having missed the French. After riding together for nearly ten miles, Sir John returned to Poitiers, and Pembroke to Mortagne.

We will now turn to the death of the most noble, generous, and gracious queen of her time, Philippa of Hainault, Queen of England and Ireland.[1]

'. . . The good Queen of England, that so many good deeds had done in her time, and so many knights succoured, and ladies and damosels comforted, and had so largely departed of her goods to her people, and naturally loved always the nation of Hainault, the country where she was born; she fell sick in the Castle of Windsor, the which sickness continued in her so long that there was no remedy but death. And the good lady, when she knew and perceived that there was with her no remedy but death, she desired to speak with the King her husband. And when he was before her she put out of her bed her right hand and took the King by his right hand, who was right sorrowful at his heart. Then she said: "Sir, we have in peace, joy, and great prosperity used all our time together. Sir, now, I pray you, at our departing, that ye will grant me three desires." The King, right sorrowfully weeping, said, "Madam, desire what ye will, I grant it." "Sir," said she, "I require you, first of all, that all manner of people such as

---

[1] *This passage is stylistically one of the gems of Lord Berners' translation, and is given in full. For the sake of clarity, the spelling has been modernised, though some of the original flavour is thereby lost.*

I have dealt withal in their merchandise, on this side of the sea or beyond, that it may please you to pay everything that I owe to them, or to any other. And secondly, sir, all such ordinance and promises as I have made to the churches as well in this country as beyond the sea, whereas I have had my devotion, that it may please you to accomplish and to fulfil the same. Thirdly, sir, I require you that it may please you to take none other sepulchre, whensoever it shall please God to call you out of this transitory life, but beside me in Westminster." The King, all weeping, said, "Madam, I grant all your desire." Then the good lady and Queen made on her the sign of the cross, and commended the King her husband to God, and her youngest son, Thomas, who was there beside her. And anon, after she yielded up the spirit, the which I believe surely the holy angels received with great joy up to heaven, for in all her life she did neither in thought nor deed thing whereby to lese her soul, as far as any creature could know. Thus the good Queen of England died in the year of Our Lord 1369, in the vigil of Our Lady in the middle of August.'

SUMMARY

274-277

In France, the abbey of Saint Salvin in Poitou was delivered up to the French, who garrisoned it. The Duke of Lancaster rode through Picardy and Normandy to Harfleur, and then returned to Calais. The English captured Sir Hugh de Chatillon, captain of Abbéville.

278

Sir John Chandos was enraged by the capture of Saint Salvin, as he was at that time seneschal of Poitou. He racked his brains to find some method of recapturing it, but Sir Louis of Saint Julien defended it successfully against all the attacks that he made on it. On New Year's Eve, Sir John was reinforced by Sir Guiscard d'Angle, Sir Thomas Percy, and nine other knights with three hundred men under them who had left Poitiers by night. No one except the lords who led them knew where they were going, but they brought scaling ladders and all the other necessary equipment with them. When they reached Saint Salvin they left their horses with the grooms and entered the dike surrounding the town at about midnight. In this situation they would very soon have achieved their object, when suddenly they heard the watchman of the fortress sound his horn. The reason for this was that a French knight had come from La Roche Posay to ask Sir Louis to join him on an expedition; but the English were not to know that this party of Frenchmen had arrived, and thought that they themselves had been seen by the guard. They therefore rode off to Chamigny, about five miles off, and from there Sir John Chandos and Sir Thomas Percy advanced towards Poitiers with their troops. On the way, however, they met the French contingent from Saint Salvin, and Sir John was determined to attack the French, of whom he thought very poorly. He called out to them scornfully, and finished by saying: 'Sir Louis, Sir Louis, and you, Keranlouet, you have become too much the masters. For more than a year and a half I have been trying to meet you, and now, thank God, I have. We will soon see which of us is the stronger in this land, you or I. I have often heard that you wanted to see me, and now that pleasure is yours. I am John Chandos, look at me well. Now, if God wills, we will put to the test your feats of arms that are so renowned.'

The French closed their ranks, and Sir John's banner advanced before him. Sir John wore a long robe down to the ground, emblazoned back and front with his arms, argent, a pile gules. Sword in hand, he advanced on foot to meet the enemy. The night before, there had been a frost, and the ground was slippery; and as he advanced, his feet became entangled in his robes, and he stumbled. At this moment a strong and bold knight, Jacques de Saint Martin by name, struck him a blow on the cheek with his lance. It so happened that Sir John had lost the sight of one eye in an accident while stag-hunting in the heaths round Bordeaux, five years before; and he did not see the blow coming. Worse still, he had not lowered his vizor, and in stumbling he fell into the blow of the lance, which penetrated as far as the brain. He fell to the ground in acute pain and rolled over twice in his agony, like a dying man. And indeed, after that blow, he never spoke again.

His followers, seeing what had happened, were like madmen. His uncle Sir Edward Clifford, leapt up and stood over his body, which the French were trying to take. He defended it so valiantly that no one dare come within reach of his sword. When the battle was over, and the superior numbers of the French and Bretons had prevailed, the latter were unable to leave the field with their prisoners, since their servants had already retired with the horses. Whereupon two hundred supporters of the English from Poitou under Sir Guiscard d'Angle arrived on the scene, and the French surrendered. The knights of Poitou were horrified to see Sir John Chandos in this state, and cried out, lamenting their loss: 'Oh, flower of knighthood, Sir John Chandos, curse the forging of the spear which has put you in danger of death.' All those around him lamented his state, and though he could hear them, he could not articulate a word in reply, but merely groaned. His servants gently removed his armour and carried him at a walking pace to Mortemer. Jacques de Saint Martin was himself so severely wounded in the battle that he died at Poitiers, and Sir John lived only a day and a night. God have mercy on his soul! For never in a hundred years was there an English knight so noble, so courteous, and so full of every virtue and good quality.

When the Prince of Wales and his knights in Guyenne heard the news, they were quite shattered, and said that they had now lost everything on both sides of the sea. Sir John was indeed a supreme loss to the English, for by his valour and wisdom the whole of Guyenne might have been recovered.

SUMMARY

279-327

King Edward sent a letter to Aquitaine, forbidding the Prince of Wales to levy taxes and charges on the inhabitants, for fear of their joining the French, and giving orders that all money previously collected in this way should be repaid. The letter was ignored.

Here ends Book I of the Chronicles, but the beginning of Book II covers some of the same ground again, in more detail. This was because each book was originally a separate work, and the first book originally contained a summary of the events down to 1397, part of which was omitted when the first and second books were put together. In addition to this, a large part of the first book was completely rewritten, twice, after its first production.

BOOK II

Book II

The wars in France from 1370 to 1375 are gone into in minute detail by Froissart, but as they consisted of small individual campaigns of the sort with which the reader is now quite familiar, they are only sum-marized here briefly.

SUMMARY

1-11

The Duke of Bourbon besieged and recaptured the castle of Belle-perche, where his mother was held prisoner, but not before she had been removed to another castle by the Earls of Pembroke and Cam-bridge. The French King and his three brothers, the Dukes of Anjou, Berry, and Burgundy, decided to make an expedition with two armies into Aquitaine, and besiege the Prince of Wales in Angoulême; also to recall Bertrand du Guesclin and appoint him Constable of France. Various preparations were made on the English as well as the French side, and the Duke of Bourbon's mother was exchanged for Sir Simon Burley. The French King made peace with his brother-in-law, the King of Navarre.

Bertrand du Guesclin came up from Leon, in Spain, to Toulouse, where he joined the Duke of Anjou; they took a number of castles from the English. The Duke of Berry invaded Limousin.

A truce was made between England and Scotland, and Sir Robert Knolles, reinforced by some Scottish mercenaries, ravaged the whole of Vermandois and Picardy, but after burning Pont l'Evêque, suffered losses at Noyon. The King of France sent for Bertrand du Guesclin. The Prince of Wales joined his brother the Duke of Lancaster at

Cognac, and though his health was so bad that he had to be carried in a litter, the Prince captured Limoges by undermining the walls, and brutally massacred the inhabitants.

Bertrand du Guesclin, now Constable of France, defeated Sir Robert Knolles at Pont Valin, in Anjou. The Prince of Wales's eldest son, Edward, died at Bordeaux in 1372, and the Prince returned to England for his health, leaving Aquitaine under the Duke of Lancaster, who captured Montpont and then returned to Bordeaux. Various knights in Poitou turned against the English, but those who remained loyal captured Montcontour. Usson, in Auvergne, was taken by Bertrand du Guesclin. Peace was made between England and Flanders, after heavy losses had been inflicted on Flemish shipping.

King James of Mallorca was ransomed from King Henry of Spain, but died after declaring war on the King of Aragon. The Duke of Lancaster married the elder daughter of the late King Pedro of Spain, whereupon King Henry made a new treaty with the King of France. The Duke of Lancaster returned to England to report to the King, who in 1372 made the Earl of Pembroke Governor of Aquitaine and Poitou. The King of France sent a Spanish fleet to intercept him off La Rochelle, and the English were totally defeated (June 23rd). Lord Pembroke and Sir Guiscard d'Angle were captured and brought before King Henry in Spain.

Owen of Wales landed in Guernsey and defeated the English. Bertrand du Guesclin took Montcontour and Saint Sévère; Poitiers and La Rochelle went over to the French, who also recovered the whole of Poitou and Saintonge.

In Brittany, the English were besieged at Becherel, and Bertrand du Guesclin led an expedition that reconquered nearly all of Brittany for the French, despite strenuous efforts on the English side. In Gascony, the Duke of Anjou captured several towns, and negotiations at Bruges ended in a truce, to last for one year.

In 1376 the Prince of Wales died, and King Edward III survived him by only a year. The King of France subsequently sent a large navy to attack the English coast, and war broke out again between France and Navarre. The Duke of Anjou won many successes against the English, particularly in Gascony.

The Scots captured Berwick, but the English regained it under the

Earl of Northumberland. The Queen of France died after giving birth
to a daughter, afterwards Duchess of Berry; the Queen of Navarre
also died, the sister of the King of France.

12

Pope Gregory XI, who was at this time on the papal throne at
Avignon, was deeply displeased by his inability to arrange a peace
between the Kings of England and France. He had given a great
deal of attention to this object, as also had the College of Cardinals,
on his instructions. He decided, as a matter of devotion, to
revisit Rome, where Saint Peter and Saint Paul had founded the
Holy See and given it increase; for he had made a vow that if
ever he were raised to the supreme honour of the papacy, he
would not occupy the papal throne anywhere other than where
Saint Peter had placed it. This Pope suffered from delicate health,
which was a constant trouble to him. And being at Avignon, he
became so involved in the affairs of France, at the insistence of the
French King and his brothers, that he was unable to give sufficient
attention to his own concerns. He therefore decided to retire
from France, to be more at his ease. He made elaborate preparations all along the Genoese coast for his journey, as befitted his
high calling; and he instructed his cardinals to make their own
arrangements, since he was set on moving to Rome. The cardinals
were astonished and highly vexed at the news, for they had unpleasant memories of the Romans, and would very willingly have
dissuaded him had they found it possible to do so.

The King of France was also deeply displeased, for it suited
him far better to have the Pope close by at Avignon than anywhere else. He therefore told his brother, the Duke of Anjou,
who was then at Toulouse, to visit the Pope and try to dissuade
him. The duke obeyed and was most gladly received by the
cardinals; but in spite of all his eloquent attempts he was quite
unable to dissuade the Pope from leaving Avignon, and the preparations for his departure to Rome continued during the duke's
visit. The Pope did, however, appoint four cardinals to remain

at Avignon, and gave them full powers to deal with all matters on that side of the Alps, excepting certain business which lay in the power of the Pope alone and could not be delegated. When the duke saw that all his efforts were in vain, he left the Pope with these words: 'Holy Father, you are going to a country where you are little loved. You are leaving the fountainhead of faith and the country where the Church is more excellent, and her voice speaks more strongly, than anywhere else in the world. By this action of yours the Church may fall into great tribulation. For if you die in that country, which according to your physicians is not improbable, the Romans, who are a strange and treacherous people, will have all the cardinals in their power and will appoint whoever they like as Pope.'

But in spite of all the duke's arguments the Pope set out for Marseille, where Genoese galleys awaited him; and the duke returned to Toulouse. The Pope, after revictualling at Genoa, landed not far from Rome. Now the Romans were delighted at his arrival, and all the principal nobles set out to meet him on horseback and escorted him triumphantly into the city. He took up residence in the Vatican, and frequently visited the church of Santa Maria Maggiore, to which he was particularly attached and which he embellished with various additions. It was in this same church that he died, not long afterwards, on March 28th, 1377. He was buried there with all the pomp and magnificence that were suitable to his rank.

Soon after his death, the cardinals met in conclave in the Vatican. As soon as they had assembled to appoint a worthy and effective successor to the papacy, the people of Rome congregated in large numbers in the district of the Vatican. They numbered over thirty thousand, all in all, and they were bent on rioting if the election did not turn out as they wished. Their leaders came several times before the cardinals and exclaimed: 'My lords cardinals, decide on your choice of Pope; you are too long about it. And choose a Roman, for we will have no other. If you do elect another, neither the people of Rome nor the consuls will recognize him, and you will all be in danger of your lives!'

The cardinals, being at the mercy of the Roman mob, became uneasy at these words, and their anxiety increased when the lawlessness of the Romans reached the point where those who were nearest the conclave broke in on it, in order to frighten the cardinals into making up their minds more quickly in favour of the wishes of the mob. The cardinals, in terror, fled for their lives. But the mob prevented them from dispersing and rounded them up willy-nilly. Finding themselves in mortal danger, the cardinals quickly came to a decision in order to appease the people, and in spite of the fact that they were acting under duress, they made an excellent choice, electing a very saintly man, a Roman who had been made one of their number by Pope Urban V, called Cardinal de Saint Pierre.

The people of Rome were delighted at his election, but their delight was short-lived, for he survived only three days. The reason for his death was this: the mob was so delighted at having engineered the election of a Roman, that in their exultation they took the good man, who was at least a hundred years old, and mounting him on a white mule, they led him up and down the streets of Rome. So exhausted was he by this treatment that on the third day he took to his bed and died. He lies buried in Saint Peter's.

The cardinals were much vexed by his death; for had he survived they had decided (keeping their intentions hidden from the Romans in the meantime) to remove the Holy See from Rome, to Naples or Genoa, out of the clutches of the Romans. But now they went back into conclave, in greater peril than ever, for the mob once again assembled and indicated clearly that they would destroy the cardinals if they did not make a popular choice. They shouted to the cardinals from outside the conclave: 'Think carefully, my lords, and give us a Roman Pope, who belongs here; or else we will make your heads redder than your hats.'

Once more, the cardinals were terrified, for to die as confessors seemed to them far preferable than to die as martyrs. To escape from danger, they made their choice; and it fell not on one of their own number but on the Archbishop of Bari, a great scholar, who had worked hard for the Church. The Cardinal of Geneva leaned out of the window of the conclave and cried out to the people: 'Be silent; you have a Roman as Pope, Bartolomeo Prignano, Archbishop of Bari.' The mob replied: 'We are satisfied.'

The archbishop was not in Rome at the time, but was summoned at once. He was delighted at the news and presented himself before the cardinals. Great feasts were held and he was. elevated to the papacy under the name of Urban VI, a name that was popular with the Romans, for Pope Urban V had held them in great affection. His elevation was made known in all the churches in Christendom, and all the royalty and nobility were informed— emperors, kings, dukes and counts. The cardinals, too, informed their friends that the new Pope had been chosen by valid election, though some of them were to regret their words later. The new Pope renewed all the indulgences granted by his predecessors, and many pilgrims made the journey to Rome to receive grace.

34

However, a number of cardinals intended, given a suitable opportunity, to hold a fresh election, for the new Pope proved to be of a wilful and obstinate disposition, and this was to the advantage neither of the cardinals nor of the Church. When he found himself established with the full papal authority, and a number of the rulers of Christendom had written to him signifying their obedience to him, he became puffed up, and set about trimming the power of the cardinals and depriving them of several of their established privileges.

This they found displeasing; they held a meeting, at which they came to the conclusion that the Pope would never be of any service to them and that he was in no way worthy or fit to govern the Christian world. It was proposed to elect another in his place, wiser and more prudent, who would govern the Church better. The Cardinal of Amiens was particularly active in the matter, and it was suggested in certain quarters that he was aiming at the papacy himself. The affair dragged on through the whole summer, for those who favoured a fresh election did not dare disclose their feelings, for fear of the Romans. As a result, a number of cardinals left Rome for their summer holidays in the surrounding country. Pope Urban stayed for a considerable time at Tivoli. But these holidays could not last indefinitely, for there were numbers of the clergy from different parts of the world at Rome, who had been promised grace and favour of various kinds. Eventually the dissenting cardinals elected a new Pope, and their choice fell on Robert of Geneva, son of the late Count of Geneva: his first promotion had been to the bishopric of Terouenne, and he had then become Archbishop of Cambrai and finally Cardinal of Geneva. The majority of the cardinals took part in this election, and the new Pope took the name of Clement.

At this juncture a valiant Breton knight, Silvester Bude by name, was in the neighbourhood of Rome. He had under his command two thousand Bretons, who in the few years previous to this time had fought most actively against the people of Florence; for Pope Gregory had attacked and excommunicated the Florentines on account of their rebellion, though by the intercession of Silvester Bude they were pardoned. Pope Clement and the cardinals of his faction sent secretly for him, and his troops, and they took up their quarters in the Castel Sant'Angelo, a fortress outside the city, to keep the Romans in check.

Pope Urban and his cardinals did not dare leave Tivoli (dearly though they wished to do so) for fear of the Bretons, for they were ruthless troops, and were ready to kill anyone who stood in their way. Seeing the danger that they were in, the Romans sent for troops from Germany and Lombardy, who skirmished continually with the Bretons. Pope Clement granted indulgences to all the clergy who desired them, and proclaimed his election all over the world.

King Charles of France, on hearing the situation, was astonished. He summoned his brothers, and the chief barons, as well as all the prelates and the rector and principal doctors of the University of Paris, to decide which of the two Popes he should recognize. The opinions of the clergy were divided, and there was no quick decision; but in the end all the prelates of France decided in favour of Clement, as did the King's brothers and the majority in the University. The King duly recognized the authority of Pope Clement and published an edict to that effect, commanding everyone in his kingdom to obey Pope Clement as God's representative on earth. The King of Spain took the same line, as did the Count of Savoy, the Duke of Milan and the Queen of Naples. The support of the King of France for Pope Clement carried great weight, for France is the fountainhead of faith and excellence by reason of the noble churches and exalted hierarchy of the country. Charles of Bohemia, King of Germany and Emperor of Rome, was still alive at this time, and resided at Prague, where he had heard of all these events with some astonishment. The empire, except for the archbishopric of Trèves, was solidly in favour of Urban, and would hear of no other Pope. But the Emperor remained neutral until the day of his death, and spoke so diplomatically whenever the subject arose that all the nobility and hierarchy were content. However, throughout the empire, and in England too, the Church supported Urban; but the whole of Scotland was for Clement. Louis, Count of Flanders, severely suppressed the Clementists in Hainault, Flanders, and Liège, for he was a confirmed Urbanist, and said that the Pope had been scandalously treated. Count Louis enjoyed such affection and loyalty in these territories that on his account alone the churches and landowners supported his views, though Hainault, with its churches and its ruler, Count Albert, remained neutral and obeyed neither Pope, with the result that the Bishop of Cambrai lost all his revenues in Hainault.

About this time Pope Clement sent the Cardinal of Poitiers, a wise and valiant priest, to preach and to explain the situation to the people of France, Hainault, Flanders, and Brabant. He had been present at the first papal election, and could confirm that the Archbishop of Bari had been elected Pope only under duress. He was graciously received by the King of France, and in Hainault and Brabant, but was advised not to visit Liège or Flanders, since the inhabitants were unshakeably committed to Pope Urban. After visiting Tournai and Valenciennes, the Cardinal went to Cambrai, where he stayed some time in the hope of hearing good news.

Thus was the Christian world divided between the two Popes. The larger number of churches supported Urban, but the richer and more obedient were for Clement, who with the consent of the cardinals sent to Avignon to have the palace put in order, for he intended to retire there as soon as possible; meanwhile, he stayed at Fondi. The Roman Campagna was full of troops, who harassed the city and attacked the Vatican by day and night, while the garrison in the Castel Sant'Angelo gave the Romans constant trouble. But the Romans, reinforced by German troops, in the end captured the Vatican, and later burned it. Those of the Bretons who managed to retire to the Castel Sant'Angelo were so hard pressed there that they surrendered it in return for their lives being spared. The Romans dismantled the fortress, and the Bretons made their way to Fondi and the flat country round about. Their leader, Silvester Bude, was highly displeased to hear that his troops had lost both the Vatican and the fortress, and wondered how to take his revenge on the Romans. He discovered from his spies that all the chief citizens of Rome were to assemble at a given moment in the capitol, to hold council. He then collected a force of Bretons and secretly advanced along byroads to Rome, entering the city in the evening by the gate leading to Naples. They arrived in the Forum just as the council had emerged from the capitol, and levelling their spears and spurring their horses they charged the Romans at full gallop, killing and wounding a large number of them, including all the chief citizens of Rome. Among the dead were seven of the more notable knights, and two hundred other rich and important men. Many more were wounded. The Bretons then retired, as it was evening, and were not pursued, partly owing to the approach of night and partly because the Romans were so terrified that they could think only of the slaughter of their friends. They passed the night in great anguish, burying the dead and ministering to the wounded. The next morning they decided on a most cruel and unjust reprisal, and attacked and killed over three hundred of the poor clergy in Rome, who were innocent of the smallest offence; in particular they showed no mercy to any Breton that fell into their hands. Such was the pitiful state of affairs at Rome on account of the two Popes; and every day, people who were in no way involved suffered severely.

The Queen of Naples came to visit Pope Clement at Fondi, and to give him encouragement, for she and her subjects supported him. This Queen had had it in mind for some time to make over to the Pope the kingdom of Sicily and the county of Provence, which were dependencies of her own crown, for him to grant as an inheritance to any high-born prince in the kingdom of France that he cared to choose, on condition that the prince should defend her against the house of Hungary, whom she held in mortal hatred. When she arrived at Fondi, she knelt before the Pope, made her confession, and then gave an account[1] of her situation as follows, keeping nothing secret:

'Holy Father, I possess several large and noble inheritances—the kingdoms of Naples and Sicily, Apulia, Calabria and Provence. But it is true that in his lifetime my father, King Louis of Sicily, Duke of Apulia, acknowledged that he held these territories from the Church. On his deathbed he took my hand and said: "Dear child, you will inherit a rich and extensive country; and believe me, many princes will compete for your hand on account of your great inheritance. I command and enjoin you to follow the advice of a great prince in ruling the countries that you inherit, and to marry one great enough to keep yourself and your possessions in peace. And if it happens by the will of God that you give birth to no heir, make over all your possessions to who-

---

[1] '*Hr history is diffrntly rlated from Froissart's account.*' Johnes.

ever is Pope at the time. For those are the instructions that my father, King Robert, gave me on his deathbed. By charging you to do this, I am discharging my duty to him."

'Holy Father, I promised on my word to carry out his wishes, in the presence of all who were in his room. And after his death, Father, I married with the approval of the nobles of Sicily and Naples, Andrew of Hungary, brother of King Louis of that country. And by him I had no children, for he died young at Aix-en-Provence.[1] After his death I was married again, to Prince Charles of Tarenti, and by him I had a daughter, but the King of Hungary, from displeasure at his brother's death, made war on Prince Charles, and annexed Apulia and Calabria. He also captured my husband and imprisoned him in Hungary, where he died.

'After this, again with the consent of my nobles, I married James, King of Mallorca, and I sent for Louis of Navarre from France to marry my daughter, but he died on the journey. King James went on an expedition to regain the island of Mallorca, his inheritance, which the King of Aragon had seized, for King James had lost his inheritance when his father was put to death in prison by the King of Aragon. I told the King, my husband, that I was rich and powerful enough to keep him in as royal a state as he wished, but he insisted so much, and gave so many good reasons for regaining his inheritance, that I consented willy-nilly to his doing as he pleased. When he left, I instructed him particularly to go and lay his case before King Charles of France, and to do as he suggested. But this he totally neglected to do, and it turned out very badly for him as a result: he went to the Prince of Wales, who was bound by an undertaking to help him, and in whom he had greater confidence than in my cousin, the King of France. However, after he had set out, I wrote to the King of

---

[1] *This Queen had her first husband murdered, and thrown out of a window at Aversa, where he lay for several days. He was eventually buried by his nurse, and a canon of Saint Januarius, in the Cathedral of Naples. The Queen's account, here as elsewhere is very far from the truth.*

France and sent ambassadors, to ask him to send me a prince of the blood to marry my daughter, so that our possessions should not be without an heir. The King granted my request, for which I was grateful, and sent me his cousin, Robert of Artois, who married my daughter.

'Holy Father, my husband the King of Mallorca died on that expedition; and I then married Lord Otto of Brunswick. Whereupon the Lord Charles of Durazzo,[1] seeing that Lord Otto would enjoy my inheritance during my lifetime, attacked us and imprisoned us in the Castel del Ovo at Naples. The sea ran so high that we thought it would engulf us, and we were so terrified that we surrendered, in return for our lives' being spared. My husband and I, and my daughter and her husband were imprisoned, and only my husband and I survived. We gained our liberty only at the cost of a treaty yielding Apulia and Calabria to Lord Charles, and now he is trying to acquire Naples, Sicily, and Provence as well. He makes alliances on every side, and he will override the rights of the Church when I am dead, and before, if he possibly can.

'It is for this reason, Holy Father, that I desire to discharge my duty before you and before God, and to fulfil the intentions of my predecessors; and I put in your hands the whole of my inheritance in Sicily, Naples, Apulia, Calabria, and Provence, for you to grant in perpetuity to whomsoever you find most suitable, who can defend them against our enemy, Charles de la Paix.'

The Pope heard her long speech with pleasure, and reverently accepted her gift, with these words: 'My daughter of Naples, we will arrange that your lands shall have an heir of your own blood, noble and powerful enough to resist all who may seek to oppose him.' Official documents were drawn up to confirm these transactions, so that the title of these possessions should be established beyond question for ever.

---

[1] *Charles de la Paix, son of Louis of Durazzo.*

35

The Queen and Lord Otto her husband, having fulfilled the purpose of their visit to Fondi, remained there as long as they felt inclined before returning to Naples. Pope Clement discovered that Pope Urban and his supporters at Rome were earnestly seeking to win over Charles de la Paix and the people of Naples to their side, and decided that it was not healthy for him to remain so near Rome any longer. He was not even sure how long the route to Avignon, by land and sea, would remain open. But his most particular reason for wishing to go to Avignon was in order to hand over to the Duke of Anjou, without prejudice, the rights that had been entrusted to him by the Queen of Naples. He made all the arrangements prudently, and in secret, and embarked with his cardinals and their families in galleys sent from Aragon. They had favourable winds and arrived safely at Marseille, to the joy of the people, and proceeded from there to Avignon. The Pope informed the King of France and his brothers of his arrival, at which they were delighted. The Duke of Anjou, ever eager for honours and large possessions, came from Toulouse, where he then lived, and joyfully received from the Pope, on behalf of himself and his heirs, those territories which the Queen of Naples had given up. He announced his intention of visiting his new possessions as soon as possible. The duke spent about a fortnight with the Pope before returning to Toulouse, and the Pope put Silvester Bude and Bernard de la Salle and Florimont in command of his troops, to attack and harry the Romans.

SUMMARY

13-34, 36-72

Meanwhile the King of France had taken into custody the two sons of his brother-in-law, the King of Navarre, who now declared war on him. The King of France captured the county of Montpellier from him and laid siege to Evreux in Normandy. The English provided garrisons for various towns in Normandy belonging to Navarre, but the French captured them all except Cherbourg and Mortagne. The English recovered some castles near Bordeaux, but after failing to take Saint Malo they returned to England.

Later, the English contingent at Bordeaux drove the Spaniards (who had besieged Pamplona) out of Navarre and invaded Castile. Peace was made between Navarre and Castile. King Henry of Castile died.

The Count of Flanders gravely offended the French king by intercepting an ambassador sent by him to King Robert of Scotland. The Duke of Anjou invaded Brittany, but the Duke of Brittany remained in England. The English and the Bretons captured a number of strongholds in Auvergne.

When Pope Clement had left for Avignon, Pope Urban appointed Sir John Hawkwood, an experienced campaigner, as commander of his troops. They defeated Pope Clement's Bretons under Silvester Bude, who was taken to Rome; Bude escaped to Avignon, where, however, he was executed for treachery at the instigation of his enemy the Cardinal of Amiens.

The *Chronicle* now turns to the affairs of Flanders, explaining the causes of the dispute between the Count of Flanders and the Flemish people. John Lyon, employed by the Count at Ghent, introduced the organization of the White Hoods, 'men who loved war better than peace, and had nothing to lose.' The Count wanted them abolished, but they murdered the bailiff of Ghent, and destroyed houses and property in the town, bringing about a state of anarchy. They also burnt Andreghen, one of the Count's favourite castles. However, John Lyon died, possibly by poison, and the men of Ghent chose captains to command them. Several other towns joined Ghent in besieging Oudenarde, and a great assault was made on the Count at Dendremonde. Eventually the Duke of Burgundy succeeded in making peace between the Flemish and the Count.

The townsmen of Ghent then appealed to the Count to come and visit them, which he did. The White Hoods razed the walls of Oudenarde and destroyed the houses of the nobles. The bitter war between the men of Ghent and the nobles broke out again; the nobles made war on the Flemish, and the Count's army inflicted heavy losses on the men of Ghent. Ypres and Courtrais surrendered to the Count, who then laid siege to Ghent; he failed to take the town, but defeated a large army under Rasse de Harzelle. Courtrai was besieged by Peter du Bois, but without success. Arnoul le Clerc attacked the Count's army, but was defeated and killed. The people of Ghent gradually gained control of the city at the expense of the nobles and Philip van Artevelde.[1]

In 1382 the Count of Flanders again besieged Ghent, but raised the siege on the death of his cousin, the Lord d'Enghien. The whole country supported the Count, except the districts of the Quatre Metiers (whence provisions were sent to Ghent) and of Aloet. The Count showed plainly that he did not wish to negotiate with the citizens of Ghent, who then marched out of the city, and defeated the Count at Bruges; they captured the town and the Count had to hide in a small house. All Flanders, with the exception of Oudenarde, then went over to the side of Ghent, and the Count retired with his supporters to Lille. Philip van Artevelde kept great state in Ghent, and besieged Oudenarde, but some of his troops burned some villages on the French frontier, which gave rise to a war with the French King Charles VI, partly because of the burned villages, and partly at the instigation of the King's uncle, the Duke of Burgundy, who was anxious to recover Flanders for the Count, who was his vassal.

During the siege of Oudenarde, the rebels asked King Charles to make peace between them and the Count, but he answered them contemptuously, and they then tried to draw the English into an alliance. This too was unsuccessful. The French King then sent commissioners to Flanders to try to make peace there, and, as a result of their reception, and after hearing the answers that they brought back, assembled an army in Artois against the Flemish. The Flemish then destroyed a number of bridges across the river Lis, and heavily guarded the entrances to their country. A small French force nevertheless succeeded in crossing the river and after defeating Peter du Bois and the Flemish, with great slaughter, rebuilt the bridge at Commines. King Charles

---

[1] *Son of Jacques van Artevelde and godson of the late Queen Philippa of England.*

then crossed the river with an army of four thousand fighting men, and the town of Ypres surrendered to him. Several other towns also surrendered, but Bruges was prevented from doing so by Philip van Artevelde.

On the eve of the great battle of Roosebeke,[1] Philip van Artevelde gave a dinner to his captains, as did King Charles to his uncles and to his principal barons. The next day, the Flemish army was utterly defeated and Van Artevelde was killed. Bruges surrendered to the French and King Charles returned to Paris, where there had been riots. The people of Paris were severely punished, and several of the leading citizens beheaded. Ghent continued the war with France, but the Count of Flanders was completely subject to the King of France, and expelled the English merchants from Bruges and Flanders.

In this year the English also made an expedition against Spain but, to their displeasure, a settlement was made between the Kings of Castile and Portugal, and the English returned home. King Richard II married Anne, daughter of King Charles IV of Bohemia. The Earl of Savoy and the Count of Anjou captured Apulia and Calabria.

73

In the previous year, great commotions and disturbances arose in England among the poorer people, and the country came near to complete ruin. Indeed, never was any country in such danger; for a rebellion was fostered similar to that stirred up in France by the Jacquerie, which did such damage to the country. It is strange how insignificant was its origin, which I will describe, from the best of my information, as a warning to mankind.

It is the custom in England, as in other countries, for the nobility to have great power over the common people, who are their serfs. This means that they are bound by law and custom to plough the fields of their masters, harvest the corn, gather it into barns, and thresh and winnow the grain; they must also mow and

---

[1] *November 27th, 1382.*

carry home the hay, cut and collect wood, and perform all manner of tasks of this kind. The peasants have to perform these duties by law, and they are more numerous in England than anywhere else. Thus the nobility and clergy are served by right, especially in the counties of Kent, Essex, Sussex, and Bedford, where they are more powerful than elsewhere.[1]

The wretched peasantry of these counties now began to rebel, saying that the servitude in which they were kept was excessive, and that at the beginning of the world no man was a slave; nor ought anyone to be treated as such, unless he had committed some treason against his master, as Lucifer did against God. But they themselves had done no such thing, and were not angels or spirits, but men of the same stuff as their masters, who treated them like beasts. This they would no longer endure: if they were to work for their masters then they must be paid.

A mad priest in the county of Kent, John Ball by name, had for some time been encouraging these notions, and had several times been confined in the Archbishop of Canterbury's prison for his absurd speeches. For it was his habit on Sundays after mass, when everyone was coming out of church, to collect a crowd round him in the market-place and address them more or less as follows: 'My friends, the state of England cannot be right until everything is held communally, and until there is no distinction between nobleman and serf, and we are all as one. Why are those whom we call lords masters over us? How have they deserved it? By what right do they keep us enslaved? We are all descended from our first parents, Adam and Eve; how then can they say that they are better lords than us, except in making us toil and earn for them to spend? They are dressed in velvet and furs, while we wear only cloth. They have wine, and spices and good bread, while we have rye, and straw that has been thrown away, and water to drink. They have fine houses and manors, and we have to brave the wind and rain as we toil in the fields. It is by the

---

[1] *This is not true. It was merely the case that the Peasants' Revolt began in these counties.*

sweat of our brows that they maintain their high state. We are called serfs, and we are beaten if we do not perform our tasks. We have no sovereign to appeal to, or to listen to us and give us justice. Let us go to the King. He is young, and we will show him our miserable slavery, we will tell him it must be changed, or else we will provide the remedy ourselves. When the King sees us, either he will listen to us, or we will help ourselves.'

With these and similar words John Ball harangued the people as they came out of mass on Sundays, and a number of ill-disposed people agreed with his theme. On being informed, the Archbishop of Canterbury again had John Ball imprisoned for two or three months, but it would have been better had he locked him up for the rest of his life, or even had him executed; but the archbishop could not in all conscience put him to death, and so he was released, and at once went back to his former errors. A number of the meaner sort in London came to hear of his words and deeds, and in their envy of the rich began to murmur to each other that the country was badly governed, and that all the silver and gold was in the possession of the nobles. These people began to rebel and to send word round the neighbouring counties encouraging those of the same opinion to come at once to London, and they would all press the King so hard that there would not be a slave left in England.

The peasants in Essex, Kent, Sussex and Bedford therefore flocked to London, to the number of sixty thousand in all. The chief rabble-rouser was Wat Tyler, and under him were two other leaders, Jack Straw and John Ball. This Wat had been a tiler of roofs; he was a bad character, and a deeply embittered man. All London, except for the rebels, was in terror. When they approached the city, the mayor and the richer citizens held council and decided to close the gates of the city and let no one enter; but they decided on reflection that there would then be a danger of all the suburbs being burned to the ground. So the city remained open to them, and they entered in troops of anything from twenty to two hundred, depending on the size of the towns from which they came. You must realize that at least three-quarters of them had no idea what they wanted, but simply followed each other like sheep or cattle—or like those shepherds long ago, who announced that they were going to conquer the Holy Land, but afterwards accomplished nothing. In the same way these poor people came to London, some of them from as far as a hundred miles off, but the greater part from the counties mentioned above. On arriving, they demanded to see the King. The gentry of the land, the knights and squires, began not without reason to be alarmed; and they collected together, for mutual support, as best they could.

At the same time as the men of Kent took the road to London, the Princess of Wales (the King's mother) was returning from a pilgrimage to Canterbury. She was in great danger from the peasants, for they attacked her carriage and caused a great commotion; she was greatly afraid that they would do violence to herself or her ladies in waiting, but God protected her and she made the journey from Canterbury to London in a single day, not daring to spend a night on the road. She found the King at the Tower of London, and with him the Earl of Salisbury, the Archbishop of Canterbury, Count Robert of Namur, the lord of Gommegny and several others, who stayed with the King out of suspicion of his subjects, though the rebels did not have the least idea of what they wanted. Before this rebellion actually broke out, it was well known at the King's palace that the revolt was coming to a head; and the remarkable thing is that the King took no steps to put things right. In order that lords and gentlemen may take warning in the matter of putting down rebels, I will give a full account of what happened.

74

On the Monday before the feast of Corpus Christi, 1381, these men left their homes and set out for London, to speak to the King and to gain their freedom, for their object was that no Englishman should remain a serf. At Canterbury they found John Ball (he was looking, in vain, for the archbishop, who was in London with the King) and with him Wat Tyler and Jack Straw. They were given a warm welcome, for the people of Canterbury were on their side; and having decided to make for London to see the King, they sent word to their supporters in Essex and Sussex, and as far as Bedford and Stafford, encouraging them to do the same, so that London would be surrounded. In this way the King would be unable to escape them; they aimed to assemble together in London from every side on the feast of Corpus Christi.

At Canterbury, they invaded the church of Saint Thomas and did great damage; they also wrecked the apartments of the archbishop, saying as they destroyed or removed his belongings: 'This chancellor of England has had his furniture cheap; he will now give us an account of the revenues of the country, and of the great sums he has raised since the King's coronation.' After raiding the monasteries of Saint Thomas and Saint Vincent, they left for Rochester, accompanied by all the inhabitants of Canterbury. They were joined by the people of the villages to right and left of the road, and they advanced like a whirlwind, mercilessly destroying the houses of attorneys and King's proctors, and of the officers of the archbishop's court.

At Rochester they were again welcomed, and they went to the castle and seized the governor, Sir John Newton, saying: 'You will have to come with us and be our commander-in-chief, and do exactly as we say.' Sir John tried to refuse, and gave a number of excellent reasons for doing so, but in vain, for they replied: 'Sir John, if you refuse, you are a dead man.' Realizing that the people were out of their minds and quite ready to kill him, he reluctantly put himself at their head. The rebels acted in the same way, in other parts of England, as far afield as Norwich and Lincoln, and forced such great nobles as Lord Morley, Sir Stephen Hales and Sir Stephen Cossington to march with them. And it is surprising how well things turned out in the end; for if they had had their way they would have destroyed the entire nobility of England; the same would have occurred in other countries, and the peasantry would have followed the example of the inhabitants of Ghent and Flanders, who were up in arms against their masters. In the same year the people of Paris rose in a similar fashion, more than twenty thousand of them arming themselves with iron mallets.

After leaving Rochester the rebels crossed the river and came to Dartford, never sparing the property of attorneys or proctors as they went. They cut off several heads on their way, and soon reached Blackheath, where they encamped on a hill, saying that they were for the King and the commons of England. When it was known in London how close they were, the gates of London Bridge were closed, and guards were set there by order of the mayor, Sir William Walworth, and other prominent citizens. The rebels, however, had over thirty thousand sympathizers in the town.

Sir John Newton was dispatched from Blackheath to speak to the King at the Tower, asking him to come and address the rebels, and informing him that all their actions were performed in his service; for the country had of recent years been sadly misgoverned, to the dishonour of the realm and the detriment of the common people by his uncles, by the clergy, and most of all by the Archbishop of Canterbury, the chancellor, from whom they wanted an account of his ministry.

Sir John did not dare refuse, but crossed the river to the Tower. The King, and those with him, were in a state of great suspense, and everyone made way for him as he landed. The King was in a room with his mother, the Princess of Wales, and his two brothers, Thomas Earl of Kent and Sir John Holland, the Earls of Salisbury, Warwick, and Suffolk, the Archbishop of Canterbury, the Grand Prior of the Knights Templar of England, Count Robert of Namur, the Mayor of London, and other prominent citizens. Sir John was well known to them, being one of the King's officers, and kneeling before the King, he said: 'Most honoured sire, do not be displeased with me for the message I bring, for my dear lord, it is not of my own free will that I bring it.' 'No, Sir John,' replied the King. 'Tell us your message; we hold you excused.' 'Most honoured Sire, the commoners of your realm have sent me to entreat you to come and speak to them at Blackheath. They want to hear no one but yourself. You need have no fears for your person; they will do you no harm, since they are and will always continue to be your loyal subjects. They will only tell you a number of things which they say you ought to hear, but of which they have not charged me to inform you. My dear lord, have the goodness to give me an answer that will satisfy them and will convince them that I have come before you; for they hold my children as hostages, and will kill them if I do not return.'

The King replied: 'You shall have an answer at once.' He then held a council, at which he was advised to say that if they would come down to the river Thames on Thursday morning he would speak to them without fail: Sir John Newton conveyed this message to them, and it gave great pleasure. The rebels, who now numbered sixty thousand, encamped and spent the night as best they could, though four-fifths of them went hungry.

Rumour had it in London that the rebels were supported by the Earl of Buckingham, who was at this time in Wales, where he held large properties by right of his wife, the daughter of the Earl of Hereford and Northampton. Some people even swore that they had seen him among them, mistaking him for a man from Kent, Thomas by name, who bore an uncanny resemblance to him. The Earl of Cambridge and the barons who were with him at Plymouth, fitting out an expedition to Portugal, also came to hear of the expedition and hurriedly left the harbour, and put to sea (though with some difficulty, against contrary winds) for fear that their expedition should be prevented by the populace, who had already attacked shipping at Southampton, at Winchelsea and in the region of Arundel. The Duke of Lancaster was on the Scots border between Roxburgh and Melrose, negotiating with the Scots. He was also informed of the rebellion and was well aware of the personal danger that he was in, for he was not popular with the common people in England. Nevertheless he arranged the treaty with Scotland most skilfully. The Scots lords, the Earls of Douglas, Moray, and Sutherland, and Sir Thomas Erskine, were also aware of the rebellion and of the extreme danger in which England lay, and they took a sterner line with the Duke of Lancaster as a result.

75

On the feast of Corpus Christi, the King heard mass in the chapel of the Tower, with all his lords, and afterwards embarked in his barge, with the Earls of Salisbury, Warwick, and Oxford, and other knights. They were rowed downstream to Rotherhithe, where over ten thousand men had assembled from Blackheath. When they saw the royal barge approaching, they set up such a hue and cry that it sounded as if all the devils in hell had been let loose. They had brought Sir John Newton with them, and they would have hacked him to pieces, as they had threatened, if the King had failed to appear.

When the King and his lords saw the hostile state of the crowd, there was none of them so bold as not to feel alarm. The King was advised not to land, but to have his barge rowed up and down the river in front of the crowd. 'Tell me what you want,' cried the King. 'I have come here to talk with you.' That part of the crowd that was nearest him answered with one voice: 'We want you to land, and then we can tell you more easily what we require.' The Earl of Salisbury then answered for the King: 'Gentlemen, you are in no fit state nor are you properly dressed to speak to the King.' Nothing more was said, and the King was conducted back to the Tower.

When the people saw that they could achieve nothing more, they returned, in a rage, to Blackheath, where the bulk of the mob still was, and explained what had happened. Then they all cried out: 'Let us go to London!' They set out at once, and destroyed on the way a number of houses belonging to lawyers, courtiers, and the clergy; and on reaching the suburbs of London, which are extensive and beautiful, they destroyed several fine houses; in particular they demolished the Marshalsea (the King's prison) and liberated all who were confined in it. Altogether, they did great damage in the suburbs and threatened those who had closed the gates of London Bridge, saying that they would burn all the suburbs, take London by force, and burn and destroy everything.

Many of the common people of London were on their side, and got together and said: 'Why refuse admittance to these good people? They are our friends, and they are acting for the common good.' The gates were opened, the crowds poured in; rushing to those houses that were the best provisioned, they fell on the food and drink that they found. In the hope of appeasing them, nothing was refused them.

The leaders of the mob, Jack Straw, John Ball, and Wat Tyler, marched through London at the head of thirty thousand men, to the palace of the Savoy, a handsome building on the way to Westminster, built on the bank of the Thames, and belonging to the Duke of Lancaster. They killed the guards and burned the palace to the ground. Not content with this outrage, they went next to the house of the Knights Hospitallers of Rhodes, which is dedicated to Saint John of Mount Carmel, and burned the house, and the church and the hospital as well. After this they went from street to street, killing all the Flemings that they found, even those in religious houses as well as elsewhere. They broke into several houses of Lombard merchants and seized the contents, nobody daring to oppose them. They murdered a rich citizen called Richard Lyon, whose servant Wat Tyler had been, in the wars of France. Wat Tyler had once been beaten by his master, and had not forgotten it; he led his men to Lyon's house, had him beheaded, and had his head carried through the streets on a pike. Such was the frenzied behaviour of the mob, and the damage they did in the city that day.

In the evening they encamped in Saint Catherine's Square, before the Tower, and announced that they would not leave until they had obtained from the King all that they wanted; and that the Chancellor of England must give them an account of all the revenue levied in England for the last five years; and that if he could not give a satisfactory account it would be the worse for him.

The desperate situation of the King and his court in the Tower may easily be imagined, for the crowd outside were howling like men possessed. In the evening the King held a council with his barons, on the advice of Sir William Walworth, the Mayor of London, and other prominent citizens. It was proposed that they should arm themselves and set out at midnight and fall upon the rabble (who numbered sixty thousand) and who would be lying in a drunken sleep in the streets; not one in twenty of them would be armed, and they would kill them like flies. The citizens of London were quite capable of doing this, for they had taken their friends and dependants into their houses, fully armed. Sir Robert Knolles was guarding his property in his house with a hundred and twenty fully armed men who would have sallied forth if it had been required of them. Sir Perdiccas d'Albret was also in London, and between them all they could have mustered between seven and eight thousand armed men. But nothing came of it, for they were too much afraid of the common people of London. The Earl of Salisbury and the King's other advisers said to him: 'Sir, if you can appease the mob with fair words, it would be better. Grant them all they ask, for if we begin something that we cannot finish, nothing will ever be recovered, for us or for our heirs, and England will be a desert.' This advice was taken, and the mayor was told to cancel his plans, which he did. There are twelve sheriffs in London, besides the mayor.[1] Nine of them were on the side of the citizens and the King, and three on that of the mob, for which they eventually paid dearly.

On Friday morning, the King gave orders to the crowd in Saint Catherine's Square to retire to a fine meadow at Mile End, where people go to amuse themselves in summer and where any who wished to do so might speak to him. Most of the common people from the villages set out, but not all; for a great part of the mob only wanted to riot, to destroy the nobility, and to plunder the city. They clearly showed that this was the chief purpose

[1] *Froissart is wrong; two sheriffs and twenty-six aldermen (including the mayor) is the correct figure, according to Johnes.*

of their rebellion; for when the gates of the Tower were opened and the King came out with his two brothers and a number of attendant lords, four hundred of the mob, led by Tyler, Straw, and Ball, dashed in by force and rushed from room to room; inside they found the Archbishop of Canterbury, Simon of Sudbury, a wise and resolute man and Chancellor of England. He had only just said mass before the King, but he was seized by these ruffians and beheaded. They also murdered the Grand Prior of Saint John, and a Dominican friar attached to the Duke of Lancaster, and one of the royal sergeants-at-arms. They stuck the four heads on pikes and carried them round the streets, eventually setting them up on London Bridge, as if they had been traitors to King and country. They also entered the rooms of the Princess of Wales, the King's mother, and cut her bed to pieces. The Princess fainted from shock, and was carried by her attendants down to the river where she was taken by boat to the King's Wardrobe: she remained there, half-dead from shock, for the rest of that day and the next night, till the King came to comfort her.

76

The King made his way to Mile End but was not accompanied by his brothers, the Earl of Kent and Sir John Holland, who did not dare show themselves to the people there, as they feared for their lives. When the King arrived, he found sixty thousand men assembled from different villages and districts of England; he advanced towards them, and asked them pleasantly: 'My friends, I am your King and your lord. What do you want? And what do you wish to say?' Those who heard him replied: 'We want you to set us free for ever, us and our descendants and our lands, and to grant that we should never again be called serfs, nor held in bondage.' The King replied: 'I grant your wish. Now return quietly to your homes, and leave behind two or three men from each village, and I will have letters written, sealed with my seal, which your deputies will peacefully bring back to you, with all your requests granted. And for your greater assurance I shall have my banner sent to every town and castle and to all the stewards of the crown.' All the innocent and well-intentioned people were quite satisfied by these words, and began to return to London. The King promised a banner to each of the following counties—Kent, Essex, Sussex, Bedford, Cambridge, Stafford and Lincoln. He gave a free pardon for all that had been done by the people of these counties, on condition that they followed the royal banner back to their homes on the terms he had mentioned. Half of the mob dispersed, and the King gave orders for thirty secretaries to draw up the letters that very day, and for the letters to be sealed and delivered.

The chief mischief-makers, however, remained: Tyler, Straw, and Ball declared that though the people were satisfied, they themselves would not depart. And with them there remained over thirty thousand who took the same view; they stayed in the city, showing no inclination to receive the King's letters, but keeping London in a state of terror. The citizens kept to their houses, with as many of their friends and attendants as they could muster. The King went to visit his mother at the Wardrobe, and comforted her as best he could.

On the same feast of Corpus Christi a large crowd marched towards London from Lincoln, Norfolk, and Suffolk. They stopped outside Norwich, where the governor of the town was Sir Robert Salle, who though not of gentle birth had been knighted by King Edward for his ability and courage. The rebels wanted him to be their leader, and threatened to sack the town if he would not come and meet them. He rode out to where they were gathered, and being at first respectfully received, made the mistake of dismounting from his horse. They then reminded him that he was not a gentleman, but the son of a mason, like themselves; and they promised to raise him so high that a quarter of England would be under his command. Sir Robert was furious: 'Get back,' he cried, 'villainous scoundrels and false traitors that you are. Would you have me dishonour myself by deserting my natural lord for such worthless scum as you? I would rather you were all hanged, and so you surely will be.' The rabble then attacked him as he tried to remount and he set about him with his fine Bordeaux sword, and killed twelve of them, with each stroke cutting off a foot, a head, an arm or a leg, so that none was so bold as to close with him. But the mob numbered forty thousand, and they shot and hurled missiles at him so fiercely that even if he had been fully armed, he would still have been overpowered. In the end he was brought down and hacked to pieces by the mob. So died Sir Robert Salle, sad though it is to relate; and all the knights and squires of England were angry when they heard the news.

On the Saturday the King left the Wardrobe and returned to Westminster, where he heard mass in the abbey with all his lords. He made his devotions at a statue of Our Lady in a little chapel that has witnessed many miracles and where much grace has been gained, so that the Kings of England have great faith in it.

The King rode past Saint Bartholomew's Church in Smith-field, and found the remainder of the rabble assembled in the horse-market. The King's banners had been given them on the previous evening, but they intended to pillage the city that very day: 'For,' said their leaders, 'so far we have done nothing. The liberty which the King has given us will bring us very little gain. Let us agree to loot this large, rich, and powerful city, before the crowd arrives from all over England. For they will come from Essex and Sussex, Cambridge and Bedford, and from Arundel, Warwick and Reading; from Berkshire and from Oxford, from Guildford, Coventry, Lynn, Stafford and Lincoln; and even from York and Durham. If we plunder the city of its gold and silver and treasures now, we will steal a march on them, and we will not regret it; but if we wait, they will snatch the spoils away from us.'

The King and his lords halted when they saw the crowd. 'Here is the King,' said Wat Tyler, 'I will go and speak to him. Do not move until I make a signal.' And waving his arms, he added, 'When I make this sign, come forward and kill them all except the King; do not hurt him, for he is young, and we will do what we like with him. We will take him wherever we like in England, and we will be masters of the whole country, without a doubt.' There was a London tailor there, John Tickle by name, who had brought sixty doublets with him; some of the mob had put on these doublets, and on his asking who was to pay for them, for he was asking thirty marks, Tyler replied: 'Keep quiet; you will be paid all right by tonight: you can trust me, that's enough security for you.' With these words he spurred on his horse and rode right up to the King, so that his horse's tail was under the very nose of the King's horse. The first words he spoke were as follows: 'King, do you see all these men here?' 'Yes,' said the King, 'why do you ask?' 'I ask because they are all under my orders, and have all sworn on their honour to obey my commands.' 'That's all right,' said the King. 'I have no objection.' Tyler, whose one object was a riot, went on: 'And do you think that these people, and all the others, as many more again, who are under my orders in London, do you think that they ought to leave without your letters? No, we will take them all with us.' 'Those are my orders,' replied the King. 'The letters will be delivered one after the other. Now, my friend, go back to your men and take them away from London quietly; for it is my intention that every village and town shall have a charter, as it has been arranged.'

Wat Tyler at that moment noticed the squire who was carrying the King's sword, and standing behind him. Tyler hated the squire, who had maltreated him in the past and had had words with him. 'What, are you here?' said Tyler. 'Give me your dagger.' 'I will not,' said the squire, 'why should I?' The King turned and said, 'Give it to him,' which the squire did, though much against his will. Tyler took it and balanced it in his hand. 'Give me that sword,' he said next. 'I will not,' said the squire, 'it is the King's sword, and you are not fit to hold it; you are only a labourer. If you and I were alone here you would not have spoken like that for a pile of gold as big as that church,' and he pointed to Saint Paul's. 'On my honour,' replied Tyler, 'I will not eat before I have your head.' At this point the Mayor of London rode up, with a dozen others all armed under their robes, and breaking through the crowd, saw how Tyler was behaving. 'Scoundrel, how dare you speak like that in front of the King?' he said. The King then grew angry, and said to the mayor: 'Arrest this man.' At the same time, Tyler said to the mayor: 'What has it got to do with you, what I say or do?' The mayor, who now had the support of the King, replied: 'You stinking wretch, is this how you talk in front of my natural lord the King? I'll not live another day if you don't pay for it.' With these words he drew a short, curved broadsword, and hit Tyler such a blow on the head with the flat of it that he fell off his horse to the ground. He was immediately surrounded where he lay, so that his own men could not see him. Then one of the King's squires, John Standish, dismounted, drew his sword and stabbed Tyler in the stomach, killing him. His followers then began to cry out 'They have cut down our captain! Come on, let us kill them all!' They drew themselves up in some kind of order and advanced, each with his bow ready to shoot. At great personal risk the King then rode out in front of his followers, forbidding any to follow him, and advanced on the mob, who were preparing to avenge their leader: 'Gentlemen,' he said, 'what do you want? You have no other captain but me. I am your King. Keep the peace.' When they saw and heard the King speak, most of the crowd were quite abashed and the more peaceful of them began to disperse. But the more rebellious ones stood firm and showed that they meant business. The King turned back and asked for advice. The mayor advised him to stay out in the fields, for nothing would be gained by running away, and support would soon be coming from London. Meanwhile a rumour had already reached the city that the King and the mayor were being killed; and between seven and eight thousand men-at-arms immediately collected at Smithfield and the neighbouring fields where the King had retired. The leaders were Sir Robert Knolles, Sir Perdiccas d'Albret, and a powerful citizen called Nicholas Bramber, the King's draper, who was knighted on the spot by the King along with John Standish, and the mayor, William Walworth. Sir Robert Knolles advised attacking the mob and killing them, but the King refused. 'Go and demand my banners back from them,' he said. 'Then we can see what mood they are in. But one way or another I will regain control of them.' 'That is right,' said the Earl of Salisbury.

The three new knights were sent ahead, and made a sign that they were coming to parley, to prevent the crowd firing at them. On approaching, the knights called out: 'Listen! The King orders you to give up your banners, and we hope that he will have mercy on you.' The banners were duly handed over, and orders were then given for all who had received the royal letters to give them back. Some obeyed, and others did not. Those that were given back the King had torn up before the eyes of the crowd.

As soon as the banners were surrendered, the crowd kept no proper order, and most of them threw down their bows and went back to London. Sir Robert Knolles was furious that they were not pursued and cut down; but the King declared that he would sure enough have his revenge, which indeed he did. After returning to London with his lords and followers, the first thing the King did was to visit his mother at the Wardrobe, where she had been in great anxiety for two days and two nights. 'Ah! my dear son, what pain and anguish I have been through for you today!' she said. 'Yes, madam, I know,' said the King. 'But now rejoice and praise God; for today I have regained my heritage and my kingdom, which I had lost.'

The King spent the whole of that day with his mother, and the lords went to their own houses. A public proclamation was made through the streets that all who were not inhabitants of London, or who had not been there for a year, should leave the city, and if any were still there by sunrise on Sunday they would be regarded as traitors and lose their heads. The proclamation was universally obeyed, but Jack Straw and John Ball were found hiding in a ruin, hoping to escape. However their own followers informed on them, and the King was delighted at their capture. Their heads were cut off and fixed, with that of Wat Tyler, on London Bridge, in place of those of the gallant men who had been murdered on the Thursday. This news was circulated in the neighbouring counties and reached the ears of the crowds who had been encouraged by the original rebels to make for London, whereupon they dared go no further, and all returned home.

SUMMARY

77-130

The peasants, who had gone home, were later punished. The Duke of Lancaster remained in Scotland until the revolt was over.

The Count of Flanders besieged Ghent without success. An expedition was made by the English against the Spaniards; France supported Castile.

Richard II married Anne, sister of the Emperor, Wenceslas of Bohemia. After a successful campaign by the Canon de Robersac, peace was made between Castile and Portugal, to the annoyance of the English.

The Maillotins revolted in Paris. The people of Ghent defeated the Earl of Flanders and captured all the neighbouring towns except Oudenarde. While besieging it they burned some villages on the French frontier, and caused the King of France to attack them. After a long campaign King Charles utterly defeated the Flemish at the battle of Rosebeek. Their leader, Philip van Artevelde, was killed. Nevertheless the people of Ghent rallied under Peter du Bois and King Charles returned to Paris to punish the rebels, beheading several of their leaders. The war with Ghent continued.

131

In the following year, the man who signed himself Pope Urban VI moved from Rome to Genoa, where he was warmly received. You have heard how he was recognized in England by Church and laity alike. And because his rival, Pope Clement, was recognized by the King of France and his entire people, Urban considered how he could obtain help from England to damage the King of France. He decided on the following method: he would send papal bulls to the archbishops and bishops of England, proclaiming that he absolved, and would absolve from all crimes and sins all those who would assist in the destruction of the Clementists. He had heard that Clement had resorted to exactly the same plan against him in France, and that (regarding matters of faith) the French called the Urbanists dogs. Urban realized that the only way that he could strike at France was through England; but in order to do so he would need considerable sums of money, for he was well aware that the English nobles would not undertake an expedition for all the absolutions in the world, unless money was forthcoming. For men-at-arms cannot live on pardons, nor do they pay great attention to them except at the point of death. And so together with the bulls that he sent for the clergy to preach about, he would make the Church contribute a whole tithe[1] to the King and the nobles, so as not to draw on the royal treasure nor to oppress the common people; and this, he imagined, would satisfy them.

As the money was to come from the Church, Pope Urban was anxious that the expedition should be commanded by a dignitary of the Church, and Sir Henry Despencer, Bishop of Norwich, was appointed. Knowing that the King of Spain was opposed to him (being closely allied to the King of France), Pope Urban declared that a similar army should be raised in Spain by the Duke of Lancaster, who called himself King of Castile by right of his wife; and he also undertook to put a tithe at the disposal of the King of Portugal who had recently gone to war with Don John of Castile. Such was the manner in which Pope Urban arranged his affairs,

---

[1] *This passage in Froissart is not entirely clear, and is obscurely rendered by Johnes. It does not mean that the Church was to pay a tenth of the cost of the campaign, but that the entire tithe revenue of the Church should be devoted to this end, so as to avoid levying extra taxes to pay for what was basically an ecclesiastical quarrel.*

and the thirty papal bulls were joyfully received in England. The clergy preached on the subject up and down the land, and the movement became similar to a crusade. The people of England, credulous as they were, believed in it readily. And there was not a man or a woman in the country who did not believe that if he failed to contribute generously towards the expedition he would also fail to end the year honourably and fail too, in the next life, to reach the gates of heaven. According to the bull, whoever gave most received the most pardons; and all who died at this time, having made their contributions, were absolved from their sins, and indeed were counted lucky to die and to gain so noble an absolution. By tithes and alms, no less than twenty-five thousand francs were collected in England.

132

The King, with his uncle and advisers, was delighted by the amount that had been collected, and decided that they had enough money to carry on war simultaneously against France and Spain. Thomas, Bishop of London, who was the Earl of Devonshire's brother, was nominated to command the Spanish expedition, in the name of the Pope and prelates of England. They were to have two thousand lances and four thousand archers at their disposal, and half of the money that had been collected. But the Bishop of Norwich's expedition was to leave first, and to enter France at Calais. They had no clear plan of campaign, nor did they know if the King of France would oppose them in the field.

The Duke of Lancaster had high hopes of his expedition, but the following consideration was against it: for a long time he had been unpopular with the people, and they were in general far more inclined to follow the bishop. In any case, France was nearer than Spain. Some of them said privately that the duke was planning his expedition more from avarice, and from a desire to gain a share in the silver and gold that had been collected from the Church and from those good people who had given alms, than from true devotion; but that the bishop represented the Pope, and had been chosen by him for the command. For this reason, the majority of the people, as well as King Richard himself, had greater faith in him.

The bishop commanded about five hundred lances and fifteen hundred others.[1] They were accompanied by a large number of priests, as the expedition was an affair of the Church and had been instigated by the Pope. Before the bishop and the captain embarked, they were summoned before the King's council, where they swore a solemn oath, in the King's presence, to fulfil the object of their expedition and not to make war on anyone who acknowledged Urban as Pope, but only on the Clementists. The King undertook to send a good marshal and a valiant man, Sir William Beauchamp, to join them at Calais when he returned from the borders of Scotland, where he was then engaged in negotiations with the Scots.[2]

The bishop and his army embarked at Dover, and arrived at Calais on April 23rd, 1383, where they were welcomed by the governor, Sir John Devereux. Those who were able to lodge in the town did so, and the rest built a camp outside. They waited for Sir William Beauchamp till May 4th, when the bishop, who was young and eager for the fray, and had never borne arms before except with his brother in Lombardy, said to his companions: 'My lords, why are we waiting? Sir William will never arrive, and the King and his uncles have forgotten us. Let us do some deeds of arms, since that is what we are here for. We must loyally employ the funds of the Church, which we are living on, and we must win some victories in the field.' 'Well spoken!' replied those who were nearest him. 'Let us tell our men that we will set out in three days' time, and let us see which way we can go. We cannot leave Calais without entering enemy country. For France surrounds us on every side, not only towards Boulogne and Saint Omer, but also in the direction of Flanders, since the

[1] *Froissart gives a list of the principal knights involved.*
[2] *The truce with Scotland was due to expire on June 21st.*

country there, too, has now been conquered by the King of France. All things considered, the most honourable thing that we can do is to recapture it. For the Count of Flanders has done a great injustice to our countrymen in expelling them from Bruges and from Flanders. Two years ago he would never have done such a thing, but now he has to obey the orders of the King of France.' This plan was adopted by the council, and orders were given to the army accordingly.

133

The knights informed the bishop that before setting out they would like the opinion of Sir Hugh Calverly, who was at that moment on a visit to his cousin, the Governor of Guyenne. The bishop sent for him on his return, and asked his opinion. 'Sir,' replied Sir Hugh, 'you know on what terms we left England; our expedition has no concern with the wars of kings, but is directed solely against the Clementists. We are the soldiers of Pope Urban, who has given us absolution from all sins if we destroy the Clementists. If we enter Flanders, even though it is now under the Duke of Burgundy, and the King of France, we will forfeit our rights, for I understand that the Count of Flanders and his subjects are as good Urbanists as we are. Besides, we have not enough troops to invade Flanders, for they are a numerous people, ready for war and thoroughly accustomed to it; indeed, they have known nothing else for the last four years. It is a difficult country to invade, and besides, the Flemish have done us no wrong. If we must make an expedition, let us make one against France: for the French are our enemies twice over. Our King is openly at war with them in the first place, and they are also Clementists to a man, holding a faith contrary to us and to our Pope. But besides all this, we ought to wait for our marshal, Sir William Beauchamp, who must soon arrive with a large force —the King's last words to us were that he would send him. My advice is therefore, since we want to make an expedition, to make for Aire or Montreuil. Nobody will oppose us yet, and the Flemish will swell our ranks, for they have lost everything, and will have everything to gain. The misfortunes that they have suffered at the hands of the French still rankle in their hearts; for they have lost their fathers and their sons in the war, as well as their friends.'

Sir Hugh had hardly finished when the bishop took him up hotly and impatiently: 'Yes, yes, Sir Hugh, you have been fighting in France for so long that you know nothing of fighting anywhere else. But where can we better succeed than by invading that rich part of the coast towards Bourbourg, Dunkirk, and Menport, and from there to the districts of Cassel, Bergues, Ypres and Poperinghe? According to the men of Ghent that we have with us, these places have never been harassed by war. We will therefore set off and gain what advantage we may, and there await the arrival of Sir William Beauchamp, if he is really coming —for we have had no news of him yet.'

Sir Hugh saw that he was rebuffed by his nobly-born commander the bishop, and made no reply, not from lack of spirit, but because he received no support from Sir Thomas Trivet nor Sir William Elmham. He therefore left with these words: 'By God, sir, if you advance, Sir Hugh Calverly advances with you; you shall not march without him.'

'I am glad to hear it,' said the bishop. 'Now get ready, for we advance in the morning.' Orders were given accordingly, and in the morning they took the road for Gravelines, to the number of three thousand armed men. They reached the town at ebb tide, and therefore passed by the port, and instead attacked a monastery that the townsmen had fortified. The town could not hold out long: it was fortified only with palisades, and defended by seamen, without officers, nor had the country any expectation of war. After two days the monastery also was captured, where the inhabitants of the town had retired with their wives and children and all they possessed; and in the end the invaders killed those who defended it, and had the rest at their mercy. The whole army was then quartered with ample provisions at Gravelines; and the rest of the inhabitants took fright at the news and retired into their fortresses, sending their wives and children to Bergues, Bourbourg, and Saint Omer.

The Count of Flanders summoned his council when he heard the news: 'I am very much astonished,' he said, 'that the English should overrun my lands and take my towns without giving me any notice, and invade my country without any declaration of war.' 'Indeed you may well wonder,' some of them replied. 'But it can only be supposed that they now regard Flanders as being under France, so far has the King of France advanced into it, and so much of our country has surrendered to him.' 'Well, what are we to do?' asked the Count. 'The best thing to do is this,' replied his council: 'Sir John Vilain, and Sir John Montieu are here, and they have pensions from the King of England. Let them go on your behalf to England and speak to the King and explain this whole affair, and ask why he has attacked you, without so much as a declaration of war. When he hears what your ambassadors have to say, I believe that he will be angry with those who have attacked you and will recall them in disgrace.' 'That is all very well,' said the earl, 'but in the meantime the army at Gravelines can do immeasurable damage in the Francomb, and who will stop them?' 'Sir,' came the answer, 'it is still desirable that a conference should be held with them, to find out what they want. Sir John Vilain and Sir John Montieu are so astute that they will soon restore peace to the country.' The Count gave his consent, and the two knights set off with their instructions both for their negotiations with the bishop, and also for their visit to the King of England and his uncles.

Meanwhile there was a popular rising in all the towns of Flanders that I have just mentioned, and the people advanced to Dunkirk to defend their frontiers and to fight the English. Their leader was Sir John Sporequin, who was governor of all the territory of the Duchess of Bar, which extended along this frontier to the gates of Ypres. This Sir John knew nothing of the Count's intended embassy to England, but together with another knight they collected twelve thousand men armed with pikes, coats of mail, jackets,[1] steel caps and helmets, all of them from the lands of the Duchess of Bar between Dunkirk and Gravelines.

The two Flemish knights reached Gravelines and came before the bishop, who outwardly gave them a fair reception; he had that day given a dinner to all the barons and knights of his army, knowing the impending arrival of the two knights, and wanting them to find the English all together.

'Sir, we are sent hither by my lord of Flanders,' said the knights.

'What lord?' said the bishop.

'The Count of Flanders,' was the reply. 'The country has no other lord.'

'In God's name,' said the bishop, 'we consider that it belongs to the King of France, or the Duke of Burgundy, our enemies, for they have just captured it by force of arms.'

'With all respect to Your Grace,' replied the knights, 'this land was officially handed over at Tournon to be held and governed by our lord the Count of Flanders. We are attached by loyalty, and by the pensions that we receive, to the King of England; and the Count has sent us to ask you for passports, so that we can go to England, to the King, and discover his reasons for making war on the Count and the people of Flanders without sending him a defiance.'

The bishop replied that he would consider their request, and give them an answer in the morning. The English conferred among themselves, and all things considered they decided not to give the two knights passports to England: it would be a long journey, and Flanders would be secure until their return, and could meanwhile be fortified. The Count, who was no fool, would have time to approach the King of France and the Duke of Burgundy, who would soon muster a force against which the English would be helpless. Sir Hugh Calverly was then asked what answer could be given to the two knights in the morning.

---

[1] 'Hocquetons': *according to Johnes, a quilted garment generally worn beneath armour, but sometimes used as the sole armour of light troops.*

He made the following suggestion to the bishop: 'Sir, you are our leader: tell them that you are in the territories of the Duchess of Bar, who is a Clementist; that you are fighting on behalf of Pope Urban and of nobody else, and that if the people of this country, with the monasteries and churches, will be good Urbanists and follow you wherever you lead them, you will see that our army passes peacefully through the country, paying for whatever it needs. But as for providing passports for England, you are not empowered to do so, for our war has nothing to do with the Kings of either France or England; we are Pope Urban's men. And in my opinion, this is a sufficient answer for them.' This solution appealed to all present, and especially to the bishop, who did not care what was said or done provided the campaign went forward. The two knights came to the bishop again the following morning after mass, and he received them with apparent friendliness, talking to them about other matters until his own knights arrived. He then addressed the two knights as follows: 'My lords, you are waiting for an answer, and you shall have one. As regards the request that you have brought from the Count of Flanders, you may return to him whenever you like; but if you go towards Calais or across to England, you do so at your own risk. I will give you no safe-conduct, for I have no authority from the King of England to do so. I am a soldier of Pope Urban, and all who are with me are the same, and are being paid to serve him. We are now in this territory of the Duchess of Bar, who is a Clementist. If her people support her, we will make war on them. If they follow us, they will share the absolution that has been given to us. For Pope Urban, on whose behalf we march, gives absolution for all offences to those who help in the destruction of the Clementists.'

When the two knights heard this, Sir John Vilain replied: 'My lord, I cannot believe that you have heard anything other than that the Count of Flanders is a loyal supporter of Pope Urban. You are therefore ill advised to make war on him or his people. His belief is that the King of England has not given you instructions to make war on him. Had he wished to do so, he is so noble, and so correct, that he would have declared war first.' The bishop was provoked by this and replied: 'Go and tell your Count that this is our last word. If he wants to send you or anyone else to England, the better to discover the King's intentions, those who go will have to take another route. For they will not pass this way, nor by Calais either.' The knights realized that nothing would induce the bishop to change his mind, and they withdrew.

134

The same day, the bishop was informed that at Dunkirk and in the surrounding district, there were over twelve thousand armed men under the command of the Bastard of Flanders. The bishop decided that the Count of Flanders was at the bottom of this expedition, though not openly connected with it, and therefore took the field with six hundred lances and fifteen hundred archers. He advanced towards Dunkirk, with the arms of the Church borne before him as gonfalonier of Pope Urban—the banner of Saint Peter: gules, two keys in saltire. His pennon had his own arms charged with a difference, since he was a younger brother of the Despencers. The Flemish took up a position in battle order, and numbered over twelve thousand men. Sir Hugh Calverly then prudently insisted on discovering if this large force did in fact support Clement, and a herald was dispatched. But the Flemish killed him before he could make his enquiry, and the English were now thoroughly roused, and said: 'Come on! This rabble has murdered our herald: they shall pay for it, or we will all die in the field.' Battle was joined, and although the Flemish defended themselves stoutly, the fire of the English archers was deadly, and they were supported to great effect by the men-at-arms, who after the discharge of a flight of arrows, broke through the enemy lines and killed large numbers at the first onslaught. In the end the English won the day, and the Flemish retired into Dunkirk. But the English followed up and pressed them so hard that they entered the town as well, and great numbers were killed in the streets as well as on the shore; though four hundred were killed on the English side as well. Very few of the Flemish escaped death or capture, and on that day at Dunkirk over nine thousand of them were killed.

The Count of Flanders was deeply distressed at the outcome of the battle, and at once sent a messenger to the Duke of Burgundy with the news, concluding that as the English had entered Flanders and killed his people, they would not rest there but would advance further and do yet more damage. The duke fortified all the frontier towns along the Flemish border, and strengthened the approaches to Artois.

SUMMARY

135-159

The English, under the Bishop of Norwich, conquered all the coast from Gravelines to Sluys, and laid siege to Ypres, assisted by the people of Ghent; they won minor successes near Commines and Emenin, and the King of France issued a grand summons to raise the siege. This was finally successful and the English abandoned all their conquests.[1] After long negotiations a truce was made between France and England covering Spain and Scotland on the French side, and Ghent on the English side, to last till Michaelmas 1384.

The Count of Flanders died, and was buried with great ceremony at Lille. King Richard's father-in-law, Wenceslas, King of Bohemia, 'noble, handsome, lively, wise, valiant, and amorous,' also died.

Fighting between England and Scotland delayed the general peace, but it was at last accepted. In spite of the truce, Oudenarde was re-captured from the people of Ghent, who asked the King of England to appoint a governor of their town. He chose Sir John Bourchier.[2]

---

[1] *The bishop's expeditionary force was highly unpopular on its return to England, and several of the leading knights—Elmham, Farndon, Trivet, and Ferrers—were heavily fined. Sir Hugh Calverley was an honourable exception.*

[2] *Ancestor of Lord Berners, the celebrated Tudor translator of* The Chronicles.

The Duke of Anjou died, and the truce was extended till May 1385. The son and daughter of the Duke of Burgundy married the daughter and son of the Duke of Hainault, though the Duke of Lancaster had intended to marry his daughter Philippa to William of Hainault.

Louis of Valois tried to marry the Queen of Hungary, but she was forced to marry the Marquis of Brandenburg. The King of France married Isabel, daughter of the Duke of Bavaria and niece of the Duchess of Brabant.

Ghent made peace with the Duke of Burgundy. The English governor, Sir John Bourchier, returned safely home, and general amnesties were declared on all sides.

Meanwhile, the truce between France and England had ended, and war had broken out again in Flanders, Spain, Portugal, Limousin, and Poitou, and also between England and Scotland. As usual, the Scots were supported by the French.

160

The French expedition to Scotland met with favourable winds, for it was the month of May, when the weather is generally calm. They followed the coast of Flanders, past Zeeland and Holland and Friesland, but before they finally reached Scotland, disaster struck one of the young French knights—a skilful man-at-arms called Sir Aubert d'Angers. He was young and able-bodied, and to show how nimble and sure-footed he was, he climbed up the ship's rigging in full armour, only to loose his footing and fall headlong into the sea. Nobody could save him, because he quickly sank under the weight of his armour, and the ship was soon at some distance from the spot. All the barons were much disheartened by his death, but there was nothing they could do to prevent it.

They continued their voyage and finally landed at Edinburgh, which is the capital of Scotland, and the principal residence of the King when he is not out of the country. They were awaited there by the Earls of Douglas and Moray, who were informed of their movements, and who met them with a warm welcome at the harbour. Of the Frenchmen, Sir Geoffrey de Chargny was at once recognized, since he had spent two months in Scotland the year before, and was easily able to introduce the French admiral and barons. The King of Scotland was away in the highlands, where he felt more at home, but three or four of his sons were there to receive the French. They explained that the King would soon arrive, and the French were satisfied with this information and found quarters in the town and the neighbouring villages. Although Edinburgh is the royal residence, and is the Paris of Scotland, it is less of a town than Tournai or Valenciennes, and contains fewer than four hundred houses, but the French found lodgings in Dunfermline, Dunbar, Dalkeith, and other villages in the neighbourhood.

The news soon spread that a large number of men-at-arms from France had landed in the country, and complaints could be heard on every side as follows: 'What devils have sent them? Can we not carry on war against the English without them? We will never have any success while these people are here, and they must be told to go away. There are quite enough of us here for our campaign, and we have no need of their company. They do not understand us, nor we them; we cannot even converse with each other. It will not be long before they have eaten up and destroyed everything there is in this country. If we let them stay, they will be more of a hindrance and a liability and they will do us more harm than the English would, if they got into the country. And what does it matter if the English do burn our houses? We can rebuild them cheaply enough in three days if we have some poles and some branches to cover them.' Such were the remarks made by the Scots; they thought nothing of the French, indeed they hated them in their hearts and abused them with their tongues for all they were worth, like the uncivilized and dishonourable people that they are.

It is fair to say that, all things considered, it was a mistake for such a large number of French nobles to have come on the expedition, and it would have been better if twenty or thirty knights had come, rather than five hundred or a thousand. The reason is this: in Scotland they never found men of substance, since the inhabitants are like savages and have no wish to he acquainted with anyone else, so jealous are they of other people's possessions, and so fearful of losing what little they have themselves; for the country is very poor. And when the English invade, as they have done several times, they have to take their provisions with them, for there is nothing to be found in the country. It is almost impossible to get iron to make horseshoes, or leather for harness. Everything comes ready-made from Flanders, and failing that there is nothing.

The French knights and barons were accustomed to living in fine castles and town houses, with comfortable, decorated rooms and good, soft beds; and when they found themselves surrounded by poverty, they began to laugh and to say, 'What is this wilderness that the admirals have brought us to? We have never known what poverty and hardship meant till now. Our mothers and fathers used to say, "If you live long enough, you will have to endure hard beds and bad nights," and now we know exactly what they meant. For God's sake let us get on with our purpose and make an expedition into England, since it will be neither honourable nor in any way profitable to make a long stay in Scotland.' They complained in this way to the Admiral of France, Sir John de Vienne, their captain, who tried to calm them by saying 'My lords, we must suffer, and wait, and speak persuasively, since we have exposed ourselves to these dangers. We still have a long way to go, and we cannot go back by England. You must take things as you find them, and you cannot always be at Paris or Dijon, or Beaune or Chalons. If one wants to live in this world and win honour, one must accept the bad with the good.'

Sir John did his best to appease the knights, and to make the acquaintance of the nobles of Scotland, but they hardly visited him at all, since, as I have said, they are unsociable people and difficult to know. The Earls of Douglas and Moray were more comfort to them than the rest of Scotland put together, but the plight of the French was such that when they wanted to buy horses, they were charged sixty or a hundred florins for what was worth only ten. Even this was difficult to arrange, and when they succeeded in getting horses there was no harness except what they had brought with them from Flanders. On top of all this, when their servants went out foraging, they found it quite easy to load onto their horses as much forage as they could carry, but on their way home the servants were frequently ambushed, beaten, and robbed, and often actually killed—so that after a time no servants dared to go out for fear of death: in one month the French lost a hundred servants, for even when they went out three or four together, not one would return.

The King of Scotland needed a great deal of pleading before he would come down to Edinburgh, and also required a large sum of money for himself and his courtiers. The Scots knights were responsible for this, and, just to make things harder and more expensive for the French, they declared that they would not make war on the English that season. Sir John de Vienne undertook not to leave the country before the King and his people were totally satisfied, and if he had not done so he would have had no help at all from the Scots. It was the least bad bargain that he could get, but however much it was to the advantage of the Scots, they remained determined that the war should be profitable only to themselves and not to the French.

SUMMARY

161-168

The Count of Valois married Margaret, daughter of the King of Hungary, and the King of France married Isabelle, daughter of Stephen of Bavaria. Sluys was captured by the Duke of Burgundy. The King of France retired from Flanders and disbanded his army, and the Duke of Bourbon also returns to Paris.

169

At last King Robert of Scotland came down to Edinburgh. He had red, bleary eyes, the colour of sandalwood, which showed that he was no valiant fighter, but would rather stay at home than go on a campaign. However, he had nine sons who were more warlike. The barons of France came to pay him their respect, and a number of Scots earls, Douglas, Moray, Mar, Sutherland and some others, were present at the occasion. The French admiral asked the King to fulfil the agreement by which the French had come to Scotland, namely to mount a campaign against England. Those of the Scottish barons who were keen to advance themselves were delighted, and replied that, God willing, they would make an expedition that would bring both profit and honour.

The army summoned to Edinburgh by the King amounted to over thirty thousand men, all mounted, and it found quarters as best it might. Sir John was impatient to give his men an opportunity to shine on the field of battle, for they had been idle for too long, and the order was soon given to move. The army set off in the direction of Roxburgh, and although the King remained at Edinburgh, all his sons accompanied the expedition. The French had brought with them two hundred full sets of armour, which were distributed among the Scots knights to the great delight of the recipients, who were otherwise ill-equipped. They encamped on the Tweed at Melrose, and after passing Lambir Law, reached Roxburgh. Roxburgh Castle, and all the land around it, belonged to Sir John Montagu, and was held for him by Sir Edward Clifford. After due consideration, the French admiral and the Scottish army passed it by, since it appeared to be heavily defended, and impregnable, and followed the Tweed in the direction of Berwick and the sea. They came to two square towers, held by two knights, father and son, by the name of Strands, and finally took them by storm, and captured the knights, who had put up a valiant defence and inflicted severe wounds on the Scots troops. The army also made an assault on Wark Castle, which was held for Sir John Montagu by Sir John Lussbourne, who had made its defences as strong as possible in expectation of an attack. Here the French showed far more valour than the Scots. Crossing the ditches against heavy resistance, they fixed their scaling ladders to the walls, and fought hand-to-hand with daggers against the occupants of the castle. Sir John Lussbourne took on the French knights himself, and apart from a German knight, Sir Alberic Gastelain, who was sadly killed, many others were wounded. But finally, owing to the great number of the assailants and the continuous vigour of their assault, the castle was taken, together with the knight and his family who were inside. The French took forty prisoners, and they burned and dismantled the castle, since they could not hope to hold such a forward position in England. They then advanced towards Alnwick, and destroyed the lands of the Percys as far as Cornhill, a strong castle near the sea, which they did not attack for they knew well that it would be a waste of effort.

To their delight, the French discovered that a large English army under the Duke of Lancaster, the Earls of Northumberland and Nottingham, and Lord Neville was hastening to meet them, and that it included the barons of Northumberland, York, and Durham. The Scots, however, advised a retreat, and wanted to await the enemy on their own borders, to which Sir John de Vienne agreed, and the army retired past Berwick in the direction of Roxburgh.

The English had known for some time of the arrival of the French in Scotland, and had made greater preparations than ever for a counter-expedition. They had loaded a hundred and twenty vessels to accompany it, with provisions, by sea; and the King took the field with his uncles the Earls of Cambridge and Buckingham, and his brothers Sir Thomas and Sir John Holland. The Earls of Salisbury, Arundel, Pembroke, Stafford and Devonshire, with other barons, and knights, accompanied the King, with an army of forty thousand lances, not counting a further two thousand lances and fifteen hundred archers belonging to the barons of the borders. The King made great haste to York, with fifty thousand archers, and hearing there was to be a battle against the Scots in Northumberland he advanced to Beverley, where the news reached him that the Scots had retired to their own country.

170

At this time an accident occurred that aroused deadly hatred between the English lords. An archer belonging to Sir Ralph Stafford shot a squire attached to the King's brother, Sir John Holland, in a quarrel over the treatment of a knight from Bohemia who had come to visit Queen Anne. Sir Ralph, though angry with his archer, tried to negotiate his pardon, but Sir John, in a frenzy, knocked Sir Ralph off his horse in the dark with his sword, and accidentally killed him. Sir John hastily took sanctuary in Beverley Minster, knowing how popular Sir Ralph had been with the army, and uncertain of the reaction of his own brother the King. Sir Ralph's father, the Earl of Stafford, was enraged by the death of his only son, a handsome and accomplished knight, but took the wisest advice of his friends, and after the funeral of his son, went to the King and with tears in eyes, fell on his knees and said in great anguish: 'King, you are King of England, and have sworn to uphold justice in the kingdom, and you know how your brother, without any reason, has killed my son and heir. I demand justice; otherwise you will have no worse enemy than me. I want you to know that the death of my son affects me so deeply that were I not afraid of breaking up this campaign by the trouble and confusion that the army would suffer, whereby I would gain more blame than honour, I would avenge him so heavily that it would still be spoken of in England a hundred years from now. But for the present I will wait till this expedition is over, because I do not wish our enemies to be assisted by my misfortune.' 'Earl of Stafford,' replied the King, 'you may be certain that I will see that justice is done beyond what the barons of my kingdom would wish or dare to judge, and never, for any brother of mine, will I do otherwise.' The Earl of Stafford's relations replied, 'Sir, you have spoken well, we thank you very much.' The earl continued with the expedition, and concealed his feelings about the death of his son, for which the barons gave him great credit.

171

Confident in the hope that Sir John de Vienne would give them battle, the King's army, which consisted by now of seven thousand men-at-arms and sixty thousand archers, pressed on northwards. Sir John had intended to fight, as he had shown by his words to the Scots: 'My lords, collect as large an army as you can. For if the English come as far as Scotland, I will fight.' And the Scots had replied, 'God be on our side!'—though afterwards they were to change their tune.

The King advanced through Durham and Newcastle to Berwick, where he crossed the Tweed and took up his quarters in Melrose Abbey. This abbey had never before been damaged, in all the wars between England and Scotland; but on this occasion it was burned and destroyed because the English were determined to lay waste to the whole of Scotland before returning home, since the Scots had now joined themselves with the French.

The French admiral then asked the Scots: 'Why do we wait? Why do we not make a reconnaissance and then fight our enemies? When we arrived, we were told that if you had a thousand good lances from France, you would be strong enough to fight. Well, you have over a thousand, as well as five hundred crossbowmen. And I can tell you that my knights are great fighters, the flower of our knighthood; they will not run away, they will stand their ground and take whatever God sends them.'

The Scots knew the strength of the English and had no intention of fighting, and this was their answer: 'In faith, my lord, we know that you and your knights are men of valour, but we hear that the whole of England has come up here, and that they have never been in such force before. We will take you to a spot where you can see their array, and if you say they must be fought, they will be, for we fully acknowledge everything you claim that we have said.' Then Douglas and the Scots lords took the admiral up to a mountain corrie, below which the English army had to pass, so that he and the French knights could see the combined strength of the English forces, which together came to six thousand men-at-arms and sixty thousand archers, servants, and followers. The Scots had no more than a thousand lances (with a thousand more from France) and about thirty thousand other men, all badly armed. And the admiral said to Douglas: 'You are right not to fight them; they are strong enough to overrun the whole country and lay it waste, but since we cannot fight, I beg you to take us by the side roads into England, so that we can take the war into their country, as they have done into yours—if such a plan is possible.' The Scots assured him that it was.

So the Scots and the French made for the English border near Carlisle, through the forests and mountains, and they burned towns, villages and houses along the border. The Scots advanced with speed, but the King, being in no fit state for campaigning, retired to the highlands, where he stayed for the whole war, leaving his people to get on with the fighting. The Scots crossed into England, and ravaged the territory of Mowbray, Earl of Nottingham, as well as the estates of the Earl of Stafford, the Baron of Greystoke and Lord Musgrave, before continuing their march to Carlisle.

172

Meanwhile, to the east of the French knights, the King of England had entered Scotland, with his army devastating the country as they went, until they reached Edinburgh, where the King spent five days. When they left, they burned the whole town to the ground except the castle, which is fine and strong and was well defended. The country round about was also laid waste, having been previously abandoned by the inhabitants, who had retired into the fortresses and deep forests, taking their animals with them. The King's large army needed quantities of provisions, which had to follow from England, by land and sea, as none were available in Scotland. They proceeded to Dunfermline, a reasonably fine town with an abbey of black friars where the kings of Scotland were usually buried.

The King moved on, after staying in the abbey, and the army burned it, together with the town as well. They then attacked the castle of Stirling, but suffered heavy losses and failed to take it; and after burning the town they marched away, ravaging the lands of Lord Erskine. The Duke of Lancaster and his brothers intended to lay waste the whole of Scotland and then to cut off the French and Scots (whose march to Carlisle had been reported to them) and kill or capture them all. They burned the town of Perth, on the Tay, where there is a fine harbour from which ships can go all over the world, and then they burned Dundee, sparing neither abbeys nor churches in the general destruction. The English vanguard advanced as far as Aberdeen, which is on the sea, on the edge of the Highlands, but they did not attack the town, though the inhabitants were gravely alarmed at their approach.

The French and Scots acted in exactly the same way in Cumberland and Westmorland, meeting with no opposition, since the men-at-arms were all with the King. They finally reached Carlisle, which is well defended by gates, walls, towers and ditches; for it is there that King Arthur generally resided, on account of the fine woods that surround it, and the great feats of arms that have happened there.[1]

In Carlisle there were several knights—among them Sir Lewis Clifford, kinsman of Sir William Neville, and Sir Thomas Musgrave—and the town, which is the capital of the district, was fortunate to have such men to defend it. The French admiral launched a heavy attack, but the defence was solid, and many notable feats of arms were achieved.

---

[1] *Froissart is thinking of Caerleon, identified by Tennyson as Caerleon-on-Usk.*

173

The King's uncles and other advisers were in favour of pursuing the French admiral and the Scots troops, assuming that they could catch up with them in the borders of Cumberland. The necessary stores had arrived, either by sea or land, and the King himself had given orders that this plan should be followed. But it was frustrated in a single evening by Michael de la Pole, Earl of Suffolk, who at that time was the King's greatest favourite and chief counsellor. Whatever his intention may have been, these are said to have been his words to the King: 'Ah, my lord, what are you thinking of? Are you to follow the plan which your uncles have made for you? If you do, you will never return: the Duke of Lancaster's one aim is that you should die, and he should be King. How dare he advise going into country like that, and crossing the mountains of Northumberland, in the middle of winter? There are thirty narrow places there where you could be ambushed, and be in the gravest peril from the Scots. Whatever they tell you, do not put yourself in such danger. If the Duke of Lancaster is so keen, let him go himself, with his own men—I would never advise you to go yourself; you have done quite enough for one season. Neither the Prince your father, nor King Edward[1] your ancestor, ever penetrated so far into Scotland as you have done. This should be enough for you. Protect yourself, for you are young and you have everything before you, and there are people who make great pretences, but who love you very little.'

The King was greatly impressed by these words, and the next day, when the lords were preparing for the march which had already been decided on, the Duke of Lancaster went to see the King, unaware of what Suffolk had said. The King was in a choleric and irascible mood, and said: 'Uncle of Lancaster, you

---

[1] *Possibly Edward III, Richard's grandfather, but more probably Edward I, the Hammer of the Scots.*

will not have your own way yet. Do you think we will ruin ourselves and our people, just for your words? It is outrageous that
you should give us such mad advice, and in future I shall ignore
it, for there is more danger and potential damage in it than any
possible profit or honour or advancement for us and our people.
If you want to make this expedition, do it yourself, but we are
returning to England. And those who love us may follow us.'

Lancaster replied: 'Then I will follow you, my lord, for there
is no man in your company who loves you as much as I do and
my brother do. And if anyone says that I wish other than well to
you and your people, I will throw down my glove to him.'
Nothing more was said, and the King gave orders to return to
England, and the duke had to change his plans. Thus did the
Earl of Suffolk prevent the expedition. Some said that the King
should have pursued the Scots, for he had all his supplies, and it
was on his way home; while others said that the risk was too great,
and they might lose more than they gained. The army left
Scotland by the same road as they had entered it, but not before
ravaging the greater part of the country.

When the French admiral heard the news, his council decided
to return to Scotland, having devastated Cumberland (though
unable to capture Carlisle) and being now short of supplies. The
French thought they had done as much damage in the bishoprics
of Carlisle and Durham as the English had done in Scotland.
When they reached the lowlands, on their way north, they found
the country ruined but the people undismayed: for, they said,
with six or eight stakes they could soon build new houses, and
could fetch their cattle back from the remote fastnesses where
they had been hidden. But whenever the French wanted to buy
anything, they were charged a steep price and there was a danger
of serious riots breaking out on this score. The Scots accused the
French of doing them more harm than the English, and when
asked to explain said: 'You have trampled on all our crops—
wheat, barley and oats—on your way through the country, and
you will not deign to keep to the roads.' The Scots demanded
compensation before the French left, or the latter would find

neither ship nor sailor to take them home again. And some of the
Scots knights complained that their timber had been cut down
and that the French had done great damage in lodging themselves.

174

The French had the greatest difficulty in finding provisions
when they had returned to the neighbourhood of Edinburgh.
There was no wine, and very little beer, or corn or barley for
making bread. Their horses were either broken down or even
killed by hunger and cold, nor would anybody buy them, or
their harness either. The knights told the admiral what he knew
to be true when they complained that they could not endure the
conditions much longer and that Scotland was no place to spend
the winter; and that if they had to wait till the following
summer, they would die of want, and if they scattered over the
countryside, they were afraid that the Scots would murder them
in their beds, judging by the way they had treated the French
foragers before.

The admiral sympathized with them, but expected that the
King of France and the Duke of Burgundy would send reinforcements of money, supplies and men, with which he could wage
war on the English the following summer, if he could but survive
the winter. But seeing the mood of the Scots, he gave permission
for those who so wished to depart. But no ships were available,
and only a few minor knights were allowed by the Scots to leave
the country, so that the rest might be still further weakened. The
French knights were told that they could not leave the country
before paying for the Scots army which had followed them. The
French were in despair, though Douglas and Moray (who were
well disposed towards them), remonstrated with the Scots and
said that they were acting neither like men-at-arms nor friends of
the kingdom of France, and that in future no Scots knight would
ever be able to set foot in France. But the other Scots knights
said to Douglas and Moray, 'Make no concessions to the French,
for you have lost as much as we have.' The admiral was therefore

told that if the French were so anxious to leave Scotland they must first pay compensation, and he found no alternative but to proclaim publicly that anyone in Scotland who had suffered loss or damage from the French should bring their claim to him. The Scots were appeased by this, and by the admiral's personal undertaking not to leave the country until he had personally settled every claim.

Many of the French knights were now able to leave Scotland and return to Flanders or any port to which they could get a passage. They arrived starving, and without either arms or food; and they cursed Scotland, and the day they had gone there. They said that no campaign had ever been harder, and that with God's help they could wish the King of France would make a truce with England for a year or two and march on Scotland and utterly destroy it, for they had never met with worse people than the Scots, and nowhere had they found such false and treacherous savages. The admiral sent a message by them to the King of France and the Duke of Burgundy, explaining the whole situation, and saying that if they wished to see him again they must send enough money to meet the Scots claims in full, since he had given an undertaking to the barons of Scotland that they would be paid.

The King of France and his council were in honour bound to ransom the admiral, since it was they who had sent him there. The money was raised forthwith, and collected at Bruges. The entire Scots claim was met, and the admiral was thus able to leave Scotland. He landed at Sluys, and while some of his knights sought better fortune in other countries, in Norway, and Denmark, and Ireland, most of them landed in France, in a state of destitution, especially the knights from Burgundy, Champagne, Bar, and Lorraine, who to avoid travelling on foot, were reduced to riding the cart-horses that they found working in the fields.

A splendid feast was given for the admiral, and he was asked many questions about Scotland, and the size of the Scots army, and that of the English. Sir John de Vienne said that if the Constable of France had accompanied him with a good company of men-at-arms and Genoese, as had been proposed, they could have taken on the English army in Scotland, and defeated them from lack of supplies. The Duke of Burgundy was inspired by this talk with a great desire to make a large-scale expedition against England.

SUMMARY

175-179

Negotiations between Ghent and the Duke of Burgundy were finally successful, against the wishes of the English governor. A peace treaty was signed.

BOOK III

Book III

≋≋

Froissart produced each of the four volumes of the Chronicles *at some interval after completing its predecessor. Thus, the third volume was not begun till 1390, two years after the completion of the second. But in it he returns to events that had occurred as far back as 1382, and gives a fuller account of them from the further details that he had by then established. This accounts for many of the inconsistencies and contradictions in the original text, which was never intended to appear as a coherent whole.*

The third volume was commissioned by Guy of Châtillon, Count of Blois, at whose court Froissart was then living.

1

It is some time since I spoke of the affairs of distant countries, but I have delayed referring to them because events nearer home were so fresh in my mind. But in Castile and Portugal, in Gascony and Rouergue, in Quercy, in Limousin and in Bigorre, there were valiant men who were not slow to further their own ends, and to make schemes and stratagems against each other without ceasing, and to undertake feats of arms that might result in the surprise and capture of towns, castles and fortresses.

I, John Froissart, had undertaken to compile this chronicle at the request and pleasure of that most noble and renowned prince Guy of Châtillon, Count of Blois, Lord of Avesnes, Beauvais, Estonnehonne and La Gande, my sovereign lord and master; and I decided that there was no likelihood of great feats of arms being performed in Picardy or on the Flemish border, since those parts of the country were at peace. I am well aware that the day will come, when I am dust and ashes, when this grand and noble history will be in great demand, and all noble and valiant people will take pleasure in it, to their own advantage. In order, therefore, to discover the truth about matters that took place far away, and to avoid sending an emissary to make my enquiries for me, I took the opportunity of visiting that great and redoubtable prince, Gaston Phoebus, Count of Foix and Béarn. For I knew that, once admitted to his court, I could not be in a better position to learn the truth about everything; for as a result of his noble and generous disposition, his court is constantly and eagerly frequented by knights and squires from distant lands. I was provided with letters of introduction by the Count of Blois, and in company with a knight called Espaing du Lyon I reached the Château d'Orthez, in Béarn, at sunset on the feast of Saint Katherine,[1] 1388. I dismounted at the Hôtel de la Lune, which was kept by a squire of the count's called Ernanton de Puy, who welcomed me warmly, as I was a Frenchman. Sir Espaing went to speak to the Count of Foix, and found him in a gallery. It was his habit to dine about that time—to rise at noon and have dinner at midnight.

SUMMARY

2-8

A brief summary of the war between Castile and Portugal is followed by Froissart's famous ride to Orthez with Sir Espaing du Lyon, who told him a number of stories about the castles visible from the road and their owners.

9

I was at once sent for, since the count, more than anyone else, loves to see strangers and hear their news. He welcomed me hospitably, and I was entertained in style for more than twelve weeks; my horses, too, were well looked after. What strengthened our acquaintance was that I brought with me a book called

[1] *April 30th.*

Méliador, which I had made for Wenceslas of Bohemia, Duke of Luxemburg and Brabant, containing all the songs, ballads, rounds and virelays which he had composed. The count was pleased by it, and every night after supper I used to read part of it aloud, amid complete silence, so keen was the count's interest. When he wanted to discuss a particular point in it, he would talk to me in good French, and not in his native Gascon. I will say something of his way of life, since I was there long enough to become familiar with it.

Count Gaston Phoebus of Foix was then about fifty-nine years old. I have, in my time, seen many kings, princes, and knights, but I have never met such a good-looking and well-formed man, with such a fine figure and such a pleasing and attractive face. His eyes were grey and deeply expressive of affection, when he felt it. He was so perfect in every way that no praise is too high for him. He loved what should be loved, and deeply detested those things that are detestable. He was wise, full of enterprise and good counsel, and never had doubtful or vicious people about him. He was prudent and devout, and prayed assiduously —a nocturn every day from the Psalms, and prayers to Our Lady, to the Holy Ghost and to the Crucifix, as well as vigils for the dead. Every day he had five francs distributed in small coin as alms, for the love of God to the poor at his gate. He was generous and open-handed, and he knew well how to take from the right source, and to distribute where there was need. Above all, he was fond of dogs, and of hunting both in summer and winter, and he willingly occupied himself both with love and with war. He allowed no extravagance, and kept an account of what was spent each month. He chose twelve of the ablest of his subjects to administer his finances, and they worked in pairs, for two months at a time. He had a chief steward to whom all the others were accountable, and who kept written accounts for him. He also had a treasury in his room from which he would take money to give as presents, for no knight or squire who visited him left empty-handed; and he constantly replenished this supply, to meet any eventuality. He was always accessible to everybody, and treated people with kindness and courtesy, though the answers and advice that he gave were brief. He had four secretaries permanently on call, and when he had letters to write or to copy, or wanted them for any other purpose, he would not call on them by their names, John, Walter, William, or whatever it might be, but would call out for any one of them quite impersonally.

When he came into the hall for supper, at midnight, it was lit by twelve torches, each carried by a servant, and giving out a brilliant light. The hall was always full of knights and squires, and tables were ready laid for anyone who wanted supper. Everyone waited till they were addressed before speaking to him. He ate a great deal of poultry, the wings and legs only, and drank very little. He was expert in music, and often made his attendants sing songs and rounds to him. He spent about two hours at table, and was always pleased to see fanciful dishes placed in front of him, which he would at once have sent round to the knights and squires.

In short, I had been in any number of the highest courts of the day, but never had I seen one which pleased me more. On every side, knights and squires of honour came and went, and one heard them talking of love and war. No form of honour was missing, and the valour of the count attracted news and information from every country one could name. It was there that I learned the greater part of the feats of arms that had occurred in Spain, Portugal, Aragon, Navarre, England and Scotland and the borders of Languedoc; for knights and squires of every nation arrived there, and I could either consult them or the count himself, since he was so ready to talk with me. Seeing that everything at the court was so fine and splendid, I was anxious to know what had become of the count's son, Gaston, and how he had died. In the end I heard the story from an old and important squire who related it as follows:

It is well known that the count had not been on good terms with the countess for a long time. The cause of the trouble was the King of Navarre, the countess's brother, who once pledged himself to ransom Lord d'Albreth (whom the count held in prison) for fifty thousand francs. The count knew that the King could not be trusted, and would not accept his security. The countess was annoyed by this and pointed out that she had herself brought with her a dowry of fifty thousand francs, and that the count would not therefore be risking his own money by accepting the King's security; 'That is true,' replied the count. 'But if I thought that your brother would fail to pay for that reason, I would not let Lord d'Albreth go until the last farthing was paid. But since you ask me, I will release him—not out of any love for you, but for the sake of my son.' Lord d'Albreth was released, and went over to the French side, marrying the sister of the Duke of Bourbon. In due course he paid the King of Navarre what he owed him for securing his release, but the King never repaid the Count of Foix. The count then told his wife to go and tell her brother that he was very much dissatisfied at the failure to pay. This she agreed to do and she was warmly welcomed by her brother on her arrival at Pamplona. She gave him the message, and the King replied; 'My dear sister, the money is yours. It is your dowry, and since I am in possession of it, it will never leave the kingdom of Navarre.' 'Ah, my lord,' replied the countess, 'You will make my husband hate me bitterly, and if you persist in this I will not dare return to Foix, for my lord will kill me for having deceived him.' The King was unwilling to let such a large sum slip through his fingers, and replied: 'I cannot say how you should act—whether you should stay or go, but it is my duty to keep this money for you, and it will never leave Navarre.'

The countess could not make him change his mind, and, not daring to go home, stayed in Navarre. The count understood the perfidy of the King, and began to hate the countess—blameless though she was—for not coming home after delivering his message. So the matter stood. Gaston, their son, grew up to be a fine boy, and was married to the daughter of the Count of Armagnac. He was now about sixteen, a handsome boy, and the image of his father. He decided to visit his mother in Navarre, but in spite of his beseeching her to return, she would not. His uncle, the King of Navarre, entertained him royally, and gave him a number of presents, the last of which was a bag of the most violent poison. 'Gaston, my nephew,' said the King, 'you must do what I tell you. You know that your father, the count, has conceived a deadly hatred for your mother. This is a great sorrow to me, and must be to you too. To put him right, you must take a little of this powder and put it in your father's food, taking care that no one sees you. As soon as he eats it he will long for your mother to be with him again, and they will love each other as much as ever. But you must not tell anyone of our scheme, or it will lose its effect.' The boy promised to do all this, and believed every word his uncle had told him.

He was warmly welcomed on his return to Orthez, and showed his father the presents he had been given, with the exception of the little bag of powder. Gaston had a little bastard brother, Evan, and like many brothers of the same age, they shared a bedroom. They even used the same clothes on occasion, and one day Evan picked up Gaston's coat from his bed and found the bag with the powder. He asked Gaston what it was, and was told sharply that it was no business of his. Gaston remained very thoughtful, and three days later happened to lose his temper with Evan over a game, and hit him. Evan ran in tears to his father, who had just heard mass, and asked him, 'What is the matter, Evan, for God's sake?' 'My lord, Gaston has attacked me, though he deserves attacking more than me.' 'Why?' said the count, whose suspicions were easily aroused. 'Well, since he has come back from Navarre he has been carrying a bag of powder next to his chest. I do not know what it is, or what it is for, but he has said once or twice that his mother will soon be more in your favour than she has ever been.' 'Oh,' said the count. 'Well, keep quiet and do not tell anyone else what you have told me.' 'I will not,' replied the child.

The count pondered deeply till supper-time, when he took his place at table as usual. His son Gaston always served him at table, and tasted the food first; and when he came near, the count noticed the strings of the little bag hanging from his neck. 'Gaston, come here.' he said, 'I have something to say in your ear.' The child approached, and his father opened his shirt, cut the strings of the bag, and held it in his hand. 'What is in this bag?' he asked. The child turned pale, trembled violently, and said nothing, for he knew he had done wrong. The count took some powder from the bag, sprinkled it on a slice of bread and gave it to a greyhound sitting by his chair. After eating the first morsel, the dog rolled over and died. The count, not surprisingly, flew into a rage, and went for his son with the knife. He would have killed him on the spot, but knights and squires dashed up and cried out, 'My lord, for God's sake, wait and see what this is before you lay hands on your son.' The count cried out, in the Gascon language: '*Zo*, Gaston, you traitor. It was for your sake, and to increase your inheritance, that I fought and incurred the enmity of the Kings of France, and Spain, and England, and Navarre and Aragon, and are you now trying to murder me? Unnatural boy, know that you will die for it.' With these words he leaped over the table, knife in hand, and would have killed him on the spot, had not the knights and squires thrown themselves on their knees in tears, and said: 'My Lord, for God's sake, do not kill Gaston. He is your only child. Keep him, and question him. Perhaps he did not know what he had got, and is not in the least to blame.' 'Put him in the dungeon,' cried the count, 'and guard him so closely that he will not escape.' This was done, and many of the boy's attendants were arrested, but some escaped out of the country, among them the Bishop of Lescar, near Pau, who was gravely suspected. Fifteen others were horribly put to death, on the grounds that they must inevitably have known the boy's secrets, and should have warned the count of what his son was carrying at his breast. Some of those who were killed were the handsomest and best young squires in Gascony, for the count was always surrounded by a splendid household.

The count was overwhelmed, and summoned all the nobles and principal people of Foix and Béarn to Orthez, and explained that he found his son guilty, and intended to put him to death. They replied with one accord: 'Saving your grace, my lord, we do not want Gaston to die. He is your heir and you have no other.' The count hesitated, and thought that two or three months' imprisonment might be a sufficient punishment, after which his son should be sent on his travels for a few years, at the end of which the crime would be forgotten, and his son would be older and steadier. The nobles made him promise not to put Gaston to death, and after giving the promise, he dismissed them.

Gaston was confined to a small and dimly lit cell in the dungeon; for ten days he hardly ate or drank anything, and after his death his meals were found untouched, so that it is strange that he survived as long as he did. The count had him kept without any guard to comfort him, and he was still dressed in the clothes he had on before. He was deeply vexed at this unexpected treatment, and cursed the day he was born to come to such an end. On the day of his death he again refused food, and the servants noticing that none of the food had been touched, went to the count and explained that his son was starving himself. The count went into the cell without a word, holding in his hand a long, narrow knife with which he had been cleaning and cutting his nails. He held it so closely in his fist that only the tip of it protruded. While opening the curtain at the cell door he had the misfortune to strike his son on a vein in his throat. All the count said was, 'Ah, traitor, why won't you eat?'; he then left the cell and went back to his room. Gaston was frightened at his father's coming, and already weak with fasting, and the point of the knife, small as it was, had cut a vein in his throat. The boy turned away and died. The servant immediately went back to the count and told him that Gaston was dead. The count could not believe it and sent a knight to confirm it, which he did. The count was then beside himself with rage and grief, and cried out: 'Oh, oh, Gaston, what a tragedy! It was a black day for us both when you went to Navarre to see your mother. Never will I be so happy again.' He then sent for his barber, and had his head shaved in mourning, and together with his household put on black clothes. Gaston's body was carried, amid tears and lamentations, to the church of the Augustinian Friars at Orthez, where he was buried. He died by his father's hand, but it was the King of Navarre who was to blame.

I was deeply affected by this sad story, and felt deeply sorry for the count, whom I found a magnificent, noble, generous and courteous lord, and also for the country, which was now without an heir. The same squire told me a story of the count's bastard brother, Sir Peter of Béarn, when I asked if he was a rich man, and married. 'He is married,' was the answer, 'but neither his wife nor his children live with him, for the following reason. He is in the habit of getting out of bed in his sleep and putting on his armour, drawing his sword and striking out as if he were on the field of battle. When his servants wake him up and tell him, he is quite unaware of what he is doing, and tells them they are lying. Sometimes they leave no armour in his bedroom, but on those occasions he makes such a tumult that it sounds as if all the devils in hell were let loose. So they find it better to leave the armour with him, because he sometimes remains quietly in bed. Of the fortune that his wife brought him she keeps the revenue from three-quarters of it and he keeps the remaining quarter. She lives with her cousin the King of Castile, and her father was the Count of Biscay, who was put to death by his cousin, Don Pedro.[1] He tried to imprison her, too, but only succeeded in seizing her lands, so that while he was alive she never enjoyed them. When her father died, she was told 'Escape, my lady, for if Don Pedro catches you he will either imprison you or kill you for he is angry that you say he had his wife murdered in her bed, who was sister of the Duke of Bourbon and the Queen of France. And your evidence is the most credible, since you were her lady of the bedchamber. That is why Florence, Countess of Biscay, fled, with only a few attendants—as anyone would flee from death— and arrived here and told my lord her story.

[1] *Pedro the Cruel, King of Castile.*

'The count, who is full of affection for ladies and damsels, took pity on her and placed her with the Lady of Corasse, who is a great baroness in this country, and provided her with everything that was fitting. His brother Sir Peter, who had not yet formed the habit of fighting in his sleep, was then a young knight in high favour, and the count arranged a marriage between them, and recovered her lands. They have a son and a daughter, but she keeps them with her in Castile, as they are still young, and she is now once more in possession of the greater part of her lands.'

'Holy Mary!' said I. 'How comes it that Sir Peter has these strange fancies, and dares not sleep alone in his room, but gets up and skirmishes about? It is indeed a strange tale!' 'Upon my word,' was the reply, 'he has often been asked, but he has no idea. The first night that it happened was after he had been hunting a wonderfully large bear in the woods in Biscay. The bear had killed four of his dogs, and wounded several others, but Sir Peter drew his Bordeaux sword and after a long fight, in which he was in great danger, finally killed the bear and brought it back to his castle at Languedudon. All who saw it marvelled at the size of the bear and at the spirit of the knight who had got the better of it.

'When Sir Peter's wife saw it, she fainted, and was carried to her room. She remained in a sad state for two days, but would not say what was the matter. On the third day she said to her husband: "My lord, I will never be well until I have made a pilgrimage to the shrine of Saint James at Compostella. Give me leave to go, I beg you, with my son Peter and my daughter Adrienne." Sir Peter agreed, and she left with all her gold, silver, and jewellery, for she had determined never to return. She made her pilgrimage, and took the opportunity of visiting her cousins the King and Queen of Castile, who entertained her well; and there she still is. She will neither come home herself, nor send back her children. The rumour is that the moment she saw the bear, she had a premonition, which caused her to faint. For her father had once hunted it and had heard a voice crying out (though he could see nobody): "You hunt me though I wish you no harm;

but you will die a miserable death." His daughter remembered this when she saw the bear, and also remembered that he had been put to death by Don Pedro without cause. She will not love her husband any more, and maintains that whatever he does to prevent it, he will not succeed. The story of Sir Peter is well known; what do you think of it?'

I replied that I could easily believe it, since we read in history that the gods and goddesses of old transformed men and women into animals and birds, as they pleased; and I told him the story of Actaeon who was changed by Diana into a stag. The squire replied that this might indeed be the case.

Of all the solemn feasts that the count kept every year, that of Saint Nicholas[1] was celebrated the most splendidly throughout his territories, more so even than that of Easter. I was there myself, and I saw the entire population of the town of Orthez, led by their clergy, process to the castle; there the count joined them and the procession returned on foot to the church of Saint Nicholas, where the psalm was chanted *Benedictus Dominus, Deus meus, qui docet manus meas ad proelium, et digitos meos ad bellum.*[2] When the psalm was finished, they began it over again, and the divine office was as splendidly performed as in the chapel of the Pope or the King of France on the special feasts at Easter and Christmas. The Bishop of Pamiers sang the mass, and I never heard the organ played more melodiously than on that day. To put it briefly, the state of the count's court at this time was perfect, and the count was so wise and perceptive that no great prince of the day could compare with him for good sense, honour, and generosity.

[1] *December 6th.*
[2] *Blessed be the Lord my God, who trains my hands for battle, and instructs my fingers in warfare.*

SUMMARY

10-17

Froissart learns further details of the fighting in different parts of France, and the war between Castile and Portugal. The Portuguese, with English support, won a great victory at Aljubarrota and a truce followed.

18

Another fact that was told me at Orthez will amaze the reader, if he considers it, namely that at Orthez, the Count of Foix knew on the very next day everything that happened at the battle of Aljubarota.

He spent three days in complete seclusion, eating little, and saying nothing. On the third evening he called his brother, Sir Arnold William, and said in a low voice:

'Our men have had a bad time of it. I am greatly distressed, because it has happened exactly as I predicted.' Sir Arnold knew his brother's character well enough to remain silent, but the count, to relieve his feelings, exclaimed, more vigorously this time:

'By God, Sir Arnold, it is just as I say, and we shall soon have news of it. Never for a hundred years has the country of Béarn suffered such losses in a day as it has now in Portugal.' These words were heard by many other knights, who remembered them ten days later when reports from the field came in, bringing fresh grief to the count, and to many others who had lost a father, a son, a brother or a friend.

'Holy Mary!' I said to the squire, 'How did the count know or even guess all this the very next day after the battle? Is he a wizard, or has he got messengers that ride on the wind? What secret art is he endowed with?' The squire laughed and said: 'He must have known it by necromancy. We in this country do not know how he does it, but we have our suspicions, which I must insist that you keep to yourself, for I would not like it known that I told you. We only speak of it discreetly among ourselves.' With this he drew me aside into a corner of the chapel at Orthez and told me the following tale.

About twenty years before, there had been in Béarn a baron called Raymond, Lord of Corasse.[1] Raymond had a lawsuit about the tithes of his church with a priest from Catalonia, who took it before the Pope at Avignon. The Pope decided in favour of the priest, who hurried back to Béarn with a copy of the judgement, sealed with the papal bull. Raymond had his doubts about the priest and said:

'Do you think that I will lose my inheritance just for this piece of paper? I do not think you are so bold as to take anything that is mine, but if you do, you will pay with your life. Go and look for benefactions somewhere else, for you will have nothing from my estates—I forbid you, once and for all, to take my tithes.' The priest knew the baron to be cruel, and did not dare persevere, but before leaving the district he came to the baron and said: 'It is by force, and not by right, that you deprive me of my church dues, and you are doing a grave wrong. I am not so strong in this country as you are, but as soon as I can I will send you a champion of whom you will be a great deal more afraid than you are of me.'

The baron replied: 'Go, in God's name, and do whatever you can. I am not afraid of you, alive or dead, and I will not lose my inheritance for any words of yours.'

The priest left, but about three months later the baron was in bed with his wife at Corasse when invisible messengers came and made a tremendous disturbance in the castle, crashing into everything they came upon, and hammering on the baron's bedroom door. His wife was very much alarmed, but the baron did not want to show fright, for he was brave enough for any adventure. The noise went on for a considerable time, in different parts of the castle, before it stopped, and next day the servants all

---

[1] *A town about twenty miles from Orthez.*

went to the baron and asked if he had heard what they had in the night. The baron replied: 'No. What did you hear?' They explained that the castle had been turned upside down, and all the crockery knocked over in the kitchen. The baron laughed and said that either they had imagined it, or it had been done by the wind.

'In the name of God,' said his wife, 'I heard it all night.'

The next night, the noises were repeated still louder on the doors and windows of the Baron's room. He jumped up and called out: 'Who is making all this noise in my room at this hour?'

The answer came: 'It is I.'

'Who sends you here?'

'The Catalan priest whom you wronged and deprived of his inheritance. I will not leave you alone until you have paid him.'

'Since you are such a good messenger—what is your name?'

'I am called Orton.'

'Orton,' said the baron, 'you are wasting your time in the services of this priest, he will only give you trouble. I want you to leave him and come and serve me.' Orton had taken a liking to the knight and said:

'You want me to?'

'Yes, but you must do no harm to anyone here. Then we will get on well.'

Orton took a great liking to the baron, and often visited him at night. When he found him asleep he would wake him up by pulling the pillow from under his head, or banging on the door or the windows. 'Let me sleep, Orton,' the baron would say.

'Not until I have told you some news,' would be Orton's reply. The baron's wife was so frightened that her hair stood on end and she hid in the bedclothes. Orton gave the baron reports from England or Hungary or Germany or wherever he had been, and the baron would learn the latest news. This continued for five or six years, until the baron could no longer keep it to himself but told the Count of Foix how he was able to give him such accurate information from all over the world. I do not know if Orton had more than one master, but he visited the baron two or three times every week and gave him information, which the baron passed on to the Count of Foix, who was delighted, since no man had a keener appetite than him for news from abroad. One day they were talking about Orton, and the count asked if the baron had ever seen the spirit. The answer was no.

'Oh,' said the count, 'I am surprised. If I were on such good terms with him as you are, I would ask him to show himself. I should much like to know—you say he speaks Gascon, like you or I?'

'He does, and since you ask, I will try and see him.'

One night, the baron was, as usual, in bed with his wife, who was now quite accustomed to Orton, and quite unafraid of him, when the spirit woke the baron by tweaking his pillow.

'Where have you come from?'

'Prague. The Emperor died the day before yesterday.'

'How far is Prague?'

'Sixty days' journey, but I can go as quick as the wind.'

'Have you got wings?'

'That is none of your business,' said Orton.

'No, but I would dearly love to see you and to know what form you take.'

'That does not concern you. It is enough that you can hear me, and that I bring you reliable news.'

'By God,' said the baron, 'I would like you better if I could see you.'

Orton answered: 'Since you are so keen to set eyes on me, the first thing you see when you get up in the morning, will be me.'

'All right,' said the baron, 'you can go now.'

In the morning the knight was getting up, but his wife was so alarmed that she said she would not get up all day; when her husband complained she said:

'If I do, I shall see Orton. I do not want to meet him or to see him.'

'Well, I will,' said the baron, and jumped up and sat on the end of the bed; but even after opening the shutters he could see nothing that he could claim to be Orton. The next night Orton came and started talking to the baron, who complained that Orton had not shown himself.

'I did,' said Orton.

'You did not,' said the baron.

'Did you not see anything then, when you jumped up?'

The baron thought, and finally said:

'Yes. When I was sitting on my bed I saw two straws turning and twisting in the draught, on the floor.'

'That was me,' said Orton, 'that was the form I took.'

'That is not enough, you must appear in a different form so that I can see you and recognize you.'

'You ask too much; you will ruin me and drive me away.'

'I will not. When I see you once properly, I will not ask to see you again.'

'Well,' said Orton, 'you will see me tomorrow. Remember, the first thing you see when you leave your room in the morning will be me.'

'All right,' said the baron. 'You can go now, I want to sleep.'

Orton left, and in the morning the baron got up and went into a gallery that looked out onto a courtyard in the castle. His eyes fell on the largest sow he had ever seen; but she was so thin that she was nothing but skin and bone, and her udder was long and thin and spotted, and her snout was sharp and lean. The baron was not at all pleased to see the sow and had his dogs set on her to destroy her. The sow gave a loud cry and looked up at the baron, who was leaning out of the window. The sow then disappeared; no one saw where she went, and no one ever saw her again. The baron went back to his room thoughtfully, and remembering Orton, said:

'I think I have seen my messenger, and I am sorry I set my dogs on him. I may never see him again, for he said several times that if I ever annoyed him, I would lose him.'

In this he was right. Orton never came again, and within a year the baron was dead. And that is the story of Orton.

'Yes,' said I, 'but why did you tell it me? Does the count also have a messenger of this kind?'

'A number of people think so,' replied the squire, 'because nothing ever happens either here or abroad without his getting to know of it, if he has a mind to. He knew what had happened in Portugal, and no one can lose even a gold or silver spoon here without his knowing at once.' I then left the squire for other company, but I did not forget what he had told me.

SUMMARY

19-24

At Orthez, Froissart heard more descriptions of the war between Portugal and Castile. At the great battle fought at Aljubarrota on August 15th, 1385, the Portuguese, with English support, defeated the forces of Castile and France, partly owing to the Castilians being jealous of their allies.

Soon afterwards, the French recaptured a number of castles held by the English in Toulouse, Rouergue, and the neighbourhood. The King of Armenia appealed to the French to help him against the Turks, who had driven him out of his kingdom.

25

About this time Otto of Brunswick came to Pope Clement at Avignon to ask for payment in consideration of the war he had fought for him against the Romans and Bartolomeo Prignano, who, as you have already heard, styled himself Pope Urban VI. He discussed various topics with the Pope and the cardinals, and received their full attention; but when it came to money, he could not obtain a penny, as the papal treasury was so empty that even the allowances for the cardinals' hats could not be paid. Otto left the Pope with his purpose unachieved, and in a state of discontent. On leaving Avignon he received one thousand francs, which he thought inadequate. Pope Clement's cause was greatly weakened, for Otto never bothered himself with it again.

In addition to this, Margaret of Durazzo, who lived at Gaeta, sent for his assistance against the people of Naples. She was the widow of Charles of Durazzo, King of Naples, who had competed with Louis, Duke of Anjou, for the crown; and she now opposed Louis's widow, the reigning Queen of Naples. Some of Otto's counsellors advised him to help Margaret in her cause, and to marry her, and thus to become king of the country; on the other hand, the young children of King Louis (who had been crowned at Bari) were the rightful heirs, and they had many friends and relations, including the King of France, and also Jeanne, the Dowager Duchess of Anjou, who would support them decisively. Otto wavered for so long that in the end neither party had his support.

At this time, Pope Urban was besieged at Perugia by the army of Pope Clement, which was commanded by Talebert, a knight of Rhodes, and Sir Bernard de la Salle. Urban was hard pressed, and on the point of being captured. Indeed, for the sum of twenty thousand francs, Count Conrad, who was in command of a large force of Germans, would have delivered him up to Pope Clement. Bernard de la Salle was sent to Avignon to inform the Pope and the cardinals, but the money could not be raised. Sir Bernard returned discontented to Perugia, the siege was conducted with less vigour on both sides, and Pope Urban escaped to Rome.

I am sure that in times to come it will be a matter of astonishment that troubles of such severity and such long duration should have befallen the Church. But in fact they were a punishment sent by God to draw the attention of the clergy to the excessive pomp and possessions which they enjoyed; yet most of them ignored it, so much were they taken up with pride, arrogance, and the spirit of competition in material magnificence. Little attention was paid to religion, which would have been severely weakened, and might indeed have disappeared from the face of the earth, if it had been less firmly rooted in human nature, and had it not been confirmed and strengthened by the Holy Ghost, who rekindles the hearts of those who have gone astray. The great landowners, who had previously been such noble benefactors of the Church, began to make a mockery of it, and do so even down to the present time.[1] The common people were considerably surprised at this state of affairs, and wondered why such great lords as the Kings of France and Germany did nothing to remedy it. There is nevertheless one point which may reassure the people and excuse the great nobles: in the same way that there cannot be the yolk of an egg without the white, nor the white without the yolk, so neither can the clergy nor the nobility exist independently of each other.[2] For the nobles are ruled by the clergy, and without their control would soon degenerate into beasts.

In the course of my travels, I have seen a good deal of mankind, but I have never met any lord, with the exception of the Count of Foix, who did not keep and support in comfort a whole entourage of jesters, pages, and court favourites. But the Count of Foix did nothing of the kind, for he was a man of great good sense and natural wisdom, which he valued more highly than anything that such people could have provided for him. I am not saying that those lords who behave as I have described are mad; they are something more than mad: they are blind in spite of having two perfectly good eyes.

King Charles of France, of happy memory, had decided in favour of Pope Clement when the papal schism first broke out; and the Kings of Castile and Scotland took the same view. But the Kings of England and Portugal took the opposite line, as did the Count of Flanders (as I have stated previously), the Emperor of Germany and the King of Hungary. All these supported Urban.

While I am on the subject of these dissensions of Church and state, and the hypocritical behaviour of the great landowners, I recall how, in my youth, in the reign of Pope Innocent at Avignon, a learned friar was kept in prison, by name Brother John of Roche

[1] *1390.*

[2] *This may seem a poor excuse for the irreligiousness of the nobility, but it is to some extent explained by the system of patronage without which Froissart could not have conducted his research.*

Teillère. This friar, as I have often heard in private, though it was never mentioned openly, made a number of remarkable prophecies while in prison about the affairs of the world, and in particular those relating to France. He foretold the capture of King John and the misfortunes of the Church that would be caused by the worldly excesses of those who governed it. I was told that he was taken to the Pope's palace at Avignon, to dispute with the Cardinals of Ostia and Auxerre. He told them the following parable:

'There was once a bird that was hatched and grew up without any feathers. When the other birds heard of this, they went to see him, for in spite of being without feathers, he was a fine and beautiful bird. They pondered on the fact that without feathers he could not fly, and that if he did not fly he could not live, and they decided that such a beautiful bird could not be allowed to perish, and every other bird presented him with some of its own feathers. The best feathered contributed the most, and soon he was able to fly, to the delight of all who had made it possible. When he saw how well feathered he was, and how all the other birds honoured him, he became proud; and he not only began to look down on those who had raised him up, he went so far as to peck them and drive them away. The other birds assembled and discussed how they should deal with this bird whom they had clothed, and who had now become so proud and puffed up that he thought nothing of them. The peacock said: "My feathers have made him too beautiful, I am going to take them back." "In God's name," said the falcon, "I shall do the same." And all the other birds followed the example of the peacock and the falcon, and began to take away the feathers that they had given. When he saw this, the bird became very humble, and realized the honour and glory which he enjoyed did not come from himself, nor did his fine feathers; for he had come into the world naked and unfledged, and had remained so until the other birds had given him feathers, which they were now perfectly capable of taking away from him, whenever they chose. He then cried out for mercy, and said that he would mend his ways and never again be guilty of vanity and pride. The other birds took pity on him when they saw how humble he had become, and gave him back their feathers, saying: "We are quite happy to see you flying about, as long as you remain humble—that is how it should be. But remember, if you ever grow proud again, we will pluck you bare, and leave you naked, as we found you."

'This, my lords,' said Brother John to the cardinals, 'is what will happen to you. For the emperors and kings and princes of Christendom have given you all your possessions that you may serve God; and you spend them on pomp and vanity and luxury and extravagance of every kind. Why do you not read the life of Saint Sylvester, the first[1] pope after Saint Peter, and consider how it came about that Constantine first gave tithes to the Church, and on what conditions? Sylvester did not make expeditions attended by two or three hundred horsemen. He lived a simple and secluded life at Rome, surrounded by men of the Church, when through the grace of God the angel announced to him the conversion of the Emperor, who until that time had been an infidel and an unbeliever. The angel also told Sylvester that he would be instrumental in curing the Emperor of leprosy, from which he was suffering so severely that his limbs were rotting away. And he afterwards cured the Emperor, by means of baptism. And that is how Constantine came to believe in God, and converted the empire to Christianity, and made over to the Church all the tithes which until then had been paid to the Emperor. He also gave the Pope many other properties and gifts, for the increase of the faith and of the Church. But it was his intention that these benefits should be properly used, humbly and not proudly, nor with vanity and presumption, whereas what happens now is the opposite. That is why the day will come when God will grow so angry with those who rule the Church that the

---

[1] *This is an obvious mistake: Saint Sylvester was thirty-second in succession to Saint Peter, and the miraculous conversion of the Emperor Constantine is elsewhere attributed to the appearance of a fiery cross in the sky, over the words* ΕΝ ΤΟΥΤΩ ΝΙΚΑ.

nobles who have conferred all these benefits on the Church will grow cold in their devotions and will perhaps even take back what they have given.'

The cardinals were quite astonished at the friar's speech, and would willingly have put him to death, had they been able to find any possible just cause for doing so. Instead, they imprisoned him at Avignon, and did not dare let him out, for his attention was always on such deep matters, and he examined the Scriptures so closely, that he might have led the world astray. However, many of the prophecies that he made in prison (for which he quoted the Apocalypse in support) afterwards came true. His proofs saved him on several occasions from a heretic's death at the stake; and some of the cardinals took pity on him and refrained from oppressing him, as they might have done otherwise.

SUMMARY

26-124

The author returns to the affairs of Portugal, and explains why the Portuguese preferred to have the Grand Master of Avis for their King rather than Don John of Castile, who had married Beatrice, daughter of the late King Ferdinand of Portugal. The chief reason was their hatred of the Castilians. After the battle of Aljubarrota, they sent ambassadors to London, who were well received, and who told the Duke of Lancaster of the events of the last years.

Parliament met at Westminster and the Duke of Lancaster was dispatched with a large army to recover Castile for the Portuguese. A number of French knights offered their services to the King of Castile, and the Duke of Lancaster could not resist attacking the French who were blockading the English garrison at Brest, and driving them off. He subsequently landed at Corunna, in Galicia. A month later he marched to Santiago, which surrendered. Meanwhile the French evacuated Corunna and joined the King of Castile, plundering the country as they went.

Great preparations were made by the French to invade England, and a fleet assembled at Sluys. In Galicia, the English took Roales and Villalobos, and, in Portugal, Pontevedra, Vigo, and Bayona. The French fleet at Sluys was delayed by the dilatoriness[1] of the Duke of Berry, and the expedition was finally postponed till the following spring [1387].

King Pedro of Aragon died in January, and his son, King John, imprisoned the Archbishop of Bordeaux, who had been negotiating for the Duke of Lancaster. The latter retaliated by invading Aragon, and the archbishop was released. The Duke of Bourbon led a French army to support the King of Castile, and meanwhile the English fleet, under the Earl of Arundel, with the Earls of Devonshire and Nottingham and the indefatigable Bishop of Norwich, defeated the Flemish fleet (raised by the Duke of Burgundy) off the mouth of the Thames. The English then landed near Sluys, and after plundering the surrounding country, returned home.

The King of Portugal married Philippa, daughter of the Duke of Lancaster, at Oporto. Braganza surrendered to the Duke of Lancaster. A French force arrived in Castile, and advised the King not to give battle until the arrival of the Duke of Bourbon's army.

Great discontent arose in England at the lack of military success, especially by comparison with the triumphs of Edward III and the Black Prince. Further French plans to invade England were hindered by the Duke of Brittany, who was eager to regain favour with the English; he also imprisoned and held to ransom the Constable of France, who surrendered various castles, and large sums of money, in return for his freedom. France was also harassed by the Duke of Guelders, and the King of Portugal and the Duke of Lancaster had further successes against Castile, and joined forces.

Froissart then gives an account (inaccurate in detail as in chronology) of events in England. The King's uncles, the Dukes of Gloucester and York, were opposed to the government of the King, and especially to the Earl of Oxford, now created Duke of Ireland. The latter left London, with the King, and went to Bristol. They then decided to make war on the King's uncles, who won a battle against them near

---

[1] *This may, in fact, have been carefully planned policy.*

Oxford. The Duke of Ireland fled to Holland, and the King returned
to London to hold Parliament.

The King of Castile would not face the King of Portugal and the
Duke of Lancaster in open battle, but the army of the latter suffered
great hardship from the climate in Castile and from the country
being already laid waste. All foreign troops gradually left Castile, and
the Duke of Lancaster, after a serious illness, retired to Bayonne.

The long feud between Brabant and Guelders continued, the former allying itself with France, the latter with England; the Duke of
Brittany made a joint treaty with England and Navarre. The French
King invaded Guelders, and an English fleet went to support the Duke
of Brittany, landing at La Rochelle.

124

. . . I have already described many of the troubles that afflicted
King Richard II through his quarrels with his uncles. As a result
of the evil counsel of the Duke of Ireland, a number of English
knights lost their lives, and the Archbishop of York was nearly
deprived of his see. By the advice of the King's new council and
the Archbishop of Canterbury, Lord Nevill, who had been in
command of the defence of the border against the Scots, was
relieved of his post. He had previously been paid sixteen thousand
francs a year for this service by the counties of Durham and
Northumberland. He was replaced by Sir Henry Percy, Earl of
Northumberland, at a salary of eleven thousand francs a year.
This caused great hatred and indignation between the two
families, who were neighbours, and were even related to each
other. The barons and knights of Scotland heard of this feud, and
decided in return for all that they suffered in the past, to make an
expedition into England, now that the English were already
quarrelling among themselves.

To conceal their plans, they called an assembly as far away as
Aberdeen, on the fringe of the highlands. And they decided in
the presence of all the barons of Scotland, to concentrate their
forces at Jedburgh Castle, a remote place near the border. On

the appointed day, in the middle of August 1388, they all assembled, without mentioning anything of their plans to their King, who in their opinion knew nothing about warfare. The knights included James, Earl of Douglas, John, Earl of Moray, with the Earls of March and Dunbar, Fife, Sutherland, Menteith, and Mar, Sir Archibald Douglas, Sir Robert Erskine, Sir Mark Drummond, Sir William Lindsay and his brother Sir James, Sir Thomas Berry, Sir Alexander Lindsay, Sir John Swinton, Sir John Sandilands, Sir Patrick Dunbar, Sir John and Sir Walter Sinclair, Sir Patrick Hepburn, and his son Sir John, Lord Montgomery, with his two sons, Sir John Maxwell, Sir Adam Glendenning, Sir William Stuart, Sir John Haliburton, Sir Robert Lauder, Sir Stephen Fraser, Sir Alexander and Sir John Ramsay, Sir William of North Berwick, Sir Robert Hart, Sir William Wardlaw, Sir John Armstrong, David Fleming, Robert Campbell and many other Scots knights and squires.

There had not been such a large gathering for sixty years, and they numbered twelve thousand lances, and forty thousand archers and other men. The Scots are not skilled in archery, but they all carry battle-axes over their shoulders with which they deal fearsome blows in battle. The lords were well pleased with the extent of their numbers and were determined to make an offensive into England to such effect that it would be spoken of for twenty years. They arranged a final base not far off,[1] from which they would set out into England.

The Earl of Northumberland, and the Governors of York and Berwick, soon found out what was afoot by sending spies, disguised as minstrels, to the gathering at Aberdeen. These spies discovered the intentions of the Scots to muster at Jedburgh, and they also noticed a great deal of movement all over the country. They reported all that they saw back to their lords at Newcastle, and secret preparations were made in Northumberland; the knights and barons retired into their castles so as not to frighten off the Scots from their intended expedition, but to be ready to

---

[1] *At Kirk Yetholm, at the foot of the Cheviots.*

fall on them as soon as they appeared. They also reckoned that if the Scots entered the country in Cumberland, by Carlisle, they in their turn would ride into Scotland and do far worse damage, for Scotland is an unenclosed country, whereas the castles and towns of England are strongly fortified.

The Scots at Kirk Yetholm captured an English squire who had been sent to spy on them, to discover their numbers and their intentions. His horse, which he had tied up to a tree, was stolen by a Scotsman (they are all thieves) and he was noticed walking away, booted and spurred, by two Scots knights. He was brought before the Earl of Douglas and was forced to answer, on pain of death, a number of questions: where the Northumbrian barons were, if they had any plans for a counter-expedition, and, if so, by what road: along the coast by Berwick and Dunbar, or by the mountains through Menteith to Stirling. This was the answer that the English squire was forced to give:

'My lords, since I clearly know the truth, I will tell you. When I left Newcastle, there was no sign of an expedition being mounted, but the barons are all ready to set out at a moment's notice, and when they hear that you have crossed the border, they will not come and meet you, for there are not enough of them to fight such a large army as they are convinced that you have.'

'How many do they say we are?' asked the Earl of Moray.

'Forty thousand fighting men, and twelve hundred lances,' was the answer. 'And if you march into Cumberland, they will take the road by Berwick to Dunbar, Dalkeith, and Edinburgh. But if you take that road yourselves, they will go round by Carlisle and enter Scotland by the mountains there.' The Scots lords exchanged silent glances, and later conferred and made other plans, while the English squire was handed over to the governor of Jedburgh Castle for safe keeping.

125

The Scots decided on the following strategy: they divided their army into two, the larger half, with the baggage, to head for Carlisle; while the rest, consisting of three or four hundred lances and two thousand archers and other fighting men, who were all well mounted, were to make for Newcastle and, after crossing the Tyne, were to enter the bishopric of Durham, burning and laying waste the country as they went. They would do a great deal of damage before they were discovered, and when that time came they would choose a favourable position, and fight it out, that being the general wish: for it was high time to repay some of the harm that had been done to them in the past.

The Earl of Douglas, with the Earls of March and Moray, led the smaller division towards Newcastle. The two divisions took leave of each other affectionately and promised not to fight a pitched battle until they were all united, when their superiority in numbers would give them a decisive advantage. They then left the forest of Jedworth, one division turning to the right, the other to the left. The Northumbrians, when their squire failed to return, guessed something of what had happened. They remained on the alert, ready to set out as soon as any word should come of the movements of the Scots. They gave up their messenger for lost.

The Earl of Douglas led his division through Northumberland and into the rich county of Durham, crossing the Tyne near Brancepeth; they then immediately began burning towns and laying waste the country. When the Earl of Northumberland heard what was happening—and indeed smoke could be seen rising from the towns that the Scots attacked and set on fire—he sent his two sons to Newcastle. But he himself stayed at Alnwick, and gave orders for everyone else to join him there; before his sons left, he gave them the following instructions: 'Go to Newcastle, and all the countryside will join you. I will stay here, for it

is on their way home. If we can surround them, we will do well.
But I do not know yet what their tactics will be.'

The two sons, Sir Henry and Sir Ralph, set out and were duly
joined by everyone fit to bear arms. The Scots continued their
destruction right up to the city of Durham, where they skirmished,
but did not stay long. They then turned back, as they had
planned, taking with them all the booty they thought worth the
trouble. The country on the borders of Durham and Northumberland is very rich, and they set fire to all the towns that were
not enclosed. They recrossed the Tyne at the same place as before
and halted outside Newcastle. All the knights of the country
were assembled there, including the Governor of York, Sir
Ralph Langley, Sir Matthew Redman, Sir Robert Ogle, Sir
Thomas Grey, Sir Thomas Halton, Sir John Felton, Sir John
Lilburne, Sir William Walsingham, Sir Thomas Abington, the
Lord of Hilton, Sir John Copeland, and many others. The town
was full to overflowing. There was continual skirmishing, and
the Earl of Douglas, after a long fight, captured Sir Henry
Percy's pennon. Douglas cried out: 'I will take this token back to
Scotland, and fly it from the tower of Dalkeith Castle for all to see
for miles around.' 'By God, Earl of Douglas,' replied Sir Henry,
'you will not even take it out of Northumberland; you may be
sure that you will never keep it or be able to boast of it.' 'In that
case you will have to come and fetch it tonight,' said Douglas. 'I
will fly it in front of my tent, and we shall see if you can remove
it.'

It was growing late, and both sides retired to their camps. The
Scots kept a careful watch, and Sir Henry was advised to postpone
his attack on their quarters. Next day, the Scots struck camp and
made for the border, stopping only to make a vigorous and successful attack on the town and castle of Ponteland, which was held
by a very valiant knight, Sir Raymond Delaval. They burned
both town and castle, and marched on to Otterburn, where they
pitched camp.

126

Very early the next morning, they made an assault on the castle, which was a strong one, and surrounded by marshes. They attacked long and fiercely, but without success; and afterwards, being exhausted, they retired to hold council. The majority was for moving on and rejoining the other division in the direction of Carlisle. But the Earl of Douglas thought otherwise: 'In defiance of Sir Henry Percy, who declared that he would recapture his pennon, which I took from him in fair fight, I will not leave this place for two or three days. We will make another assault on the castle, which it is quite possible to take. We will thus gain twice as much honour, and we will see if he comes for his pennon within that time. If he does, it will be defended.'

Everyone agreed to this, as was only fitting; for Douglas was their supreme commander, and they held him in the highest regard. They built huts out of branches and leaves, and fortified their camp in the marshes, where they also penned the cattle which they had captured.

The Percys were deeply mortified at the loss of their pennon, and Sir Henry had not forgotten his defiant words. But the English imagined that the troops led by Douglas were only the vanguard of the Scots, and the more experienced and prudent knights were against Sir Henry's pursuing them. Their argument went as follows: 'Sir, the fortunes of war are uncertain; if the Earl of Douglas has captured your pennon, he has won it dearly, for he has come right up to our gates, and was well resisted. Another time you will win as much or more from him. You know as well as we do that the whole power of Scotland has taken the field. We are not strong enough to take them on, and they may be merely trying to draw us on by a trick. If they are forty thousand strong, as it is reported, they will surround us and have us at their mercy. It is better to lose one pennon than two or three hundred men, and to risk the whole countryside; for if we lost, it would be defenceless.'

The Percys had been restrained by these words, but fresh reports were brought by other knights who had been able to discover the full extent of the Scots army, as well as their plans and the place where they had chosen to encamp. Whereupon Sir Henry was delighted, and cried: 'To horse! To horse! For by the faith I owe to God and to my father, I will go and recover my pennon, and we will turn the Scots out of their camp before night-fall.' All the knights and squires who heard of the plan joined him. The Bishop of Durham had also collected a large army, and was expected at Newcastle that very evening; but Sir Henry already had six hundred knights and squires at his disposal, and at least eight thousand foot soldiers, and, thinking that this was a large enough force to defeat the Scots (who did not number more than about three hundred mounted lances and perhaps two thousand other fighting men), he would not wait for the Bishop.

By the time the English arrived at Otterburn, the Scots were already at supper, and indeed some of them were asleep, for they had had a hard day attacking the castle, and were planning a fresh assault in the cool of the early morning. The English mistook their servants' quarters for the main camp and forced their way in, shouting 'Percy! Percy!' The alarm was soon given, and the Scots, who had been expecting an attack, had time to send some infantry to prolong the first skirmish while their lords armed themselves. They formed into three companies under the pennons of the three chief barons, and although it was now night, the moon shone brightly, for it was the month of August, and the weather was fine.

The Scots had planned in advance what to do in the event of being attacked; and it is a great advantage to an army, if it is attacked by night, to have examined the ground and to have arranged its defence beforehand, and to have assessed the chances of victory or defeat. The English scattered the servants, but, on advancing into the camp, found fresh troops ready to resist them; and the chief part of the Scots army had made a detour along the side of the moor and fell on the English flank, shouting their battle cries and taking their opponents by surprise. The English rallied, however, and cries of 'Percy!' and 'Douglas!' echoed on every side. The battle raged cruelly, and many were dashed to the ground at the first onslaught of the lances. The English were the more numerous, and in their great desire to be the victors, they stood their ground and drove back the Scots to the brink of defeat. The Earl of Douglas, who was young and strong and eager to shine in battle, and afraid of nothing, made his standard-bearer advance, shouting 'Douglas! Douglas!' Sir Henry and Sir Ralph Percy, eager to avenge the capture of their pennon, hurried to the spot, crying out 'Percy! Percy!' The two banners met, and great deeds of arms were performed, but the English strength in numbers prevailed, and the Scots were driven back. Sir Patrick Hepburn and his son, of the same name, fought gallantly, and brought great honour on their knighthood and their country; and without their vigorous defence the banner of Douglas would have been lost. This brought not only great credit on themselves, but on their memories, and on their descendants to this day.

I met at Orthez, in the year after the battle, two valiant knights who had fought on the English side, Sir John of Châteauneuf and Sir John of Cautiron, and I afterwards met at Avignon a knight and two squires who had fought for Douglas. And in my youth I travelled all through Scotland myself, and spent fifteen days at the castle of Dalkeith with William Earl of Douglas, father of that Sir James, of whom we are now speaking. I therefore had my information from both sides, and they agreed that this battle was as stubborn and hard fought as any battle in history. This I easily believe, for both English and Scots are excellent fighters, and they do not spare each other when they meet. As long as they have lances, axes, swords or daggers, and the breath to wield them, they fight on. When one side has won, they are so proud of winning that they ransom their prisoners on the spot, and with great courtesy. But in the heat of battle, they spare each other nothing; and indeed, in this battle, as valiant deeds were performed as have ever been done.

127

The following paragraph from the translation by Lord Berners is a perfect example of his style at its best, and there is perhaps no need to give a more modern rendering of the passage. The scene could not be more vividly described; only the spelling has been brought up to date.

'Knights and squires were of good courage on both parties to fight valiantly: cowards there had no place, but hardiness reigned with goodly feats of arms, for knights and squires were so joined together at hand strokes, that archers had no place. There the Scots shewed great hardiness and fought merrily with great desire of honour. The Englishmen were three to one: howbeit, I say not but Englishmen did nobly acquit themselves, for even the Englishmen had rather been slain or taken in the place than to fly. Thus, as I have said, the banners of Douglas and Percy and their men were met each against other, envious who should win the honour of that journey. At the beginning the Englishmen were so strong that they reculed back their enemies: then the Earl Douglas, who was of great heart and high enterprise, seeing his men recule back, then to recover the place and to show knightly valor he took his axe in both his hands, and entered so into the press that he made himself way in such wise, that none durst approach near him, and he was so well armed that he bare well off such strokes as he received. Thus he went ever forward like a hardy Hector, willing alone to conquer the field and to discomfit his enemies: but at last he was encountered with three spears all at once, the one strake him on the shoulder, the other on the breast and the stroke glinted down to his belly, and the third strake him in the thigh, and sore hurt with all three strokes, so that he was borne perforce to the earth and after that he could not be again relieved. Some of his knights and squires followed him, but not all, for it was night, and no light but by the shining of the moon. The Englishmen knew well they had borne one down to the earth, but they wist not who it was; for if they had known that it had been the Earl Douglas, they had been thereof so joyful and so proud that the victory had been theirs. Nor also the Scots knew not of that adventure till the end of the battle; for if they had known it, they would have been so sore dispaired and discouraged that they would have fled away. Thus as the Earl Douglas was felled to the earth, he was stricken into the head with an axe, and another stroke through the thigh: the Englishmen passed forth and took no heed of him: they thought none otherwise but that they had slain a man of arms. On the other part the Earl George de la March and of Dunbar fought right valiantly and gave the Englishmen much ado, and cried 'Follow Douglas,' and set on the sons of Percy: also Earl John of Moray with his banner of men fought valiantly and set fiercely on the Englishmen, and gave them so much to do that they wist not to whom to attend.

Of all the battles and encounterings that I have made mention of here-before in all this history, great or small, this battle that I treat of now was one of the sorest and best foughten without cowardice or faint hearts. For there was neither knight nor squire but that did his devoir and fought hand to hand. . . .'

The sons of the Earl of Northumberland, who commanded the army, acquitted themselves valiantly. Sir Ralph narrowly escaped the same fate as Douglas, when he advanced so far ahead that he was surrounded and severely wounded. Being also winded, he surrendered to Sir John Maxwell, who was from the household of the Earl of Moray. On being asked who he was (for it was dark), Sir Ralph was so weak from loss of blood that he could hardly answer. 'Well, Sir Ralph,' was the reply, 'rescued or not, you are my prisoner. I am Maxwell.' 'I submit,' said Sir Ralph, 'but attend to me, for I am so badly wounded that my boots and breeches are filled with blood.' Maxwell looked after him, and hearing the cry of Moray nearby, and seeing the Earl's banner approaching, he said: 'My lord, I present to you Sir Ralph Percy, a prisoner. But take good care of him, for he is very badly wounded.' The Earl was delighted, and said, 'Maxwell, you have well earned your spurs.' Sir Ralph's wounds were dressed, and the battle raged on; none knew who would win, and there were many rescues and counter-attacks that never came to my knowledge.

128

The young Earl of Douglas had performed wonders. When he was wounded, he lay where he fell, for the blow on his head was mortal. His men had kept as close to him as they could, and now his cousins Sir James Lindsay and Sir John and Sir Walter Sinclair, gathered round him, with other knights. They found with him a gallant knight who had kept up with him, and who was his chaplain, but who had valiantly exchanged the chapel for the battlefield, and had several times turned back the English with his battle-axe. In reward for his services, he was later made an archdeacon, and Canon of Aberdeen; his name was Sir William of North Berwick. He, too, had been severely wounded, and with him was Sir Robert Hart, who had fought by his side all night and now lay beside him, with fifteen different wounds on his body from lances and other weapons. Sir John Sinclair asked the Earl; 'How goes it, cousin?' 'Not very well,' was the reply. 'But thank God, few of my ancestors have died in their beds. You must avenge me, for I am as good as dead. My heart beats more and more faintly. Walter, you and Sir John Sinclair raise my banner, for it is certainly on the ground; it fell from the hand of David Campbell, my valiant squire who refused a knighthood from me today, though he was the equal of any knight in courage and loyalty. Shout "Douglas" but do not tell friend or foe that I am not with you. For our foes would be encouraged and our friends disheartened.'

Sir James Lindsay and the Sinclair brothers followed these instructions, and succeeded in rallying a number of the Scottish troops, who drove back the English, killing and bringing down many of them. The Scots advanced as far as the banner of Douglas, which had been borne forward by Sir John Sinclair, and, as the attack gathered force, they were joined by most of the rest of the Scottish army, including the Earls of Moray, March, and Dunbar with their banners and men. They were greatly encouraged by the retreat of the English, and their lances and battle-axes rained blows on the stout helmets of the enemy.

To tell the truth, the English were exceedingly tired before the battle began, for they had come by forced march from Newcastle that same day, a distance of thirty-two miles, and although their spirit was still eager, they were out of breath, whereas the Scots were fresh, and well rested. In their final attack, they drove the English so far back that there was no question of their rallying. Sir Henry Percy had the misfortune to be captured by Lord Montgomery, a most valiant Scots knight. They had fought for a long time hand-to-hand, without interference, for every knight and squire was fully engaged with the enemy. All the chief knights on the English side, whose names I mentioned earlier, were taken prisoner, with the exception of Sir Matthew Redman, the Governor of Berwick, who, seeing that there was no hope of a rally and that knights and squires were fleeing and being captured on every side, succeeded in riding off towards Newcastle; nor could he have regained, single-handed, all that was lost. Of all who fell or were taken on the English side, none fought better than a squire called Thomas Felton, who after prodigious feats of arms against the Earl of Moray's standard, was killed while fighting a cousin of the Earl of Douglas, Simon Glendinning by name.

The battle was extremely hard fought from beginning to end, but the behaviour of the Scots throughout was chivalrous in the extreme; whenever they took a prisoner, they treated him like one of themselves. If the Scots had been numerous enough, not one Englishman would have escaped either death or capture. But they felt anxious at the large number of English troops in the country, and tended to stick together in large companies in order to maintain solidarity and to guard the prisoners that they took. Equally, if the Scots had been reinforced by those of their number that had set off for Carlisle, they would have captured both the Bishop of Durham and the city of Newcastle.

129

After the Percys had set out from Newcastle, that same evening it occurred to the Bishop of Durham while he was at dinner that he would not be acting honourably by remaining in the town while his countrymen took the field. Accordingly, he set out at once at the head of his own troops, amounting to seven thousand men in all, of which five thousand were infantry and two thousand cavalry. Everyone was astonished at his decision, as it was already night, none of them were armed, and indeed many of them had already gone to bed, having marched a considerable distance that day. But they had not advanced three miles before they met troops who had fled from the battlefield, and who told them what had happened, whereupon the general alarm was overwhelming, and panic seized the bishop's men, who began to run away themselves. The bishop decided to retire to Newcastle, on the grounds that the Scots army must indeed be a considerable one if it had put to flight such a large English force. Whereas if the bishop's force had remained steady, and forced the runaways to join them, it is the opinion of many that they could have defeated the Scots.

Sir Matthew Redman, the Governor of Berwick, was pursued for over three miles by Sir James Lindsay. Eventually, Sir Matthew's horse stumbled, and he leaped off; after a vigorous single combat, Sir Matthew surrendered, and offered to present himself within fifteen days at any place in Scotland that Sir James cared to name. It was decided on Edinburgh. Sir James then took the wrong road, it being now dark, and had the misfortune to fall in with the Bishop of Durham and five hundred of his men, whom Sir James mistook for his own side. The bishop captured Sir James, and took him back to Newcastle.

130

The Scots meanwhile retired to their camp, and next day the bishop again set out from Newcastle at the head of his men. On hearing of his approach, the Scots decided to hold their ground, as it was a strong position to defend, and if they had retired they would have been unable to take their prisoners with them, many of them being wounded. They made the prisoners swear to acknowledge their capture, whether they were rescued later or not. They then ordered their minstrels to blow their horns and to make as much noise as possible. On expeditions of this kind, the Scots infantry all carry horns slung on their shoulders, in the manner of hunters. The horns are all of different sizes, and when they are all blown together, in different keys, they can be heard four miles away by day, and six miles away by night, to the terror and consternation of their enemies, and the great delight of themselves. The Scots commanders now ordered music of this kind to be played. The bishop was less than a mile away when this happened, and the noise was as if all the devils in hell had gathered together. Drums were also beaten, and the English, who had never heard anything like it before, were very much frightened. The noise stopped abruptly and then, when the English were only half a mile away, started up again. However, the bishop advanced steadily to within two bowshots of the Scots, who began to make more noise than ever, while the bishop was able to see the strength of the Scots position. After some deliberation, the English knights found it inadvisable to attack, for defeat seemed more probable than victory. They therefore returned to Newcastle.

The Scots retired for food and drink, and made preparations to depart. They allowed Sir Ralph Percy, who was seriously injured, to go to Newcastle to have his wounds better attended to, on the understanding that, as soon as he could ride a horse, he would surrender himself at Edinburgh.

I have been told by people on the Scots side that one thousand

and forty men on the English side were killed or captured in the battle, and a further eight hundred and sixty in the subsequent pursuit, as well as a thousand more wounded. The English rallied several times in the course of the pursuit, when they considered the circumstances favourable, and turned on their pursuers, which accounts for their additional losses. Of the Scots, only about a hundred were killed, and two hundred captured.

The Scots returned to their own country by way of Melrose, where the Earl of Douglas was buried. The Scots were most considerate and accommodating in the matter of ransoms, as I learned from a knight who had been captured by the Earl of March, and who was full of praise for the earl for allowing him to settle his ransom at his own convenience. I believe that the Scots were richer by two hundred thousand francs from the ransoms, and not since the battle of Stirling, when they had pursued the English for three days, had the Scots won so decisive a victory.

When Sir Archibald Douglas and the Earls of Fife and Sutherland, who were near Carlisle, heard the news, their natural delight was mixed with disappointment at not having been at the battle themselves. They decided to rejoin their companions who had already returned to Scotland.

SUMMARY

Book III: 131–143 *and*
Book IV: 1, 3–9

The King of France[1] set out to bring the Duke of Guelders to heel, and was graciously received by the duke's father, the Duke of Juliers, who persuaded his son to recant his letter of defiance. Peace was also made between the King of France and the Duchess of Brabant.

The Earl of Arundel, with twenty-seven ships, tried to land near La Rochelle, but was chased off by Louis of Sancerre. Catherine, daughter of the Duke of Lancaster, was married to the son of the King

---

[1] *Charles V.*

of Castile. Charles VI, who had just come of age, warned Castile to make no alliance prejudicial to France.

The Duke of Guelders was captured in Prussia, and although rescued by the knights of the Teutonic order, returned to keep faith with the squire who had captured him.

The King of Castile's answer satisfied the King of France, and the Earl of Arundel returned to England.

Froissart attended the marriage of the Duke of Berry. Peace was made between England and France for three years.

The Duke of Ireland was banished by the King of France at the request of the Duke's father-in-law, the Lord of Coucy. The King then decided to tour his country and visited his uncle the Duke of Burgundy. From there he went on to call on the Pope at Avignon, and from there to Languedoc and to Montpellier.

BOOK IV

Book IV

2

On Sunday, August 20th, 1389, the crowds in Paris and outside the gates were remarkable to behold. The nobles of France who were to escort the Queen's litter assembled at Saint Denis in the afternoon. The road was lined by twelve hundred citizens of Paris, mounted on horseback, and dressed in crimson and green silk uniforms interwoven with gold thread. The Queen led the procession herself, attended by the Duchesses of Berry, Burgundy, Touraine, and Lorraine, the Countess of Nevers, the Lady de Coucy and the other ladies in order of precedence, all in open litters, which were beautifully decorated. Only the Duchess of Touraine, to be different from the others, rode on a horse with the most magnificent trappings. The procession moved at a foot pace.

The Queen's litter was escorted in front by the Dukes of Touraine and Bourbon, in the middle by the Dukes of Berry and Burgundy, and at the back by Lord Peter of Navarre and the Count of Ostrevant. The Duchess of Touraine followed between the Count de la Marche and the Count of Nevers. After them, in an open litter, were the Duchess of Burgundy and her daughter Margaret, Countess of Nevers, attended by Henry, Lord of Bar, and William, the young Count of Namur, as outriders. Next came the Duchess of Orléans in an open litter, escorted by Sir James of Bourbon and Sir Philip of Artois. Then the Duchess of Bar and her daughter, escorted by Sir Charles d'Albreth and the Lord de Coucy. These were followed by many more ladies and knights. Sergeants-at-arms and officers of the King had been posted to keep the road clear, for the crowd was so great that it seemed as if all the world was there.

At the gate of Saint Denis there was a tableau of a starry sky with children dressed as angels singing sweetly and melodiously. In front was an image of Our Lady, with the Holy Child playing with a windmill made out of a large walnut. The top of the sky was decorated with the arms of France and Bavaria, with the sunburst that was to be the King's badge at the ensuing tournaments. This sight gave great pleasure to the Queen and her ladies, and also to the others who passed by it. The Queen then advanced to the fountain in the Rue Saint Denis, which had been decorated with fine blue cloth covered with gold fleurs-de-lis. The pillars round it were adorned with the arms of the chief barons of France, and instead of water, the fountain flowed with great streams of wine mixed with honey and spices. All round it, girls in fine and rich dresses, wearing caps of gold, sang most sweetly—a pleasure to hear and a pleasure to see. They carried great golden bowls with which they supplied any who wished it with draughts of wine, and the Queen paused to admire them, as did all her retinue.

Below the Monastery of the Trinity, scaffolding had been erected to support a castle and a battle scene between the Saracens, under Saladin, and the Christians. All the famous lords who had been on the crusade were represented with their long coats of arms, as they were worn at the time. A little above them were figures of the King of France and the Twelve Peers, all armed. When the Queen approached, the figure of King Richard, the Lionheart, left his men and asked the figure of the King of France leave to attack the Saracens. Then battle was joined, and lasted for some time. It was watched with great pleasure. At the second gate of Saint Denis there was another representation of the starry heavens, with the figures of the Holy Trinity. And against the backcloth of the sky, more children were singing, dressed as angels. As the Queen's litter passed through the gate, the gates of Paradise opened above her and two angels came out, holding in their hands a rich crown of gold studded with precious stones which they gently placed on the Queen's head, singing sweetly the following verse:

The Queen of France enters Paris

Dame enclose entre fleurs de lys,
Reine estes-vous de Paris,
De France et de tout le Pays:
Nous en rallons en paradis.

And opposite the Chapel of Saint James, on the right, there was some scaffolding supporting a kind of room, lined with rich hangings in which organ music was beautifully played. The whole of the Rue Saint Denis was covered with a canopy of rich cloth and silk, as if it were all available for nothing, as at Alexandria or Damascus. I, the author of this book, was present there myself, and I was amazed at where this great quantity of stuffs had come from—for all the houses along the Rue Saint Denis, all the way to the Châtelet and even to the Pont de Nôtre Dame, were hung with tapestries depicting historical scenes, which were much admired and enjoyed. The procession slowly passed all these sights, and when it reached the gate of the Châtelet it halted to see some more fine pageants that had been arranged there.

There was a wooden castle with turrets, so well made that it would have lasted for forty years. At every gap in the battlements there stood a knight in full armour, and inside was a magnificent bed with rich covers and curtains, as if ready for a king. It was called the Bed of Justice, and in it lay a figure of Saint Anne. In front of the castle was a large space containing a warren, full of bushes, in which were collected a large number of hares, rabbits, and small birds, which darted in and out of the cover in alarm at the crowd. And out of this wood, on the side of the Queen's procession, came a white stag which ran towards the bed; from another part of the wood an eagle and lion appeared, cunningly devised, and proudly approached the stag. They were followed by twelve maidens, richly adorned, with golden chaplets on their heads, carrying drawn swords. They took their places between the lion and stag and the eagle—seemingly to defend the stag and the Bed of Justice. The Queen and the nobles were delighted by this tableau, and then passed on to the Pont de

Nôtre Dame, which was decorated in the most lavish way imaginable, with another canopy representing a starry sky, with green and crimson hangings. The streets were decorated as far as Nôtre Dame, and it was late by the time the Queen reached the cathedral, for the whole procession had never broken out of a walking pace. The whole bridge was hung with green and white sarsenet, and before reaching the cathedral the Queen and her procession passed a number of other pageants with which they were delighted, and which I will describe.

A whole month previously, a masterly acrobat from Geneva had tied a rope from the highest tower of Nôtre Dame across to the highest house on the Pont Saint Michel, passing right over the rooftops. As the Queen and her ladies passed, the acrobat emerged onto a scaffold on the tower and sat on a kind of saddle, holding a lighted torch in each hand. He then slid down the rope, singing and juggling with the torches, to the great admiration of the crowd. The torches could be seen all over Paris, and up to a distance of three miles.

At the door of Nôtre Dame the Queen was greeted by the Dukes of Berry, Burgundy, Touraine, and Bourbon, who escorted her from her litter. Her ladies also alighted and all trooped into the cathedral, where the bishop and the clergy sang loudly in praise of God and the Virgin Mary. The Queen was escorted to the high altar, where, after kneeling in prayer for a little, she presented four sheets of cloth of gold, and the crown that had been given earlier, to the treasury of Nôtre Dame. Sir John de la Riviere and Sir John le Mercier immediately brought an even more splendid crown, with which she was crowned by the bishop and the four dukes.

The Queen and her ladies then returned to their litters, and as it was now dark the procession was lit up by five hundred candles. In this way they proceeded to the palace, where the King, Queen Joan,[1] and her daughter were awaiting them. The

---

[1] *According to D. Sauvage's edition of Froissart, this was the widow of Charles le Bel, whose daughter married Philip Duke of Orleans, brother of King John.*

ladies all had rooms prepared for them there, but the lords returned to their own houses after the dancing. Next day the King gave a grand dinner for all the ladies, and the Archbishop of Rouen, John de Vienne, said high mass, at which the Queen was anointed and sanctified Queen of France in the usual way. She was again attended by the four dukes. After mass, the entire company assembled in the great hall.

The great marble table which is never moved from the hall was on this occasion covered with a large oak board, four inches thick, on which dinner was served. Raised above the main table, against one of the pillars, was the King's own table, which was large, fine, and richly arranged, and covered with gold and silver plate, to the envy of all who saw it. Below the King's table there was a wooden barrier, with three entrances in it, which were guarded by sergeants-at-arms and ushers to prevent anyone entering except those who were serving at the table. For the truth is that there was such a great crowd in the hall that one could turn round only with great difficulty. There were also a number of minstrels who played away as best they could. The King, clergy, and ladies washed and sat down in the following plan.

At the head of the King's table were the Bishops of Noyon and Langres, and next to the King the Archbishop of Rouen. The King wore an open coat of red velvet trimmed with ermine, with a very rich gold crown on his head. Next to the King, and a little above him, was the Queen, who was also richly crowned. Next to the Queen was the King of Armenia, then the Duchesses of Berry, Burgundy, and Touraine, Madame de Nevers, Bona de Bar, Lady de Coucy and Marie de Harcourt, and at the very end Lady de Sally, wife of Sir Guy de la Tremouille. There were two other tables seating five hundred ladies, but the crush was so intense that they could hardly be served. The food was plentiful and sumptuous, but I will give no account of it. But there were also various most ingenious devices which could have given great pleasure if they had been properly executed.

In the middle of the palace a square wooden castle had been erected, forty feet high and twenty feet square, with a tower at each of the four corners and a higher one over the centre. The castle represented the city of Troy, and the central tower was the palace of Ilion, with the pennons of King Priam, noble Hector and his other sons all displayed, as well as those of the other kings and princes who were besieged in the city with them. The castle rested on four wheels, which were turned ingeniously from within. Opposite it there was a partition, draped with the banners of the Kings of Greece and of the other chiefs who took part in the siege of Troy. It was also on wheels, but appeared to be moved by an invisible power. In support of them there was a ship containing a hundred men-at-arms. The men from ship and partition fiercely attacked the castle, which was stoutly defended. But the battle could not last long owing to the density of the crowd, and the people being stifled by the heat and the crush. One table, at which a number of ladies were sitting, near the door of the parliament chamber, was even knocked over, and the guests had to extricate themselves as best they could. The Queen was almost fainting, and a window behind her had to be broken open to let in air. Lady de Coucy was also overcome, and the King had the banquet stopped and the tables removed, to give more room. Wine and spices were served, and after the King and Queen retired to their rooms everyone left the hall. Some of the ladies stayed in the palace and others, including Lady de Coucy, retired to their houses to recover.

At five o'clock the Queen, accompanied by her four duchesses, left the palace in an open litter and processed to the King's palace on the Seine, the Hôtel de Saint Pol. The procession following the Queen and her ladies amounted to no less than a thousand horses. Although the Hôtel is very large, a great hall had been erected outside it, made of wood, covered with Normandy cloth. There were tapestries on the walls depicting strange stories, which were much admired. The Queen remained in her room, but the King gave a supper in this hall for the ladies, after which they danced all night till dawn, when they went home to rest, as well they might.

The Duchess of Touraine had only recently come to France,

from Lombardy, to marry the duke; she was called Valentina, daughter of the Lord of Milan. She had never been in Paris before the Queen's solemn entry, and both she and the Queen were given wonderful presents by the townspeople. On the Tuesday, before dinner, forty of the most notable citizens, all dressed in the same uniform, brought a present to the Queen at the Hôtel de Saint Pol, having displayed it all over the streets of the town. The present was in a richly worked litter, carried by two strong men dressed as savages. It was covered with a silk canopy, beneath which the jewels inside could be easily seen. When they reached the King's chamber they found it open and ready to receive them—for they were expected, and no one is more welcome than the bringer of gifts. The litter was laid on two trestles and those who had brought it knelt down, and their leader addressed the King as follows:

'Very dear Lord and noble King, your people of Paris present you with all these jewels in their joy at the happy event of your reign.'

'Thank you very much,' said the King, 'they are fine and rich.'

When they had gone the King said to Sir William des Bordes and another knight:

'Let us have a closer look and see what they are.'

The presentation consisted of four pots, four saucers and six dishes, all made of gold, and weighing a hundred and fifty marks.

The Queen also received a presentation in the same way, which consisted of a ship made of gold, two large flagons, two boxes for sweets, two salt-cellars, six pots, six saucers, all of gold; and a dozen lamps, two dozen plates, six large dishes and two bowls, all of silver, weighing three hundred marks. The litter in which they were brought was carried by two men dressed as a bear and a unicorn.

The third presentation was made to the Duchess of Touraine, and was made by two men disguised as Moors, with blackened faces, and wearing rich robes and white turbans, like Saracens or Tartars. The litter was also magnificently decked out with a silk cover, and it was escorted by twelve citizens of Paris in the same splendid uniforms. It too, contained gold and silver plate: a ship, a large pot, two saucers, two large dishes and two salt-cellars, all of gold; and in silver, six pots, six dishes, two dozen plates, two dozen salt-cellars, and two dozen cups, weighing two hundred marks, both of gold and silver. The Duchess was naturally delighted by this magnificent present, and gracefully thanked the representatives who had brought it, and the citizens of Paris who had paid for it. These gifts were presented on the Tuesday, and their great value indicates the substance and power of the people of Paris. I myself saw these presents, and I was told that they had cost sixty thousand golden crowns. Afterwards the King and Queen and nobles dined privately, for the great tournament was to be held at three o'clock in Saint Katherine's Field. The thirty knights who took part in it were called the Knights of the Golden Sun.

10

During his stay in Toulouse, the King of France paid close attention to matters of state, appointing new seneschals and officials, and making a number of reforms of a kind that endeared him to his people. He granted the Lord d'Albreth the right to quarter the arms of France with his own, and the Lord d'Albreth gave a dinner costing a thousand francs. Soon afterwards the King decided to leave for Paris, and after the Archbishop of Toulouse, with the citizens of the town, and the ladies, had taken leave of him, he set out for Montpellier, which he reached next day, after staying the night at Châteauneuf d'Auroy. He spent three days amusing himself at Montpellier, but was then eager to return to the Queen at Paris. As a joke, he said to his brother, the Duke of Touraine: 'My dear brother, I wish that we were in Paris, athough our attendants can remain here where they are. For I long to see the Queen, just as you must long to see your wife.' 'Well,' said the duke, 'wishing will not get us there: it is too far.' 'You are right,' said the King. 'But I feel I could get there quite soon if I chose.' 'It can only be done by hard riding,' said the duke. 'I could get there too, on my horse.' 'Who will be there first?' said the King. 'We'll have a bet on it.' 'Certainly,' replied the duke, who was always eager for money. The bet was struck for five thousand francs, and both were to leave the following day, at the same time, accompanied by only one knight or servant each. They set out the next day, the Lord of Garencières with the King and the Lord of Vienville with the duke. All four were young and active, and they rode night and day, changing horses as they went and riding in carts when they needed to sleep. They spared themselves no exertion, and left all their retinue behind. The King took four and a half days to reach Paris, but the duke won the bet, by only taking four days and eight hours. It was a close-run thing, and the King only lost by sleeping for eight hours at Troyes, in Champagne. At one point the duke took to the water and went by boat down the Seine as far as Melun; there he remounted and rode on to Paris, where he went straight to the Hôtel de Saint Pol, where the Queen and the duchess were residing. He immediately asked after the King, and was delighted to hear that he had not arrived. 'Madam,' he said to the Queen, 'the King will not be long.' And indeed he arrived soon after. The duke went up to him and said, 'Sir, I have won the bet, and you must pay up.' 'You are right,' said the King. 'I will pay.' They told the ladies all the adventures that they had met with on the way, and how they had taken only four and a half days to cover the distance between Montpellier and Paris, which is four hundred and seventy-seven miles. The ladies treated it as a joke, and laughed, but they realized how strenuous the journey had been, and that only their youth and courage could have carried them through. The Duke of Touraine insisted on being paid in ready money.

11

About this time occurred the death of Pope Urban, at Rome, which caused deep sorrow among the Romans, by whom he was

greatly loved.[1] He was buried with all due solemnity in Saint
Peter's, and the cardinals retired into conclave before the news
of Pope Urban's death had reached Pope Clement at Avignon.
This news only arrived there ten days after Pope Urban's death,
and Pope Clement and his cardinals were filled with the hope
that the schism in the Church might now be ended, and discussed the situation at length. They fondly hoped that the
cardinals at Rome would be in no hurry to go into conclave, but
that they would make overtures to Avignon. They informed the
King of France of the death of Pope Urban (whom they called the
antipope) and begged him to support Pope Clement, and to
write to that effect to his cousins, the Kings of Germany and
Hungary, the Count of Vertus, and the Duke of Austria (who
had all supported Pope Urban), asking them to help restore peace
to the Church, on the grounds that there should be no dissension
in the faith, and since there is only one God in Heaven, so there
can and ought to be only one supreme pontiff on earth.

The King of France put the position to his uncle the Duke of
Burgundy, explaining that he had been on the point of mounting
a large expedition against Rome, and destroying the unbelievers;
but now that the antipope was dead, Pope Clement's cardinals
were asking for his support. The duke replied: 'It is quite true
that Urban is dead, but we know nothing of the state of opinion
among the cardinals at Rome. They may again be forced to
choose a pope at the dictates of the people of Rome, as they did
before in electing the Archbishop of Bari. Do not act hastily,
therefore, but wait and see. It may be that the cardinals at Rome
will be unable to agree among themselves; alternatively, they may
conceal their purpose from the Romans, and decide to acknowledge Pope Clement, provided that he satisfies their pride by
moving to Rome, which he would be quite willing to do. But not
till this seems likely should you write to those of your cousins who

---

[1] *Pope Urban VI died on October 18th, 1389. Far from being loved by the
Romans, he was 'detested for his violent and tyrannical conduct,' according to
Johnes.*

hold different religious opinions to your own and ask them to help put an end to the schism in the Church, and to restore its unity.'

The King found this advice acceptable, and decided to take no immediate action. The students at the university were quite preoccupied with discussing how the cardinals would act, and their usual studies were neglected. Pope Clement, as they knew, had written to the King and to the Dukes of Touraine and Burgundy, and also, in general terms, to the university, asking for their support. Those who supported Clement said that the King should write to the other Christian leaders—the Kings of Germany and Hungary, the Duke of Austria and the lord of Milan—and all others who took the opposite line over the papacy, and persuade them to return to the true fold. On three successive days the chief students of the university went in a body to the Hôtel de Saint Pol, where the King was living, and begged him to agree to the Pope's requests and so bring the schism to an end. But they were not admitted, and no answer was given them, to their great dissatisfaction.

However, a few days later, news came that the cardinals at Rome had elected Boniface, the Cardinal of Naples, to the papacy.[1] The King of France and his lords were sadly disappointed, and the Duke of Burgundy pointed out how little would have been achieved by those letters that the King had wanted to write. 'It has all turned out as I predicted,' he said. The King agreed. Pardons were offered by Pope Boniface to all the clergy in the countries that supported him, and those who wished to gain them set out for Rome at considerable danger, for on the boundaries of Ancona and of the Romagna Sir Bernard de la Salle was making war on the Romans on behalf of Pope Clement. He kept a lookout for these pilgrims, and did them a great deal of harm, quite a number of them being killed or lost.

[1] *Pietro di Tomacelli, Pope Boniface IX.*

SUMMARY

12-42

The castle of Ventadour, in Limousin, surrendered to the forces of the Duke of Berry. A great tournament was held at Saint Inglivère, near Calais, and three French knights took on all comers for a month.

The Vicomte de Meaux, by order of the King, besieged and captured Amerigo Marcel, captain of the brigands who were terrorizing the borders of Limousin, and took him to Paris, where he was executed, in spite of all his appeals for help.

The merchants of Genoa were at this time suffering greatly from the pirates who were based at Mahedia,[1] in Africa. The merchants asked for French support in an expedition against them, and the Duke of Bourbon agreed to take command. The fleet sailed from Genoa in June 1390, and laid siege to the town.

The Saracens made several sorties against the besiegers, and the town was stormed, but without success. Sixty French knights were killed, but the Saracens were unaware of the extent of this reverse. The heat was oppressive, spirits fell, and the Genoese would gladly have come to terms with the Saracens. At the approach of winter the siege was raised. The Saracens were from then on masters of the Straits of Gibraltar, and ships going to Flanders or England had to pay them tribute.

Jousts were held in London, and English ambassadors went to Paris to propose a meeting between the Kings of England and France with a view to a lasting peace. The King of Castile died, and was succeeded by his son Henry, who had married the Duke of Lancaster's daughter.

The Count of Armagnac went on an expedition to Lombardy to help his brother-in-law Bernabo Visconti against Galeas Visconti, Duke of Milan. The count was captured at the siege of Alessandria and died.

---

[1] *A port, seventy miles from Tunis, later razed to the ground by Andrea Doria, at the command of the Emperor Charles V, and never rebuilt.*

Summary

Sir Peter of Craon fell from the royal favour in France, and took refuge with the Duke of Brittany. Gaston of Foix, one of Froissart's chief patrons, died suddenly after hunting. After making a treaty with him based on a double alliance by marriage, King Charles asked the Duke of Brittany to give up Sir Peter of Craon, and on his refusal the King prepared an expedition against him. The Duke of Touraine exchanged his duchy with the King for that of Orléans.

The King went first, at the head of his army, to Saint-Germain-en-Laye, where he stayed a fortnight. The King had been ill, and according to his doctors he was not yet in good health, but he was so anxious to set off that he did his best to conceal the fact, partly in order to get his army on the road. His uncles, the Dukes of Berry and Burgundy, lagged behind, and if they had been able to do so, would have refrained from joining the expedition, but they were in honour bound to take part.

After a fortnight the King set out for Chartres, spending four days with Lord de la Rivière at Auneau on the way, where he was magnificently received. His troops were augmented daily from every side, and the King declared that he would not return to Paris until he had made the Duke of Brittany see reason. The Dukes of Berry and Burgundy, who would have followed a more moderate line, were much put out by the youthful eagerness of the King. After a week at Chartres the King advanced to Le Mans, now followed by men from Artois, Beauvais, Picardy and the Vermandois. But there was without doubt a section of the army that was not truly hostile to the Duke of Brittany, and did all they could to obstruct the expedition and harass the King. The court remained at Le Mans for three weeks, for the King was feverish and not fit to ride. The doctors said that the King was overwhelmed by public business, and that rest and quiet were absolutely necessary. His uncles remonstrated with him, but the King only replied that he felt better when he was riding than when he was doing nothing: 'Whoever advises me to the contrary,' he added, 'displeases me and shows no love for me.'

43

The King was, however, persuaded to send four knights to the Duke of Brittany, instructing him to send Sir Peter of Craon to the King at Le Mans, when they would try to make the duke's peace with the King, and prevent the expedition from harming either the duke or the country of Brittany. The duke answered prudently as follows: 'I would be quite happy to assist Sir Peter of Craon and hand him over to the King, but, may God help me, I do not know where he is or what he is doing. I therefore wish to be excused in this matter. I heard, a year ago, how Sir Peter hated Sir Olivier de Clisson with all his heart, and how he would fight him to the death at the first opportunity. I asked him if he had sent his challenge to Sir Olivier, and he replied that he had; and that he would kill him just as soon as he could lay hands on him. That is all I know of the matter, and I am amazed that His Majesty wants to make war on me over it. With all respect to him, I do not see that I have done anything for which he could make war. Nor, please God, will I ever break any of the pacts or alliances that we have made, either in respect of the marriages of our children or of anything else.'

The knights took this message back with them, but although the Dukes of Berry and Burgundy were entirely satisfied by it, the King thought exactly the opposite, and declared that having come thus far he would under no circumstances return to Paris without having dealt with the Duke of Brittany. Such was the King's hatred of Sir Peter whom he was sure the Duke was harbouring.

A rumour then reached Le Mans that the Queen of Aragon, Yolande de Bar, who was a first cousin of King Charles, had imprisoned an unknown knight at Barcelona. From the fact that he refused to give his name, it was supposed that he was Sir Peter of Craon. Queen Yolande wrote a most friendly letter to the King saying that the knight had on his arrival at Barcelona hired a ship at great expense to take him, or so he said, to Naples, and that she supposed, in view of his great anxiety to be free, that he was indeed Sir Peter. She asked the King to send her some people who knew Sir Peter by sight, and undertook not to release her prisoner until she heard from the King.

This letter might have brought the whole expedition to a halt, but the friends of Olivier de Clisson suspected that it was a fraud, and that Sir Peter was, so far from being in prison, under the safe protection of the Duke of Brittany. However, the King was persuaded by the Duke of Burgundy to send to Barcelona. Meanwhile the Duke of Brittany was growing anxious, not knowing either in what fortified place he could safely make his own headquarters, nor whom he could trust among his own knights and squires. He almost repented of what he had done, but thought that he would soon be able to tell who his real friends were when the King entered the country.

But although war seemed inevitable, events took a quite unexpected turn, to the great advantage of the duke. As the old saying goes, 'The lucky are never poor.' But had it not been for an extraordinary and pitiful misfortune which overtook the King of France, nothing could have saved the duke.

44

After spending three weeks at Le Mans, and having received the duke's message, the King decided to march on Brittany. His intention was to expel the duke from his duchy for ever, and to install a governor until his children should be of an age to rule there themselves. The King left Le Mans at ten o'clock on the morning of an exceedingly hot day, in the middle of August. He had spent the weeks at Le Mans in unremitting labour, toiling almost unaided at matters of state, without having been in good health, even at the beginning: all the summer he had been weak in body, and dizzy as well—eating and drinking little, and suffering almost every day from attacks of a fever, which was naturally aggravated by his exertions. The insults to which his constable had been subjected in Brittany also preyed on his mind, but he would listen neither to his doctors nor to his uncles, and utterly refused to postpone the expedition.

The story goes that while he was advancing through the forest of Le Mans, an incident occurred that should have made the King stop and hold council. A man, bareheaded and barefoot, dressed in a rough white coat (which he wore as an indication of being not entirely sane) dashed out from the trees, seized the reins of the King's horse, and said to him: 'King, go no farther; turn back, you are betrayed.' This had a considerable effect on the King, and his nervous condition deteriorated still further. The King's men rushed up and knocked the reins out of the man's hands, and let him run off, taking him for a half-wit. They were afterwards severely blamed for not questioning the man and discovering if he really were mad, why he had spoken out and where he had come from. However, the man ran off and was never seen again.

The King and his army reached the edge of the forest about midday, and entered a stretch of open, sandy country. The sun blazed overhead, and horses and men were overcome by the heat; even the most hardened campaigner suffered. The misfortune which then befell the King was evidently sent by the hand of God, the severity of whose punishments causes mankind to tremble. Indeed, there are examples of them in the Old Testament as well as in the Gospels. Have we not seen how Nebuchadnezzar, the King of the Assyrians, ruled in such power that nothing on earth exceeded it? And suddenly, at the height of his glory, God, the King of Kings, the Lord of Heaven and earth, who created and ordained all things, decreed that he should lose both his mind and his kingdom. For seven years he remained in this condition, living on acorns and berries, like a pig. At the end of this period of penance God restored his faculties, and he declared to Daniel the prophet that there was no God but the God of Israel, and beyond any doubt God the Father, the Son, and the Holy Ghost, the three persons of the Trinity in one substance, were, are, and always will be omnipotent, as it was in the beginning.

There is therefore no reason to be surprised at whatever is brought about by the Divine Will.

To return to the present case, the hand of God fell that day on the King of France—some say through his own fault. His state of health was such that if he was going to ride long distances on horseback, he should have done so only in the cool of the morning or the evening. Those of his advisers who allowed this state of affairs to occur were afterwards much blamed.

The heat was exceptional, even for that time of year, and the King was dressed in a black velvet jacket, and wore on his head a single scarlet hood, ornamented with a chaplet of large and beautiful pearls which the Queen had presented to him on his departure. Behind him rode two pages in single file, wearing Montauban caps of polished steel that glittered in the sun. The second page carried a vermilion lance, decorated with silk, for the King, with a broad, bright, sharp blade, one of a dozen that Lord de la Rivière had brought the King from Toulouse. As they rode, the attention of the pages, who were only children, began to wander, and the one carrying the lance fell asleep. The lance fell from his hand, and crashed suddenly onto the helmet of the page in front. The King, who was riding just in front, gave a great start and shook all over, as his mind was still on the words of the madman whom they had met in the forest. He imagined that a host of enemies was attacking him, and in his distracted state he drew his sword and turned on the pages, no longer recognizing either them or anyone else. Thinking he was on the field of battle, surrounded by enemies, he drew his sword and dealt out blows with it right and left, not caring on whom they fell, and shouting out: 'Forward! Advance on these traitors!' The pages thought that it was their negligence that had enraged the King, and spurred their horses off in different directions. The King was incapable of recognizing anyone, even his own brother and his uncle, and he went for the Duke of Orléans with drawn sword: the duke fled in terror, with the King in pursuit. The Duke of Burgundy, hearing the pages cry out, looked in their direction and saw what was happening. With reason, he was amazed and cried out for help: 'Help! My lord has lost his mind! After him for God's sake, and stop him! Fly, my dear nephew Orléans, or my lord will kill you!' The duke fled, and those who were riding a little apart, hearing all the shouting and commotion, thought that they were hunting a wolf or a hare, until they heard of the King's condition. The Duke of Orléans escaped, and knights and squires quickly surrounded the King and let him rain blows on them till he was exhausted; for, naturally, the more he exerted himself, the weaker he became. Several knights were knocked down, because they did not attempt to defend themselves, but I never heard that anyone was killed in this adventure.[1]

At last, when the King was exhausted, and running with sweat, one of his chamberlains, a Norman knight who was also one of his closest friends, Sir William Martel, came up behind him and threw his arms round him. The sword was taken from the King's hand by other lords, who lifted him from his horse, and laid him on the ground; they then removed his jacket to give him air. His brother and his three uncles came up, but he gave no sign of recognizing them, merely rolling his eyes and saying nothing. The princes were dumbfounded, and eventually decided to call off the expedition and return to Le Mans. They kept many of their thoughts to themselves, but later, on their return to Paris, they left those who were not in their good graces in no doubt as to their intentions. It was a pitiful sight for the King of France, the most noble and powerful prince in the world, to be suddenly deprived of his senses in this way.

The King was conveyed in a litter to Le Mans, where physicians examined him. A rumour soon spread that he had been poisoned, but the Duke of Burgundy established beyond doubt that this was not the case. He bitterly regretted the whole expedition, thinking that he and his brothers would be blamed for what had happened to the King in the course of it, though in fact they had done all they could to prevent his setting out.

---

[1] *According to* Les Grandes Chroniques de France, *four men were killed, and the* Anonyme de Saint Denis *adds a fifth.*

SUMMARY

45-51

The King was moved to the castle of Creil, near Compiègne, on the Oise, but at first made little improvement. The Three Estates appointed the Dukes of Berry and Burgundy to act as regents, and stern measures were taken against the King's late advisers. Olivier de Clisson and Montague escaped, but Le Mercier and De la Rivière were arrested, and only escaped execution by the intervention of the young Duchess of Berry. Sir Olivier was deprived of his office in his absence and banished from France.

Under the care of his physician, Guillaume de Harseley, the King of France gradually recovered his health and his faculties.

52

You have read earlier that a truce had been made for three years between England and France, and that two ambassadors, the Count of Saint Pol and the Lord de Chastelmorant, having brought documents duly signed and sealed from England, later returned from Amiens to London, with the Dukes of Lancaster and York, to discover the intentions of King Richard and the English Parliament, with regard to a permanent peace being settled, to replace the existing three years' truce. The French knights were told on reaching London that nothing could be done till Parliament met at Michaelmas, when the matter would be discussed, and in the meantime they returned to France. But when the news of the illness of King Charles reached England, the whole matter was deferred. Nevertheless King Richard and the Duke of Lancaster were most anxious for peace, and had it rested with them, the delay would have been avoided. But the commoners of England were for war rather than peace, and they had the support of the King's youngest uncle, Thomas, Duke of Gloucester, and the Earls of Essex and Buckingham; the latter was Constable of England, and he enjoyed great popularity in the country. Like other, younger men who were anxious to distinguish themselves in the field, he wanted war, whereas the Duke of Lancaster, older and wiser, took the view that the war between France and England had lasted long enough, and that a good peace, scrupulously kept, would benefit the whole of Christendom, which had suffered a great deal and had been considerably weakened. He also pointed out the threat of Bajazet, who was massing his forces on the frontier of Hungary, and indicated that this was the proper theatre of war for young knights.

Great importance should be attached to the Duke of Lancaster's well-intentioned words. For he had several times invaded and overrun France, at small benefit to himself. His campaigns had always been physically arduous to himself, and though he had burned and laid waste the country through which he went, it had always quickly recovered. His view was that the war, as conducted at present, might go on for ever, but that a reverse at any time might prove extremely serious for England. The fact that the King favoured peace had not escaped his notice.

I cannot be altogether sure about the rights and wrongs of this matter: but it is sometimes pointed out that the two daughters of the Duke of Lancaster were both married to European kings—one to the King of Castile, the other to the King of Portugal. The King of Castile was young, and peace with France was certainly to his advantage, and made his own reign calmer; it was also necessary that the peace between Castile and France should not be disrupted by England. For, if it were, France would at once fall on Castile, to which she had open access through the territory of Yolande de Bar, Queen of Aragon, who was herself French by birth. She also ruled in Catalonia. The Basque provinces, and Béarn, were also open to the French, for when the Count of Foix died, his heir in Béarn, the Vicomte de Châteaubon, had sworn and sealed a right of entry of this kind to the French. In addition to his wife's being French, the King of Navarre also had a brother in Paris who acted consistently in the interest of the two kings.

The final result of the long discussion at Westminster was that the truce should last till June 1394. The French ambassadors returned with the document signed and sealed, and the peace was strictly preserved.

In spite of the death of his excellent physician, the King's recovery was complete, and he returned to Paris, to the Hôtel de Saint Pol, in the middle of the winter. Carols, dances and other amusements helped the court to pass away the long winter nights. The Vicomte de Châteaubon came to Paris to do homage to the King for his inheritance in Béarn, and with him came Evan of Foix, a bastard son of the late count, with whom the King struck up a warm friendship, appointing him one of the knights of his bedchamber, and granting him twelve fine horses at the charge of the crown.

53

Not long after this, the marriage of one of the Queen's ladies in waiting was celebrated at court. In the course of the celebrations, a young squire from Normandy arranged the following amusement to entertain the King and the ladies of the court. In the evening, he prepared six linen suits, each made all in one piece, covered with the finest flax, of the consistency of human hair. The King and five knights dressed up in these, and being apparently covered in hair from head to foot, they had the appearance of savages. This masquerade gave great pleasure to the King, which he expressed to the squire. The whole affair was arranged so secretly that only the servants who dressed them knew of it. Sir Evan of Foix, with great forethought for what might happen, advised the King to give orders that no torches should be brought near the disguised figures, because if a spark should fall on one of the suits, the flax would instantly catch fire, and the wearer would be burned to a cinder. The King firmly approved of this advice, and gave orders for all the torches to be hung down one side of the room in which the ladies were sitting, and for nobody to come near the six savages who were soon to appear.

These instructions were followed, and the men in disguise capered about the room, until soon afterwards the Duke of Orléans came in, with four knights all carrying torches, in ignorance of the orders that had been given, and quite unaware of what was happening. The duke first watched the dancing, and then joined in himself, just as the King and the other 'savages' came in. Their disguise was complete, and nobody recognized them as the five knights danced round, all fastened together, with the King at their head, though not attached to them.

The attention of all was fixed on them, and the orders about the torches were forgotten. Fortunately for him, the King soon went and sat down to show himself to the Queen and the young Duchess of Berry, his aunt, who amused herself by trying to discover who he was. But at that moment a terrible accident occurred, through the youthful high spirits of the Duke of Orléans, who, if he had known the consequences, would never have acted as he did. But in his anxiety to discover the identity of the 'savages,' he took up a torch and held it too near to one of the flax suits. The flax burst into flames, which were increased by the pitch with which it was attached to the linen. The five 'savages' were also tied together, and the suits fitted them closely; the fire was so strong that scarcely anyone dared approach, though some knights did indeed try to come to their help, but they only succeeded in severely burning their own hands. The cries of the unfortunate knights were dreadful to hear.

One of the five knights, Jean de Nantouillet, remembering that there was a pantry near by, succeeded in breaking away from the others, and plunged himself into a large tub of water which was used for washing the dishes and cups. He was the only one of the five to survive, and even he was very ill for some time.

The King had told the Queen of the disguise that he was going to wear, and on hearing the cries of anguish, she was terrified, and fainted. Complete confusion reigned, but the Duchess of Berry saved the King by covering him with her gown, and preventing the flames from reaching his flaxen suit. The King was anxious to leave her, and she made him change his clothes and show the

Queen that he was unscathed; when she saw that he was safe, the Queen trembled with joy. The bastard son of the Count of Foix, when he was already blazing, cried out: 'Save the King! Save the King!' And it was only by the grace of God that he had left the other revellers and gone to talk to the ladies: had he not done so he would inevitably have lost his life.

This sad tragedy occurred about midnight on the Tuesday before Candlemas, 1392, in the ballroom of the Hôtel de Saint Pol. The Duke of Orléans was the sole, and unwitting, cause of the disaster, and reproached himself bitterly for it. The people of Paris were disturbed by the danger in which the King had found himself, and openly criticized his frivolous behaviour. On the advice of his uncles, the Dukes of Berry and Burgundy, the King, attended by his nobles, processed on horseback through Paris to Nôtre Dame, where he heard mass and made his offerings. The people had been in great commotion, but the affair was gradually forgotten; masses and prayers were said for those who had died, and money was given to charity. But oh, Count Gaston of Foix, if you had been alive to hear of the cruel death of your dearest son, how you would have grieved! You loved him so much that I do not know how you could have been consoled. All the lords and ladies of France were deeply shocked and distressed by the accident.

It must however be realized that Pope Boniface and his cardinals at Rome rejoiced when they heard the news. At a meeting of the Consistory, it was stated that this was a second punishment sent by God to the French for having supported the anti-pope at Avignon, Robert of Geneva, whom they regarded as false, presumptuous and proud, and as never having done a single good deed in his life. The Pope and the College of Cardinals decided to send a learned friar secretly to the King of France to try to bring him and his people back to the true path of reason and salvation. They held that, being the greatest king in Christendom, he ought to glorify and support the Church more than anyone else, instead of going astray as he had done. Having first discovered whether the King of France would receive him, they selected and instructed a Franciscan friar for this arduous undertaking.

SUMMARY

54-58

The Lord de la Rivière won the support of the Duchess of Berry, who saved his life, in spite of the efforts of the Duchess of Burgundy. The Lord de Coucy declines the post of Constable of France, which was filled by the Comte d'Eu, on his marriage to the daughter of the Duke of Berry. Sir Olivier de Clisson, the previous Constable, waged war on the Duke of Brittany, but a treaty was concluded between the Kings of France and England, through the efforts of their respective uncles, though it was nearly broken off as a result of the dispute over the papal succession. The King of France relapsed into a state of weak mental health.

59

On September 16th, 1394, Robert of Geneva, who had been elected Pope under the name of Clement VII sixteen years earlier, died at Avignon. I do not propose to discuss whether he occupied the papal throne rightly or wrongly, for the question is beyond my capacity to judge. The King of France began to recover his health, to the great joy of his subjects and more especially of his Queen. She was an excellent lady, whom God loved. She had suffered deeply on account of the King's illness and had given alms lavishly, and arranged processions both in Paris and in other parts of the country.

The cardinals at Avignon elected as Pope the cardinal and papal legate Peter de la Luna, a Spaniard. He was in fact a holy man, who had led a blameless life of contemplation; but his election had been made subject to the approval of the King of France and his council, and without it the election could not have been upheld. But consider how low the Church had fallen as a result of the schism, that those authorities who should have been free and independent could only act with the support of those who should have been in obedience to them! All the necessary solemnities for a papal coronation were observed at Avignon, and the new Pope took the name of Benedict XIII. He offered a general pardon to all clergy who came to Avignon, and on the advice of the Sacred College he wrote to the King of France informing him of his election. I heard that the King paid little attention to this letter, not having yet decided whether to support him as Pope or not; and in order to be sure of having the best advice available, he summoned before him all the most learned and acute lawyers and clerks in the University of Paris. Headed by Master John of Gignincourt and Master Peter Playons,[1] they gave their views that the Christian faith was being corrupted by the schism in the Church, and that this situation should not be allowed to continue, since the whole of Christianity suffered by it, and the clergy most of all. It was also unfitting, they said, for the University of Paris to be sending to Pope Benedict at Avignon lists of those of the clergy who wanted pardons. The King found their advice reasonable, and decided that no further lists were to be sent to Avignon until the whole question of the papacy was settled.

The Duke of Berry strongly supported the new Pope, who was similarly recognized by all those clergy who were dependent on the Duke. But the Dukes of Burgundy and Orléans, and many of the other chief nobles, concealed their true feelings on the subject for the time being. Pope Benedict refused no pardons in his anxiety to increase the power and importance of the papal court at Avignon. The Duke of Brittany willingly fell in with the King's views, for he had in the past been so outraged by what he had heard from his cousin, the Duke of Flanders, about the rebellion in the Church that he was strongly disinclined to support Pope Benedict, in spite of the Breton clergy doing so. And when high offices of the Church fell vacant in France, the King filled them without reference to Pope Benedict, who was greatly surprised by

[1] *There are several versions of this name.*

this behaviour, as were the cardinals who had elected him. They also began to feel anxious that the King might deprive them of their revenues from the church property in France, and they decided to send a legate to the French court, to discover the King's intentions with regard to the Church and to assure him that they had elected Pope Benedict only subject to the King's approval, and that if he so wished, they would dethrone the Pope and elect another.

I have already mentioned that Pope Boniface sent a friar from Rome to visit the King of France. He arrived at Paris about this time, quite humbly and without the pomp and circumstance of a legate. The King received him and willingly listened to what he had to say. The legate from Avignon also arrived about this time; he was an eloquent and able envoy, and he too was listened to attentively by the King and his court. The supporters of Pope Benedict naturally took care to push forward the legate from Avignon and arranged frequent audiences for him. The King's council finally reached the following decision, though it was only with great difficulty that they persuaded the University of Paris to support it: that everything possible should be done to make both Popes resign their offices, and all the cardinals likewise, and then to form a council from among the most learned and sapient of the clergy from all over Christendom—from the German Empire, from France, and from the other countries as well. Then, without favour or bias being shown in any direction, the Church could regain, through unity, its former and proper strength and stability. They saw no other possible method of ending the schism, such was the pride and self-interest of the great nobles everywhere.

This proposal was made in the presence of the King and the Dukes of Orléans and Burgundy and their advisers. It was approved, and the King followed the line taken by the University. He willingly undertook to send letters to the Kings of Germany, Bohemia, Hungary, and England; and he thought that he could depend on the Kings of Castile, Navarre, Aragon, Sicily, Naples, and Scotland to obey whatever Pope he and the kingdom of

France obeyed. Special messengers were dispatched, but answers were not forthcoming as soon as was expected. At this time the learned clerk, Master John of Gignincourt, died at Paris, at the Sorbonne. He was deeply mourned and regretted by the King, the court and the university alike, for his ability was unequalled, and he could have done much for the reform and unity of the Church.

I must also mention at this time a clerk at Avignon, who was well versed in science and in law, and was auditor of the papal palace. He was a native of the archbishopric of Rheims, and his name was Sir Jean de Varennes. He was in high favour for the services that he had rendered to Pope Clement and to others as well, and he was on the point of being made a bishop or cardinal; he had also been chaplain to a cardinal who was known, at Avignon, as Saint Peter of Luxemburg. Sir Jean, for all his high position, resigned all his appointments and rewards, remaining only Canon of Rheims, an office which was worth only about a hundred francs to the incumbent if in residence, and only thirty to an absentee. He left Avignon to return to his native country, and settled at the village of Saint Lie, near Rheims, where he led a most devout and admirable life, preaching the faith and works of Our Lord. He fervently supported the authority of the Pope at Avignon, and denied that of Pope Boniface. He was eagerly visited and sought out by the people, on account of his holy and sober way of life, his daily fasts, and the excellence of his sermons. Some said, however, that he had been sent by the cardinals at Avignon to propagate their cause and to advertise the holiness of his life, which would have entitled him to be elected to the papacy. Sir Jean would not allow people to call him the Holy Man of Saint Lie, but simply the Auditor. He lived with his mother, and said mass devoutly every day. He asked for nothing, and all that was given him he distributed for alms, to the glory of God.

60

At this time the King of England's council proposed an expedition against Ireland. King Richard had agreed to truces being made with France and her allies, but with the exception of Ireland, as his predecessors had always claimed it as their right. His grandfather, King Edward III of happy memory, had signed himself King of Ireland and had always made war on its people in spite of all his commitments in other quarters. And so, to keep those knights and squires of England occupied who were eager for feats of arms, and to increase the honour and glory of the kingdom and to preserve its rights, King Richard mounted a great expedition, with men-at-arms and archers, and set out for Ireland, declaring that he would not return until everything should be settled to his satisfaction. It was also arranged that the Duke of Lancaster, who in his time had strenuously exerted himself on land and sea to increase the fortunes of the kingdom of England, should mount a separate expedition. With five hundred men-at-arms and a thousand cavalry, he was to set out, either from Plymouth or Southampton, for Guyenne and Aquitaine. It was the intention of King Richard and his council that the Duke of Lancaster and his heirs should be Lords of Aquitaine, and hold the whole country, in perpetuity, with all its domains and castles, just as his father King Edward had done, and all the former Dukes of Aquitaine. They were at this time held by King Richard, but with the reservation of paying homage to the Kings of England, the Duke of Lancaster and his heirs were to enjoy all other rights, lordships, rents and revenues. This was duly and fully confirmed by the King, under his seal. The duke was delighted by this gift, as well he might be; for the lands of Aquitaine are amply sufficient to keep their lord in great state. The deed of this gift was engrossed, examined and passed by the council.

61

Preparations for both expeditions went forward, but both departures were delayed for about two months by the illness of Anne, Queen of England. To the great distress of the King and his household, she made no improvement, but left this world on the feast of Whitsun, 1394. The King and all who loved her were most deeply grieved by her death. She was buried at Westminster, but her funeral was delayed, since the King wished it majestically and magnificently arranged.[1] Quantities of wax were brought, at great expense, from Flanders, to make candles and torches, and the illuminations at the funeral were more sumptuous than had ever been seen before, even on the death of Queen Philippa. Queen Anne was the daughter of the King of Bohemia, who was also Emperor of Rome and Germany, and King Richard could never forget her, so much had they been in love, ever since they were married, as little more than children. She bore him no offspring. Thus the King, the Duke of Lancaster and the Earl of Derby were all left widowers in the same year, and there was no talk of the King marrying again, for he would not hear of it.

Meanwhile the preparations for the Irish expedition went on uninterrupted. The expedition eventually sailed from Bristol and from Holyhead, and landed at Dublin, which had always been held for the English crown, and whose archbishop was with the King at this time. The King set out for Wales in July and tried to distract his mind from the loss of his Queen by means of hunting expeditions on the way. He was attended by his uncles, the Dukes of York and Gloucester, his half-brother the Earl of Kent, and the latter's son, Sir Thomas Holland; also by the Earls of Rutland, Salisbury, Arundel, Northumberland, Devonshire,

---

[1] '*On the 7th of June, Queen Anne died at Sheen in Surrey. . . . The King took her death so heavily that, besides cursing the place where she died, he did also, for anger, throw down the buildings, unto the which former Kings, being weary of the city, were wont for pleasure to resort.*' Stowe's Chronicle.

and Nottingham, Sir Thomas Percy, the high steward of England, Sir John Arundel, and other knights and squires. A large force was also left to defend the Scots border, for the Scots are an accursed race, who observe truces only when it suits them. The King's other half-brother, Sir John Holland, Earl of Huntingdon, had not yet returned from a pilgrimage to Jerusalem and to the shrine of Saint Catherine on Mount Sinai. Having reached Paris, he heard of an impending battle between the King of Hungary and the Sultan Bajazet, which, farther delayed his homecoming. The Duke of Lancaster set out from Plymouth with his expedition, and set sail for Bordeaux.

The King's army, which numbered four thousand men-at-arms and thirty thousand archers, embarked at three ports—Bristol, Holyhead, and Haverfordwest. It was a month before they all landed at Dublin. There was also a valiant English knight in Ireland, the Earl of Ormonde, who had inherited property there from his ancestors, though his claim to it was disputed. The army landed without loss and found quarters in an uninhabited tract of country within a radius of thirty miles from Dublin. The army guarded their encampment carefully against the Irish, and had they failed to do so they would have regretted it. The King, with his uncles and clergy, lodged in Dublin, and were well supplied with provisions of every kind; for the English are expert in war, and well able to forage and to look after themselves and their horses when the need arises.

62

And in very truth I, John Froissart, Treasurer and Canon of Chimay in the County of Hainault and the diocese of Liège, formed a strong desire to go and see the kingdom of England. I was at Abbeville at the time, and a truce had been completed between England and France and their allies on both sides. I had several reasons in mind. First, I had in my youth been brought up at the court of King Edward III and Queen Philippa, among their children and the courtiers of the King. The honour and nobility of the court was of the highest and best, as was their generosity and courtesy towards myself. Secondly, I wanted to see the country, for I had an irrational feeling that I would live longer for having seen it. I had been intending to go there for twenty-seven years, and even if I could not revisit those lords whom I had met before, I would take great pleasure in meeting their heirs, who would be able to help me in verifying all that I had written about the history of the country.

I spoke of my intention to my dear patrons, Albert, Duke of Bavaria and Count of Hainault, Holland, and Zeeland, and Lord of Friesland, and to his son William, at that time Count of Ostrevant; to that dear and deeply honoured lady, Joan, Duchess of Brabant and Luxemburg; and to the much respected Lord Enguerrand, the Lord of Coucy, as well as to that gallant knight, the Lord of Gommegnies, with whom I had arrived at the English court in my youth, together with many other knights who stood as hostages for King John of France, as I have related before. All these that I have mentioned gave me letters of introduction to the King and his uncles, except the Lord of Coucy, who through his close connection with France could only write to his daughter, the Duchess of Ireland. I had also collected all the love poems that I had written over the past thirty-four years, and had them well written out and illuminated. I was also eager to see once again King Richard, whom I had not seen since his christening in the cathedral at Bordeaux. I had intended, after that ceremony, to follow King Richard's father, the Prince of Wales, on his expedition to Spain; but when we reached Dax, the Prince had sent me back to his mother in England. I wished, therefore, to see King Richard and his uncles, and I took with me a beautiful illuminated book, bound in velvet, with clasps of silver gilt, as a present for the King. I spared no pains; for when a man undertakes something willingly, he counts neither the cost nor the trouble. I obtained horses and equipment, and set out from Calais for Dover on July 12th. When I arrived I found nobody whom I remembered from my last visit to England: the inns were all kept by new people, and those who had been children in my day were now grown men and women. They did not know me, nor I them. After resting for a day and a night, I set out for Canterbury, to visit the shrine of Saint Thomas and the magnificent tomb of the Prince of Wales. After hearing high mass and making my offering at the shrine, I returned to my inn to hear that the King was arriving next day on a pilgrimage to the shrine, after a campaign of nine months in Ireland. He duly arrived with a large retinue of lords and ladies, but when I met them they were all new faces.

The times had changed greatly in twenty-eight years. None of the King's uncles was with him, as they were all three otherwise occupied. I was at first dismayed: if I could have found my old friend Sir Richard Sturry, who had been a knight of the bedchamber to King Edward, and held the same office under King Richard, as well as being a member of his privy council, I would have been relieved. However, he was at his house in London. I then decided to go to Sir Thomas Percy, the High Steward of England. I found him well-disposed and agreeable, and he offered to present myself and my letters to the King. I was delighted, for one must have friends and intermediaries to be introduced to so great a prince as the King of England. The King had already retired, and I returned to my inn. Next day I returned to the archbishop's house, where the King had stayed, and from where he was preparing to set off for Leeds Castle. Sir Thomas Percy advised me not to announce my arrival for the present, but to join the King's company; he undertook to see that I was properly lodged when the King and his court reached Leeds Castle, which they were to do in two days time.

I did as he advised, and spent the first night at an inn at Ospringe, where I made the acquaintance of a knight of the bedchamber, Sir William de Lisle, who had remained there that morning instead of following the King, as he had a pain in the head. Seeing that I was a foreigner and a Frenchman—for they consider everyone French who speaks the *langue d'oil*,[1] wherever he

---

[1] *At that time the* lingua franca *of what is now the northern half of France.*

may come from—he treated me with great courtesy and friendliness, for that is the English custom. When I had told him my business, and explained Sir Thomas Percy's instructions to me, he replied that I could not have had better advice, and that the King and the Duke of York would be at Leeds on Friday, at dinnertime. I was delighted, since I had letters to the Duke of York as well, and he would remember me from the household of his father King Edward, and would help to establish my position at King Richard's court.

On the Friday morning Sir William de Lisle and I rode out together. He had been with the Irish expedition, and I asked him the truth about Saint Patrick's Purgatory at Lough Dergh, in Donegal.[1] This is how he described it: 'When my companion and I entered the cave, we went down three or four steps, but were soon overcome by the heat. We sat down on the steps, which are made of stone, and soon fell asleep.' I asked if he had had strange dreams, or if he had known where he was. He replied that both of them had indeed had strange dreams, more than they would have had in their own beds. They were let out in the morning, as they had requested, and soon afterwards the whole experience began to seem as if it had all been a dream. I should have liked to question Sir William further, but at this point we were overtaken by other knights, who held him in conversation until we reached Leeds, where we found the King and his court. I gave my letters of introduction from the Count of Hainault and

---

[1] *On a visit to Donegal in 1818, J. A. Buchon, an editor of the* Chronicles, *went to Lough Dergh. His description can be rendered as follow : 'Saint Patrick's Purgatory consists of a cave sixteen feet long by two feet wide; it is not high enough for a tall man to stand upright. Here, after fasting for nine days, and completing a series of processions and genuflexions, the pilgrims contemplate the punishments undergone by souls in purgatory. For two days they live on water alone. And if neither the mental disturbance nor the physical privations that they suffer are sufficient to induce hallucinatory visions, there are not lacking monks to remedy the defect.'*

Modern pilgrims find Lough Dergh less artificial, but not much more comfortable.

the Count of Ostrevant to the Duke of York, who was also at the court. The duke remembered me and greeted me warmly: 'Stay here with us and our people, Sir John,' he said. 'We will show you every kindness and attention. We remember the old days, when you were in the Queen my mother's household. We have not forgotten those times.' I thanked the Duke warmly for his kind words, and after receiving more hospitable attention from Sir Thomas Percy and Sir William de Lisle, I was taken by them to the royal apartments, where the Duke of York presented me to the King.

The King received me graciously, and carefully read the letters that I had brought him. He welcomed me by saying that since I had been at the court of his grandparents when they were King and Queen, I still belonged to the royal household. But on the advice of Sir Thomas Percy I did not present my book to the King on this occasion, as he was occupied with matters of state. The council were at this point considering two questions of great importance. First, negotiations with France on the possible marriage of King Richard to the Lady Isabel, the eldest daughter of the French King: the ambassadors that were sent to make this proposal were the Earl of Rutland, who was the King's first cousin, the Archbishop of Dublin, the Earl Marshal, the Bishop of Saint David's, and Sir William Scrope. Secondly, a deputation of knights had come from France and were pressing the King, since his return from Ireland, for an answer to their petition in connection with his gift to the Duke of Lancaster of the entire Duchy of Aquitaine. These |lords, together with the principal cities and towns of the duchy, maintained that such a gift was invalid, and therefore void, on the grounds that Aquitaine was a fief, inseparably attached to the English crown. To decide these matters, the King summoned the chief barons and prelates of the country to meet him on the feast of Saint Mary Magdalen[1] at his palace at Eltham, which lies halfway between London and Dartford, seven miles from each. After four days the court left

---

[1] *July 22nd.*

Leeds for Rochester, on the way to Eltham, and I set out in their company.

63

In the course of our ride, Sir William de Lisle and Sir John de Grailly explained to me at some length the two reasons for the council that was to be held at Eltham. First, the Duke of Lancaster had sent two knights from his own council, together with two skilled lawyers to plead his case before the King and his council. The people of Aquitaine and Bordeaux had stated that they were glad to welcome the duke as the son of their former lord, King Edward of happy memory, but not in any other capacity, that is to say as ruler of the country. The people of Bayonne had received him in the same spirit, namely insisting that the duke should solemnly undertake on oath that he and his people would act peacefully during their stay, and not take anything by force, but pay in ready money for their requirements, and refrain from extending the powers of the crown to oppress the people of the country. The duke had replied that so far from harming or oppressing anybody, he had merely come to guard and defend them as his inheritance; and he begged that the will of the King of England should be complied with. The dispute had dragged on, and the duke had eventually agreed to abide by the arbitration of the Parliament of England, whether favourable to himself or not. The Gascons also sent representatives to argue their case before the King.

I heard also that the Duke of Gloucester[1] was to be present, and would strongly support the Duke of Lancaster's claims; for he would always prefer the Duke of Lancaster, who took precedence over him, to be out of the country. The Duke of Gloucester had a good head, I was told, but was proud and overbearing; yet in spite of this he was popular in the country, and was influential enough to have caused the execution of Sir Simon

---

[1] *Thomas of Woodstock, youngest son of King Edward III.*

Burleigh and the banishment of the Duke of Ireland, the Archbishop of York, and other knights of the King's council. The Duke of Lancaster was more feared than loved in England.

The second reason for the meeting of the council was the desire of King Richard to remarry. If the Duke of Burgundy or the Count of Hainault had had daughters, I learned that King Richard would willingly have chosen one of them. But as it was, his thoughts had turned to the eldest daughter of the King of France. It was a matter of astonishment in England that the King should be so eager to marry the daughter of his chief enemy, nor did it add to his popularity. He seemed indifferent to this, however, and it had long been known how anxious he was for a lasting peace between the two countries. He took the view that the wars between the two countries had lasted too long, that too many valiant men had been killed on both sides, too many misdeeds had been perpetrated, and too many Christian people ruined or destroyed, to the great weakening of the Christian faith. The King's advisers had tried to dissuade him on the grounds that the lady would not be old enough to be a bride for five or six years. He replied that she was getting older every day, and in any case that since she was so young, he would be able to educate her and bring her up according to his own views, and according to English ways, and that he himself was young enough to be able to wait until she was grown up. As Sir John de Grailly told me, nothing could alter the King's intention; he added that I might see many strange things in the course of my visit.

Parliament was held at Eltham, in the presence of the King and his uncles, the knights and representatives of the towns of Gascony, as well as those of the Duke of Lancaster. They sat for four hours, and I cannot say exactly what passed, as I was not admitted to the session, nor was anybody who did not belong to it. Afterwards, however, I found Sir Richard Sturry, whom I had looked for in vain at Leeds, and he remembered me at once, though the last time he had seen me had been in Brussels, twenty-four years before. I asked him, as we walked up and down outside the King's chamber, if he could tell me what Parliament had decided, and after pondering for a few minutes, decided that it was not worth keeping secret something that would soon be common knowledge. Sir Richard Sturry then explained to me how the lords of Gascony had put their case before the King and council. They had opposed the grant that had been made to the Duke of Lancaster, on the grounds that the cities and lands in that country had received, from various kings of England, certain privileges, which the successors of those kings had, without exception, sworn to respect. As soon as any king of England came to the throne, he swore, with his hand on the missal, to preserve those rights and not to allow them to be infringed. To prove their point, they read aloud to the King a charter duly engrossed and sealed with the great seal of England, which he had granted them. The charter was in French as well as Latin, and was perfectly understood by all those present. The names of eleven great barons and prelates who had been nominated as sureties were also read out.

When they heard the letter read out, the members of the council looked first at each other, and then at the King, but not one of them said a word. The man who had read the letter then addressed the King in the following words: 'Most beloved and renowned Sire, and you, my dear lords, I am instructed by the representatives of the principal towns, and the inhabitants of Gascony, to lay this statement before you, and to affirm their dependence on the English crown, as this charter indeed shows. And if Gascony decided to receive the Duke of Lancaster as her King, and to be freed from paying homage and allegiance to you, the loss to the English crown would be serious. For although at the moment the Duke of Lancaster may be the King's man, and carefully respects the privileges of the crown, that love and loyalty may in the course of time fade and disappear as a result of the marriages that his heirs may make. For it is necessary that marriages should be arranged between the great ruling families for the preservation not only of their territories but also of the love of their subjects. An heir of the Duke of Lancaster may some day marry a daughter of the King of France, or of one of the

Dukes of Berry or of Brittany, or of Anjou or of Maine, or the King of Navarre, or the Count of Armagnac or of Foix, thus putting the whole of Guyenne in opposition to England, and perhaps making foreign alliances that would be ruinous to England. The King of England would then have great difficulty in recovering what rightfully belonged to the crown. Therefore, most beloved and renowned King, and you, my dear lords, be kind enough to consider these points that I have brought up. For the whole of my country is unanimous in its desire to remain in obedience to our redoubted lord and King, and to remain loyal in our attachment to the crown of England.'

The lords and prelates then approached the King, headed by his uncles and the Earls of Derby and Arundel. Those who had come from Aquitaine were asked to leave the chamber, and the King asked the opinion of the council. The prelates referred the question to the King's two uncles, as the matter concerned them more closely. They too begged to be excused at first, on the grounds that the matter was of general importance and should be considered in open council, not as being restricted to the royal family. Eventually the Duke of Gloucester was persuaded to give his opinion, which was that it would be a serious thing to revoke a gift freely made by a king with the full support of his council, and legally enacted in every way, for the sole reason that his subjects were rebellious. And that the King was not in fact lord and master of his inheritance if he could not dispose of it as he pleased. There were various comments on this speech, some boldly to the effect that it was not reasonable, though no one openly contradicted the duke, for he was too much feared. The Earl of Derby, who was the Duke of Lancaster's son, spoke next, in warm support of the Duke of Gloucester, saying, 'Good uncle, you have spoken well; your exposition of the matter is just and reasonable, and I support you.' At this point the council adjourned, and private discussions began between the various lords present. However, neither the emissaries from Guyenne nor the Duke of Lancaster's knights were recalled into the council chamber.

The King did not make up his mind at once, but intended to

reassemble the council after dinner, to decide how to act to the best advantage of the crown. He also made the Archbishop of Canterbury speak on the subject that he had broached to him that morning, namely of sending emissaries to France to negotiate the marriage of the King to the daughter of the King of France, who was still only eight years old. It was now decided whom to send on this mission, although the princess was already betrothed to the Duke of Brittany's son, and it would be difficult to break the engagement, since the agreement had been signed and sealed by the King of France and his uncles and the Duke of Brittany. Nevertheless the emissaries set out, having obtained passports from the French King.

As for the requests made by the people of Aquitaine and Guyenne, to preserve their ancient rights and privileges and in particular their allegiance to the British crown, the unanimous voice of the people of England, and that of perhaps four-fifths of the council, supported their case. But the Duke of Gloucester opposed them, making it clear that he would rather see the Duke of Lancaster in Aquitaine, since he had too much power in England, and too much influence with the King. Gloucester paid little attention to his other brother, Edmund, Duke of York, since he took little interest in public affairs, and was largely concerned with leading an agreeable life. He had, besides, recently married a young and beautiful wife, the daughter of the Earl of Kent, and spent much of his time with her. Gloucester, on the other hand, was malicious and wily, and was always asking favours from his nephew the King, and complaining about poverty, even though he was a great lord: he was High Constable of England, Earl of Hereford, Essex, and Buckingham, and in addition he had an income from the royal exchequer of four thousand nobles. Nor would he ever exert himself for his King or his country unless he was well paid for it. It was thus very much to his interest that the Duke of Lancaster should remain in Aquitaine, so that he could continue to have his own way in England. In order to show his superiority, the Duke of Gloucester left the council chamber as soon as he had given his opinion, and had dinner prepared for himself and the Earl of Derby; they were also joined by the Duke of York. Afterwards Gloucester took leave of the King and left for London. Further discussions were held next day, but the representatives of Aquitaine could get no answer to their petitions.

64

I have described these proceedings at length partly to give a fuller account of the truth and partly because, being in England at the time, I heard a first-hand account of them from Sir Richard Sturry. On the Sunday, after all the members of the council had left except the Duke of York, Sir Thomas Percy and Sir Richard, I was presented to the King, who desired to see the book that I had brought him. I gave it to him in his chamber, and laid it on his bed. He opened it and read it with considerable pleasure, as well he might, for it was beautifully written and illuminated, and bound in crimson velvet with ten silver-gilt studs, and roses embroidered in gold in the centre. The King asked the subject of my poems and I replied that they were concerning love. The King was delighted, and read out several of the poems, for he read and spoke French fluently. He then handed it to one of his knights, Sir Richard Credon, and told him to put it in his private library. The King was most affable to me about the book.

On the same day an English knight called Sir Henry Cristall,[1] noticing how much attention was being paid to me by the King and the lords, and also having seen my book, made my acquaintance. He knew that I was interested in history, and enquired if I had heard any account of the King's recent campaign in Ireland, which had brought the four Kings of that country, all great lords, under allegiance to the English crown. When he heard that I had not, he offered to tell me what had happened himself, so that I could record it for posterity to my own satisfaction. Sir Henry was at this time about fifty years old. His account went as follows:

[1] *The different texts give half a dozen variations on this name.*

'It is not recorded in living memory that a King of England ever undertook an expedition on so large a scale, and with so many men-at-arms and archers, against the Irish. He remained in their country over nine months; the expense involved was considerable, but it was willingly borne by the kingdom at large, for the city merchants and the great towns of England thought it well worth while when they saw the King return home in honour and glory. Only men-at-arms and archers had gone on the expedition, four thousand of the former and thirty thousand of the latter. They were all paid regularly every week, and were consequently well satisfied. I must tell you that Ireland is one of the worst and most unfavourable countries in which to carry on warfare; it abounds in deep forests and in lakes and bogs, and much of it is uninhabitable. It is often impossible to come to grips with the people, for they are quite ready to desert their towns and take refuge in the woods, and live in huts made of branches, or even among the bushes and hedges, like wild beasts. And when they hear of the approach of an invader, they retire into such remote and impenetrable fastnesses that it is impossible to come up with them. It happens quite often, however, that from their minute knowledge of the country they find a favourable opportunity for attacking their enemies; they are very alert on such occasions, and no man-at-arms, however well mounted, can overtake them, so light are they on their feet; they can even leap up onto a horse and drag the rider to the ground, or else pin his arms behind him so that he cannot escape, for their own arms are immensely strong. They have pointed, two-edged knives, with broad blades, and they never regard an enemy as dead until they have cut his throat, like a sheep. They then cut out the heart and carry it off; some people, who are well acquainted with their customs, say that they actually eat the human heart, and regard it as a great delicacy. They never allow prisoners to be ransomed, and when they have the worst of any skirmish, they scatter and hide in hedges or bushes, or underground, and seem to disappear without trace.

'No knight has greater experience of warfare in Ireland than

Sir William Windsor; but even he was unable to discover the national characteristics of the people, for they are a hardy race, rough and proud, and their moods and habits are unpredictable.[1] They pay no attention to outward appearances, nor do they have any respect for nobility; for although they are governed by Kings, of which there are several in the country, they have no experience of noble or civilized behaviour, but prefer to remain in that state of savagery in which they are brought up. But in fact four of the more powerful of the Kings of Ireland[2] have submitted to the King of England, but out of goodwill and friendship rather than compulsion. The Earl of Ormonde, whose lands march with theirs, took great pains to persuade them to go to Dublin, where King Richard was staying, and to submit themselves to him and to the English crown. This was generally considered a great achievement for the expedition, for King Edward I, of happy memory, was never able to succeed in the way that King Richard has now done. Yet although honour has been won, the practical gain is small, for nothing can be done with such savage and primitive people. I will give an example of their savageness, so that you may compare them with other nations. I speak from personal experience, as I had some Irish under my care and guidance at Dublin for about a month: by the order of the King and his council I was to instruct them in English manners and procedure. I know their language as well as I know English or French, for I was brought up among them: Thomas, father of the present Earl of Ormonde, brought me up in his own household, out of his high regard for my horsemanship.

'It so happened that he once set out on an expedition against the Irish, with three hundred lances and a thousand archers (for the English kept up a constant war against them in the hope of

[1] Or, as Lord Berners puts it: 'They be hard people and of rude engine and wit and of divers frequentations and usage.'
[2] O'Neill, O'Hanlon, O'Donnel, and MacMahon swore allegiance to Richard II at Drogheda, as did the principal chiefs of Leinster, O'Brien, O'Nolan, O'More, O'Murrough, and MacMurrough.

subjecting them to their rule). The Irish had formed an ambush against us, but were so heavily attacked by our archers when they emerged from it that they had to retreat, for they are only lightly armed. The earl set off in pursuit, and I was especially well mounted that day, and kept up with him. But it so happened that my horse took fright and bolted, and as I passed through the Irish, one of them leaped up behind me and held me fast, though without harming me in any way with lance or knife. He rode behind me for two hours, until we reached a very remote spot, near a large thicket, where we were joined by the rest of the Irish. The English would never give chase for such a long way, and he seemed delighted to have taken me prisoner. His house was in a town called Elphin, which was defended with a wooden palisade and a moat of stagnant water. His name was Bryan Costeret. He was a handsome man, and I afterwards made a number of enquiries about him, from which it appears that he is still alive, though now very old. He kept me with him for seven years, and gave me his daughter in marriage, by whom I had two daughters.

'In the seventh year of my captivity, Arthur MacMurrough, King of Leinster, raised an army against Lionel, Duke of Clarence, who was King Edward's son. A fierce battle was fought near Leinster, and the English won the day. The Irish fled, and the King of Leinster escaped. My wife's father was captured, and he was mounted on my horse, which was recognized as having belonged to the Earl of Ormonde. The English thus discovered first that I was alive and secondly that I had been honourably entertained, and married to the daughter of my captor.

'The Duke of Clarence and Sir William Windsor, and all our people, were delighted; and my father-in-law was offered his freedom in return for that of myself with my wife and children. He refused the terms at first, so fond was he of his daughter and me, and our children; but in the end he saw no alternative, and agreed, provided that my elder daughter remained with him. I returned to England and settled with my wife at Bristol, on the Severn. Both my daughters are now married: the one in Ireland has three sons and two daughters, and her sister has four boys and

two girls. We have always spoken Irish in the family, and I have
taught it to my children; and that is why I was chosen by our
lord the King to instruct those four Irish Kings in the customs of
the English. I must admit that their manners were rough and
coarse, and any impression I made on them was only on the
surface; they always revert to their own uncivilized habits.

'I will tell you what I was charged to do: King Richard
wanted the Irish Kings to adopt the habits, the appearance and
the dress of England, and he also wanted to knight them. A large
and fine house was found for them in Dublin, and I was commanded to live there with them, and never to leave the house
except when absolutely necessary. For three or four days we
grew to know each other, and I said nothing to try to change
their ways. When they sat at table they sometimes made grimaces
which I did not find attractive, and I was determined to put a
stop to them. They made their minstrels and servants sit at the
same table with them, and eat and drink from the same plates
and cups. This, they said, was the national custom: with the
exception of their beds, they shared everything communally.
This went on for three days, but on the fourth I had the tables
arranged and laid properly, and I put the four Kings at a high
table, with the minstrels at a lower one, and the servants somewhere else again. They pretended to be annoyed at this, and
looked at each other, and refused to eat, saying that their old
custom had been broken. I replied, laughing, to appease them,
that their custom was not reasonable and did not accord with
their rank; and I explained the orders that the King had given
me. And after that they cheerfully complied with English customs,
inasmuch as they had put themselves under allegiance to the
King of England.

'They had another habit, which I knew was common in their
country, of not wearing breeches. So I had some made for them
and for their people, to which they soon grew accustomed. And
I broke them of various other unsuitable habits, both as regards
dress and other things as well. At first I had difficulty in persuading them to wear clothes of silk trimmed with fur, for till then

they considered a rough Irish cloak sufficient. They always rode without saddles or stirrups, and I had great trouble in getting them to use them.

'I once questioned them about their religious faith, but they were not at all pleased: they replied that they believed in God and in the Trinity, just as we did. I asked which Pope they supported, and they replied without hesitation, the Pope of Rome. I said that the King wanted to make them knights, according to the traditional custom of England and France, and I asked if they would accept an order of chivalry. They replied that they were already knights, and that that was quite enough. I asked how and when their knighthood had been conferred, and they said that the King knights his sons when they reach the age of seven; and that if a boy's father is already dead, he is knighted by his nearest relation. The young knights begin to learn to tilt with a light lance against a shield set up in a field. The more lances a boy breaks, the more honour he gains, and it is on this principle that they are knighted, more especially the sons of kings. I already knew about the early training of their knights, and I explained that this method of being knighted in childhood would not seem adequate to the King of England, and that he would grant them the honour in a different form. They asked how, and I explained that the ceremony would take place in church, in full and solemn dignity. They were duly impressed.

'About two days before the King wished to perform the ceremony, he sent the Earl of Ormonde to Dublin, since he knew the Irish language well, having estates in the country. There he was shown every respect, which he reciprocated, and the purpose of his mission, namely to give the Irish greater confidence in the King's intentions, was fulfilled. He spoke to them with great friendliness, and asked if they were satisfied with my behaviour towards them. They answered, gracefully, that I had explained to them the customs and manners of England, for which they were duly grateful. This answer pleased the Earl of Ormonde and he proceeded to tell them something about the order of knighthood they were to receive, explaining every detail of what was expected of those on whom it was conferred, and letting them understand its full importance. The four Kings, whose names were as follows, were once again delighted: they were O'Neill, King of Meath, O'Brien, King of Thomond, Arthur Mac-Murrough, King of Leinster, and Conor, King of Connaught. They were knighted by King Richard in the cathedral of Saint John the Baptist at Dublin on the feast of the Annunciation,[1] which was a Thursday. The previous night they spent in vigil in the cathedral, and they were solemnly knighted in the morning after mass, along with three Englishmen. The Kings were richly dressed, as befitted their rank, and they dined afterwards at King Richard's table, where they were looked on with great curiosity by the English and others who were present. For they were strange figures, different in appearance from the English and from the people of other countries. One is naturally inclined to gaze at any novelty, and it was certainly something quite new, at that time, to see these four Kings of Ireland.'

Such was Sir Henry's account, and I answered as follows: 'Sir Henry, I can well believe you, and I would give a good deal to have been there. I had indeed arranged to come to England at that time, but the death of Queen Anne made me postpone my visit. But one thing astonishes me: how did these four Kings put themselves so readily under obedience to King Richard, when his valiant great-great-grandfather, King Edward I, who was such a redoubtable man, and so much feared and renowned on every side, never succeeded in making them submit to him, but was always at war with them? You said that it was by a treaty, and by the grace of God. Now the grace of God is of great value to those who receive it, but nowadays few lords can extend their territories in any other way than by force. When I go home to Hainault, I shall be questioned very closely on this point, for my lord Albert, the Duke of Barana, who is also Count of Hainault, Holland and Zeeland, together with his son William, also call themselves lords of Friesland, which is a large and powerful

[1] *March 25th.*

country, which their predecessors have always claimed to rule. But the Frieslanders refuse to acknowledge them or to submit to them.'

Sir Henry replied: 'Sir John, I cannot truly explain it in full, but the general opinion is that the Irish were very much frightened by the large expedition that the King brought from England and that had been in Ireland for nine months. The coast was so strongly held by them that no provisions or other goods could be landed. Now the inhabitants of the more remote parts of Ireland were quite indifferent to this, for they neither know nor wish to know anything about commerce, since they live quite simply, like wild beasts. But those who live on the coast opposite England are more like ourselves, and are used to trade. Now King Edward I, of happy memory, had so many wars on his hands—in France, in Brittany, in Gascony, and in Scotland—that his forces were all split up in different places, and he never had a large number to send to Ireland. But when the Irish now saw such a large force entering the country, they found it advisable to acknowledge the King of England. And long ago, when King Edward the Confessor was on the English throne, he defeated the Danes three times, at sea; and he was more loved and feared by the Irish than any King of England either before or since. For this reason, King Richard laid aside his own banners which bore the leopards and fleur-de-lis, and carried instead the arms of Edward the Confessor, which were a cross *patencé* or, on a field gules, with four doves argent on the shield or banner. We have heard that this pleased the Irish very much, and that they were more inclined to submit to him, since the ancestors of these four Kings had paid homage to Edward the Confessor. They also considered King Richard to be a prudent and conscientious man, and therefore paid homage as their ancestors had done before them.

'That is how our King achieved his object in Ireland; and you must remember it and set it down in your chronicles when you return home.'

I replied: 'Henry, you have spoken loyally, and it shall be done.'

Upon this, we left each other, and soon afterwards I enquired from March Herald what Sir Henry's arms might be, as he had treated me so courteously, and had had the four Kings of Ireland under his care for more than fifteen days. His arms were argent, a chevron gules between three besants of the second per pale, two and one.

65

I was able to spend as much time as I pleased at the court of King Richard, and not always in the same place; for the King moved about a good deal, to Eltham, Leeds Castle, Kingston, Sheen, Chertsey and Windsor. All this time he was in touch with the Duke of Lancaster, and with the people of Aquitaine, who were still reluctant to recognize anyone as their lord except the King of England. And it was finally decided by the council that King Richard should keep for himself the gift which he had tried to bestow on the Duke of Lancaster, in spite of the wishes of the Duke of Gloucester, who was anxious that his brother should have Aquitaine. But the kingdom of England had its doubts about what might happen in the future, and accepted what the people of Bordeaux and Bayonne said, namely that if Aquitaine ceased being under the English crown, it would be greatly to the disadvantage of the realm. And the people of Bordeaux and Bayonne and of the borders of Gascony had exerted themselves considerably to protect the honour of England, and they did not now wish to see her suffer any disadvantage. The council eagerly urged these considerations on the King when the Duke of Gloucester was absent, though nobody dared speak out in his presence. . . .

SUMMARY

65-73

The English embassy to France brought back a hopeful answer about the possibility of a match between King Richard and the little Princess Isabel, although there was also some feeling against the marriage in France. Great efforts were made by Robert le Monnet, a squire of Normandy, also called Robert the Hermit, to bring about peace between England and France. On returning from the East he had seen a vision, and he frequently spoke with the King of France, and also with the English lords at Lelinghen, and also in England with the Duke of Gloucester and others.

In Paris, the Lord de la Rivière and Sir John le Mercier were released from prison but banished from the neighbourhood of Paris. Peace was made between the Duke of Brittany and Olivier de Clisson, and with the protection of the Duke of Burgundy, Peter of Craon returned in secret to Paris.

The King of Hungary appealed to the King of France for help against the Turks, who threatened his country. An army was sent under the Count of Nevers (the son of the Duke of Burgundy), with the Count of Artois and the Lord de Coucy.

The Duchess of Anjou, who was also Queen of Naples, brought an action in the Parliament of Paris against Sir Peter of Craon for a hundred thousand francs. He was released from other charges in order to stand trial, judgement was given against him and he was put in prison until the money should be paid.

The marriage between King Richard and the King of France's daughter was finally arranged. The Duke of Lancaster married his mistress Catherine Swynford, which caused great indignation at court. The Duchess of Gloucester and the Countesses of Arundel and Derby declared that they would never meet her: being second in rank only to the Queen, she would have taken precedence over them.

74

We will now turn to the expedition made that summer[1] by the Count of Nevers and other French lords into Hungary. He arrived at Buda with a large number of valiant men from France and other countries, and the army was well received by the King of Hungary, as indeed it deserved to be. Before taking the field, the King of Hungary wished to learn some news of the movements of Bajazet, the Sultan of Turkey, who had given him warning in February to muster his forces, since he was going to cross the Danube before the end of May with a large army and give battle. There was much speculation about how he would do this, but the general opinion was that Bajazet was a very valiant and capable man, and obviously much addicted to warfare; and that he would do what he had said. But if his threat came to nothing, and he failed to cross the Danube, the Hungarians thought that they ought to invade Turkey. The King of Hungary could raise a hundred thousand men, including foreigners, and they would be enough to conquer the whole of Turkey and to go as far as the Persian Empire. If they defeated Bajazet they might even conquer Syria and the Holy Land, and deliver Jerusalem from the hands of the Sultan and the enemies of God. The Kings of England and France would then in the following summer raise such a large joint army that nothing would be able to withstand it.

So said the French knights in Hungary. When May came there was no sign of Bajazet, and the King of Hungary, who had been joined by the Knights of Rhodes, sent scouts, who knew the country, across the Danube, but they could only learn that Bajazet was still in Asia, either at Damascus or Antioch or Alexandria. The King then called a council, at which the Lord de Coucy, speaking for the French, said that if Bajazet had failed to keep his word, that was no reason for them to stay idle; they should achieve some feats of arms, since that was the purpose of

[1] *1393.*

their being there. All the French, German, Bohemian, and other troops agreed to set out against the Turks, and if the latter were under the command of Bajazet, the invaders would have the opportunity of winning greater honour.

The French lords set out from Buda in magnificent array, over which no expense was spared, under the guidance of the Constable of Hungary, who knew the country. There were sixty thousand horsemen in the army, and only a few followers on foot; the Hungarian crossbowmen were also mounted. Barges, pontoons and boats had been prepared to take them over the river Danube, which is the boundary between Hungary and Turkey, and the crossing took eight days. They decided to besiege the city of Nissa, which is in the middle of a plain bordered by the Morava. This river is navigable, and is a tributary of the great Danube, which extends for four hundred leagues from its source to where it flows into the sea. It would be the most valuable river in the world to Hungary and the neighbouring countries if only the boats that use it could pass out into the sea. But this they cannot do, because near the mouth of the river there is a large mountain which divides the stream into two halves and where the noise is so tremendous that it can be heard seven leagues away. For this reason no vessel dares approach it.[1]

The river Morava is bordered on both banks by fertile lands, to the great advantage of the inhabitants; and good wines are made in the vineyards. The wine is put into goatskins by the Turks, who are forbidden by law, on pain of death, to drink it; they sell it instead to the Christians. They do however eat the grapes, and they make agreeable drinks out of various fruits and spices, and for refreshment, in the hot weather, they drink quantities of goat's milk.

The King of Hungary's army remained in front of Nissa without opposition, and they found all the fruit ripe, which was very convenient. In the end they took the town by storm, with

[1] *Buchon observes that the falls of the Danube are close to Belgrade, nowhere near the mouth of the river.*

373

great slaughter of men, women, and children. The Christians took no pity on anyone. King Sigismund then advanced towards the large and strong city of Nicopoli, but before reaching it his army spent fifteen days besieging Rachowa, which they finally captured and destroyed. On their way to Nicopoli they also encamped near the town and castle of Belgraltchi, and the French contingent under the Count of Nevers (who had been knighted by the King of Hungary) laid siege to the place. The town was taken after resisting for four days, but the castle held out under its lord, whose name was Corbadas, and who was valiantly supported by his three brothers, Maladius, Balachius and Ruffin. Many of the inhabitants of the town took refuge in the castle, and after a week's fruitless efforts, the French decided that they were achieving nothing, and raised the siege; for they knew that King Sigismund was anxious to go on to Nicopoli. Before rejoining the Hungarians, however, the French burned the town to the ground.

Corbadas, Lord of Belgraltchi, was pleased by the departure of the French, and spoke philosophically to his brothers as follows: 'We shall now be undisturbed for the rest of the year. If my city has been burned and destroyed—well, it can be rebuilt. But what surprises me is that there is no news of our lord the Sultan Bajazet, although he told me that he would be in this country at the beginning of May. He fully intended to cross the Bosphorus, enter Hungary and give battle to the Christians. He even sent word of his intentions to the King of Hungary, who has now acquired the support of the French and has himself crossed the Danube and entered Turkey, where he will do great damage to Bajazet's possessions, for we have no resources with which to resist him. Furthermore, they will now certainly lay siege to Nicopoli, and although it is strong enough to hold out for some time, it can do so only if it is well defended. We are four brothers, and we are not only knights but also blood relations of Bajazet, and we should therefore attend to his interests. I propose, therefore, the following plan. My brother Maladius and I will go to Nicopoli and help with its defence. Balachius will remain here to defend Belgraltchi, and Ruffin will go at once across the sea to Bajazet and explain to him how matters stand, and tell him of the army that has invaded Turkey, that he may send a sufficient force against the Christians to protect his possessions. Otherwise he will not only lose the kingdom of Armenia that he has won, but all his original lands as well. For, from what we hear, the King of Hungary and his allies are set on great deeds.'

This was agreed on; meanwhile, the Christian army, amounting to a hundred thousand, laid siege to Nicopoli. The inhabitants of the town were overjoyed at the arrival of Corbadas and Maladius, and Ruffin set out in secret to find Bajazet, who was in Cairo, seeking the aid of the Caliph of Baghdad. He realized that there must be exceptional news from Turkey, and asked Ruffin what had happened. When he heard the answer, Bajazet repeated the story to the Caliph, who replied: 'We must make arrangements: I will provide troops to withstand them, for we must defend our religion and our inheritance.' 'That is true,' said Bajazet. 'For the present we will let the King of Hungary have full rein, but he will pay in the end. When I first heard of this expedition from my good friend the Duke of Milan, who sent me at the same time a dozen gyrfalcons and peregrine falcons, I learned the names of some of the French barons who were coming on the expedition. And if I can capture those that he named, their ransoms would be, together, worth a million florins. They are the Duke of Burgundy's son John; Philip of Artois, who is Count of Eu and Constable of France; John of Bourbon; Henry and Philip of Bar, who are cousins to the King of France; Enguerrand, lord of Coucy; Boucicault, the senior Marshal of France; Guy de la Tremouille, the lord of Sully; and John de Vienne, High Admiral of France. Besides these there are five hundred other knights of France, all valiant men. The Duke of Milan advised me, if it comes to a battle (as it most certainly will), to make use of every tactical and strategic advantage, since our enemies are such valiant campaigners that not even the meanest of them would fly to save his life. They have come on this expedition for glory, and to gain honour. I will satisfy their appetite for battle before three months are up, if they have not had enough before.'

SUMMARY

75, 77-80

Froissart here digresses to give an account of the rise of the Visconti family in Milan and Lombardy. The three Visconti brothers Matthew, Galeas, and Bernabo, who founded the fortunes of the family, had an uncle who was Archbishop of Milan in 1347, at the time when Charles of Luxemburg was elected Emperor in succession to Louis of Bavaria. The Archbishop entertained the new Emperor so magnificently that he was created Lord of Milan; he also lent the Emperor a hundred thousand ducats. When the Archbishop died he was succeeded by his nephew Sir Matthew, who aroused the jealousy of his two indigent brothers, but died[1] before their plot against him had come to anything.

The surviving brothers strengthened their position further, Galeas marrying, in 1350, Blanche, sister of the Count of Savoy, and Bernabo, three weeks later, marrying Beatrice, sister of the Duke of Brunswick. The brothers remained on good terms, dividing the towns of Lombardy amicably between them and each ruling over Milan in turn for a year at a time. The people were taxed heavily, the towns were garrisoned by foreign mercenaries, and the country was so strong that nobody dared try to encroach on it.

When Sir Galeas heard of the difficulty that King John of France was having in raising money for his ransom to pay the King of England, he arranged that his own son, John Galeas, should marry one of the daughters of the King of France in return for six hundred thousand francs being paid to the King of England. They had a son, and also a daughter, Valentina, who married Louis, Duke of Orléans and Count of Blois and of Valois, the second son of Charles V of France. The only man to attack the Viscontis with any success was the Marquis of Montferrat, with the aid of Sir John Hawkwood and his English mercenaries.

On the death of Sir Galeas, his son John Galeas ruled at first with prudence and restraint, but later captured his surviving uncle, Sir

---

[1] '*From the effects of his own intemperance.*' Johnes.

Bernabo, in an ambush, and informed him that 'one lord was enough for Lombardy.' He put his uncle to death, and seized many of his children, though one of them married the Duke of Austria and Bohemia; their daughter Isabel married King Charles VI of France.

Sir John Galeas was as materially-minded as his father;[1] and when the schism opened in the Church, these lords of Milan laughed at both the Popes, as did other great lords. His daughter Valentina, Duchess of Orléans, shared his worldly cravings, and wanted her husband to be King of France, even arranging for a poisoned apple to be thrown on the floor in a room where the Dauphin and her own son, who were about the same age, were playing. It was eaten not by the Dauphin, but by her own son, who died on the spot. The French court was outraged, and people in Paris said openly that if she was not prevented from having access to the King, she would be forcibly removed and put to death, since she had obviously put a spell on him. This idea was supported by the King's refusal, in his illness, to see the Queen or indeed anyone else except the Duchess of Orléans. The Duke removed her from Paris, first to a castle near Beauvais and then to Neufchatel, on the Loire.

Sir John Galeas was much annoyed by his daughter's treatment, and sent ambassadors to France saying that if any knight accused her of treason, he would be challenged to mortal combat. The King of France was by this time restored in health, and little attention was paid to the ambassadors. Sir John Galeas was furious at their reception and sent a defiance to the King of France, but by the time it had arrived most of the French knights had already set off for Hungary. To spite the King of France, the Duke of Milan therefore formed an

---

[1] *Froissart says: 'He renewed all the taxes and other methods of extortion that he had at first abolished, and added new ones, for which he was more feared than loved. He followed the errors of his father, and refused to adore and believe in God. He deprived religious houses of their revenues and appropriated them to himself, saying that the monks lived too luxuriously on rich food and delicate wines, instead of rising at midnight to fulfil their ritual duties. This, he said, was not how Saint Benedict had ordained that they should live; and in future they could live on eggs and thin wine, so that their voices might ring out clearer and louder in choir.'*

377

alliance with Bajazet, and regularly informed him of affairs in Europe. This explains the otherwise extraordinary alliance between the Duke of Milan and the infidel Turk.

76

Bajazet did not stay long at Cairo once he had obtained the support of the Caliph of Baghdad, who undertook to raise the best army that he could find; for if the French should invade and conquer Turkey, all the neighbouring countries would tremble, for their faith would be destroyed, and they themselves would be subjected to the Christians. To this, death itself would be preferable. Bajazet and the Caliph sent word to several Saracen kings, in Persia, Media, and Tartary, and even to Lithuania, beyond the boundary of Prussia. The Saracen kings and lords realized that they would be opposed by the full flower of Christian chivalry, and selected their troops with the utmost care, choosing only those of the greatest ability and experience. Naturally, this could not be done quickly, but when all was ready Bajazet set out, followed by large bodies of troops from the places named above. All were spoiling for a fight and eager to show their strength against the Christians, who meanwhile kept up the siege of Nicopoli.

The garrison was numerous, and they defended the town valiantly, but they were much surprised at having no news of Bajazet, though the Emperor of Constantinople had written to say that he was still in the region of Alexandria. The besieging army was easily and cheaply supplied with provisions from Hungary. In the course of the siege, the Lord de Coucy and a number of other French lords decided to make an expedition farther into Turkey, for they had been too long in the same place, and the siege could be easily kept up by the King of Hungary and the rest of the troops. They therefore set out with about five hundred lances and the same number of crossbowmen, all on horseback. They took with them guides who knew the country, and accompanied by some of the best mounted Hungarian cavalry they set out to see what they could find. That very same week, the Turks also took the field with an army of twenty thousand, for they were determined to stop the Christians from burning and laying waste the country. They advanced as far as a pass through which the Christians would have to go in order to reach the plain, and waited there for two days. They were on the point of returning when the Christian outriders came galloping up. The Turks remained quiet and held their fire. The outriders rode up quite close and although they could not establish exactly the numbers of the Turkish army, they saw that it was very large. They reported this news to the Lord de Coucy, who took the view that having come thus far it would be disgraceful not to fight a battle.

Between the Christian and Turkish armies was situated a small wood, near which the Lord de Coucy halted his troops and announced the following plan to Sir Reginald de Roye and the Lord de Saint Pye: 'To draw the Turks out of their ambush, you must advance with a hundred of our lances, while we post the rest in this wood. When they see such a small force, the Turks will leave their ambush, and you must allow them to pursue you past this wood. When they have passed you must turn and stand, and we will dash out from the wood. They will then be trapped and we will have them at our mercy.'

This plan was put into operation, and when the Turkish army passed the wood, the Christians charged out of the wood, crying 'Our Lady for the Lord de Coucy!' The Turks halted, quite bewildered at finding themselves surrounded; they defended themselves as best they could, but there was little that they could do. The French performed valiant feats of arms, and cut down all who opposed them. The corpses were piled high on the ground where they fell, and the Christians took pity on none. Any who escaped were lucky indeed, and in the evening the Christians returned to their camp outside Nicopoli.

The praises of the Lord de Coucy resounded on every side for his victory over fifteen thousand Turks, but the Comte d'Eu was by no means impressed. He said that the engagement had been undertaken purely out of vanity and that the Christians had been put in great danger—not least his own company—by attacking such an immensely superior force. In addition, the commander-in-chief, the Count of Nevers, should have been informed, since he too was eager for the fray, and anxious to acquit himself with honour.

That is what the Comte d'Eu, out of jealousy, one must suppose, said about the Lord de Coucy. And for the rest of the campaign he was never on good terms with him again, although he could see that the Lord de Coucy was held in the highest esteem and affection by the other knights, both by the French ones and the foreigners, as indeed was only to be expected, for he was closely related by blood to the King of France, and bore for arms the royal fleur-de-lis with a bar. He was also Constable of France. This was the beginning of the hatred of the Comte d'Eu for the Lord de Coucy, which was eventually to do such harm to the Christians.

81

The city of Nicopoli was by now on the point of surrender. The assault made on it by the Christians had been severe, and there was still no news of Bajazet to comfort the beleaguered garrison. The King of Hungary now addressed the knights of France and Burgundy as follows: 'My lords, thanks to God we have had a good campaign; our feats of arms have been successful and we have beaten the Turks. Nicopoli is as good as ours; it is so undermined and surrounded that it can hold out no longer. All things considered, I recommend that we advance no farther this season, once the city is in our hands. We will retire across the Danube into Hungary, where I have a number of cities, towns and castles all ready to receive you, in return for your support in this war against my bitter enemies the Turks. We will re-equip ourselves with stores for the next campaigning season, and we will communicate the position to the King of France, so that he will send us reinforcements for next year. Let us hope that he will even come here in person when he knows the size of our army and the extent of our successes; for he is young and vigorous, and fond of battle. Whether he comes or not, we will next summer by God's grace cross the Bosphorus, regain Armenia and advance into Syria, capturing the ports of Beirut and Jaffa, and conquering Jerusalem and the whole of the Holy Land. If the Caliph stands in our way, we will fight him, and he will not get away without a battle.'

The King of Hungary and the French lords regarded Nicopoli as theirs, but things turned out differently. During the whole of that summer Bajazet had been recruiting an army of Saracens and infidels, and had found troops from as far away as Persia. All the great lords of his religion had put themselves at his disposal in the fight against Christianity, and an army of them amounting to over two hundred thousand had crossed the Bosphorus, without the Christians having any idea either of their numbers or of their intentions; and they succeeded in approaching quite close to Nicopoli without arousing the suspicions of their enemies. Bajazet was as great an expert in warfare as could be, and he was brave and enterprising into the bargain. He had a considerable respect for the ability of the Christians, and the stratagem he adopted was as follows: he drew up his main army in a triangular form, with a vanguard of eight thousand Turks a league ahead of it, to conceal it. The vanguard's orders were to advance slowly and to give the impression of constituting the entire army until they should actually meet the Christians, when they were to retire gently towards the main army, which in turn was to attempt to close with the Christians, and defeat them.

The date was Michaelmas Eve,[1] 1396, and the King of Hungary and his lords were at dinner when news was brought that the Turks were at hand. Neither the French nor the Hungarian scouts were aware of the whole truth, for they did not have the courage to establish the presence of any more than the vanguard of the enemy. Most of the French army, too, was at dinner

[1] *September 28th.*

when the messenger came and called out to the Count of Nevers and the other French lords: 'Come quick and arm yourselves! Do not be taken by surprise! The Turks are almost upon you!' Most of the Christian knights, in their eagerness for the fray, were delighted by what they heard. Heated by the wine that they had been drinking, they called for their horses and armour and made for their banners and pennons, which were quickly raised by the standard-bearers. The banner of Our Lady was unfurled, and that valiant knight Sir John de Vienne took his place beside it. In their great eagerness for battle, the French were the first in the field; they were drawn up in fine style, and had very little fear of the Turks, for they were unaware of their numbers, nor did they know that Bajazet himself was in command of them. At this point the King of Hungary's marshal[1] rode up to the French lords and begged them, on behalf of the King, not to engage with the Turks until they should hear further from him. The King doubted whether the scouts and spies had reported the full extent of the Turkish army. In about two hours, the marshal added, they would have fuller information from other scouts who had been sent further afield. The Turks would certainly not take the initiative in attacking until they were all concentrated in one place. These were the instructions of the King of Hungary and his council.

The French barons considered these instructions, and the first to be asked his opinion was the Lord de Coucy, who found them perfectly reasonable. Whereupon the Comte d'Eu, piqued at not having been the first to be consulted, took the opposite view, from a mixture of pride and malice, saying: 'Yes, yes, the King of Hungary wants all the honour and glory of the day for himself. He has put us in the van, but now he wants to remove us. You may believe this message if you like, but you will not persuade me.' And turning to his standard-bearer he added, 'In the name of God and Saint George, they will see what stuff I am made of today.'

[1] *Numerous versions of this knight's name appear in the various texts.*

The Lord de Coucy thought this a very foolish speech and asked the opinion of Sir John de Vienne (who had under his charge the banner of Our Lady, the Sovereign of all, on whom they all depended). The answer came as follows: 'Lord de Coucy, when truth and reason cannot be heard, rashness and folly must reign. Since the Comte d'Eu is set on fighting, we shall have to follow him; but we would be much stronger with the King of Hungary than we are without him.' Meanwhile the enemy were approaching fast, and the two wings of the Turkish vanguard, each of them sixty thousand strong, began to close in. The Christians were encircled, and even if they had wished to retreat it would have been impossible, so strong and densely packed were the enemy wings. The more experienced knights and squires realized that they could not win the day, but all the same they advanced beneath the banner of Our Lady. The knights of France were so sumptuously armed that each of them might have been a king. But I am told that when they advanced against the Turks, they were not more than seven hundred in number. Think of the folly, and the pity of it! If they had only waited for the King of Hungary, who had at least sixteen thousand men, they could have done great deeds; but pride was their downfall. Never since the battle of Roncesvalles, where the twelve peers of France were killed, did the French suffer such a terrible loss. Nevertheless, before they were overcome, they inflicted terrible losses on the Turks, though most of the knights and squires realized that they were only advancing to their doom. They routed the Turkish vanguard and came to where Bajazet had taken up a position with his main army in a great valley. Then the French wanted to retire, but they were hemmed in on every side. The battle raged furiously, and the French held out for a long time.

News reached the King of Hungary that the battle had already begun, and that the French had disobeyed his instructions. He was furious, as indeed he had reason to be, and he knew that the day was lost. He said to the Grand Master of Rhodes, who was with him: 'We will lose the day by the pride and vanity of the French. If they had done as I said we would have had enough men to fight the enemy.' The King turned and saw his own troops now put to flight, and the Turks pursuing them; and he knew that there would be no recovery. Those around him said: 'Sir, save yourself! You are either taken or slain! All Hungary is lost! The pride of the French has lost us the day, and they will all be taken or killed—not one will escape. Escape, Sir, if you can!'

The King was highly incensed not only at having to flee, but also at being defeated through the pride of the French. Indeed, it was a disastrous day for both countries. As you know, when an army flees, it is pursued. The Hungarians fled in complete disarray, and the Turks followed, killing and capturing all they could. However, the King of Hungary and the Grand Master of Rhodes, with the help of God, found a little boat on the Danube belonging to the Grand Master, and they got into it, with only five others, and reached the other bank. Had they not done so, they would certainly have been either killed or captured, for the Turks pursued the fugitives right up to the river bank and made a terrible slaughter of them.

The Lord de Montcaurel, a valiant knight from Artois, had his young son with him, and seeing that the day was lost, he said to his squire: 'Take my son and escape; there is a way through over there. Save my son for me, and I will wait for the end here with the others.' When he heard these words, the son at first refused to go and to leave his father. But the father prevailed in the end, and the squire took the boy away, out of danger, to the river. But there the boy, in his misery for his father, fell into the river between two barges, and was drowned; for no one could save him. Sir William de la Trémouille was killed after carrying out tremendous feats of arms, and Sir John de Vienne also fell at last after distinguishing himself equally; he was found on the field with the banner of Our Lady still held tight in his fist. The entire French force that was engaged in the campaign for Nicopoli was defeated and scattered as I have described. The truth is that the French knights and squires and their allies from other countries acquitted themselves heroically in the field, and if they had been supported in the same way by the Hungarians the day would have turned out differently. But in fact the French were responsible for the disaster, since it was through their pride that all was lost. There was present at the battle a knight from Picardy called Sir James of Helly who had spent some time in Turkey in the service of Amurath, the father of the Sultan Bajazet of whom we are dealing. This knight could speak Turkish, and when he saw that the day was lost he was determined to be taken prisoner and ransomed, for he knew that the Saracens in their greed for gold and silver would spare his life. Many other French knights were saved by the great richness of their armour, and indeed they were arrayed like kings, and were thought by the Saracens to be much greater lords than in fact they were.

SUMMARY

82-91

All the French prisoners were executed with the exception of nine great lords from whom Bajazet could expect notable ransoms. Bajazet dispersed the greater part of his forces, and the survivors of the Christian army suffered great hardship on their journey home. The King of France was informed of the disaster by Sir James of Helly, and sent presents to Bajazet to dissuade him from maltreating his prisoners. The King of Hungary would not at first allow these presents to be carried through his country, on the grounds that it was degrading for the King of France to send presents to the infidel.

The King of France still suffered from annual fits of madness, and the Duchess of Orléans was still in exile, on the grounds of having used sorcery and of putting a spell on him. Her father, the Duke of Milan, was enraged at these accusations, and war might have ensued but for the arrival of the news of Nicopoli. Strenuous efforts were made to ransom the French knights.

In England, the Duke of Gloucester secretly encouraged the people to demand the abolition of various taxes originally imposed in time of war. King Richard's unpopularity grew, and a rumour was spread that he might give up Calais to the French. The Duke of Gloucester, whose chief object was to renew the wars with France, continued to stir up the people against the King, who finally had him arrested.

The Lord de Coucy and the Comte d'Eu died in Turkey before their release could be arranged, but ransoms were agreed on for the other French prisoners, who then returned by sea to Venice, and thence to France. With the death of the Comte d'Eu in Turkey, Lord Louis of Sancerre was made Constable of France, and was followed as Marshal of France by Lord Boucicaut. The Count of Blois, one of Froissart's chief patrons, died.

92

You have already heard how, in England, King Richard had lured his uncle the Duke of Gloucester out of his castle at Pleshy, and had him arrested, between ten and eleven o'clock at night, by the Earl Marshal. The Duke cried out after the King, who was riding away, to deliver him from his peril, for he knew in his heart that his position was desperate. But the King turned a deaf ear and rode off to London, where he stayed the night in the Tower. The Duke of Gloucester, however, had quite a different lodging, and was forced willy-nilly onto a barge and thence onto a ship lying in the Thames, and with the aid of wind and tide was brought to Calais the following evening. The duchess and her children were naturally most alarmed when they heard the news, and on the advice of Sir John Lackingay sent messages to the Dukes of Lancaster and York. They were furious at the arrest of their brother, and sent back word to the duchess not to be too downhearted, for the King would not dare treat the duke except in accordance with the law.

Next day the King left the Tower and rode to Eltham. In the evening of the same day the Earls of Arundel and Warwick were taken to the Tower by the King's orders, to the general surprise and indignation of the people. But the common view was that the Dukes of York and Lancaster could put things right whenever they chose, and could have prevented the arrest of their brother, had they foreseen it; however, they would regret their indolence, and only by instant action would they be able to prevent a disaster.

The Duke of Gloucester was much alarmed at finding himself confined in the castle at Calais, and asked the Earl Marshal why he had been brought there, and if he could go and see the garrison and the troops and townspeople. The Earl Marshal answered as follows: 'My lord, I would not dare do as you ask, for I must guard you under pain of death. My lord the King is angry with you at the moment, and wishes you to be detained here in our charge. This must be carried out until we have other news, which please God may be soon, for, so help me God, I am much disturbed by your troubles and would certainly help you if I could, but you know the oath of allegiance that I have sworn to the King, and which I am in honour bound to keep.' The Duke realized the danger that he was in, and made his confession, in a devout and contrite fashion, to a priest who had said mass before him. He thanked God for everything that had been bestowed on him, and repented of all his sins. It was as well that he did so, too, for his end was nearer than he knew. Just before dinner, when the tables were laid in the castle and the duke was on the point of washing his hands, four men came out of the next room and putting a towel round his neck they strangled him, two of them pulling at each end.[1] They then undressed the body, put it between the sheets, with the head on a pillow, and covered the bed with fur coverlets; they then went back to the great hall and let it be known that the Duke had had an apoplectic fit and had been put to bed with considerable difficulty. This story was soon spread round the town, and while some believed it, others did not.

Two days later it was announced that the Duke of Gloucester had died in his bed in the castle at Calais. The Earl Marshal,

---

[1] *It is in fact known that Gloucester was smothered in a feather bed, not strangled. One of the murderers, Hall by name, later confessed the exact circumstances. See Parl. Plac. viii, pp. 452-3.*

being closely related to him, went into mourning, and so did all
the knights and squires in Calais. The news reached Flanders
and France before being known in England, and the French
welcomed it warmly, for they held that there would never be
good relations or peace between England and France while the
Duke of Gloucester was still alive; and they remembered how he
had been far more obstinate in the peace negotiations than any
of his brothers, and they regarded his death as being no loss, nor
did they care how it had happened. Likewise in England there
were many knights and squires who had been afraid of his rough
and ready methods and who now did not grieve at his death.
Some remembered how he had caused the exile of the Duke of
Ireland, others how he had been responsible for the execution of
Sir Simon Burleigh who had been such a noble and valiant
knight and had served the Prince of Wales and the kingdom of
England so well. Other knights, too, had been put to death at his
instigation, Sir Robert Tresilian, Sir Nicholas Bramber, and Sir
John Standish among them. Thus was the duke little mourned in
England, except by his own particular followers. His body was
embalmed at Calais and taken across in a coffin to England,
where it was landed at Hadleigh Castle, on the Thames, and
carried from there to the castle at Pleshy. The duke was buried
there in the church that he had founded and dedicated to the
Holy Trinity. The Duchess of Gloucester and her son Humphrey,
and her two daughters, were deeply distressed when the duke's
body was brought back, and the duchess had a double reason for
her anguish, since her uncle, Richard Earl of Arundel, had been
publicly beheaded in Cheapside by order of the King, and in his
presence. The execution was performed by the Earl Marshal,
who was Arundel's own son-in-law, and who bandaged the eyes
of the victim himself.

The Earl of Warwick was only saved from a similar fate by
the intercession of the Earl of Salisbury, who was in favour with
the King. His life was spared on condition that he should be
kept in custody, for the King would not pardon him absolutely,
since he had joined with Gloucester and Arundel in plotting to

break the truce between England and France, and the treaty between the two countries specified the death penalty for anyone who should try to infringe it. Salisbury and Warwick had been companions in battle from an early age, and Salisbury made an eloquent plea for his pardon, giving as an excuse his extreme age, and the fact that he had been deceived and misled by Gloucester and Arundel; he added that Warwick was innocent of complicity in what had happened and that the family of Beauchamp, of which Warwick was the head, had never been guilty of treason, either by thought or deed, against the King. Warwick was banished to the Isle of Wight, and was allowed to take with him all the money and possessions that he required.

The Dukes of York and Lancaster immediately suspected that their nephew the King was responsible for the death of their brother Gloucester. They felt that although he had opposed the treaty with France, he had done so only by word, in the heat of the moment, and had not supported his word by action—they felt that there was all the difference between words and deeds, and that for words alone he had not deserved to die. These two brothers had considerable support, in particular from the family of the Earl of Arundel and from the Earl of Stafford. The King was living at Eltham at this time, and had sent for all his vassals; he had also raised a force of ten thousand archers in Kent and Sussex, and he sent word to London that the Duke of Lancaster should not be admitted to the city. The citizens replied that they could see no reason why the Duke of Lancaster should be excluded from the city, and the duke moved there with his son the Earl of Derby. The Earl of Rutland, who was there too, and who was a great favourite with the King, was anxious to make peace between the two parties, and admitted that his uncle Gloucester had been in the wrong on several occasions in regard to the King. And the people of London came to realize the great harm that could arise from dissension between the King and his uncles, and from the formation of factions. What had been done could not be undone; and the Duke of Gloucester had to some extent caused his own death by speaking out too freely in his determination to break the truce that had been signed and sealed between England and France. The people of London concealed their true feelings and the wisest among them saw that there was nothing to be done; they were also in awe of the power of the King of France, and were anxious that their trade should not suffer. They began to attempt to mediate between the King and the Duke of Lancaster, who was naturally enraged at the death of his brother. But it occurred to him that his nephew the King was married to the daughter of the King of France, and the two daughters of the duke himself were married to the Kings of Spain and Portugal, and they might suffer deeply if the King of England became involved in a war. The duke, therefore, had to change his tune and fall in with the sentiments of the people of London and the leading clergy, who had been mediating between the King and his uncles. A peaceful settlement was reached with the King, on condition that he should be guided entirely by the counsel of the Duke of Lancaster, and never act against it. Afterwards, however, he broke this promise and followed the worst advice, for which, as you will hear, he suffered to the full. And although he came to terms with his uncles after the death of the Duke of Gloucester, he then began to rule more fiercely than ever. He held his court at Pleshy in Essex, a place which had belonged to the Duke of Gloucester and should have been inherited by his son Humphrey. But the King took possession, since it is the law in England that the King takes charge of the estates of anyone who loses his father before reaching the age of twenty-one, and that only on coming of age can the heir take possession. The King took charge of Humphrey, and of his inheritance, and made him come and live with him, together with his mother and two sisters. He deprived Humphrey of the post of Hereditary Constable of England, which his father had held, and gave it instead to the Earl of Rutland. The King began to keep state far more extravagantly than any king of England had ever done before, and lived at the rate of a hundred thousand nobles a year. He also made the son of the Earl of Arundel, who had been beheaded, his ward, and attached him to his court. One of the late Duke of Gloucester's knights, whose name was Cerbel, was also beheaded for speaking out too freely against the King and his council, and Sir John Lackingay was also in some danger until he left the establishment of the Duchess of Gloucester and went to live elsewhere. At this time there was nobody in England, however great, that dared speak out about the actions or intentions of the King. The King chose his own advisers, and the knights of his chamber encouraged him to act in accordance with their own interests. The King maintained at his expense a bodyguard of two thousand archers, since he still did not feel safe from his uncles nor from the family of the Earl of Arundel.

93

A great assembly was held at Rheims and attended by the Emperor[1] and by the King of France and all the principal nobles of France and the Empire, to resolve the schism in the Church. Not wishing the true cause for the assembly to be known, they gave out that the Emperor had come to arrange a marriage between the son of his brother, the Marquis of Brandenburg, and a daughter of the Duke of Orléans. The King of France gave orders to his officers to pay all the expenses of the Emperor and the Germans during their stay at Rheims. The Germans therefore had ten barrels of herrings and eight hundred carp delivered to them every day, for it was Lent. The expense to the King of France, therefore, was immense. When the two monarchs met, they paid each other elaborate compliments, which they were well versed in doing—more especially, that is to say, the King of France, for the Germans are by nature a rude and gross people, except for a certain skill and ingenuity where their own interests are concerned. At the top of the King's table at dinner sat the Patriarch of Jerusalem, next to him the Emperor, then the King of France and the King of Navarre. The German lords sat at the other tables and were waited on by the lords of France, none of

---

[1] *Wenceslas of Luxemburg, Emperor of Germany.*

whom sat down at table. The Dukes of Berry and Bourbon, the Count of Saint Pol, and the other great barons waited at the King's table, and the Duke of Orléans provided all the plate. There were gold and silver furnishings everywhere, as plentiful as if they had been made of wood, and after this splendid and sumptuous dinner I am told that the King made a present to the Emperor of all the gold and silver plate that had been used, and everything on the sideboards as well, together with all the ornaments, tapestries, and other furnishings in the dining hall and also in the room to which the Emperor retired after dinner to take wine and spices. The value of this gift was estimated at two hundred thousand florins, and the other German knights were given magnificent presents of gold and silver plate as well. The Germans and all the other foreign knights who were assembled were astounded at the wealth and power of France.

The marriage was agreed on, but the consultations on the papacy were kept secret. I later discovered that the Bishop of Cambrai was chosen to go as an ambassador to Pope Boniface at Rome, and negotiate with him in the names of the King of France and the Emperor, and try to induce him to agree to a new papal election, and to stand by the result, whether re-elected or not. The bishop was instructed to make the same declaration to Pope Benedict at Avignon, and to threaten both Popes with degradation and with the effective annulment of all the rights of the Church; the bishop was to state that the Kings of England, Scotland, Spain, Portugal, Navarre, and Aragon all supported the King of France in this matter, and that the Emperor had the backing of his brother the King of Hungary, and of all Bohemia and of the rest of Germany as far as Prussia. The monarchs, after making a pact not to make any variation in carrying out what they had agreed upon, left each other in the friendliest spirit and returned home. The Duke of Burgundy had refused to attend at Rheims, on the ground that it was a waste of time to make any pact with the Germans, since they would never keep to any promise or undertaking that they might give. But his attitude made no difference to the arrangements that were made.

The bishop set out, and the King of France sent ambassadors to England, to inform his son-in-law King Richard of what had been settled. The ambassadors were most warmly received, and when King Richard heard their object, which was that he should remain neutral in the dispute between the two Popes, he instantly promised to do so. The King of France was delighted when the ambassadors returned with this news. The King of Navarre came to Paris to try to regain his inheritance of Evreux, which the King of France had seized from his father. In spite of every attempt, however, he could not succeed, and left Paris abruptly to return to Navarre, highly disgruntled with the King of France and his council. We will now leave France and Germany and return to England.

94

The temperament of King Richard was such that if he took a liking to anybody, he would immediately raise him up to a position of extraordinary power and influence; nor did anybody dare to speak out against these whims; nor had there been so credulous a King in England since time out of mind. His favourites, however, never learned from the fate of those who had preceded them: the Duke of Ireland was exiled, Sir Simon Burleigh was executed for the advice he gave the King, and the same fate overtook Sir Robert Tresilian, Sir Nicholas Bramber, Sir John Waller, and several others, though it was the Duke of Gloucester who played the chief part in their downfall. And when Gloucester himself died, there was little regret among the King's entourage, who thought that there would now be nobody to oppose their wishes. His immediate advisers, and the Earl Marshal in particular, who was the arch-favourite of the moment, could no longer conceal their pride and presumption. In order to please and flatter the King still more, the Earl Marshal told him all that he heard, so that the King might realize what a good and trustworthy servant he was, and that his position of favour with the King, already stronger than that of anyone else, might be reinforced still further. But thinking to advance themselves, people are often deceived, and so it was with the Earl Marshal. It happened like this:

Henry, Earl of Derby and the late Duke of Gloucester had married two sisters, daughters of the Earl of Hereford and Northampton, the Constable of England. Their children were therefore first cousins on their mother's side, and second cousins on their father's. And although many of the great barons were outraged by Gloucester's death, the King's power had now become absolute, and they did not like to show in public the displeasure that they confided to each other. For the King had given it to be understood that anyone who spoke out against the deaths of Arundel and Gloucester would be regarded as a false traitor, and would incur his displeasure. This announcement had its intended effect, until the Earl Marshal and the Earl of Derby happened one day to have a conversation about the King and the counsellors that he trusted. The Earl of Derby said the following words, in all good faith, and not thinking that they would ever be repeated—not that there was in fact anything wicked or treacherous about them: 'Holy Mary, dear cousin, what is our cousin the King up to? Will he drive all the nobles out of England? There'll soon be nobody left. He shows quite clearly that he does not want to advance the fortunes of the kingdom.' The Earl Marshal seized on these words, but did not reply to them; he thought however that they overstepped the mark, and that Derby was quite capable of stirring up great trouble in England, for nobody was in greater favour with the people of London. The devil got into his head, and since what is fated to happen cannot be avoided, he decided to repeat what he had heard before the King and a number of the nobles. He knelt before the King and spoke as follows:[1] 'Very dear and renowned lord, I am of your own blood, I am your liegeman, and Earl Marshal of England; and I have sworn on my oath, with my hand held in yours, that I could no longer remain where anything was said against you, or that

[1] *Cp. Shakespeare*, Richard II, *Act I, Scene 1. See p. 163.*

could in any way be harmful to your royal majesty; and that if I heard or saw anything of the kind, and did not reveal it to you, I should be rightly held a villain and a traitor.' The King then said: 'Earl Marshal, why are you saying this? We would like to know.' 'Dear and most renowned lord, it is because I do not wish to allow nor to conceal anything which could hurt you. Let the Earl of Derby come forward and I will speak out.'

The Earl of Derby was called up, and the King made the Earl Marshal rise, for he had so far addressed him on his knees. Thinking no harm, Derby was challenged by the Earl Marshal as follows: 'Earl of Derby, I charge you with having offended by thought and word against your natural sovereign lord the King, in saying that he is unworthy of ruling the realm, on the grounds that he abuses his kingdom without regard to law or justice, and that he unreasonably drives out those valiant men who ought to be helping him to protect and uphold the country. And therefore I throw down my challenge, and wish to prove, my body against yours, that you are a false and wicked traitor.'

Derby was amazed and taken aback by these words, and was so surprised that he did not ask the duke, his father, nor any of his friends what he should do. But after thinking a little, he stepped forward, holding his hood in his hand, came before the Earl Marshal and said: 'Earl Marshal, I say that you are a false and wicked traitor. All this I will prove with my body against yours, and here is my gage.'

The Earl Marshal saw that he was being called out, and to show that he wanted a duel with the Earl of Derby he picked up the gage and said: 'Earl of Derby, I put your word before the King and these lords. I will show that your words are false, and that what I have said is true.'

Each lord then withdrew and joined his friends; the usual wine and spices were not served, and the King showed his great displeasure by shutting himself up in his room. Soon afterwards, however, he sent for the Earls of Huntingdon and Salisbury, and asked their advice. They replied: 'Sir, send for your constable and we will tell you.' The Earl of Rutland, Constable of England, was sent for, and was instructed to forbid the Earl Marshal and the Earl of Derby to leave the country without leave from the King.

As you may imagine, the whole court was in a state of turmoil. The Earl Marshal was much blamed, but what he had said could not be retracted; indeed, he pretended to make light of the whole affair, so high and mighty had he become, and so proud and presumptuous was his heart. The various lords departed to their homes. Whatever face he may have put on it the Duke of Lancaster was very angry, and felt that the King should not have reacted as he had to the Earl Marshal's words, but should have disregarded them. And the more sensible of the barons of England agreed with him.

The Earl of Derby remained at his house in London, and a number of great lords stood as sureties for him, for his reputation was high with his father, the Duke of Lancaster, and his uncle, the Duke of York, as well as the Earl of Northumberland and many other high barons. The Earl Marshal held court in the Tower of London, and both lords provided themselves with all that they would need for the encounter. Derby sent to the Duke of Milan for armour of a special kind, which the duke most willingly provided. To honour and please the Earl of Derby still more, in addition to the very best of his plated and mailed armour he sent the four best armourers in Lombardy back to England with the knight who had been entrusted by Derby with the errand. The Earl Marshal sent to Germany for his equipment, and both lords were put to considerable expense, for each tried to outdo the other; but the greater splendour was shown in the end by Derby, for the Earl Marshal was not as vigorously helped and supported by the King as he might have expected. In fact the King's advisers spoke to him as follows: 'Sir, you should not interfere in this matter too much. Hide your feelings and let the affair take its course. The Earl of Derby is extremely popular in the country, and especially with the people of London. And if they see you taking the Earl Marshal's side, you will lose their affection and regard.' The King knew that this advice was true, and followed it.

The duel was to be a matter of life and death, fought before the King and the chief nobles; it was much spoken about, and different views were held everywhere. Some people, especially in France, said: 'Let them fight it out! These English knights are too proud; in the end they will all destroy each other. Really, they are the most perverse people under the sun, and the most presumptuous.' But others, more profound, said: 'The King of England is neither wise nor well advised to allow two such noble and distinguished knights—both of them, moreover, related to him by blood—to come to hate each other like this, and all on account of a few words quite unworthy of serious consideration. What he should have said, when these words were first brought to his attention, is this: "You are both closely related to me and to each other. I forbid you to indulge in hatred and malice against each other, and I command you to behave like friends and cousins, which you are. If you do not find satisfaction in your lives in this country, then go abroad, to Hungary or some other country where adventures and feats of arms are to be had." ' If the King had said this, and taken steps to pacify these lords, he would have acted wisely and offended nobody.

The Duke of Lancaster was much annoyed and disturbed by the way in which the King his nephew handled his affairs. He did not know who to confide in, but like a wise man, he took thought for the future, and said to those whom he trusted best: 'The King will ruin everything by the time he has finished. He listens readily to bad advice, which will ruin him and the country as well. If he lives long he will gradually lose everything that we and our predecessors have taken so much trouble to gain. He allows feuds to spring up between those great nobles who should love and serve and honour him and guard and protect the country. He has put my brother to death, and the Earl of Arundel, just because they told him the truth. He will listen to nobody who wishes him well, or speaks or advises wisely, unless it is by pure whim. He could find no better way of destroying his country than by permitting hatred among the nobles and the principal towns. The French are too clever for him: for every misfortune that we suffer they would wish us ten, for the only way that they can recover what they have lost, and succeed in their designs, is through our troubles. It is obvious, and always has been, that a kingdom divided against itself is ruined and destroyed. We have seen it in France, in Spain, in Naples and in the Papal possessions. And the present schism between the two Popes is destroying them every day. Again, we have seen it in Flanders, and at the present time the kingdom of Friesland, already involved in war by our cousins in Hainault, is also torn by internal strife. And unless God prevents it, the same thing will happen here. The signs are unmistakable. The King allows my only son and heir to fight with the Earl Marshal over a trifle. And, as his father, I do not like to say a word against it, since his honour is involved, and mine too; and he is certainly a strong enough knight to stand up against the Earl Marshal. But at best, even if they both survive they will never be on good terms again.'

All this time, the Duke of Lancaster never went near the King, and equally saw very little of his son. In this he acted wisely, for he knew that no lord was better loved by the people of England than his son, and especially by the people of London, who had given him the following assurance: 'Earl of Derby, take comfort in the fact, that however this business turns out, you will emerge from it with honour, in spite of the King and his entourage. We understand how things are: the present situation has been engineered out of envy, and in order to get you out of the country, since it is obvious how highly esteemed you are by all men and women alike. And even if you leave the country in sorrow, you will return in joy; for you are more worthy to rule than Richard of Bordeaux. Anyone who wishes to reach the bottom of the matter of your own origin and his, will find that you have a better right to the crown than Richard has; although we have paid homage to him as our King for twenty years. But that was arranged through the efforts of your grandfather, King Edward III of happy memory, who suspected that something of this kind would happen. And there was once a great difference between him and your maternal grandfather, Henry, Duke of Lancaster, but through the mediation of the great lords of the day they made up their quarrel. For King Edward was so valiant, and so successful in all his enterprises that he enjoyed the love of all his people, high and low; and your grandfather Henry of Lancaster never wished him anything but well. Indeed, he was such a loyal servant of the King that he is still remembered for it by all who knew him or heard tell of him from others. If King Richard would only consider all this, he might repent of not having ruled differently.'

With these and similar words the nobles of England and the people of London assured the Earl of Derby of their affection and support, by which he was of course well pleased. He attended to the preparations for his duel and wrote asking his friends from all over England to be present at the occasion. However, the King was undecided whether or not to let the duel take place, although he had allowed the challenge to be made and accepted in his presence. And although he was more feared as King than he had ever been before, he kept his bodyguard of two thousand archers with him day and night, and paid them every week at his own expense. He confided in nobody except his brother, the Earl of Huntingdon, and the Earl of Salisbury: his cousin the Earl of Rutland, the Duke of York's son, was in his favour, but apart from a few other knights of the chamber, he paid no attention to any of the other nobles.

When the day drew near, the King was asked in confidence if he would allow the two knights to fight it out. He replied as follows: 'Yes, why not? I intend to see for myself how they fight, and perhaps we may learn from the outcome something of which we are at present ignorant, but which is of vital importance to us. There is no one in England so great that he can anger me with impunity; for if I allowed myself to be ruled in any respect by my subjects they would soon want to dominate me completely. Some of my own family have, I know, held secret consultations about my government. The greatest and most dangerous of them all was the Duke of Gloucester, for there was no man in England more wrong-headed. But now he is in peace, and I can deal with the others well enough. But why do you ask me this question?' 'Sir,' they replied, 'we wish to advise you loyally, and we sometimes hear things said which do not come to your notice. For you stay in your palace, whereas we go about in London, and in the country too; and things are said that concern you very urgently, and that may concern us as well. There is still time to act, and we beg you not to delay.' 'How is that?' said the King. 'Speak out, and spare me nothing; I wish to do everything that is right, and to maintain justice in my kingdom.' 'Sir,' they replied, 'it is a common rumour throughout the country, but especially in London, that you are responsible for this duel and that it was you that induced the Earl Marshal to fight the Earl of Derby. The people of London in general, and many of the nobility and clergy as well, say that you are on the way to destroying your royal line, and the kingdom of England as well, and that they will not endure it. And if the people of London combine with the nobles against you, how will they be stopped? Your only strength is in your men; and they are now more suspicious of you than ever, since by your marriage you have allied yourself to the King of France. For that you are much less loved by your people. And if you make these two earls confront each other in single combat, you will no longer be in command. It will be the people of London who will rule, through their alliance with the Earl of Derby's powerful connections. The Earl Marshal is so much hated, especially by the Londoners, that they would willingly put him to death. Three-quarters of the people of England say that when you heard the words which passed between the two earls you should have stopped their quarrel by telling them that they were both of them your cousins and your liegemen and that you commanded them to keep the peace; and that you should have taken Derby by the hand and invited him to your room, showing him every sign of cordiality. But since you failed to do this, the rumour is that you strongly support the Earl Marshal against Derby. Consider well what we are telling you, for it is the truth; and you have never needed good advice more urgently than you need it now.'

The King paled when he heard these words, for they were

spoken too seriously to be contradicted. He stood at the window for a little time, leaning there in silence. And when he turned again to the people who were addressing him (the Archbishop of York and the Earls of Huntingdon and Salisbury, with the King's brothers and three other knights) he said: 'I have carefully heard what you have said and I would do wrong to disregard your advice. You must consider what I should do.' 'Sir,' was the answer, 'the matter that you have spoken about is so perilous that you must hide your own feelings and break off this business if you are to preserve your own honour and the country's peace. And you must pay more attention to the kingdom at large than to the heated and presumptuous words of two knights. It is generally believed that the Earl Marshal has behaved very badly, and is still doing so, and that by means of this quarrel with the Earl of Derby he wants to turn the country upside down and stir up every kind of trouble. He must suffer for it, therefore, and the Earl of Derby must be acquitted. All in all, we recommend that you summon them both in front of you, before they take up arms, and order them to abide by whatever you decide. And their sentence shall be that the Earl Marshal shall be banished from England for ever, and Derby for a period of ten years. When Derby leaves the country, you should reduce his exile by four years, to please the people; but he must expect no further concession. That is our advice; and you must make sure that they do not engage in the duel, or every kind of trouble could result.' The King thought for a little and said: 'Your advice is loyal and I shall follow it.'

95

Soon afterwards the King summoned a large council at Eltham, and after the two earls had bound themselves to abide by the King's decision, whatever it might be, he spoke out exactly as he had been advised to do. The lords present approved of the sentence and said that the Earl of Derby could easily leave the country for two or three years, and although he had already made expeditions to Prussia, to the Holy Sepulchre, to Cairo, and to Saint Catherine's on Mount Sinai, he could find other places to visit. His two sisters were married to the Kings of Spain and Portugal, and he could easily visit them, and would be gladly received by the nobility there, for at that moment all warfare was at an end. Being so active, he could lead an expedition from Castile against the infidels in Granada; indeed, he would spend his time far better in that way than in remaining idle in England. Or he could go to his cousin, the Count of Ostrevant, in Hainault, who would be delighted to welcome him, since he was at war with the people of Friesland. And there he could easily have news of · his country and his children. In fact he could not fail to be satisfied, wherever he went. And one day the King of England would recall him, for he was the finest flower in the land, and the King could not force him to stay away too long if he was to retain the affection of his people. The Earl Marshal, on the other hand, had been harshly treated, by being deprived of any hope of ever returning to England again; but to tell the truth, he deserved it, for having started this mischief in the first place. So said the knights and squires to each other, when the King himself passed sentence on the Earl Marshal and the Earl of Derby.

SUMMARY

96-99

The Earl of Derby's exile was reduced to six years, and he left England for Paris, where he was made welcome at court. He declined the invitation of his cousin, the Count of Ostrevant, to pass the time of his exile at Quesnoy, in Hainault. The Earl Marshal went to Flanders, and then to Lombardy.

The King of France and the Emperor of Germany proceeded with their plans for the union of the Church. The Bishop of Cambrai was sent by them to Pope Boniface at Rome, who held a convocation of the College of Cardinals. They advised him to agree to attend a general council, provided that Pope Benedict at Avignon should first give up his claim to the papacy. For commercial reasons, the Romans were extremely anxious not to lose their Pope. The same bishop was also sent to Pope Benedict at Avignon, the Emperor having sent a message to the King of France inviting him to depose the Pope at Avignon first, and undertaking to follow his example with the Pope at Rome.

99

... The Bishop of Cambrai and the Marshal of France set off for Avignon, and after leaving the marshal at Lyon on the way, the bishop reached Avignon and took up his lodging in the wood-market. Some of the cardinals fully realized the purpose of his visit, seeing that he came from the King of France, but they kept their peace and waited to see what he would say, and how Pope Benedict would react.

After taking some refreshment, and changing his clothes, the bishop visited the Pope, and treated him with respect, yet with less honour than if he, and the rest of the world, had regarded him as Pope; in spite of the fact that Pope Benedict had, by the recommendation of the lords of France, given him the bishopric of Cambrai. The bishop, who was eloquent both in French and Latin, explained whom he had come from, and what was his business. Pope Benedict turned pale and said: 'I have worked hard for the Church, my election to the papacy was valid, and yet they are now trying to depose me. I will not submit to it as long as I live. I want the King of France to know that I will pay no attention to his orders, but that I will retain my name and my rank until I die.' 'Sir,' replied the bishop, 'saving your reverence, I thought you had more wisdom. Arrange a meeting with your cardinals, that you may take counsel, for without them you cannot hope to prevail against the power of the Kings of France and Germany.'

Upon this, two cardinals who had been appointed by Pope Benedict, seeing that things could not turn out well, came up to the Pope and said: 'Holy Father, the Bishop of Cambrai is right. We beg you, do as he asks.' The Pope agreed, the audience ended and the bishop went back to his lodgings, without communicating with the cardinals. In the morning, the bell of the consistory was rung, and all the cardinals in Avignon were summoned. The bishop was present at their meeting and stated, in Latin, the reasons for his mission. When he had finished, the answer given to him was that the cardinals would consider the matter, but that the bishop should not be present while they did so. After he had left the meeting, the debate lasted a long time, for some of the cardinals thought it very hard to undo something that had been effected without irregularity. But the Cardinal of Amiens made the following speech: 'My lords, willy-nilly we will have to obey the Kings of France and Germany, since they have made an alliance together, and without them we cannot exist. We might well be able to withstand the Emperor, if the King of France were on our side, but he is not. He demands our submission, and if we do not submit he will deprive us of the income from our possessions, without which we cannot live. The truth is, Holy Father, that we raised you to the papacy in order that you should reform and unify the Church to the best of your ability, all of which you have always undertaken to do, until today. Give us therefore a moderate and reasonable answer now, which will enable us to praise you; for you must know your own mind better than we can.' Here several of the cardinals joined in together: 'Holy Father, the Cardinal of Amiens is right, and we beg you to state your intentions.' Then Pope Benedict replied as follows: 'I have always desired the unity of the Church, and I have worked hard for it. But since by the grace of God I am Pope, and have been elected by you, as long as I live I will remain Pope, and I will not renounce or submit before count or duke or king, nor will I agree to any treaty or agreement or arrangement which deprives me of the papacy.'

The cardinals now rose from their places: some of them were displeased with what had been said, and left for their lodgings without taking leave of the Pope; but those who approved of his answer, and were still in the Pope's good graces, remained with him.

The Bishop of Cambrai saw how the conclave broke up, and entering the consistory he went up to Pope Benedict, who was still seated on his throne, and said to him, with no great ceremony: 'Sir, give me your answer—I must have it now. You have held your conclave, and you must tell me what you have heard and seen and discovered from it; and then I must return.'

Pope Benedict, still looking displeased at what the Cardinal of Amiens had said, replied harshly to the bishop as follows: 'Bishop, I have held a council of my fellow cardinals, who created me Pope. I was elected with all the necessary rites and solemnities, and I am acknowledged by all my subjects; and Pope I will remain, as long as I live. I will never abdicate, though it cost me my life; for I have never done anything to forfeit the protection of Heaven. You will tell our son the King of France that until now we have regarded him as a good Catholic, but that now he is being misled into the path of error. Sooner or later, he will regret it. But, I beg you, tell him from me to think carefully, and to do nothing that could trouble his conscience.' On saying this, the Pope retired to his room, and the bishop to his lodgings. After a modest dinner, the bishop set out to rejoin the Marshal of France, the Lord Boucicaut. He spent the night at Bagnols-sur-Cèze, and found the marshal at Saint Andrieu, within thirty miles of Avignon.

100

When the marshal heard from the bishop what the Pope had said, he gave the bishop leave to return to the King, for there was nothing more for him to do in that region. The marshal then summoned all the knights and men-at-arms in the neighbourhood, sending even as far as Montpellier, and ordered the Seneschal of Beaucaire to close all the approaches to Avignon, both on land and on the Rhône, so that no supplies should reach the city. The marshal's orders were readily obeyed, by some out of obedience, but by many in the hope of plundering the city of Avignon. The marshal quickly gathered such a large force that he sent a declaration of war to Benedict in his palace, and to the cardinals and all the people of Avignon.

This was a heavy blow for Avignon; the people knew that they could not long withstand the King, and a council was held of the cardinals and all the citizens of the town. They resolved to go and speak to Pope Benedict and point out to him that they were in no position to carry on for long a war with the King of France, since in order to live they had to carry on their trade, both on land and by river. Benedict answered them angrily as follows: 'Your city is strong and well equipped. I will send for troops, from Genoa and elsewhere, and from my son the King of Aragon. He is a Gonfalonier of the Church, and must come to serve my cause, for two reasons: he is related to me by blood, and he also owes obedience to me as Pope. You are too easily alarmed. You go and defend your town and I will defend my palace.' The cardinals and citizens could get no other answer, and each returned to his lodgings. The Pope had, long before this, laid in a store of wine, grain, lard, oil, and all the other provisions necessary for a fortress. And his character was so proud and cruel that it would have taken more than the present situation to disturb him. . . .

SUMMARY

100-113

The Marshal of France collected a large army and prepared to lay siege to Avignon. The town soon opened its gates, through the inhabitants' fears for their property. The King of Aragon would not come to Benedict's help, for fear of offending the King of France, who was his wife's first cousin. Benedict eventually came to terms, on condition that he need not leave Avignon until there was unity in the Church. The French army dispersed, and the Marshal of France planned an expedition against the Turks, who were again threatening Hungary. The Earl of Derby, who was living at the French court, wanted to join it. The King of France wanted King Richard to support him in his neutrality between the two Popes. Richard would have agreed, but the people of England were solidly in favour of Pope Boniface.

The Duke of Lancaster advised his son, Derby, against going to Hungary, and shortly afterwards he died. The King was pleased, and confiscated part of his estates; he also prevented Derby from marrying the daughter of the Duke of Berry, accusing him of treason. King Richard held a joust at Windsor, which was however very poorly attended by the nobles; he then left for Bristol, intending to cross over to Ireland, with twenty thousand knights and squires and ten thousand archers. The people of London were very dissatisfied with the King, and the whole country was in a thoroughly disturbed state. The Earl of Northumberland and his son were banished for declining to join the expedition.

The people of London finally sent the Archbishop of Canterbury to recall the Earl of Derby from France. The archbishop travelled as a simple pilgrim, and Derby agreed to return. He first visited the Duke of Brittany, who provided him with three shiploads of men-at-arms; they crossed from Vannes to Plymouth, and set off for London. They were met by a crowd of Londoners at Guildford, who greeted Derby most warmly.[1] After reaching London he soon set out for Bristol, passing through Oxford and Cirencester, and the King (who was now referred to in London as plain 'Richard of Bordeaux') left Bristol and retired to Flint Castle.[2] Henry surrounded the castle with troops

---

[1] *'A joie, à bien et à prospérité nous vienne le désiré, monseigneur Derby et de Lancastre!'*

[2] *Froissart's account is unfortunately full of inaccuracies. Henry in fact landed at Ravensburn—on July 22nd, and went straight to Bristol, not to London. He then went to Flint by way of Ludlow and Chester (August 9th). Meanwhile the King returned from Ireland and landed at Milford at the end of July. Hearing that Henry was at Bristol, he re-embarked and sailed round the coast of Wales to Harlech, where he landed and then went on to Conway Castle. Here he was met by Northumberland, and deceived into falling into the hands of Henry at Flint. Froissart seems to be unaware that the King reached Ireland, nor does he mention Northumberland's treachery.*

The events of this period lead up to so dramatic a climax, and form such an

and the King agreed to give himself up and return to London as Henry's prisoner. The Lady de Coucy, chief lady in waiting to the Queen, was advised to leave the country, and did so.

113

. . . The Queen of England's circumstances were now so reduced that she had neither man, woman, nor child to wait on her. Her own attendants from France had been sent away, and so had many of the English ones who favoured the King. They were replaced by ladies-in-waiting and other attendants who were forbidden to mention the King's name, even to each other.

The Duke of Lancaster and his men left Chertsey and passed through Sheen, and from there they took the King to the Tower of London under cover of darkness, together with such of his knights and men that he wanted with him. When the people of London discovered in the morning that the King was in the Tower, they were very pleased, but they were full of indignation that he had been brought there in secret and at night; and they were all very angry that the Duke of Lancaster had not taken the King through the streets of London, not so that he could be acclaimed and honoured, but to receive the insults of the crowd. Such was the hostility and hatred that was now felt towards him. Consider what a terrible thing a rebellion against the sovereign is—more especially among the English, for there is no holding them; there is no more dangerous, proud and presumptuous populace in the world. And of all the English, the people of London are the worst, and, to tell the truth, the strongest both in numbers and resources. For within the walls of London there are at least twenty-four thousand men, fully armed from head to foot, as well as thirty thousand archers. This is a powerful force,

---

important part of English history, that a translation of Froissart's account of them would have been given in full here, were the account not so extremely inaccurate.

for they are tough, bold and strong-willed, and the more blood they see shed the more cruel and less squeamish they become.

114

The Earl of Rutland, who was the Duke of York's son, was at this time Constable of England. He was at Bristol, with his brother-in-law Lord Despencer, when he heard that Conway Castle had been captured, and the King taken to London. In considerable alarm they left Bristol and went to Caerphilly, a beautiful property belonging to Lord Despencer on the borders of Wales, having first dismissed all their men-at-arms. There they waited for further news. The Duke of York remained in his own castle, and although he had taken no part in public affairs for a long time, and had no intention of doing so, he was much displeased that there was such dissension in the country, and such differences between his nephews and other relations.

When the King was imprisoned in the Tower, the Duke of Lancaster immediately recalled the Earl of Warwick from his place of exile in the Isle of Wight. He then sent word to the Earl of Northumberland and his son Henry, summoning them to come to him, which they did. Next, he took great pains to lay hands on the four murderers of his uncle, the Duke of Gloucester, at Calais. After a relentless search, they were all taken and imprisoned in solitary confinement in London. Richard of Bordeaux was detained in the Tower of London, where, in the reign of King Edward III, King John of France had been detained with his court. It was decided that Richard must give up all his royal prerogatives, if he was going to abuse them in this way; for the news of his detention would very soon be known all over Christendom, since he was now being dethroned after ruling for twenty-two years. A record of his reign was then compiled, in twenty-eight sections, and the Duke of Lancaster, with a chosen body of his counsellors, went to the Tower and entered King Richard's chamber. They treated him without ceremony, and read out to him the record[1] of his reign, to which he made no reply, for he knew that the indictment was true. He only pointed out that everything had been done with the full knowledge of his council. On being asked for their names, he gave them, in the hope of escaping by laying the blame on his advisers. This he had succeeded in doing in the past, but his enemies were not allowing him to do so again. The Duke of Lancaster returned home, and the mayor and principal men of law went to the Guildhall, where a large public gathering assembled, with the expectation of seeing justice done. In this they were not disappointed.

First, the same account of the events of the reign that had been read to King Richard was now read out again in public, and it was stated that the King had in no way contradicted it, but had observed that everything (including the deaths of Gloucester, Arundel and Sir Thomas Corbet) had been ratified by the advice of four knights of his chamber. They had been advising the King for a long time, and their actions were irremediable, and demanded punishment. For it was through their influence that the court of justice at the Palace of Westminster, and the other royal courts all over England, had been closed, as a result of which many wrongs were done. Bands of thieves had roamed over the country, robbing merchants on the highways and poor men in their homes. England was in danger of being lost beyond any hope of recovery, and the loss of Calais and Guines to the French seemed inevitable.

When the account of the King's reign was read out in public, many of the mob were amazed and astounded, and some of them began to murmur as follows: 'These crimes deserve punishment and Richard of Bordeaux must lose his throne; a public example must be made of him. He is not worthy to wear the crown; he should be stripped of all his honours and should live in prison on bread and water for the rest of his life.' And while some of the crowd made these and similar remarks to each other, others cried

---

[1] *This is to be found, in full, in R. Holinshed's* Chronicles of England, Scotland and Ireland (*1577*).

out loud: 'Sir Mayor, and you others who are there to uphold the law and preserve justice, do your duty and spare no man. As you can see, the facts speak for themselves, and the guilt of these men is proclaimed by their very actions.' Accordingly, the Mayor of London and the officers of the law retired to their judgement chamber, and the four knights were condemned to death. They were each attached to two horses, at the foot of the Tower of London, and dragged bodily through the streets, in full view of King Richard, who was watching from a window. At Cheapside their heads were cut off and set on spikes over the gates on London Bridge. Their bodies were dragged off and hung on gibbets. The names of the knights were Sir Bernard Brocas, Lord Marclais, Sir John Derby (the Receiver of Lincoln) and his steward Lord Stelle. The knights remaining in the Tower saw them dragged off to their execution, and their anxiety and distress can be imagined, since they could not expect that their own fate would be any different—so obvious was the savage spirit of the people of London. The four knights had their heads cut off on a fishmonger's slab in Cheapside. The crowds then dispersed to their homes.

King Richard was overcome with despair: he could see that his power had vanished and that he was at the mercy of the mob. Every man's hand was against him, or if he had any supporters, they were powerless even to show themselves, far less to turn their loyalty into action; so strong was the general feeling against the King. His companions said to him: 'Sir, we have little hope of surviving. When we surrendered to your cousin Lancaster at Conway Castle, he guaranteed that you and the twelve knights with you would remain unharmed as his prisoners. Of those twelve, four have just been shamefully put to death, and we cannot expect anything else for ourselves, for the people of London have him so much in their power that he cannot act against their wishes. God would be very merciful if he let us die a natural death here, for a shameful, public ordeal is a terrifying thought.'

At this, the King wrung his hands, and began to weep and to curse the day when he was born to come to such a miserable end. Some of his knights tried to comfort him, and one of them spoke as follows: 'Sir, you must take heart. We know quite well, and so do you, that this world counts for nothing, and the fickleness of fortune is amazing, for king and beggar alike. Your father-in-law, the King of France, cannot help you at the moment—he is far away. But if you could escape from this present peril, and if we could all emerge with our lives, it would be a triumph; for in a year or two, your fortunes might well change.'

'What must I do?' said the King. 'There is nothing I would not do to save us.'

'Sir,' was the answer, 'truly, from all appearances, the people of London want to crown your cousin Lancaster king; it is for this that they have sent for him and given him their support. But as long as you are alive, he cannot be crowned without your consent. Supposing you send for your cousin, and offer him terms, in exchange for our lives. Say that you are willing to abdicate the crown in his favour, and he will be appeased, and so will the people of London. Ask for your life to be spared, so that you may live here or elsewhere, either by yourself or with your knights, either in England or abroad. But if you lose your life, you lose everything.' The King pondered on this advice and decided to follow it, for his danger was great. He let his guards know that he would willingly speak to the Duke of Lancaster.

115

The Duke was soon informed, and he left his house in the evening and went down to the Tower in a barge, accompanied by his knights. He entered the Tower by a postern gate, and went straight to the King, who received him with great humility, indicating that he was aware of the great danger that he was in. The King addressed the duke as follows: 'Cousin, I have been taking stock of my position, which is indeed low, and as for continuing to rule the country and to wear the crown, I cannot think of it any longer. And if God helps my soul, I would like to leave this life by a natural death, and I would like the King of France to have his daughter back, for we have never had much happiness together. Since I brought her here, I have never enjoyed the same love and honour from my people as I did before. Cousin, I am well aware, on reflection, that I have treated you and my other royal cousins badly, and I know that I will never be forgiven, nor find peace, again. For these reasons I give up to you freely and willingly my inheritance and the crown of England, and I beg you to accept them.'

The Duke of Lancaster replied: 'The three estates of England must hear of this. I have summoned the prelates and nobles of the country, and representatives of the chief towns, and within three days there will be enough of them here for you to make your abdication in the proper way. By this action you will appease much of the hatred that is felt for you; for it was to undo the harm caused by the abeyance of justice in this country that I was sent for from abroad. The people want to crown me king, for there is a general feeling in the country that I have, and have always had, a better right to the crown than you. This was pointed out to your grandfather, King Edward of happy memory, when he brought you up to be king, but his love for the Prince of Wales his son was so strong that nobody could change his intention that you should be king. And if you had followed the example of the Prince, and listened to good advice, as a dutiful son should, you would still be king now. But you have always done the opposite; and the general feeling, in England and elsewhere, is that you were the son not of the Prince of Wales but of a priest or canon. And I have heard from various knights of the court of my uncle the Prince that he was dissatisfied at his marriage, for your mother was first cousin to King Edward, who had stood godfather to the two children that your mother had when she was married to Sir Thomas Holland. The Prince began to dislike her for not having children by him, and although she had married him through her own skill at scheming, and knew well how to hold him, she was still afraid that the Prince might want to divorce her. She succeeded in becoming pregnant, and gave birth to you and to another child, of whom we cannot judge. But in your case, your character and behaviour are so utterly inconsistent with the prowess and gallantry of the Prince, that it is said in this country and abroad as well that you are the son of a priest or canon. For there were at Bordeaux, at the time of your conception and birth, many young and handsome clergy in the Prince's court. This was the local belief. And you have certainly shown it in your conduct, for you are always thinking how to please the French and make peace with them to the disadvantage and dishonour of England. Indeed my uncle Gloucester and Lord Arundel gave you wise and loyal advice, and wanted to guard the honour of the country and follow the policies of their fathers, and you rewarded them by putting them to a traitor's death. But as for me, I will take you under my protection and prolong your life, out of compassion, as long as I can. And I will intercede for you with the people of London, and with the heirs of those whom you have put to death.'

'Thank you very much,' replied the King. 'I have greater faith in you than in anyone else in England.'

'Rightly,' said the duke. 'For without my intervention you would have been seized by the people and suffered a disgraceful death, as a result of those wicked acts that have caused the present trouble and danger that you are in.' The King listened patiently to the duke's attack, and did not know what to answer, for he saw that it was not a time for argument or taking a strong line, but for meekness and submission. He was as humble as could be, and beseeched the Duke to save his life. The duke remained with him for two hours, going into his misdemeanours in detail. He then returned home, by barge, and on the next day finished dispatching the general summons for the assembly of the three estates. His uncle, the Duke of York, arrived in London, with his son the Earl of Rutland and the Duke of Northumberland with his brother Sir Thomas Percy, along with many prelates, archbishops, bishops and abbots. All of them were warmly welcomed by the Duke of Lancaster, who rode to the Tower of London at their head.

King Richard was released from his room and entered the great hall in full kingly regalia, with the crown on his head and the sceptre in his hand. He came in alone and unattended, and spoke as follows: 'I have been King of England, Duke of Aquitaine and Lord of Ireland for twenty-two years, and these thrones, dominions, and inheritances, together with this crown and sceptre, I now hand over freely and willingly to my cousin Henry of Lancaster; and I invite him, before you all, to accept the sceptre.'

With these words he held out the sceptre to the duke, who handed it to the Archbishop of Canterbury. King Richard then removed the gold crown from his head, and put it in front of him, saying: 'Cousin Henry, Duke of Lancaster, I give you this crown with which I was crowned King of England, and all the authority appertaining to it.'

The duke took it and handed it in turn to the archbishop. These actions concluded, the duke called for a notary public and asked for an official act to be drawn up and witnessed by the temporal and spiritual lords who were present. Soon afterwards, Richard of Bordeaux returned whence he had come, and the Duke of Lancaster and the knights with him mounted their horses and rode away to their homes to await their summons to the Parliament that was to be held at Westminster. The crown and sceptre were packed up and put in the treasury at Westminster Abbey.

116

On the last day of September in the year of Our Lord 1399, Henry, Duke of Lancaster held a Parliament at Westminster, outside London. Most of the lords temporal and spiritual were present, together with representatives from a number of the principal towns. The duke proceeded to claim the kingdom of England on three counts: first, by conquest, secondly, as the rightful heir, and thirdly because Richard of Bordeaux had freely and openly abdicated in his favour, in the presence of illustrious witnesses, at the Tower of London. Henry then required the people of England to state their will. The people replied that it was their unanimous wish that he, and no one else, should be their king. He asked twice more if it was really their wish, and they cried out with one accord: 'Yes.'

Henry then sat down on the royal throne which was raised up on a dais in the middle of the hall, and covered with cloth of gold, so that he could be seen by one and all. And when he took his seat, the people all raised their hands, promising him their faith and homage. The Parliament was concluded, and the coronation was fixed for Monday the thirteenth of October, the feast of Saint Edward. On the Saturday before, the new King went from Westminster to the Tower of London with a large retinue. And forty-six squires, who were to be knighted next day, kept watch all night; each of them had a room to himself, and a bath in which he bathed.[1] Next day they were knighted by Henry at mass, and presented with long green coats with narrow sleeves, lined with miniver, similar to a prelate's robes. The knights wore a double tassel of white silk decorated with knots of the same colour hanging down from the left shoulder. Henry returned to Westminster after dinner on Sunday. He went bareheaded, wearing round his neck the order given him by the King of France; and he was escorted by the Prince, his son, with six dukes, six earls, eighteen barons, and a total of between eight and nine hundred knights. The new King wore a short jacket of cloth of gold, in the German style; he was mounted on a white horse, and he wore the blue garter below his left knee. The streets were lined by the nobility, with the retinue of each lord dressed in his livery, as the King rode past. There were six thousand in the cavalcade, and the streets were hung with decorations of many different kinds. In Cheapside there were nine fountains flowing with red and white wine.

That night the new King had a bath, and in the morning he

---

[1] *The custom of the ceremonial bath, representing purification before the receipt of an order of chivalry, is found in other European countries from the earliest times. The English Order of the Bath was founded by Richard II, who created four knights. Henry IV created twenty-five on his accession, and the later history of the order begins, after a period of comparative eclipse, with its revival by George I.*

went to confession (as he had good need to do[1]) and heard three masses, as was his custom. All the assembled prelates, and many other clergy, came in procession from Westminster Abbey to the palace to escort the King to his coronation. All the nobility joined in the return procession, the dukes, earls, and barons in long scarlet robes, and mantles trimmed with ermine, and hoods of the same material. The dukes and earls wore three bars of ermine, about nine inches long, on the left shoulder, the barons two. The knights and squires all wore uniform scarlet robes. In the procession to the abbey, the King had a canopy of blue silk carried over his head, supported on silver poles, with gold bells at the corners. It was borne by four burgesses of Dover, whose right it was to perform this function. On one side of the King the Sword of Mercy was carried by his son the Prince of Wales, and on the other the Sword of Justice, carried by Henry Percy, Earl of Northumberland, who was now Constable of England in the place of the Earl of Rutland, who had been dismissed. The Earl of Westmorland, Marshal of England, carried the sceptre. At nine o'clock the procession entered the abbey, in the middle of which a platform had been erected, covered with scarlet cloth. On it was a royal throne, in cloth of gold, on which the King took his place, in full regalia with the exception of the crown. The Archbishop of Canterbury then mounted the platform, and, from its four corners in turn, told the people that God had granted them a man to be their lord and sovereign. He then asked if it was their wish that the new King be consecrated and crowned. With one accord they all answered 'Yes!' raising their hands, and promising their loyal homage. The King then came down from the platform, and advanced to the altar to be consecrated. This ceremony was performed by the two archbishops and ten other bishops: the King was stripped of his royal trappings, down to his shirt, and was anointed on the head, the chest, the shoulders, the back, and the hands. A bonnet was placed on his head, while the

---

[1] *This comment is omitted in later MSS., along with other asides unfavourable to Henry IV.*

clergy chanted the litany used for the blessing of a baptismal font. The King was then dressed in the church vestments of a deacon, and put on the red velvet slippers of a prelate, with spurs with a point but no rowel. The Sword of Justice was then unsheathed and blessed, and handed to the King, who replaced it in the scabbard. He was then invested with it by the Archbishop of Canterbury, and crowned by him with the crown of Saint Edward, which is arched and surmounted by a cross. After mass was over, the King left the Abbey with the same procession as before. The King retired to his room and then came into Westminster Hall for dinner.

The King sat at the top table, with the two archbishops, and seventeen other bishops, and the Earl of Westmorland with the sceptre at the end of the table. Next to the King sat the Prince of Wales, who carried the Sword of Mercy, and on the other side sat the Constable of England, who carried the Sword of Justice. At the second table sat the Five Peers of England, at the third the chief citizens of London, at the fourth the newly created knights, and at the fifth a number of other knights and squires of honour. Halfway through dinner a knight by the name of Dymoke entered the hall on horseback; both knight and horse were fully armed and arrayed in crimson, and in front rode another knight, acting as his lance-bearer. Dymoke had his drawn sword in his hand, and a naked dagger at his belt. He handed the King a paper to the effect that if any knight, squire or gentleman wished to say or maintain that King Henry was not the true King, he was ready to challenge him to fight, either in the King's presence, or at any time appointed by the King. The King had this challenge proclaimed by a herald in six different parts of the hall, but it was not taken up. After dinner was over, the King took wine and spices and then retired to his rooms, and the rest of the knights dispersed to their houses. The King spent that night, and the following day, at Westminster.

You must know that the Earl of Salisbury took no part in these celebrations. He was under close arrest, and the King's advisers, as well as many other knights, especially those in

London, wanted him to be beheaded publicly in Cheapside, on the grounds that he had taken a message from Richard of Bordeaux to the King of France and his court, openly stating that King Henry was a false and wicked traitor; and that this crime was unforgivable, and must be punished by death. King Henry's nature was mild and calm, and he was disinclined to execute him, accepting his defence that he had only obeyed, willy-nilly, the orders of the four knights mentioned above who had already been executed. But the King's council would not listen to this, and said he deserved to die, and the people of London were of the same opinion. The earl remained in prison, in great danger of his life.

King Richard's brother, Sir John Holland, Earl of Huntingdon, was still at this time Governor of Calais, and he was well informed of all that was going on: how his brother had been taken and imprisoned in the Tower, where he was condemned to spend the rest of his life, having abdicated in favour of King Henry. Huntingdon was naturally displeased by what had happened to his brother, but weighing up the situation, found that he could not take on the whole power of England single-handed. Also, his wife was King Henry's sister, and she said to her husband, on his return from Calais to England: 'My lord, you must contain your anger, and do nothing that could turn out to your disadvantage. The King my brother can confer great benefits on you, and you can see that the whole country has come over to his side. If you commit yourself to any rash course, you will be ruined. Hide your feelings, I beg you, for King Henry is just as much your brother as Richard was. Stay at his side, and you will find him a good and valuable friend. There has never been a richer King in England, and he can be very generous to you and your children.' The Earl took the point of what his wife said, and went and did homage to his brother-in-law, the new King, promising fealty and service. The King was delighted to receive him, and he afterwards succeeded in persuading the King, with the help of other friends, to accept the defence offered by the Earl of Salisbury, whose mission to France was forgiven, and whose popularity with the King and the rest of the country was restored.

SUMMARY

117-120

News from England was brought to the French court by the Lady de Coucy, and King Charles was naturally much displeased. The Duke of Bourbon tried without success to win over Bordeaux and other towns in Aquitaine to the French. King Charles's council sent two ambassadors to visit Isabel, wife of Richard II. King Henry gave an assurance that she would suffer no indignity of any kind.

The Earls of Huntingdon and Salisbury suffered a change of heart and led a rebellion against King Henry. They spread a rumour that King Richard had escaped from the Tower, and they dressed up a young priest to impersonate him. A fight took place at Cirencester, at which Huntingdon and his nephew, the Earl of Kent, were killed. Salisbury and Despencer were executed, along with many other partisans. The King of France collected an army to invade England.

121

Soon after this a true report circulated in London that Richard of Bordeaux was dead. I have not been able to discover the true circumstances of his death.[1] His body was laid on a litter covered in black material, drawn by four black horses, and escorted by four knights and two attendants, all in black. The procession left the Tower (where Richard had died) and went at walking pace to Cheapside, which is the most important street in London. There it halted for two hours, and Richard's body, with the head resting, uncovered, on a black pillow, was seen by upwards of twenty thousand people. Some pitied him, but others said that he had long deserved his end.

Now consider, you lords, kings, dukes, earls, prelates and men

---

[1] *Nor has anyone else: he may have died either by voluntary or enforced starvation, or possibly by the hand of Piers Exton.*

of high estate and long lineage, how remarkable and variable are the vicissitudes of fortune. King Richard ruled in England for twenty-two years in great prosperity, and in great state. There was never a King of England who spent more on his household—a hundred thousand florins a year. For I, John Froissart, Canon and Treasurer of Chimay, had the opportunity of observing it, when I spent three months at his court. The King entertained me royally, because in youth I had served as a clerk and a page in the court of his grandfather the noble King Edward III and his Queen, Philippa of Hainault. And when I took leave of King Richard, at Windsor, I was presented with a silver-gilt goblet, weighing over two marks, and containing a hundred nobles, by Sir John Bulliver on behalf of the King. This present was of great value to me, and will continue to be so for the rest of my life.[1] I have an obligation to pray for his soul, and it is with a heavy heart that I write of his death; but this history has been composed, to the best of my ability, to give a full account of events as they occurred.

In my time, I saw two events which though very different from each other, were of the greatest significance. I was sitting at table in Bordeaux when King Richard was born. It was a Wednesday, at ten o'clock. And Sir Richard de Pont-Chardon, who was at that time Marshal of Aquitaine, came over to me and said: 'Froissart, write it down and record it that the Princess of Wales has given birth to a fine son. He is a King's son, for his father has been made King of Galicia by Don Pedro, and is even now leaving for that country to conquer it. He is of a royal line, and he will be a king himself.' The gentle knight of Pont-Chardon made no mistake, for Richard was King of England for twenty-two years. But when the knight told me the news, little did he know what the King's last end would be. I have often

---

[1] *Another who benefited by Richard II's generosity was Geoffrey Chaucer, who, according to Rymer's* Foedera *(volume dealing with 1399, published 1717), was in that year awarded a pension of twenty pounds a year for life, payable half at Easter and half at Michaelmas.*

thought about these things since. For when I first went to England in the service of King Edward and Queen Philippa, they lived with all their children at a manor belonging to the Prince of Wales at Berkhamsted, about thirty miles outside London. I took leave of the Prince and Princess of Wales, who were departing for Aquitaine, and I heard an old knight called Sir Bartholomew Burghersh say as follows: 'We have a book in this country called Brut,[1] and it states that neither the Prince of Wales, nor the Dukes of Clarence or York or Gloucester will ever be King of England. The crown will return to the house of Lancaster.' Well, as author of this history, I have seen both these knights proved right: Richard of Bordeaux was King of England for twenty-two years, and yet in his lifetime the crown returned to the house of Lancaster, when King Henry was crowned King. He laid no schemes to acquire the crown, nor would he have become King if Richard had behaved towards him as he ought. But the people of London made him king out of indignation at the wrongs that he and his children had suffered at the hands of King Richard.

When the litter that carried King Richard's body had stopped in Cheapside for two hours, the little procession moved on and rode out of London. The four knights, who had been on foot, had their horses waiting with grooms. They rode as far as the royal manor of King's Langley, which is thirty miles outside London. There King Richard of Bordeaux was buried, and may God have mercy on his soul.

News of Richard's death spread everywhere, having been expected for some time; for it was known that he would never come out of the Tower alive. His death was concealed from his Queen, and orders were given that she was not yet to be informed of it; these orders were followed for a considerable time. All these events were widely known in France, where those knights and squires who were eager for war daily expected orders to attack the frontiers. But the inner councils in both countries decided that peace was more advantageous to them than war. Envoys

[1] *The so-called* Roman de Brut, *by Robert Wace.*

were sent by both sides to Calais to prolong the truce, although the King of France was not in good health, and had not been since the tribulations of his son-in-law King Richard had begun. At the news of Richard's death the French King's health became worse still, and most of the government was in the hands of the Duke of Burgundy, who came to Saint Omer. The Duke of Bourbon, with Sir Charles d'Albreth, Sir Charles de Hangiers and Sir John de Chastelmorant were at Bourbourg, and the prelates with the French negotiators were the Patriarch of Jerusalem and the Bishops of Paris and Auxerre. On the English side there were the Earls of Northumberland, Rutland and Devonshire, Sir Henry Percy, and Sir Evan FitzWarren, with the Bishops of Winchester and Ely.

The French wanted Richard's widow to return to France, but the English said that they would rather she lived on her dowry in England, and that if she had lost her husband they would find her another one, handsome, young and agreeable, whom she would love. For Richard of Bordeaux had been too old for her. Her new husband would be the new Prince of Wales, King Henry's son. The French could not agree to this, as they knew that their King would not have it. He was in very weak health, and no doctor could diagnose the disorder from which he suffered. This question was therefore shelved, and the matter of the truce was brought up. There had already been peace for four years, and it was prolonged for another twenty-six, making thirty years altogether. Letters were written and sealed by those who had been authorized to do so by the two Kings; after which every man returned to his home.

I have omitted to say what had become of the Earl Marshal, through whom all these troubles originated. When the news of King Henry's accession and King Richard's death reached him, he took it so badly that he became ill, retired to bed, fell into a frenzy and died.

Such were the dire troubles that befell the greatest of the English lords in 1399.

122

In that year, too, Pope Benedict, who had received so much support from the French, was deposed. The same fate also overtook the King of Germany, as a result of his misdeeds; for the electors of the empire, together with all the other dukes and barons of Germany, united in driving him out into Bohemia, of which country he was King. In his place they elected a wise and valiant man from Bavaria, called Robert of Heidelberg. He came to Cologne and was crowned there, for the people of Aix would not allow him into their town; nor would the Duke of Guelders recognize his authority, to his great displeasure. The new King undertook to restore the unity of the Church. All this time the King of France and his council were negotiating with the people of Liège, who supported the Pope at Rome. Through the efforts of Sir Baudouin of Montjardin (who had a part in the government of the whole bishopric of Liège, and was a knight of the King's chamber) the whole country adopted a neutral attitude to the question of the papacy, as the King of France desired. The people of Liège sent word to such of their clergy as were in Rome at the time, that unless they returned to Liège by a specific day, they would be deprived of all their ecclesiastical benefices. When they heard this, they all returned to Liège, to the discomfiture of Pope Boniface who sent a legate into Germany, to remonstrate with the people of Liège and bring them back into his fold. The legate, however, dared not go any farther than Cologne, and merely sent letters on to Liège. These were read, and the following answer was given to the messenger: 'Do not bring us messages of this kind again, unless you want to drown. For anyone who brings such a message as this will be thrown into the Meuse.'

Bibliography

Of the three principal editions in old French, that of Luce is the best and contains fewest obvious mistakes, though unfortunately it only takes the text as far as 1385. After some thought I have followed this text as far as it goes, and used Buchon's edition for the rest of the translation.

Of the translations, that of Berners is splendid. Commissioned by Henry VIII, it was undertaken by a descendant of that Sir John Bourchier who was Governor of Ghent in 1384, and who is mentioned in the *Chronicles*. The style is always fresh and vigorous, even if the content is often obscure, and not free from error. The abridged edition of this version, published in 1899, is an easily manageable book, and gives a good idea of the whole. Ker's introduction to these selections is excellent, and I have in many cases followed him in omitting passages of lesser interest. The only translation in modern English is that of Johnes, which although useful in being the only complete one in existence, sometimes seems rather stilted and portentous to the modern reader: while it is not in the idiom of today, it also lacks the force and immediacy of Berners, who was after all writing little more than a hundred years after the events that he describes.

Of the descriptive general books, Mary Darmesteter's is charming and very readable for the period, even if the author's fancy leads her to read more into certain passages of the *Chronicles* than they may perhaps contain. This, however, is largely a matter of opinion. Coulton's special number of *Studio* is presumably hard to come by except in a few libraries, but it is the work of a real and deeply knowledgeable scholar. It is profusely illustrated with reproductions (of a poor quality by modern standards) of the illuminations in a fifteenth-century manuscript of Book IV of Froissart's *Chronicles* (Harley Manuscripts 4379 and 4380 in the Department of Illuminated Manuscripts in the British Museum).

Shears's book deals with all the various aspects of Froissart's life, whereas Coulton's is chiefly confined to his activities as a chronicler. Shears gives a clear and useful picture of the background of this age and the chapter on 'The Chivalry of the Fourteenth Century,' which is based on an essay by the author in an earlier collection published in 1928 under the title *Chivalry*, does something to correct too starry-eyed a picture of the period.

THE CHRONICLES

Printed Editions in French

Siméon Luce, G. Raynaud, L. and A. Mirot, eds. *Chroniques de Froissart*. Paris, 1869-1899. 13 v. Still in progress. Vol. I part 1 describes variant texts; part 2 up to Vol. VIII contains Book I of the *Chronicles*; Vols. IX-XI, Book II; Vols. XII-XIII, Book III. The summaries in Vols. I-XI provide correct dates, names, and places.

J. A. C. Buchon, ed. *Les Chroniques de Sire Jean Froissart*. Paris, 1835. 15 v. Contains important appendices and supplements.

(Baron) Kervyn de Lettenhove, ed. *Oeuvres de Froissart*. Brussels, 1867-1877. 25 volumes. In Vols. I-XVI there are a highly conjectural biography and variant texts, inconveniently arranged and not always reliable. Vols. XX-XXIII are an index of proper names useful as a Who's Who for the period, and XXIV-XXV form a similar geographical index.

English Translations

Sir John Bourchier, Lord Berners, tr. *The Chronicles of Froissart*. London, 1523-1525. Reprinted frequently.

Thomas Johnes, tr. *The Chronicles of Froissart*. London, 1803-1810. 5 v. Reprinted frequently. Johnes's is the only modern translation.

William Paton Ker, ed., Berners tr. *The Chronicles of Froissart*. London: D. Nutt, 1901-1903. (Tudor Translations.) 6 v. This is the best edition of Berners. The index is translated from Kervyn de Lettenhove.

Condensations and Selections

William Anderson, ed., Berners tr. *Froissart's Chronicles*. Centaur Press, 1963.

426

Julia Bastin, ed. *Jean Froissart, chroniqueur romancier et poète.* Brussels, 1941. An anthology, with introduction.

J. Buchon, ed. *Les Chroniques de Sire Jean Froissart.* Paris, 1824-1826. 3 v. There are several reprintings. This is an outmoded condensation, but conveniently compact.

H. P. Dunster, ed. Johnes tr. *Chronicles of England, France, Spain.* London: J. M. Dent, 1906. (Everyman's Library). Condensed into one volume.

A. H. Diverres, ed. *Voyage en Béarn.* Manchester, 1953. Selection from Book III of the *Chronicles*; with introduction.

G. C. Macaulay, ed. Berners tr. *The Chronicles of Froissart.* London: Macmillan, 1899. 1 v. (The Globe Edition.) A useful condensation.

G. Paris and A. Jeanroy, eds. *Extraits des chroniqueurs français.* Paris, 1922. 11th ed. Excellent brief introduction.

RELATED BOOKS

Jean le Bel. *Chronique.* J. Viard and E. Deprez, eds. Paris: Société de l'Histoire de France, 1904-1905. Jean le Bel's chronicles were used by Froissart in his Book I.

Honoré Bonet. *The Tree of Battles.* France, 1387. G. W. Coopland, tr., Liverpool, 1949. Dedicated to Charles VI, 1387; an illuminating description of the contemporary concept of war.

James Douglas Bruce. *The Evolution of Arthurian Romance.* Gottingen, 1923. Vol. II, p. 286. The relation of *Méliador* to the genre.

G. G. Coulton. *The Chronicler of European Chivalry.* London: The Studio, 1930. A copiously illustrated biography of Froissart.

Mary Darmesteter. *Froissart.* Paris, 1894. E. F. Poynter, tr., London, 1895.

Jean Froissart. *Méliador.* A. Longnon, ed., Paris, 1895-1899. 3 v.

Jean Froissart. *Oeuvres de Froissart: Poésies.* A. Scheler, ed., Brussels, 1870-1872. 3 v. These volumes are numbers XXVI-XXVIII in Kervyn de Lettenhove's *Oeuvres de Froissart.*

Johan Huizinga. *The Waning of the Middle Ages.* London: E. Arnold, 1924.

H. N. Humphreys. *Illuminated Illustrations of Froissart.* London, 1844 and 1845. Both the 1844 and 1845 series are included in the reissue, 1855.

Bibliography

William Paton Ker. *Essays on Mediaeval Literature*. London: Macmillan, 1905. This includes Mr. Ker's preface to his edition of the *Chronicles*.

F. S. Shears. *Froissart, Chronicler and Poet*. London: Routledge, 1930.

Robert M. Smith. *Froissart and the English Chronicle Play*. New York: Columbia, 1915.

M. Wilmotte. *Froissart*. Brussels, 1948.

BIBLIOGRAPHICAL GUIDES

R. Bossuat. *Manuel bibliographique de la litterature française du moyen age*. Melun, 1951. *Supplement*, Paris, 1955.

D. C. Cabeen, ed. *Critical Bibliography of French Literature*. Syracuse, N.Y.: Syracuse U.P., 1952. U. T. Holmes, ed., Vol. I, pp. 215-216.

C. P. Farrar and A. P. Evans. *Bibliography of English Translations from Mediaeval Sources*. New York: Columbia, 1946.

A. Molinier. *Les sources de l'histoire de France*. Paris, 1904. Vol. IV, pp. 5-18. Includes reliable biographical summary.

A. Potthast. *Bibliotheca historica*. 2nd ed., Berlin, 1896. Vol. I, pp. 472-474. Lists early editions and translations.

ARTICLES

Anon. 'Froissart and His Patrons.' *Times Literary Supplement*, 11 Dec., 1937, 933-934.

H. Braddy. 'Froissart's Account of Chaucer's Embassy.' *Review of English Studies*, XIV (1938), 63-67.

F. Davidson. 'Froissart's Pastourelles.' *Modern Language Notes*, XIII (1898), 229-231.

Margaret Galway. 'Froissart in England.' *University of Birmingham Historical Journal*, VII (1959), 18-35. (Contains new suggestions on the date of Froissart's birth, and his association with Queen Philippa.)

F. L. Ganshof. 'Jean Froissart.' *Société Royale d'Archeologie de Bruxelles: Annales*, XLII (1938), 256-272.

E. Hoepffner. 'La Chronologie des "Pastourelles" de Froissart.' *Mélanges offerts à M. Emile Picot*, II (Paris, 1913), 27-42.

G. L. Kittredge. 'Chaucer and Froissart.' *Englische Studien*, XXVI (1899), 321-336.

Bibliography

L. Mirot. 'Jean Froissart.' *Revue des Etudes Historiques*, CIV (1937), 385-400.

C. Oulmont. 'Nos trésors littéraires méconnus.' *Minerve Française*, IV (1920), 565-580.

P. Philippeau. 'Froissart et Jean le Bel.' *Revue du Nord*, XXII (1936), 81-111.

C. A. Sainte-Beuve. *Causeries du lundi*, 24 and 31 Oct., 1853. A famous appreciation; there have been various reprintings.

(Sir Walter Scott.) Review of Johnes's Froissart, Vol. I, in *Edinburgh Review*, V (1805), Art. vii.

Roland M. Smith. 'Five Notes on Chaucer and Froissart.' *Modern Language Notes*, LXVI (1951), 27-32.

B. J. Whiting. 'Froissart as a Poet.' *Mediaeval Studies*, VIII (1946), 189-216.

Index

Index

Wace, Robert, author of the *Roman de Brut*, 422 (fn)

Wake, Sir Thomas, marshal of the army, 17 19 24 55

Waleran, brother of Marquis of Juliers, and of Archbishop of Cologne, 71 85

Wales, 18 242 351 407 (fn 2) 409
Princess of, 190 193; son Richard born at Bordeaux (1367), 195 239 241 246 421 422

Waller, Sir John, executed, 393

Walsingham, Sir William, 308

Walworth, Sir William, Mayor of London, 241 245; knighted at Smithfield (1381), 251

Wardlaw, Sir William, 305

Wardrobe, the King's, 246 247 248 251

Wargny, Sir Robert of, governor of Caen, 15 134

Wark castle, 118; taken and burnt by the French and Scots, 267

Warwick, 248
Earl of, Constable of England, Marshal of England, 54 90 95 141 147 157 172 173 241 243 386 388 389 409

Welsh, 148

Welshmen, 149

Wenceslas of Luxemburg, Emperor of Germany, 391 392 402 404

Westminster, 133 244 248 342 351 416 418
Abbey, 214 416
palace of, 53 54 410; coronation of King Edward III, 23
parliament at, 302 341 357 415

Westmorland, 272

Earl of, Marshal of England, (1399), 417 418

White Friars, abbey of, at York, 25

White Hoods, organisation of, 234

Wight, Isle of, 389 409

Willoughby, Lord, 141 166

Winchelsea, 8 99 242

Winchester, Bishop of, 423
bishopric, 210

Windsor, 53 55 64 114 128 129 213 370 407 421
Sir William, 364 365

Wissant, near Calais, 25 (fn) 27 43 44 53 55 152
Sir Jacques of, burgher of Calais, 155
Sir Peter of, burgher of Calais, 155

Woodstock, Thomas, Duke of Gloucester, youngest son of King Edward III, *see* Gloucester

Wykeham, William of, chaplain to King Edward III, Bishop of Winchester, 210

Yolande de Bar, Queen of Aragon, 336 337 342

York, city of, 24 25 27 42 115 248
vale of, 25
Barons of, 268
Archbishop of, banished by the Duke of Gloucester, 358 401
Edmund, Duke of King Richard II, married the daughter of the Earl of Kent, 303 304 341 351 355 356 361 362 386 389 396 409 414 422

Ypres, 49 73 99 107 112 131 133 235 236 257 258 262

Zeeland, 106 263